CONTENTS

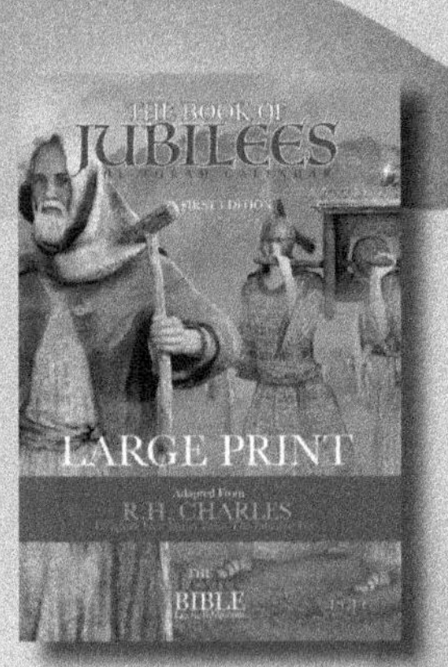

The Book of Jubilees:
7" x 10"

2nd Esdras:
7" x 10"

First Enoch:
7" x 10"

Bible History Illustrated:
7" x 10"

Apocrypha: Vol. 1
7" x 10"

9 Books In 3 Years!
And Over 500 Teaching Videos.

MIND-BLOWING REVELATIONS

APOCRYPHA

SCROLLS FOUND IN QUMRAN AND THOSE NOT PRESENT

ApocryphaTest.com

Full Publishing With Torah Test For:

The Book of TOBIT

Wisdom of SOLOMON

Book of SUSANNA

Prayer of AZARYAH

Bel & The DRAGON

Testing The Books of:

ESTHER & Additions | JUDITH | 1-2 MACCABEES

Text Adapted From The 1611
KING JAMES VERSION
REVISED ENGLISH

Compiled, Edited, Commentary, Maps, Charts, and Research By
Timothy Schwab, Anna Zamoranos and The God Culture Team

Back Cover: The ancient Tower of David in the Old City of Jerusalem, Israel.

To order additional copies of this book, contact:

The Levite Bible By The God Culture
TheGodCulture@gmail.com
Facebook: The God Culture - Original
www.ApocryphaTest.com
www.LeviteBible.com
www.TheGodCulture.com

FOREWARD

By Timothy Schwab
Author, Publisher, Researcher, Speaker, Singer/Songwriter,
Founder of The God Culture, Non-Pharisee and proudly so...

In Vol. 1, we covered the meaning of this fallacious term "apocrypha" leading to hidden books. Most of these should never have been transferred into a new category in 382 A.D. or so, by the Catholic Jerome. It is bewildering that the Protestant Church actually accepts the word of that Catholic hypocrite on this further censoring these same books especially when some of these so-called defer to Jerome as the expert. They could not be more uneducated. There has never been anything credible about this false paradigm. In fact, the four books we have tested so far including Wisdom of Sirach, Book of Baruch, Letter of Jeremiah, and Prayer of Manasseh, prove to be inspired scripture and Bible Canon kept by the Temple Priests who were exiled to Qumran/Bethabara. Fragments from all four texts were found there.

In addition, 1st Esdras was also discovered and mislabeled as ProtoEsther, yet not a single such fragment is Esther, but all are distinctly 1st Esdras including Ezra by name even. 2nd Esdras is definitively quoted in prophetic interpretation within the local community writings in at least two very significant references to the Final Eagle Empire of Ezra's vision *(2Esd. 11 13)*, and no other book could harmonize. His prophecy is there meaning 2nd Esdras was present.

All of this is meticulously solidified in archaeology in Qumran which we assessed in Vol. 1 as well as The Book of Jubilees: The Torah Calendar, The First Book of Enoch: The Oldest Book in History, and 2nd Esdras: The Hidden Book of Prophecy With 1st Esdras. This will be our first publishing in this series that will not include that research because it is already published in the others. This Torah Test is thorough enough one can draw conclusions as to the legitimate, historically documented Bible Canon that the Bible endorses. Forget about Josephus, the Pharisee and royal Hasmonean, whose list is an admission of guilt deviating from the authority, which he never was. Set aside the listing from the Greek Septuagint from Egypt where no sons of Zadok lived at that time of translation, thus, the wrong scholars to be included as authentic in origin. There is only one group the Bible certifies to the First Century to keep Bible Canon and they and their Canon are found in archaeology in Qumran/Bethabara with that exact calling demonstrated and repeated. They were endorsed by Yahusha as He chose to launch His ministry there where scripture was then kept. He is the Word.

We now advance into the rest of the 1611 King James Apocrypha with a comprehensive Torah Test for each. The books which pass the test, as most do, will be detailed in this Introduction. The four books which fail the test are separated in the back of this book for good reason. We will not publish those books here as there is no need, but we will provide ample detail of their shortcomings. By the end of Vol. 2, we will all have enough data to assess which books of the Apocrypha are inspired scripture and which ones are not. Scholars fall short in their assessments.

In the case of the Book of Tobit, we expound in research just after that book's publishing, addressing much illiterate ridicule from scholars who cannot read and do not know scripture, history, nor science. We will answer the beguiling inquiry from the blind with the light of the truth regarding the 2,000-year-old medical practice recorded by Tobit as healing blindness from infection from bird droppings specifically. That infection not only occurs but amounts to a significant percentage of similar blindness from ancient to modern times. Who is the Archangel Raphael and is he recorded elsewhere in scripture? What was the species of Tigris fish that had to be large enough to feed Tobias for about ten days, and somehow possessed a religious value to a Nephilim as sacred for the smell to ward him away? Can demons smell when in physical form and how does that work? What is very shameful for any scholar, is most cannot even answer these questions because their research on this topic has remained scant and inadequate. Many are out there demonstrating they have no education on either of these questions and that is sad.

Daniel's exploits are further disseminated in Bel & The Dragon. Bel is Bel Marduk, the Sumerian god also known as Ba'al in Samaria especially. Not only does Daniel triumph over those priests having them put to death, he kills the famous, historically-chronicled dragon of Bel Marduk. We cover the history, even with ancient Assyrian historic relief of this actual dragon, after that book's publishing as well. Indeed, we do not find this detail in Daniel 1-12 and that is because this was once chapter 14 of the Book of Daniel. Daniel is the likely writer of this account as well as Susanna which was found in the Qumran scrolls. We will test the fragments and demonstrate that too ending such illiterate, polarizing debate. Once one understands the magnitude of what Daniel did here in this account and adds it to the other miracles of the rest of his book, there is no question it coalesces, and the entire account of Daniel emerges more credible than ever before. We find this with many of these books where they enhance understanding of other portions of scripture just as inspired texts should. This is why we need them.

We will vet ancient dragons as a concept to find even archaeology of the image of the exact dragon Daniel killed. That will include the possibility of dragons breathing fire which if a scholar has a problem with this book over that, they better throw out Job as well. They would not and that would be insane, but it proves they are not consistent in applying standards in testing which creates an environment for fraud. They undermine their credibility when they apply such.

For the Prayer of Azaryah *(Babylonian name: Abednego)*, we will apply additional testing as well at the end of the book. It is fascinating to find that Daniel set up this prayer just before inserting it in the original Book of Daniel according to history. He says they prayed, and we have that prayer. Is there anything in the prayer that offers embellishment or flies in the face of scripture? We find nothing. Instead, the name of YHWH, Yahuah, is used over 40 times in this one chapter. The content reads exactly as the prayer of a prophet would.

In the case of Susanna, we will not only prove it was found in Qumran among Bible Canon in the same cave as Daniel, but we will offer a deeper case following its publishing. With this account, one learns that Daniel was a great prophet and judge from a young age which coalesces with everything we read about him. In his discernment, he is used to save Susanna from unjust judges whom he exposes. This is who Daniel was throughout scripture. The fact it ever became separated out and treated as a book on its own when Daniel wrote it as Chapter 13, required fraud on the part of Pharisees and the Catholic Church which is a recurring theme in the treatment of the Dead Sea Scrolls. That is a paradigm of willing ignorance attempting to conceal what this find makes evident. They changed the Bible.

For Wisdom of Solomon, we will cover the evidence that Solomon wrote more than what is catalogued in our modern Canon and the book tests as historic Bible Canon teaching great wisdom. It was indeed written by Solomon who identifies himself accordingly. There is nothing credible that stands against this book as inspired scripture and nothing can change that.

After testing five of the remaining nine books of Apocrypha in Vol. 2 added to the six from Vol. 1 and 2nd Esdras: The Hidden Book of Prophecy, we find that eleven of fifteen adequately prove as inspired scripture. Again, the other four will be tested in the back of this book as they each fail including the Additions to Esther (and Esther), 1st and 2nd Maccabees, and the Book of Judith. Those are texts that never should have been included in scripture even in vague association. They are lies, full of conflicts, and even occult doctrine. No wonder so many view Apocrypha as scary as these fake books were thrown in to make it appear so spuriously.

Of course, Esther is also included in our modern Canon in blatant fraud we will expose as well. However, the eleven never should have been in the category of hidden in the first place. They were not hidden in the B.C. era, nor the first century, and those who did reclassify them, will answer for their misconduct of abomination. Imagine even Martin Luther wrote that Esther and Maccabees were occult accounts he wished never came to us in our Bibles. He also admits Judith is a false history and fiction. We will offer an exhaustive examination of these books.

In the culmination of this Introduction, we provide a smackdown with no holds barred in response to the unschooled speculation called scholarship on this topic of Apocrypha. We will respond directly to Blue Letter Bible's scholar proving every one of his attempted points illiterate, or not even a position at all. In the end, he does not even offer a position against Apocrypha as little he provides is even true. He is propagating a paradigm who cannot accept these books even willing to repeat lies he has not bothered to assess. We wish we did not need to, but we must. The journey to awakening begins now. Yah Bless.

Will America Disappear?

The Prophet Ezra Forecasted the Continuation of the Vision of Daniel's Fourth Beast in the Final Eagle Empire Including the End of the British Empire, The American Superpower, And the Rise of the Final Eagle Head. Hair-raising Prophecy. You Will Never Be the Same!

Our Test and Publishing of 1ˢᵗ & 2ⁿᵈ Esdras These Have Never Been "Apocrypha"

Available Free in eBook or Purchase Internationally on Amazon or Shopee PH. All Links at:

2Esdras.org

Also, Watch Our Revealing 26-Week Series: **Answers In 2ⁿᵈ Esdras**

INTRODUCTION

Is the "Apocrypha" or Portions Scripture, Inspired and Canon? Continued From Vol. 1.

Criteria set forth by Blue Letter Bible with our stricter additions. [1]

1. Prophetic Authorship

"For a book to be considered canonical, it must have been written by a prophet or apostle or by one who had a special relationship to such (Mark to Peter, Luke to Paul). Only those who had witnessed the events or had recorded eyewitness testimony could have their writings considered as Holy Scripture." Note: The Temple Priests curated scripture and that should matter to scholars too as their library was found in Qumran/Bethabara.

2. Witness of the Spirit, Quoted as Doctrine In Scripture

"The appeal to the inner witness of the Holy Spirit was also made to aid the people in understanding which books belonged in the canon and which did not." BLB quotes Pinnock who claims the canon is a matter of *"historical process"* (Clark Pinnock, Biblical Revelation, Grand Rapids: Baker Book House, 1973, p. 104). [2] We would agree but Pinnock ignores the most obvious such history. The Levite Library or Bible canon found in Qumran/Bethabara serves as a time capsule for the Old Testament canon long before the Catholic Church, nor counsels, nor even Pharisee party in Yahudaea. Every book in the modern Old Testament canon was found there except Esther. It is Levite Priests, sons of Zadok, who were the keepers of scripture and the Qumran/Bethabara community identifies as such over 100 times.

3. Acceptance

"The final test is the acceptance of the people of God." BLB notes this is to accept Jesus and the Apostles which we agree for New Testament but this would also be to accept His people in the time of the Old Testament.

4. In Agreement with the Whole of Scripture (Our Addition)

Does it agree with scripture in whole? Even the Gospels have minor details to iron out in understanding and reconciliation, but how does it compare? The conclusion may surprise.

1. PROPHETIC AUTHORSHIP: WHO WROTE THESE BOOKS?

For 1ˢᵗ and 2ⁿᵈ Esdras, please see our extensive Torah Test published in 2ⁿᵈ Esdras: The Hidden Book of Prophecy With First Esdras available free in eBook at 2Esdras.org. See Vol. 1 for first half of this examination.

Continued from Vol. 1, each of these credible books erroneously classified as "Apocrypha" are clear whom authored them. The question comes from scoffers calling themselves Bible Scholars who will claim they can't prove authorship. That remains their shortcoming, and not the text itself which they ignore, and do not believe. Who ever said these books rely on their approval or disapproval when we have the ancient record that proves they even lie to cover up this atrocity? Who do they think they are? It is a false paradigm they establish to ensure failure, yet they have failed us.

When a book tells you who authored it, or a prophet known to author similar or the same accounts, is included as a main character in the story, only one playing games of willing ignorance would try to reject them on such lame basis. They are removing scripture and that is unacceptable. When those books are also found among the only scroll library endorsed as Bible Canon kept by the exiled Temple Priests or even strongly associated in ancient times as part of another book which was found there, one is not thinking when they claim they have the right to remove them from the Bible, or even separate and hide them as "Apocrypha." No scholar has such authority, and never has. The Old Testament Canon was already established before the Pharisees and Hasmoneans usurped the Priesthood and religion in Judaea in 165 B.C. and long before there was a Catholic Church, nor Counsels. Who cares what they voted when they had no right to vote on the already established Old Testament which we now have firm evidence of its contents in terms of books found in archaeology?

WISDOM OF SOLOMON:

Solomon typically identifies himself in the books he wrote, and Wisdom of Solomon is really no different. In this case, rather than by name or as son of David, Solomon writes in the first person in the first verse of Chapter 7, *"I, myself..."* and then, he launches into the story which befits that of King Solomon and no one else truly adheres. He identifies as a king essentially *(7:5, 8)*. Then, this king prayed for understanding and the spirit of wisdom was given to him by Elohim. That is very specific to Solomon's account. This king preferred wisdom over *"scepters, thrones and esteemed riches" (7:8)* which in the beginning of his reign certainly suits Solomon as well as the end once he overcame his dark period, repented and returned placing wisdom as the priority once again. Ecclesiastes is extremely consistent on that.

This king places wisdom above gold and silver *(7:7, 9)* for which King Solomon was famous in receiving such in tribute from all the kings of Arabia *(1Ki. 10:15; 2Ch. 9:14)*, but also in the entire narrative of Ophir, Sheba and Tarshish *(1Ki. 9-10)* as well as the building of the Temple with its gold. He admits, at first, he did not understand the wisdom was the *"mother of them (riches)..." (7:12)*. Solomon *"learned diligently,"* and did *"communicate her (wisdom) liberally:"* he did *"not hide her (wisdom's) riches" (7:13)*. It is rather hard to fathom that some scholars cannot seem to put this together and then, question whether it should even be titled Wisdom of Solomon as it has been for thousands of years. Who do they think they are to attempt to rewrite history when antiquity well establishes that fact. King Solomon wrote the aptly titled *Wisdom of Solomon* indeed. He said so as no other character corresponds with this and there is good reason why it has always been attributed to Solomon adequately.

Furthermore, Solomon is attested as writing far more content than is recorded in his three books, Proverbs, Song of Songs *(Solomon)* and Ecclesiastes in the modern Canon. 1 Kings defines he spoke 3,000 proverbs and 1,005 songs. With this in mind, one would think scholars would be asking where the other writings exist. They mostly do not bother. Here we have an entire book they have censored and disallowed in ignorance. Josephus affirms these same numbers yet forgets that his list of supposed Canon is missing many of these *(Antiquities, 8:2:5)*. Oops!

> *1 Kings 4:29 KJV*
> *And **God gave Solomon wisdom** and understanding exceeding much, and largeness of heart, even as the sand that is on the sea shore. And **Solomon's wisdom excelled** the wisdom of all the children of the east country, and all the wisdom of Egypt. For **he was wiser than all men**; than Ethan the Ezrahite, and Heman, and Chalcol, and Darda, the sons of Mahol: and his fame was in all nations round about. And **he spake three thousand proverbs: and his songs were a thousand and five**.*

When scholars cannot produce a better answer as to where all these thousands of verses are found, yet ignore the very obvious text under their noses, one must wonder what their real agenda is. No one can be that stupid. They are blinded by a paradigm which keeps them entrapped in ignorance.

THE BOOK OF TOBIT

Tobit could not be more definitive that Tobit, the one of a detailed lineage even, wrote his own book and when. He identifies himself in the first person. For a so-called scholar to claim someone wrote it hundreds of years later because they cannot understand these simple words, do not believe them and scoff preferring to accuse the Temple Priests of forgeries and giving false authors, proves a standard against the Bible. That is not Bible scholarship. There is no one more deserving of the title of "willing ignorance" awarded by 1 Peter 3. Worse, they set a false litmus test requiring the original text of Tobit be found from about 700 B.C. for them to understand that is exactly when it was written, as it says it was. Tobit was in captivity and defines the era to what can only be a short period in history and nothing else. In fact, Tobit perfectly affirms valid history which timeline we provide after the full publishing of the book. He is criticized for that too because scholars do not actually know history and seem incapable of charting a simple timeline. His is perfect.

Indeed, the book's ending was completed evidently by Tobias, his son once Tobit died. Does that really require any kind of leap in logic as it is his story too? They do the same with Moses forgetting, though supposed Bible scholars, that Moses was not only a prophet, he prophesies in that same passage of the future after his death. Instead, they prefer to scoff forgetting the precedence that scribes copied these scrolls over often to preserve them. They are admitting they do not even know the Bible paradigm and prefer Nephilim rocks instead. These are occultists and not Bible scholars.

> **Tobit 1-2a KJVA**
> **The Book of the words of Tobit, son of Tobi'el, the son of Anani'el, the son of Adu'el, the son of Gaba'el, of the seed of Asa'el, of the Tribe of Naphtali, 2 Who in the time of Shalmaneser king of the Assyrians, was led captive out of This be which is at the right hand of that city, which is called properly Naphtali in Galilee above Asher. I, Tobit...**

Tobit firmly wrote this book with Tobias, his son as the ending author. He was a sage and holy man in the time of the Assyrian captivity, and this is a precious book we all need. Due to an extreme lack of understanding by modern scholars who many do not seem to know the basics of what demons are in physical form, before disembodied, there are many deceivers out there who ridicule this book. We address this at the end of the full publishing of Tobit where we deal with the plausibility of the story as well as whom the Angel Raphael is, the fish bile that healed Tobit's eyes even found in medical journals since ancient times to the modern era, the fish smell and the type of Tigris fish that would deter a Nephilim or demon in physical form even for religious reasons scholars simply do not know, etc. Essentially, we see one flawed, illiterate ridicule after another on this book. When you realize the religious significance of this particular fish found in Sumerian Nephilim worship, and other aspects that have been widely attacked in gross negligence by scholars undeserving of readership, you will be entertained by the level of ignorance from supposed academics. These are not difficult to analyze if one attempts to reconcile the account rather than ridicule it as many scholars bellow. When they do so without ample research to support their poor opinion, they make themselves as fools and we will always call them out here as the Bible always does.

THE BOOK OF DANIEL INCLUDED SUSANNA, BEL & THE DRAGON AND PRAYER OF AZARYAH:

Many recorded the three books of Susanna, Bel & The Dragon and Prayer of Azaryah as part of the Book of Daniel in the First Century or so *[84, 85, 74, 81]*. We find Susanna fragments in the Qumran Scrolls as it was there with Daniel even prior. No fragments of Bel & The Dragon or Azaryah were found there but they are only one chapter each and associated with Daniel historically. Many scholars overlook this because they do not understand the significance of Qumran.

*"Your letter, from which I learn what you think of the **Susanna in the Book of Daniel, which is used in the Churches**. This, then, is my defense. I might, especially after all these accusations, **speak in praise of this history of Susanna, dwelling on it word by word, and expounding the exquisite nature of the thoughts.**"*
– Origen's Letter to Africanus [75] 2nd-3rd Century

Some scholars will respond in ignorance that Origen numbers only twenty-two books in Bible Canon, yet they forget Daniel and it's three addendums were one book to Origen. They are reading Origen in fragments just as they read the Bible, and this is why their understanding remains shallow as that is their negligent method of understanding. However, he very clearly defended Susanna as inspired scripture here as part of the Book of Daniel. Notice, Origen states Susanna is in the Book of Daniel and not separated. Some decided to separate it and the other two books later which set up their removal but that is not the Bible way. What they did was attack the Book of Daniel removing three chapters of content which affirm the rest of Daniel and two of them, Susanna and Bel & The Dragon, appear to be written by Daniel himself. The other was written by Daniel's best friend and partner in ministry and prophecy. We will demonstrate examples.

In Protestantism generally, scholars made up a new rule as a false litmus test. They claim that if a Bible text is not found in archeology in Hebrew, it cannot be Bible Canon. Even R.H. Charles realized the hypocrisy and lack of logic involved in such a false test. Yahuah said He would preserve His Word and He has – in Heaven. The Heavenly Tablets kept in His presence serve as the origin of all scripture. In Jubilees and First Enoch throughout, Enoch and Moses used those as the basis for portions of their writings. Revelation agrees there are Heavenly Tablets, and so do you because you do want your name written on the Heavenly Tablet called the Book of Life, we are certain.

*"**Protestant divines have been inclined to regard original composition in Hebrew as one mark of canonicity, though they have never formulated any rigid doctrine to that effect.**" [81, Charles, p. 627]*

THE BOOK OF SUSANNA (BOOK OF DANIEL 13):

The Prophet Daniel is included in this account of Susanna, a righteous woman wrongly accused by corrupt judges whom Daniel enters to rescue in the end of the story. The author is likely Daniel, and this is why this was once part of the Book of Daniel as Chapter 13 *(Modern Daniel ends at 12 now)* in ancient times which we will assess next. One cannot ignore the historic precedent as such and no scholar can deny the Prophet Daniel, if proven author, is an inspired author. Fragments of this book were also found in Qumran and history is well established as inspired scripture. We will test those specifically in the next section. Daniel wrote the first half of Daniel in the third person in similar fashion to this story consistent with the timeframe.

BEL & THE DRAGON (BOOK OF DANIEL 14):

In the story of Daniel and the Lion's Den in the Book of Daniel, we are missing details and perspective as to the buildup of such a drastic response requiring far more than mere jealousy. With Bel & The Dragon this is explained. Daniel killed their god. Bel & The Dragon was once in Daniel as Chapter 14 *(Modern Daniel ends at 12 now)*. This book truly serves to define this as well as additional exploits of Daniel that set this prophet apart even more so as a young man. Once again, the author was likely Daniel who wrote the first half of Daniel in the third person in similar fashion to this story consistent with the timeframe. We will examine this in the historicity next.

However, there is reference to the Prophet Habakkuk perhaps as an author of Bel & The Dragon. If so, this still qualifies as prophetic authorship, and it would be no surprise this would be placed with Daniel as it his story.

"In the LXX it (Bel & The Dragon) is called 'Part of the prophecy of Habakkuk the Son of Jesus of the tribe of Levi' – Charles, p. 652. [91]

PRAYER OF AZARYAH (BOOK OF DANIEL INSERTED AFTER 3:23):

Azaryah is an incredibly well-known Bible character as that is the original Hebrew name of Abednego, his Babylonian given name in captivity *(Dan. 1:7)*. Imagine Daniel's best friends, Shadrach, Meshach and Abednego and fellow compatriots in prophetic events, not having a book of affirmation? That is a much further quandary for scholars when one ponders it. Here we have Azaryah *(Abednego)* writing the account of the fiery furnace in Daniel 3 as a second witness and the author could not be more credible. He was an eyewitness even more than Daniel as he was in the furnace. When Pharisees and the Catholic Church removed this scripture, they eliminated the witness to one of the greatest Bible events and miracles.

This is why this book as well was included as part of the Book of Daniel historically inserted after Daniel 3:23 as inspired scripture which we will establish in the historicity next. Daniel's story includes these three partner prophets in ministry even identifying them as promoted when Daniel was as they became essentially provincial governors *(Dan. 2:49, 3:12)* before the fiery furnace account. They were promoted again after that event *(Dan. 3:30)*. Azaryah is the author of this text, and this is the prayer he prayed while in the fiery furnace. There is nothing in the prayer that represents anything other than scripture and there is no better authority on the event including Daniel. If Azaryah is not the author of this small book, then, Daniel is where he was operating as a scribe for Azaryah. In either event, it belongs with Daniel as it has been since antiquity.

BOOKS NOT FOUND IN QUMRAN: ESTHER & ADDITIONS, 1ˢᵗ & 2ᴺᴰ MACCABEES, AND JUDITH:

These books were not found in Qumran and for good reason. We decided to create separate sections in the back of this book to conduct a thorough and deep testing of each. For Esther, we will assess the entire book as to whether it ever should have been considered Bible Canon when the Temple Priests did not view it as scripture. There are Additions to Esther considered Apocrypha which we will test as well, but we will not limit this to additions as a full testing reveals why this book was not found among the true Temple Priests. We are also fully aware of the recent claims by illiterate Pharisee scholars who try to allege that "Proto-Esther" fragments were found in Qumran in a sham. These clearly cannot read and are unaware of the story trying to stretch the narrative erroneously and they even try to make a male titled Priest Eza or Ezra into Esther in dumfounding manner. The challenge for them is these fragments all match the account in 1ˢᵗ Esdras, not Esther, which they try to ignore, but no longer can. Not a single fragment of Esther was found there. The claim is bogus. We cover that in detail in the Vol. 1 Torah Test.

Regarding Maccabees, this book was not found in Qumran either and there is no record of its existence as a story until Josephus really, who is also the first to reference a book called Esther as well. It sure is interesting how that works. Neither of these are referenced in the New Testament nor their added Feast Days they supposedly expand into nine Feasts from the seven well-established throughout the Old and New Testaments. No one was keeping Hanukkah nor Purim in the Bible paradigm in any of the Old nor New Testaments and we will test those as well.

Finally, the story of Judith is definitively fiction offering a false history even according to Martin Luther. In all three of these cases, one will find neither quoted in the New Testament including the supposed new Feast days *(See full test)*. The following is a summation of our Torah Test of all fifteen books called "Apocrypha."

APOCRYPHA

HISTORICITY SUMMATION
2. WITNESS OF THE SPIRIT

See also, 2nd Esdras: The Hidden Book of Prophecy, free in eBook at 2Esdras.org. See Vol. 1 for first half of this examination.

Notice all dates confirm these credible texts found in Qumran precede the New Testament.

Having proven the exiled Temple Priests who were ordained to keep Bible Canon lived in Qumran/Bethabara, we now have a foundation by which to test ancient texts. As the keepers of scripture left a Library of Bible Canon behind found in 1947 and beyond, this becomes a strong start for a first testing. There is much confusion with many occult books purporting to be inspired scripture. If they are not found in Qumran/Bethabara at least by concrete association, they should be set aside and treated differently until a full test is conducted which no scholar appears to have executed in this age. Scholars continue to treat this find with gross negligence using classifications such as Apocrypha and Pseudepigrapha. They ignorantly declare the holy Temple Priests kept fraudulent writings which has always been a lie. They did not need to create new stories to scare people.

Even this erroneous category of Apocrypha is mixed. The term merely refers to books outside of the Pharisee Canon which is meaningless and exposes the church is generally using that Pharisee Canon for the Old Testament today. However, those scholars fail to ask why they are following the Pharisees whom Yahusha outright rebuked regarding their ignorance of scripture. Their leaven and oral traditions *(Talmud)* transform Torah into anti-Torah *(Mark 7:9)*. How do we determine which is inspired and which is not? Though each requires a more extensive Torah Test we will execute for the rest next, the first criteria we can apply to root out truly false books is whether the text is found at least in fragments or quoted in content in the Levite Library of Qumran/Bethabara. That is where the only divinely-ordained Bible Canon was kept to the First Century. This will complete the testing for the 1611 King James Version Apocrypha.

BOOK:	QUMRAN TEXT FOUND:
FOUND IN QUMRAN:	
√ **1ˢᵗ Esdras** *(Proto-1stEsdrasᵃᶠ)*	*100 B.C.: 4Q550 (4QProto-Estherᵃᶠ). Cave 4. Aramaic. Are All 1ˢᵗ Esdras NOT Esther. [Vermes, pp. 619-20][22][88]*
√ **2ⁿᵈ Esdras** *(Used In Interpretation)*	*100 B.C.: 1QpHab, Cave 1 [Vermes, pp. 510-11]; 100 B.C.: 1QSb, Cave 1 [22: Vermes, pp. 389-390][22]*
√ **Wisdom of Sirach** *(Ecclesiasticus)*	*73 B.C.-4 A.D.: 2QSir/2Q18: Cave 2. Hebrew; 11Q5 (11QPsa): Cave 11. Sir. 51. Mas1H (MasSir). [Vermes, pp. 307, 641], 4Q416 VI 5, 13. [22][93]*
√ **Wisdom of Solomon** *(Used In Interpretation)*	*100-1 B.C.: Portions of 4Q Instruction: 4Q415– 418, 423; 1Q26. Cave 4 [100][95]*
√ **Book of Tobit**	*100-1 B.C.: 4Q196-200: Cave 4; 11QapPsᵃ, fr. 5: Cave 11. Hebrew & Aramaic. [Vermes, pp. 596-601][22]*
√ **Book of Susanna**	*4Q551: Cave 4. Aramaic. [Vermes, p. 651][22]*
√ **Prayer of Manasseh**	*50 B.C.: 4Q381: 33, 8: Cave 4. Titled "Prayer of Manasseh" which is a match in content to the KJVA; 2 Chr. 33:19 cites Manasseh's prayer was "written among the sayings of the seers (prophets)." Hebrew. [Vermes, p. 319][22]*
√ **Letter of Jeremiah**	*100 B.C.: 7Q2: Cave 7: Greek but closer to Hebrew tradition. [Vermes, p. 472][22]*
BY ASSOCIATION:	
Once Part of Jeremiah: √ **Baruch** *(Chapter 6 found in Qumran)*	*Letter of Jeremiah is the 6ᵗʰ Chapter of Baruch. Thus, Chapters 1-5 tie to Qumran as well. These were one book as an addendum to Jeremiah in that age. [81, 76, 78, 84, 79, 77, 80] 7Q2: Cave 7 [22]*
Once Part of Daniel: √ **Prayer of Azaryah** *(Abednego - The Song of the Three Young Men)* √ **Bel and the Dragon** *(Daniel's exploits)*	*Once an extension of the Book of Daniel with Susanna (found in Qumran) as Chapters 13 (Sus.), 14 (Bel.) and inserted after 3:23 (Azar.) in documented history. Separating them as separate books to attack them is not scholarship. [84, 85, 74, 81]*
NOT FOUND IN D.S.S.:	
✗ **Judith**	*See Deconstructing the Book of Judith in back.*
✗ **Book Of Esther** *Purim & Additions*	*See Testing the Book of Esther & Purim in back.*
✗ **1ˢᵗ & 2ⁿᵈ Maccabees** *Hanukkah*	*See Examining 1ˢᵗ & 2ⁿᵈ Maccabees & Hanukkah in back.*

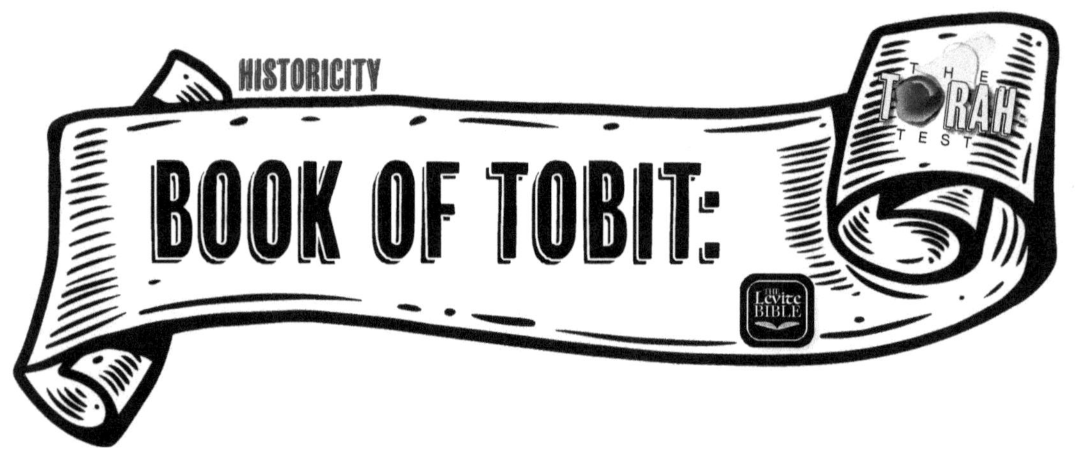

QUMRAN, FIRST CENTURY B.C.:

Qumran fragments labeled 4Q196-200 [22], are attributed to the Book of Tobit very directly and in abundance. These remnants are dated "palaeographically" to 100 B.C.-20 A.D. meaning they roughly guess based on the writing and other texts found with it. It is not a scientific dating with instruments and typically far earlier than the text would likely even date if examined, if Rockefeller could afford such dating of course. It appears not. It is a guess from a group of proven propagandists who misrepresent things like the presence of idols and sin in Tobit's time and claim that must date them to the era of Hellenism and nothing else. No one could ignore that Tobit lived in the idol and sin capitol of Nineveh in his actual time around 700 B.C. or let us not refer to them as academic nor scholarly, as that would require profound illiteracy. However, their dates do not matter for this is merely a copy which is the tradition of the scribe in ancient Israel they forget in dealing with any text not in the Pharisee Bible Canon. They do not treat Genesis the same way. Tobit tells us even a period in which the text was written period.

These fragments from Cave 4 correlate to portions of Chapters 1, 2, 3, 5, 6, 7, 8, 9, 10, 12, 13, and 14 [22, Vermes, pp. 594-601]. Considering Tobit is only 14 chapters and portions of 12 chapters were found, it is unbelievable any scholar would dare deny Tobit as inspired scripture based on historicity. This was long before the Catholic Counsels, nor Protestantism and antithetical to Pharisaism which all have no say to overrule the legitimate Temple Priests' Bible Canon already in place before either existed in Judaea period. Tobit was written in the era of the captivity of the Northern Kingdom in Assyria as the book makes no room for any other authors – only he and his son. We will address the plausibility of the story of Tobit and Tobias at the end of that publishing of that book in detail including a timeline. If you have read or heard this is in question, it is a paradigm steeped in unenlightened behavior who attempts such and their questions could have been answered by themselves if they were capable of even a little credible study.

"Tob^a, Tob^c and Tob^d are palaeographically dated to the first century bce and Tob^b, as well as the Hebrew Tob^e, to the turn of the era (30 BCE-20 ce)."
– Vermes, p. 594 [22].

Also, multiple fragments of what are titled Apocryphal Psalms (III) (11 QapPs^a= 11Q11) were found in Cave 11 in Qumran. Among them, were two very distinct references to the Archangel Raphael who does not appear, at least by name, in the entire modern Bible Canon. The first is by name quoting the Book of Tobit indisputably. Though a small amount of text, the account of Tobit is apparently mentioned here as that is the only Bible text in which Raphael is documented other than First Enoch. More specifically, it is the only account where "Raphael healed them," referring to Tobit's blindness and Sarah's demonic oppression.

Though Enoch does affirm Raphael is the Angel of Healing, he tells more of his binding of the Watcher Fallen Angels and has no accounts with specifics of Raphael healing multiple humans. Only Tobit does. There are no other options here for fragment 5 as it must be a song about the inspired Biblical account found in Tobit. No more words are needed to determine that. This means the Temple Priests applied Tobit as inspired scripture even in their own songs or they would never include fiction. To say they did, is to misapply the entire character of a Temple Priest in illiterate ignorance and many scholars are guilty of such.

"[Ra]phael healed them. Amen, amen. Selah." – Apocryphal Psalms (III) (11 QapPsa= 11Q11), fr. 5, Vermes, p. 317. [22]

For the other account of Raphael in this same column, though not by name, Vermes is clearly unaware of First Enoch in content in this respect. This is very obviously when Raphael bound Azazel, leader of the Watcher Fallen Angels and cast him into the pit or Tartarus originating in First Enoch which is also being applied as inspired scripture *(see The First Book of Enoch: The Oldest Book in History, free in eBook at FirstEnoch.org)*. This is the Temple Priests quoting First Enoch 10, especially verse 4, in the form of a song also applying it as inspired. As they are the anointed keepers of Bible Canon, this is more significant than any Pharisee or Catholic Counsel which neither can overrule the Temple Priests who already established Old Testament Canon long before the Pharisees even entered Judaea and before there was even the origins of a Catholic Church. The notion they get to outvote the Temple Priests is one of the very dumbest false paradigms we face today.

"In col. III a 'powerful angel' is mentioned (Raphael in First Enoch) who seems to be charged with defeating the demon (False, this is Azazel the Watcher Fallen Angel, not a demon) and casting it to the 'great abyss' and the 'nethermost [hell]' (Tartarus)." – Vermes, p. 316. [22].

Vermes is referring to this fragment demonstrating, even though he catalogued the scrolls, his understanding is profoundly lacking. He also translates YHWH as The LORD in ignorance as well hiding the name of Yahuah which is even worse. The fact that we continue to observe a record of learning disability on the part of these scholars with these scrolls is perplexing.

> *"The Lord (YHWH, Yahuah) will strike you with a [grea]t b[low] for your destruction and in His anger He will send against you a mighty angel [to execute] all His decisions, who will be [without] mercy on you ... against all these, who [will take] you [down] to the great abyss, [and to] the nethermost [hell.] ... dark [in the gr]eat abyss ... no more on the earth. ... for ever, and ... by the curse of Abaddon (the bottom of hell) ... the furious anger of the L[ord] (YHWH, Yahuah) ..."*
> *– Apocryphal Psalms (III) (11 QapPsa= 11Q11), fr. 4., Vermes, p. 317 [22].*

> *"Caves 4 and 11 revealed the Book of Tobit in Aramaic and in Hebrew..."*
> *– Vermes, p.11 [22]*

Partial manuscripts of Tobit were found in both Hebrew and Aramaic in the Dead Sea Scrolls. The most ancient archaeological evidence suggests Hebrew as the origin and Tobit originated in Northern Israel where he spoke and wrote Hebrew as his primary language, not Greek, nor Aramaic. Aramaic became the language of many in Samaria after Tobit's people, the Northern Tribes of Israel, were taken away and replaced by occult imposters from the East. They spoke Aramaic largely, not the Northern Lost Tribes who spoke Hebrew originally. Certainly, Tobit would have picked up at least some Aramaic in Nineveh, but he was born and raised in Israel where he spoke Hebrew. He would have written in his native language.

For scholars to confuse this very elementary timing is another example of their inability to even read basic history and the Bible whether alone claim to be able to interpret it. This is why they understand little and their conclusions veer in unthinkable directions. Tobit lived centuries before there was a Greek Empire even and long before the Hellenistic era scholars love to date many texts in ignorance without any science. Of course, that entire argument is a paper tiger shrouded in falsehood. There is no scripture that Yahuah said He preserves His Word in Hebrew on Earth. He does so in Heaven on the Heavenly Tablets. That is a false paradigm scoffers use to try to censor what the true Temple Priests defined as inspired Bible Canon even leaving their library as a preserved time capsule for us to rediscover in the days of increasing knowledge as Daniel predicted *(Dan. 12:4)*.

We know from the Book of Jubilees and First Enoch the practice of recording Biblical accounts on the Heavenly Tablets kept by the Angel of the Presence, an Archangel, is known fact *(Jub. 1:27-29, 2:1; 1 En. 81:1-2)*. As well, the language of Heaven is documented as Hebrew since Creation *(Jub. 12:25-27)* and Heaven was not confused at Babel. So, if they demand the originals, they better stop censoring texts that originate in those Heavenly Tablets for one. They also need to refrain from advocating a Pharisee Canon over the Biblically anointed one they don't even know. This is affirmed in Revelation with Heavenly Tablets such as The Book of Life *(Phil. 4:3; Rev. 3:5, 13:8, 17:8, 20:12, 15, 21:27, 22:19)* we all love to quote, as well as by Luke and Paul *(Acts 7:53; Gal. 3:19)* and the Qumran exiled Temple Priests *(4Q180, p. 553 [22]).*

TOBIT: NEW TESTAMENT, FIRST CENTURY:

The Book of Tobit is also quoted directly and indirectly in content in the New Testament. R.H. Charles compiled several. One can disagree with one here or there as being more compelling. However, this cache of references as a whole certainly proves as affirmation that the scrolls in Qumran were inspired Bible Canon quoted by Messiah and the Apostles. It only takes one such quote.

Tobit:	*New Testament: Charles, p. 199. [81]*
13:6 same uncommon Greek phrase	*1Tim. 1:17*
With 4:9 same	*1Tim. 6:19*
With 4:21 same	*1Tim. 6:6*
4:15 (LXX)	*Eph. 5:18*
12:10 they that sin are enemies to their own life	*Rom. 6:23 Wages of sin is death*
4:8 give according to that little	*2 Cor. 8:12 according to that a man hath*
4:7, 16 let not your eye be envious, when give alms	*2 Cor. 9:7 let him give; not grudgingly*
12:10	*Gal. 4:10*
4:15 drink not wine to make thee drunken	*Eph. 5:18 be not drunk with wine*
11:9	*Luke 15:20*
12:8	*Matt. 6:1-18*
4:9	*Matt. 6:20*
4:15 what you hate, do not do to others.	*Matt. 7:12, Luke 6:31 do unto others...*
6:7	*Luke 11:41*
6:16	*Matt. 25:35*
4:12	*1 Thess. 4:3*
1:3	*Acts 9:36b*
2:1	*Acts 2:1 (Pentecost)*
3:16	*Acts 9:18*
12:12	*Acts 10:4*
8:3	*Rev. 20:2*
8:16	*Rev. 21:10-12*
8:18	*Rev. 19:1-7*

It is rather monumental that Paul's famous doctrine "the wages of sin is death..." from Romans 6:23 very closely fits Tobit 12:10 *"they that sin are enemies to their own life..."* as its origin. In terms of giving, Paul clearly derived the tone of Tobit 4:8 in 2 Corinthians 8:12. However, in the famous "golden rule" of Messiah, "do unto others..." of Matt. 7:12, once again, that significant doctrine has an origin in Tobit 4:15 *"...what you hate, do not do to others."* These are not possibly, "maybe," but definitive examples of the New Testament quoting the Book of Tobit.

In Matthew 22:25 *(Cf. Mark 12:20; Luke 20:29)*, the Pharisees thought they were clever in ridiculing the story from Tobit much like many modern scholars. Understand it was not in their Pharisee Canon which the church generally follows for the Old Testament in error today, instead of the one from the Biblically ordained Temple Priests who did include Tobit as Canon. They speak of seven brothers who each die and the next of kin takes the wife of the former passing one wife through the seven men. That sounds like quite the fairy tale that Yahusha would not even need to answer unless there is some sort of basis they were trying to exploit. One woman married to seven husbands who all died consecutively. That is unprecedented as having any origin in any scripture unless one is familiar with the story of Tobit as Yahusha was, but the Pharisees were not really. In Tobit *(3:8, 7:1)*, Sarah was being harassed by a living Nephilim, which is a demon, who strangled each of her seven consecutive husbands in the marriage bed. We vet this at the end of the Tobit.

This is a definitive reference to the Book of Tobit that the Pharisees, who do not treat Tobit as scripture, confuse and embellish for the purpose of tricking Yahusha by undermining scripture, He quotes even, at the same time. They failed. Tobit's son Tobias becomes the eighth husband but survives as the Archangel Raphael assists him in driving away the Nephilim. In answer to this retelling of Tobit in error, Yahusha says to the Pharisees, who do not understand Tobit nor treat it as scripture according to Josephus in 90 A.D.: "Ye do err, not knowing the scriptures, nor the power of God." They were not only trying to entrap Him in a custom they did not understand, but specifically in the story of Tobit, they denied as scripture including the miracles it documents because they err. He goes on to address the issue of whose wife she would be in the resurrection because this is based on a true story. None of us will have spouses in the resurrection so the question demonstrated the Pharisees were ignorant and He put them in their place. This is Pharisees trying to slam Tobit over 2,000 years ago. Unfortunately for them, they got slammed instead but that does not stop them from continuing this same failed argument today.

In Matthew 11:25, Yahusha uses a term that directly matches Tobit 7:18 as "Lord of heaven and earth." This can be found a little differently in Genesis 14:22 and 24:3, but is the exact same, even in Greek as Tobit which appears a direct quote.

In Tobit 11:9, after all he had been through even losing his sight, an aged Tobit declares he is ready to die after seeing his son's safe return. This rings very similar as the origin of Luke 2:29 where Simeon pronounces the same after he meets Yahusha as a child. That was backed by Biblical precedence in Tobit.

Revelation draws on Tobit with great significance. In Chapter 1, verse 4, John references this message from Yahusha and *from the seven Spirits which are before his throne."* You will not find the concept of seven Archangels in the entire modern canon nor their names other than a couple because the modern church has followed the Pharisees and censored it in ignorance. They removed the origin of John's words making his statement questionable, they'll say, yet they are too stupid to connect that it only becomes so because they removed the origin. However, this is an ancient truth originating in First Enoch Chapters 20 and 40 and Tobit. In either event, at least one of these books is being quoted by John the Apostle in monumental doctrine, of which the church has lost understanding. They even try to debate Tobit's identification of the Archangel Raphael which is well recorded in First Enoch, and both have always been inspired fact and John just said so. We also document Raphael, the Angel of Healing and one of the Angels of the Presence in Yah's throne room at the end of the Book of Tobit. Raphael is also recorded in the Dead Sea Scrolls as well.

Tobit 12:15 KJVA
*I am **Raphael one of the seven holy Angels**, which **present the prayers of the Saints**, and which go in and out **before the glory of the Holy One**.*

In fact, in the verses that precede this in Tobit 12 as well as 15 *(above)*, Tobit further describes Raphael as the Angel of Healing, an Angel of the Presence, but also, as the Angel who does *"bring the remembrance of your prayers before the holy one."* Essentially, Raphael is also an Archangel who intercedes on behalf of mankind.

Tobit 12:12-14 KJVA
*Now therefore, when you did pray, and Sarah your daughter in Law, I did **bring the remembrance of your prayers before the holy one**, and when you did bury the dead, I was with you likewise. And when you did not delay to rise up, and leave your dinner to go and cover the dead, your good deed was not hid from me: but I was with you. And now **Elohim has sent me to heal you, and Sarah** your daughter in law.*

Some scoffers even try to use this against Tobit because they cannot read the Book of Revelation. This is a Bible bedrock doctrine with no origin really in the modern Old Testament yet again. There is a mention by Zechariah 1:12-13 where an angel speaks to Yahuah and has a conversation, but it does not read as a supplication. Scholars should be seeking this out, but they would not like the answer. Revelation 8 documents this practice in the End Times where a powerful Angel, likely Raphael, offers up the prayers of ALL the saints on the altar before the very throne of Yahuah. That is how Heaven operates as fact and this incredibly significant theology originates in the Book of Tobit.

Revelation 8:3-4 KJV
And another angel came and stood at the altar, having a golden censer; and there was given unto him much incense, that he should offer it with the prayers of all saints upon the golden altar which was before the throne. And the smoke of the incense, which came with the prayers of the saints, ascended up before God out of the angel's hand.

Furthermore, Hebrew 13:2 states: *"Be not forgetful to entertain strangers: for thereby some have entertained angels unawares."* Who did? Many scholars use the stories of Abraham and Lot to justify this declaration from the author of Hebrews. The problem is both of those stories are not such examples. Abraham and Lot were both aware they were entertaining angels. In Lot's account, the other people in Sodom even knew those were angels which is why they wanted their daughters to procreate with them bringing the return of their ancient gods, the Nephilim, especially the Titans. To what scripture does Hebrews refer? It is the Book of Tobit where Tobit and Tobias entertain an angel unaware. Raphael conceals his identity to the end *(12)*. Yes, Angels do that. This is the likely origin of Hebrews in this regard.

In Revelation 21, the first Heaven and Earth pass away and a second is made new. In verse 2, New Jerusalem comes down from Heaven to Earth. John further describes this Holy City with the streets paved with gold. The church loves this concept from the pulpit as it should. However, why is it that pastors do not know, John was quoting the Book of Tobit and documenting that gold will come from a certain land? In fact, how is it they do not know the significance of Ophir, the land of gold above the Garden of Eden in End Times prophecy? *(see The Search For King Solomon's Treasure: The Lost Isles of Gold and the Garden of Eden, free in eBook at OphirInstitute.com).*

Tobit 13:17 KJVA
And the streets of Jerusalem shall be paved with beryl, and carbuncle, and stones of Ophir.

There is no debating the historicity of the Book of Tobit as inspired scripture and Bible Canon whether a scholar likes the story or not. Of course, most do not understand it because they have never bothered to test it and its content which vets as factual, credible and accurate. We test the plausibility of Tobit at the end of the publishing of that book. However, once again, the 1611 King James translators also document this synergy between Tobit and the New Testament.

1611 KJV ANCHORS NEW TESTAMENT ORIGINS TO TOBIT:

Even the Original 1611 Authorized King James Version cites Tobit in the margin note as the origin of four New Testament passages with their parallels. This includes three times that the 1611 KJV anchors the words of Yahusha to the Book of Tobit as well as two references by the Prophet Ezra drawing from Tobit in about 400 B.C. Tobit lived and wrote around 700 B.C. thus, it becomes the origin and not the other way around. That further entrenches that date as accurate as the Book of Tobit defines itself. However, the negligence of translators who missed many other such cross-references especially those in Revelation regarding New Jerusalem is rather unimaginable. However, Messiah quoted Tobit according to the 1611 KJV.

Tobit:	*New Testament: 1611 KJVA Anchor*
4:12	*1Thess. 4:3*
*4:15 ***Yahusha Quoted Tobit****	*Matt. 7:12; Luke 6:31*
*4:16 ***Yahusha Quoted Tobit****	*Luke 14:13; Matt. 6:1*
14:5	*Ezra 3:8, 6:14 (Later O.T.)*
4:7 & Sirach 14:13 (One or the other is the origin)	*Luke 14:13***Yahusha Quoted Sirach or Tobit****

For us, there are others we feel Charles and the 1611 KJV may not have found but this is good enough for the connection in secondary evidence. One fascinating controversial scripture is Luke writing of Paul's citation of Yahusha in Acts 20:35 *"how he said, It is more blessed to give than to receive."* Yahusha did not appear to have said that in the Gospels anywhere and many scholars scoff instead of reconciling. However, it is a direct quote of Tobit 12:8: *"It is better to give alms than to lay up gold."* Did Luke attribute the quote to the wrong person? Perhaps. Does that undermine the whole of scripture? Only for an idiot who is incapable of elementary understanding in these days of scoffing.

These documents are thousands of years old, copied over and they have survived. Yes, there has been manipulation but, most of this can be unraveled today using the Hebrew and Greek to understand what the word or phrase used means. When we, then, review parallel passages that must agree and do, the original meaning is usually evident. Instead, we find scholars too often who will take such and exploit them as enemies of the Bible undermining its integrity in an illiterate paradigm which ultimately hates the Bible and operates as Pharisees. Luke's quotation most certainly derives from scripture from Tobit and is thus, accurately inspired whether one finds a direct passage of Messiah saying so or not. The so-called fact checkers who need to be checked, use this tactic often in fraud.

TOBIT: 135-570: AFTER THE APOSTLES:

We begin not only with Tobit found in Qumran with fragments dated 100 B.C.-20 A.D., but the continued references in the New Testament even by Messiah demonstrate Tobit has always been Canon. We, then, find Tobit very early in the church. In fact, Polycarp of Smyrna, Bishop of one of the 7 ekklesias of Turkey mentioned in Revelation as Yahusha's, is known to have been a disciple directly to John the Apostle *(Irenaeus: Adversus Haereses, Against Heresies 3.3, 180 A.D. and Tertullian: De praescriptione hereticorum 32.2, 177 A.D.)*. In fact, John had ordained Polycarp as bishop of Smyrna *(Jerome: On Illustrious Men, De Viris Illustribus, 393 A.D.)*. In this handoff of the mantle from John to his disciples, Polycarp wrote concerning the Book of Tobit citing passages 4:10 and 12:9 around the first half of the second century. Tobit has always been Bible canon, and this is continued as factual tradition as the Bible practice.

> *135: Polycarp of Smyrna, Disciple of John the Apostle:*
> *"...Polycarp apparently cites Tobit exactly. The juxtaposition of almsgiving with deliverance from death is unusual enough to make influence from Tobit almost certain... Polycarp then would be the first writer to use this short formula in reference to Tobit. ...Polycarp is exactly reproducing the quotation from Tobit which includes either Tobit 4:10 or Tob 12:9." – Berding [92]*

135: Polycarp of Smyrna, Disciple of John the Apostle: Epistle to the Philippians 10 quotes Tobit 4:10, and 12:9. [84][81]

198: Clement of Alexandria: The Stromata 6.12 quotes Tobit 12:8. [89][81]

204: Hippolytus: Commentary on Daniel, 6:55 cites Tobit 3:17. [81]

248: Origen: Contra Celsum 5.19, Origen quotes "As is written in the book of Tobit" quoting Tobit 12:7. [84][81] De Principiis, Book III cites Tobit, "by the angel that accompanied Tobias." [90]

252: Cyprian, Treatise 4,32 quotes Tobit 12:8 . Treatises, 11:11 (A.D. 257) quotes Tobit 13:6 [81]

305-384: Pope Damasus I: Divine Scriptures included Tobit. [84]

350: Cyril of Jerusalem: Catechetical Lectures, 4:33 "Jeremiah one, including Baruch [1-5] and Lamentations and the Epistle [of Jeremiah-Baruch 6]" treating Baruch and Letter of Jeremiah as Bible canon part of Jeremiah. [81]

357: Athanasius: Defense before Constantius, 17 quotes Tobit 4:18. [81]

368: Hilary of Poitiers: Prol. in libr. Psalm Epistle of Jeremiah included as canon with Tobit. [81]

382: Council of Rome: Decree of Pope Damasus listed the Old Testament to include Wisdom... Ecclesiasticus [Sirach]... Jeremias one book (with Baruch 1-6)... Daniel one book (with Susanna, Bel, and Azaryah)... Tobit... [81]

387: John Chrysostom: Concerning Statues, 7 quotes Tobit 4:15. [81]

393: Council of Hippo: Canon 36 included Tobit. [81]

396: Ambrose: Epistle 63:16 quotes Tobit 12:8,9. [81]

397: Council of Carthage III: Canon included Tobit. [81]

430: Augustine: De Doctr. Christiana, 2:8 and Speculum include Tobit as canonical. [81]

461: Pope Leo the Great: Sermon 10:4 quotes Tobit 4:7. [81]

550: Pseudo-Gelasian: His list of canon includes Tobit... [81]

570: Cassiodorus: "...in his enumeration of the books of the Bible {De inst. Div. litt. 14) also includes Sirach and Wisdom among the books of Solomon, and therefore regards them as canonical; so also Tobit..." [81]

Once again, in Origen's Letter to Julius Africanus approximately 2nd Century, Origen recites Tobit for paragraphs as inspired Bible Canon responding to an assault from one learned yet illiterate of the Word. In fact, Origen rips into Africanus on numerous points including his claiming the prophets never quote other prophets which is completely the opposite of the truth. It is as if Africanus was so educated, he could no longer read simple basic sentences and we find this in modern scholarship routinely. It is sad but true. He responds:

"I cannot understand how, with all your exercise in investigating and meditating on the Scriptures, you have not noticed that the prophets continually quote each other almost word for word [75]."

In plain English, Origen told Africanus, he couldn't believe he could be so illiterate. These kinds of outright lies masked as debate of the unlearned claiming to be learned in response to delivering the truth, are exactly what we observe almost daily when we restore the Word to the ancient understanding. Though we do so with enormous support, and no one could review our research and say otherwise, they try to reduce the topic to the answer of a 5-year-old essentially exclaiming "nuh uh." They'll take a 432 page book and frame it as only quoting one or two scriptures when it references over 1,000 and yet, in the form of a court jester, they attempt debate on gnat-straining in the face of an extremely strong position. They do not have to agree with it, but they do need to grow up and respond as adults rather than many of the childish responses we see. What is sad is they are not even embarrassed by their ignorance, but their senses have been so dulled down by occult education even in the church, that they do not even recognize themselves. Yahusha does not recognize most of those either and they will find that out on the Day of Judgment unfortunately.

Some modern scholars do this same when they focus on the Greek copies of Tobit only as the supposed original language demonstrating their ignorance on the topic. Jerome said he translated it from an Aramaic copy but that is not good enough for scoffers who only wish to agitate. They mix and confuse and settle nothing. In fact, often they do not even commit to one position but leave us with indecisive ignorance.

Is the Book of Tobit inspired Bible Canon? The answer is simple – Yes! No one has ever put forth a credible debate otherwise. The Biblically ordained keepers of Bible Canon, kept it, quoted it themselves and taught it as such. The Prophet Ezra even quotes it around 400 B.C. The account most certainly gains status as inspired scripture in the New Testament including the words of Yahusha. The 1611 King James Version renders Tobit the origin of New Testament passages. Polycarp, Bishop of Smyrna and direct disciple of John the Apostle, kept and quoted Tobit as Bible canon continuing the practice of John who also quoted it. This tradition continued with concrete basis in foundation as the Book of Tobit was and remains Bible Canon and inspired scripture even through to today in some circles.

As we complete the Torah Test for Tobit, you will find it passes the test. The next question we will address very directly and in detail is the plausibility of Tobit. We have reserved that research to follow the publishing of the Book of Tobit. Though we all hear and read scoffing on this account, there is not a single truth to that criticism from supposed experts who cannot even tell the truth. Those scholars prove they cannot and have not researched their questions. That is the worst of scholarship as they are supposed to prove positions not just raise questions and leave them unanswered. That is not scholarship, it is confusion, and we all know its author.

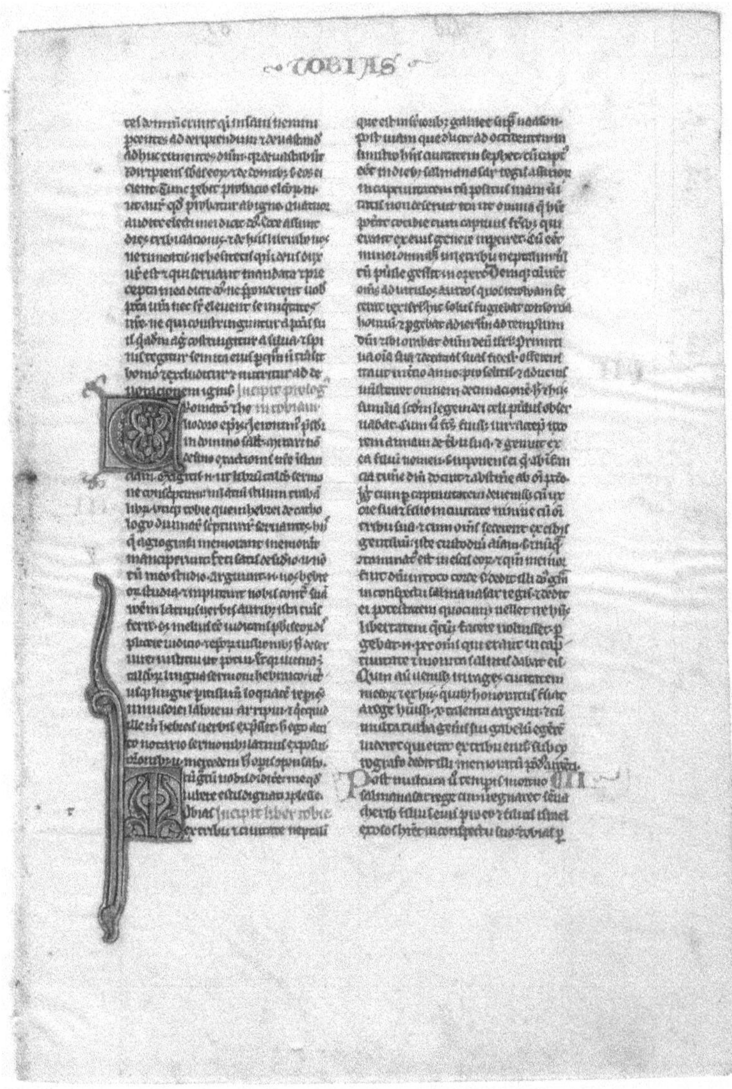

Leaf from a vellum manuscript of Tobit, c. 1240. Example of a 'pocket Bible' produced in Paris. Public Domain.

QUMRAN, FIRST CENTURY B.C.:

One of the most mischaracterized figures in ancient history is King Solomon. One will read that he was a magician, had an affair and child with the Queen of Sheba while already in his first marriage and holy at the time of the building of the Temple, and many things that fit no Bible narrative at all. Those stories originate in occult accounts, and they are never accurate and never Bible. Though he certainly entertained some dark years due to his following his pagan wives, Solomon repented in the end and was known for wisdom.

Let us not forget as Josephus *(Antiquities, 8:2:5)* and many Bible scholars have, that 1 Kings 4:29 defines King Solomon spoke 3,000 proverbs and 1,005 songs. When one considers those books attributed to Solomon in the modern Pharisee Canon, it falls short missing some of this content once existent in the Bible Canon of the Temple Priests. Josephus proves himself wrong as do most scholars on this.

Also known as the "Book of Wisdom" or simply as "Wisdom" in some translations and quotes, direct fragments of the Wisdom of Solomon were not found present in Qumran. However, it was used by the author of local community documents such as 4QInstruction. It appears this book was included in the original Greek Septuagint which dates in origin to the 300-200 B.C. era. Unfortunately, many scoffers would claim we do not know if Wisdom of Solomon was originally there even though it carried through tradition for thousands of years. However, with the connection to Qumran, there is no debate on that point. It was certainly perceived and used as inspired scripture in that time and more importantly than Egyptian translators or the Pharisees such as Josephus, by the actual Qumran/Bethabara exiled Temple Priests. They are the final word on the Old Testament Canon from the time of Moses and really Jacob to the First Century.

On this book, we find few scholars who appear to really breach the discussion as to whether there are references demonstrating commonality to the Wisdom of Solomon in Qumran. They all know there is a significant find in Qumran that they title "4QInstruction" which, they admit, is loaded with wisdom literature. Some, but few, even take it further and illustrate the passages from 4QInstruction that originate in Wisdom only to then retract backwards and clarify they do not intend to suggest that Wisdom of Solomon is found in Qumran or should be considered canon. The pressure is extremely obvious. Let us forgo such paradigms meant to limit knowledge. In other words, its message is found there and the clear origin of portions of this writing were there used as inspired scripture.

The author of 4QInstruction, which is considered fragments 4Q415, 4Q416, 4Q417, 4Q418, 4Q418a, 4Q423, and 1Q26 essentially dated to about the first century B.C. to first century A.D., used the Wisdom of Solomon as well as the Wisdom of Sirach, Proverbs, etc. in composing these documents. This entrenches a solid foundation that Wisdom of Solomon as well as Sirach, which is also found in Qumran directly, was read and known in that time by the keepers of Bible Canon. If they read and used it, why would any church attempt to change what was used as inspired by the only experts of Old Testament Canon? Who are they to change it?

One such scholar, Benjamin Wold, tests the similarities between Wisdom of Solomon and 4QInstruction found in Qumran. These excerpts show there truly is a connection though as a scholar, he does not call for an induction into Bible canon which no one needs anyway. If the Temple Priests used it as inspired in interpretation, there is nothing left to debate. It is inspired.

"Similar ideas and tropes found in the Wisdom of Solomon and 4QInstruction (4Q415–418, 423; 1Q26) have considerable significance for the study of early Jewish sapiential literature." [95]

"To not live according to the judgment of one' spirit (l. 18) results in corruption which is described as becoming fleshly. This too echoes what is found in Wis 2:21 where wickedness blinds the fool who reasoned falsely. [95]

"...and the righteous will be rewarded for their faithfulness (4Q417 1 i 14, 26; cf. Wis 4–9)." [95]

"The creation of a singular humanity in 4QInstruction, one that has it within their remit to comprehend the difference between good and evil, aligns more closely with mystery accessible by human reason as found in Wis 2:22. Whereas the speaker of the Wisdom of Solomon declares his mortality, that he is "a descendant of the first-formed child of earth" and "molded into flesh" (Wis 7:1), 4QInstruction emphasizes spirit and describes fleshly corruption. In the Wisdom of Solomon, although humankind was created for incorruption (Wis 2:23), a type of corruption (namely, death) occurs "through the Devil's envy" (Wis 2:24). The Wisdom of Solomon also makes a negative association of the body and the soul; in Wis 9:14–15, he declares that "the reasoning of mortals is worthless," because "a perishable body weighs down the soul." However, this is followed in Wis 9:17 with a statement that the one who has "learned your counsel" is the one to whom wisdom was "sent by your holy spirit from on high."

– Benjamin Wold. Journal for the Study of the Pseudepigrapha. Sage Journals [95]

Another scholar, Matthew Goff, offers some great research on this topic. Let us be clear he never commits that the Wisdom of Solomon should be considered as a Qumran text though he certainly demonstrates it was used by the writer of 4QInstruction in part whether he can see that fully in his paradigm or not. That, however, is not necessary. He and much of scholarship are steeped in the false view that Wisdom was written later. We will obliterate that when we show the many quotes in the New Testament as well as synergies between Solomon's Ecclesiastes and Wisdom of Solomon. The Original 1611 Authorized King James Version anchors several New Testament passages to Wisdom of Solomon in origin as well including the words of Yahusha, and we find it quoted around 74 A.D. by the disciple of Paul, Barnabas and in 80 A.D. by Clement of Rome *[91]*. This is an undeniable pattern of use from Qumran to Messiah and His Apostles to the next the generation and of course, we have catalogued a large cache of references that continue beyond that.

"The Wisdom of Solomon's reliance on post-exilic Palestinian traditions can now be assessed in light of the full publication of the Dead Sea Scrolls. Of particular importance is the largest sapiential text from Qumran, 4QInstruction (1Q26; 4Q415-18, 423), which was published in 1999.1 4QInstruction is normally dated to the second century BCE. It is a Hebrew wisdom text with an apocalyptic worldview. Not surprisingly, the composition has rejuvenated the study of the apocalyptic aspects of the Wisdom of Solomon." [100]

Wis. 7:17-18: "unerring knowledge of what exists, to know the structure of the world and the activity of the elements; the beginning and end and middle of times," an assertion that parallels 4Q418 123 ii 3-4(cf. Wis. 3:9)." [100]

"One should pray for understanding (Wis. 7:7-22; 4Q416 2 iii 11)." [100]

"Who can attain genuine knowledge of God and the cosmos? According to the Wisdom of Solomon, the righteous, who are sharply distinguished from the wicked. In 4QInstruction the answer is the elect... distinguished from the rest of humankind. 4Q418 81 states that God has separated the addressee from the "fleshly spirit..." (Note: The righteous and the elect are the same group and the rest of humankind are the wicked. There is no question regarding this.) [100]

*"In 4Q416 1 the natural world trembles in reaction to the advent of God to **destroy the wicked**. The "**heavens will be afraid**" and the "**[s]eas and depths**" **will be in terror**" (**Wis. 11:11-12**)." [100]*

4Q416, fr. 1 , 10-15: (Vermes, p. 425-426.) [22]
*"From heaven **He judges the work of wickedness** and all the sons of truth will be accepted...*
*...[until] his end and all those who have wallowed in it **shall be frightened and***

scream. For heaven ...The waters and abysses shall be frightened, and all the spirits of flesh shall be laid bare. And the sons of heaven ... its [judgment. And all injustice will yet come to an end and the age of trut[h] will be completed... ...in all the everlasting ages. For He is the God of truth, and from the beginning of years ... to establish righteousness between good and ev[il]. [For] his is a fleshly [inclination and his foundation..." –

He anchors this as a cross-reference to Wisdom 11:11-12 which matches, but there is a far better fit for this in Wisdom.

Wisdom of Solomon 11:11-12
Whether they were absent, or present, they were vexed alike. For a double grief came upon them, and a groaning for the remembrance of things past.

This is also affirmed far more closely in Chapters 4-5 of Wisdom and a very clear association becomes overwhelming.

Wisdom of Solomon 4:17-5:3
For they shall see the end of the wise and shall not understand what Elohim in his counsel has decreed of him, and to what end Yahuah has set him in safety. They shall see him and despise him, but Elohim shall laugh them to scorn, and they shall hereafter be a vile carcass, and a reproach among the dead forevermore. For He shall rend them, and cast them down headlong, that they shall be speechless: and He shall shake them from the foundation: and they shall be utterly laid waste, and be in sorow: and their memorial shall perish. And when they cast up the accounts of their sins, they shall come with fear: and their own iniquities shall convince them to their face. Then shall the righteous man stand in great boldness, before the face of such as have afflicted him, and made no account of his labors. When they see it, they shall be troubled with terrible fear, and shall be amazed at the strangeness of his salvation, so far beyond all that they looked for. And they repenting, and groaning for anguish of spirit, shall say within themselves, This was he whom we had sometimes in derision, and a proverb of reproach.

When assessing the use of the term "mystery" in 4QInstruction, there also appears a strong connection to Wisdom of Solomon.

"Though not as prominently, the Wisdom of Solomon, like 4QInstruction, uses the term "mystery" to refer to knowledge about God and the cosmos that one needs to be pious and just. The work claims that the wicked do not know "the mysteries of God" (Wis. 2.22 cf. 1QS iii 23)." [100]

1QS iii 21b-25a: (Vermes, p. 101.) [22]
The Angel of Darkness leads all the children of righteousness astray, and until

*his end, all their **sin, iniquities, wickedness,** and **all their unlawful deeds** are caused by his dominion **in accordance with the mysteries of God.** Every one of their chastisements, and every one of the seasons of their distress, **shall be brought about by the rule of his persecution;** for all his allotted spirits seek the overthrow of the sons of light.*
Wisdom of Solomon 2.22
As for the mysteries of Elohim, they knew them not: neither hoped they for the wages of righteousness: nor discerned a reward for blameless souls.

Goff spends a considerable amount of text on the parallel interpretation of Genesis 1-3 through the Wisdom of Solomon and 4QInstruction which synergy is evident. There is no doubt the Qumran author was using the Wisdom of Solomon in his wisdom accounts.

"See, for example, 4Q287 4 2; 4Q422 1 i9-10; 4Q504 8 4-6. Wis. 9:2-3 praises God who has "formed humankind (Adam) to have dominion over the creatures you have made, and rule the world in holiness and righteousness, and pronounce judgment in uprightness of soul..." [100]

Citing Wis. 2:23: "The immortality of the righteous is presented as a restoration of Adam's original condition. This has a Palestinian parallel in the conviction held by the Dead Sea sect that it's members will attain the "glory of Adam." Footnote: "1QS iv 7, 22-23; CD iii 20; 1QH iv 15 (cf. 4Q171 3 1-2)"
– Matthew Goff, Journal for the study of Judaism. [100]

"4QInstruction utilizes Gen. 1-3 to understand humankind in ways that are similar to the Wisdom of Solomon..." "The author of 4QInstruction may have understood Adam as immortal but never asserts this as explicitly as Wis. 2:23." The Wisdom of Solomon also has significant points in common with the two types of humankind laid out in the Hagu passage. The spiritual people of 4QInstruction and the righteous of the Wisdom of Solomon are associated with "the image of God" trope of Gen 1..." [100]

"Both the Wisdom of Solomon and 4QInstruction oppose those who attain eternal life with a type of humankind that is associated with the physical death of the body." 4Q416 1 12 compared to Wis. 5:17-23.
Wis. 5:9-14 to 4Q418 69 ii 6.
4Q418 103 ii 9; 4Q416 2 iii 7-8; 4Q418 55 11 to Wis. 7:1. [100]
"'We are tired of works of truth [we] are weary of...' Do [they] not wal[k] in eternal light? ... [gl]ory and an abundance of splendor are with them." (4Q418 69 ii 13-14; cf. 4Q418 55 8-11; 4Q417 2 i 10-12) "Eternal joy is a foil to the "eternal pit." (4Q418 69 ii 6; cf. 4Q418 126 ii 6-7) "Wis. 3:7 states with regard to the righteous that "in the time of their visitation they will shine forth, and will run like sparks

through the stubble." '... in Wis 2 v. 13 reads: "He professes to have knowledge of God, and calls himself a child of the Lord." "... v. 16 the righteous man "boasts" that God is his father." "...If the righteous man is God's son, he will help him, and will deliver him from the hand of his adversaries" (Wis. 2:28)." [100]

The similarity in language becomes very apparent in certain passages.

"lots of angels" "for himself as a first-born son" (4Q418 81 4-5) [100]

Wisdom of Solomon 2:13-18
*He professes to have the knowledge of Elohim: and **he calls himself the child of Yahuah**.*
*...and **makes his boast that Elohim is his father**.*
*...For if the just man be **the son of Elohim**, he will help him, and deliver him from the hand of his enemies.*
Wisdom of Solomon 18:13
*...upon the destruction of the **firstborn they confessed the people to be God's children**.*
Wisdom of Solomon 5:5
*How was **he counted among sons of God**? How is **his lot among saints**?*

Though lined with unbiblical Jewish theology introducing concepts not in either such as "cosmos" which is a term and understanding never found in the whole of these two texts, nor the Bible, this is a revealing comparison truly identifying the Wisdom of Solomon used in interpretation in Qumran. There are far too numerous examples to ignore, and we will not.

"Both Ben Sira and the Wisdom of Solomon, for example, emphasize divine judgment (e.g., Sir 23:16–21; Wis 3:10)."
– Goff, Society of Biblical Literature. p. 19. [101]

There are other such affinities one can find in just a simple reading of the two in parallel which should be no surprise in a writing known for wisdom drawing from ancient sources.

*"Do not reckon an **unjust man** as a help, nor **one filled with hatred** ... [apart from] the wickedness of his deeds at his visitation."*
– 4Q417, fir. 2 i, Vermes, p. 428. [22]
Wisdom of Solomon 10:3
*But when an **unrighteous man fell away from her in his anger**, he perished himself in the rage with which **he killed his brother**.*

"And without pardon, how can the poor [stand firm before Him]?"
– 4Q417, fr. 2 i, Vermes, p. 429. [22]
Wisdom of Solomon 6:6
For the man of low estate may be pardoned in mercy...

Though Wisdom of Solomon direct fragments are not found in Qumran, it is clear the community read and used it as inspired. When our modern Canon is not following this firmly established precedent, one must wonder what the agenda of modern scholars may be.

WISDOM OF SOLOMON: SIMILARITIES WTIH ECCLESIASTES:

In the case of Wisdom of Solomon, we have other books written by Solomon to which this has affinity especially Ecclesiastes. This is exactly what one would expect as King Solomon wrote it. Whether one says this is Wisdom quoting Ecclesiastes or the other way around, is of no consequence as no one can prove it either way and it is unnecessary rhetoric, not testing. This does not prove when the book was written but offers secondary support that this thinking matches Solomon as the probable author as it should.

"The relationship of the Book of Wisdom to Ecclesiastes is generally admitted."
– R.H. Charles, p. 525. [81]

Wisdom:	Ecclesiastes: Charles, p. 525. [81]
2:1, 'Short and sorrowful is our life.'	2:23, 'All his days are but sorrow, and his labour is grief.'
2:2, 'By mere chance were we born.'	3:19, 'The sons of men area chance ' (R.V. margin).
'Our name shall be forgotten and no one shall remember our works.'	1:11, 'There is no remembrance of the former generations.'
	2:6, 'For of a wise man, as of a fool, there is no remembrance for ever.'
	9:5, 'The memory of them (i. e. the dead) is forgotten.'
2:6-10	9:7-9
2:9	3:22, 5:18, 9:9
2:6-10	9:7-9

WISDOM OF SOLOMON: NEW TESTAMENT, FIRST CENTURY:

Wisdom:	New Testament: Charles, p. 526-527. [81]
12:12	Rom. 9:19-23
15:7	Rom. 9:21
8:6	Gal. 4:3
11:23 b that God's longsuffering is meant to lead sinners to repentance	Rom. 2:4 ' not knowing that the goodness of God leadeth thee to repentance.'
9:15	2Cor. 5:1
5:17 ff.	Eph. 6:1 iff.
15:3	John 17:3

"The fact that St. Paul knew and used the Book of Wisdom makes it far easier to admit its influence on other parts of the New Testament. The parallels to St. John and St. James adduced by other scholars and rejected by Grimm have now more to be said for them. Mr. Gregg quotes a large number of parallels to St. John, the most interesting being • This is life eternal, that they should know thee' (St. John xvii. 3) and Wisd. xv. 3. Prof. J. B. Mayor in his commentary on St. James, p. lxxv, gives twelve passages from Wisdom, echoes of which may be found in the epistle."
– R.H. Charles, p. 527. [81]

As with the Wisdom of Sirach, we find James (Yacob) also had a close relationship with the Wisdom of Solomon. R.H. Charles noted Professor J.B. Mayor catalogued an extensive list of passages where James, the brother of Yahusha, quoted Wisdom.

Wisdom:	Book of James: Mayor, p. 76-77. [93]
1:1-3	1:6-8, 2:4, 4:3
1:11	4:11, 5:9
2:4	4:14
2:10, 12-20, 15:14, 17:2	2:6, 5:6
2:23	3:9
3:4-6	1:2-3, 12-13
5:8, 15-16	4:6, 16, 1:10-12
7:7-10	1:5
7:18, 29	1:17
9:6	1:5
9:17	1:2-5, 3:15, 17
11:9	1:2-3, 12

The Book of John including Messiah's words demonstrate a very strong knowledge of Wisdom of Solomon as well. This is undeniable. There are many such passages that cross-reference catalogued by The Rev. J. A. F. Gregg, M.A in 1909.

Wisdom:	*Book of John: Gregg, p. 54-56. [99]*
9:9	1:1 In the beginning
8:3, 9:4	The Word was with God
7:12b, 22a, 8:6	1:3 All things...made by him
6:12	1:5 The light shineth
7:29-30	Darkness overcame it not
7:10	1:9 The true light
7:27b	1:12 As many as received him
7:25-26, 22	1:14 Glory as of the only begotten
7:11-12	1:16 Of his fulness
3:14	Grace for grace
9:17	1:18 He hath declared him
9:6	3:5, 15:5-6
9:10	3:13 That came down from heaven
16:5, 18:20	3:36 The wrath... abideth
8:3, 9:9	5:20 Loveth the Son, and sheweth
6:21	5:23 Honour the Son
7:27	5:26 To have life in himself
8:13, 17	5:57, 14:19 He shall live by me
16:12	6:63 The words
8:21, 9:4	6:65 Except it were given
2:12	7:7 Me it hateth, because I testify of it
3:9	8:31-32, 7:17 If ye continue..., ye shall know
2:24	8:44 A murderer (cp. 1 John 3:8, 12)
7:25 Nothing defiled can find entrance into her	8:46
6:18b	8:51 If a man keep..., he shall never see death
4:6	9:2
17:21	12:35 Darkness come upon you
12:19	13:15 An example
6:18a	14:15 If ye love me, keep
6:16	14:21 Will manifest myself
9:17b	14:26 Holy Ghost, whom the Father will send
14:22	14:27 Peace, not as the world giveth
7:28	16:27 , 14:6 Loveth you, because ye... loved me
15:3	17:3 Life eternal, that they may know thee
4:10-11	17:15 Not that thou shouldest take them
	out of the world
6:3	19:11 No power at all, except... from above

In their research, McClintock and Strong truly tie Wisdom of Solomon as the origin of some New Testament concepts. Whether it is quoted verbatim is impertinent as Solomon's Wisdom written prior becomes the basis of this thinking. If the Apostles and even Messiah were firmly steeped into the Wisdom of Solomon, there is no debating it's value as inspired scripture. Though many scholars have attempted over the years, they do so in ignorance.

"Thus it tells us that God is not the author of death, but made both man and all creatures in the image of his own eternity, and delighted in the whole of his creation (1:13.14; 11:24), which he made for perpetual duration (2:14; comp. Rom. 8:20-21)." – McClintock and Strong Biblical Cyclopedia [96]

Wisdom of Solomon 1:13.14
*For **Elohim made not death**: neither has He pleasure in the destruction of the living. For **He created all things**, that they might **have their being**: and the generations of the world were healthful: and there was **no poison of destruction in them**: nor the **kingdom of death** upon the earth.*
Wisdom of Solomon 11:24
*For you love all the things that are, and **abhor nothing which you have made**: for never would you have made any thing, if you had hated it.*
Wisdom of Solomon 2:14-15
He was made to reprove our thoughts. He is grievous unto us even to behold: for his life is not like other men's, his ways are of another fashion.
Romans 8:20-21 KJV
*For **the creature was made subject to vanity, not willingly**, but by reason of him who hath subjected the same in hope, Because the **creature itself also shall be delivered from the bondage of corruption** into the glorious liberty of the children of God.*

"Death entered into the world through the envy of the devil (Wisd. 2:24). We have here the first instance on record where the serpent which tempted the protoplasts in Paradise is identified with the devil (ver. 24), thus confirming the explanation given of Ge 3; Ge 1-15 in Joh 8:44; Re 12:9; Re 20:2."
– McClintock and Strong Biblical Cyclopedia [96]

Wisdom of Solomon 2:24
Nevertheless through envy of the devil came death into the world: and they that do hold of his side do find it.

Wisdom of Solomon is the first instance in scripture that we find this concept that it was satan's envy that sin and death were brought into the world. This is standard doctrine for most churches today and it did not originate in the New Testament where the modern Canon first explains it. Instead, it derives from the earlier Wisdom of Solomon 2:24. This is an extremely significant understanding, and Wisdom is the origin of these New Testament interpretations of Genesis 3. If the New Testament quoted Wisdom of Solomon, why do our churches ignore it? How one calling themselves a scholar not know this?

John 8:44 KJV
Ye are of your father the devil, and the lusts of your father ye will do. He was a
murderer from the beginning, and abode not in the truth, because there is no truth
in him. When he speaketh a lie, he speaketh of his own: for he is a liar, and the
father of it.
Revelation 12:9 KJV
And the great dragon was cast out, that old serpent, called the Devil, and Satan,
which deceiveth the whole world: he was cast out into the earth, and his angels were
cast out with him.
Revelation 20:2 KJV
And he laid hold on the dragon, that old serpent, which is the Devil, and Satan,
and bound him a thousand years,

In this case, the words of Yahusha Himself in Matthew as well as Paul and John all derive from the Wisdom of Solomon. When we restore these ancient texts, we find even the notion even more appropriate that scripture interprets itself.

> *"The book of Wisdom, moreover, shows that the doctrine of immortality and a future*
> *judgment was most emphatically believed and was generally current among the*
> *Jews (1:15; 3:4; 6:18-19; 8:17); that the Israelites believed that the wicked attract*
> *death by their painful deeds (1:16); that the saints, who are the children of. God*
> *(2:13, 16, 18), will ultimately judge the world and rule over the nations thereof*
> *(3:8; comp. Mt 19:28; 1Co 6:2; Rev. is 26; 3:21; 20:4-6)."*
> *– McClintock and Strong Biblical Cyclopedia [96]*

Furthermore, these scholars found Wisdom of Solomon as the origin of Paul and though he never tells us where such thinking originated, even Josephus.

> *"The body is regarded as the seat of sin (1:4; 8:20) and as a mere hindrance and*
> *prison of the soul (9:15; comp. 2Co 5; 2Co 1-4; Josephus, War, 2, 8, 11)."*
> *– McClintock and Strong Biblical Cyclopedia [96]*

This is extremely compelling that the Wisdom of Solomon was quoted in the New Testament and most importantly, whether attributed to that book or not, the doctrine is there. Many scholars choose to ignore this thinking from R.H. Charles, McClintock and Strong, J.B. Mayor, Gregg, and others but how exactly can they also ignore the 1611 King James anchors as well as even more definitive examples. In Romans 9:21, we see a direct quote of the potter and the clay making two kinds of vessels from Wisdom 15:7.

> *Romans 9:21 KJV*
> *Hath not the potter power over the clay, of the same lump to make one vessel unto*
> *honour, and another unto dishonour?*

Wisdom of Solomon 15:7
For the potter tempering soft earth fashions, every vessel with much labor for our service: yes, of the same clay he makes both the vessels that serve for clean uses: and likewise also all such as serve to the contrary: but what is the use of either sort, the potter himself is the judge.

In Matthew, Yahusha makes reference to the "gates of hell (Hades)" and the power over them. We do not find a direct derivative in the Old Testament for this precedence except in the Wisdom of Solomon. Yahusha was quoting Solomon.

Matthew 16:18 KJV
*And I say also unto thee, That thou art Peter, and upon this rock I will build my church; and **the gates of hell shall not prevail** against it. (Cf. Rev. 6:8, 20:13, 20:14)*
Wisdom of Solomon 16:13
*For you have **power of life and death**: you lead to the **gates of hell, and bring up again**.*

When the Pharisee leadership mocked Yahusha when He was on the cross *(tree)*, they knew exactly what they were saying as they were quoting prophecy from Wisdom of Solomon. They were not making up a charge to level at Him, they were trying to twist scripture and they well knew that the true Temple Priests read and used Wisdom of Solomon. Imagine the lunacy of a scholar forgetting that Messiah quoted this book claiming He quoted a false writing by a false author that was not written when it says it was written by whom it says it was. They accuse the holy Temple Priests ordained to keep scripture of tampering, forging, impersonating and several other unthinkable things but they do not think through the ramifications of their idiocy. They are the ones in their platform, who changed scripture and continue to hide it. Most of the entire paradigm is that of scoffers, not Bible scholars.

Matt. 27:43 KJV
*Likewise the **chief priests also, mocking with the scribes and elders**, said, "**He saved others; Himself He cannot save**. If He is the King of Israel, let Him now come down from the cross, and we will believe Him." "He trusted in God; **let Him deliver Him now if He will have Him**; for He said, '**I am the Son of God.**' "*
Wisdom of Solomon 2:18
*For if the **just man** be the **son of Elohim, he will help him**, and **deliver him** from the hand of his enemies.*

When Yahusha says Yahuah is His Father, such can be assumed from Old Testament prophesies. However, there are none more direct than the Wisdom of Solomon in this regard.

John 5:17-18 KJV
*But Jesus answered them, **My Father worketh hitherto, and I work.** **Therefore the**
Jews sought the more to kill him, *because he not only had broken the sabbath,* ***but***
said also that God was his Father, making himself equal with God.
Wisdom of Solomon 2:16
We are esteemed of him as counterfeits: he abstains from our ways as from filthiness:
he pronounces the end of the just to be blessed, and makes his boast that Elohim
is his father.

John 15 is Messiah's definition of salvation as a relationship. However, he quotes the Wisdom of Solomon in the imperfect branches with unprofitable fruit, or those not abiding in Him, shall be broken off. A full reading of John 15 fully identifies the same wisdom, and the origin is Wisdom of Solomon. Imagine Yahusha uses Solomon's wording, and a supposed Bible scholar claims it is a false book in ignorance accusing our Messiah as quoting a false book. The book is not false and cannot be, those scoffers most certainly are.

John 15:6 KJV
*If a man abide not in me, he is **cast forth as a branch,** and is withered; and **men**
gather them, and **cast them into the fire,** and they are burned.*

Wisdom of Solomon 1:5
*The **imperfect branches shall be broken off,** their fruit unprofitable, not ripe to
eat: yes, meet for nothing.*

In fact, when matching Romans 1:18-25 with Wisdom of Solomon 13:1-10, there is very apparent symbiosis between the two writings on the knowledge of the Creator and the ignorance and sin of idolatry.

We have a very close match with Romans quoting the tone and tenor of Wisdom 13 in multiple portions. Elohim's existence is evident in nature clearly seen by considering His works or understood by the things He made. There is no doubt Paul was entrenched in Wisdom of Solomon as inspired scripture.

Romans 1:20 KJV
*For the **invisible things of him from the creation of the world are clearly seen,** being
understood by the things that are made, even **his eternal power and Godhead;** so
that they are **without excuse:***

Wisdom of Solomon 13:1
*Surely vain are all **men by nature,** who are **ignorant of Elohim,** and could not
out of the **good things that are seen,** know Him that is: neither by **considering the**
works, did they acknowledge the work-master;*

Solomon was well familiar with idols, and he did not need to live in the age of Hellenism to do so which forms one of the most illiterate paradigms by scholars who try to date this work and others based on that incredibly inept claim. We find the same rebuke in Romans emanating from Wisdom.

Romans 1:23 KJV
*And changed the glory of the **uncorruptible God into an image made like to corruptible man**, and to birds, and fourfooted beasts, and creeping things.*
Wisdom of Solomon 11:15
*But for the **foolish devices of their wickedness**, wherewith being **deceived**, they **worshipped serpents void of reason**, and **vile beasts**: you did send a multitude of unreasonable beasts upon them for vengeance,*
Wisdom of Solomon 12:24-27
*For **they went astray very far in the ways of error**, and held them for **gods** (which **even amongst the beasts** of their enemies were despised) being deceived as **children of no understanding**. Therefore unto them, as to children without the use of reason, you did send a **judgment to mock them**. But they that would not be reformed by that correction wherein he tarried with them, shall feel a judgment worthy of Elohim. For look, for what things they grudged when they were punished, (that is) for them whom they thought to be gods, [now] being punished in them; when they saw it, they acknowledged Him to be the true Elohim, whom before they denied to know: and therefore came extreme damnation upon them.*
Wisdom of Solomon 13:10
*But miserable are they, and **in dead things is their hope**, who **called them gods which are the works of men's hands**, gold and silver, to show art in, and resemblances of beasts, or a **stone good for nothing**, the work of an ancient hand.*
Wisdom of Solomon 14:8
*But that which is **made with hands, is cursed**, as well it, as he that made it: he, because he made it, and it, because **being corruptible it was called Elohim**.*

As we focus out on the larger picture, it becomes evident that Paul is speaking from the framework of Wisdom of Solomon here largely. Idol worship leads to all kinds of sexual perversion in both these books in tandem but in origin from Wisdom of Solomon.

Romans 1:24-27 KJV
*Wherefore **God also gave them up to uncleanness** through the lusts of their own hearts, to **dishonour their own bodies** between themselves: Who **changed the truth of God into a lie**, and **worshipped** and served the creature more than the Creator, who is blessed for ever. Amen. For this cause **God gave them up unto vile affections**: for even their women did **change the natural use** into that which is **against nature**: And likewise also the men, **leaving the natural use of the woman, burned in their lust one toward another**; men with men working that which is **unseemly**, and*

receiving in themselves that recompence of their error which was meet.
Wisdom of Solomon 14:12
*For the **devising of idols was the beginning of spiritual fornication**, and the invention of them the corruption of life.*
Wisdom of Solomon 14:24-27
*They **kept neither lives nor marriages any longer undefiled**: but either **one slew another traitorously**, or grieved him by **adultery**: So that there reigned in all men without exception, **blood, manslaughter, theft**, and **dissimulation, corruption, unfaithfulness, tumults, perjury, Disquieting of good men, forgetfulness of good turns, defiling of souls, changing of kind, disorder in marriages, adultery,** and **shameless uncleanness.** For the **worshipping of idols** not to be named, is the beginning, the cause, and the end of all evil.*

Apparently, Paul also quotes Wisdom when he asks: who has known the mind of the Lord? He continues that he may instruct or counsel him. This is a very direct correlation to Wisdom of Solomon.

1 Corinthians 2:16 KJV
*For **who hath known the mind of the Lord, that he may instruct him**? But we have the mind of Christ.*
Wisdom of Solomon 9:13
*For what man is **he that can know the counsel of Elohim**? Or who can think what the will of Yahuah is?*

For there are many gods worshipped by pagans indeed but there is only one Father and Son who created all things including them whether they recognize it or not. This admonition is in complete agreement and coalesces as Wisdom of Solomon is the origin of Paul's words here.

1 Corinthians 8:5-6 KJV
*For though there be **that are called gods**, whether in heaven or in earth, (as there be **gods many, and lords many,**) But to us there is but one God, the Father, of whom are all things, and we in him; and one Lord Jesus Christ, by whom are all things, and we by him.*
Wisdom of Solomon 13:3
*With whose beauty, if they being delighted, **took them to be gods**: let them know how much better Yahuah of them is; for the first Author of beauty has created them.*

One cannot get more direct than a very clear quote of Wisdom 19:7 by Paul in 1 Corinthians. Our fathers were under the cloud passing through the sea is no doubt a perfect match here with Wisdom of Solomon as the origin.

1 Corinthians 10:1 KJV
Moreover, brethren, I would not that ye should be ignorant, how that all our fathers were under the cloud, and all passed through the sea;
Wisdom of Solomon 19:7
*As namely, **a cloud shadowing the camp, and where water stood before dry land appeared, and out of the Red Sea** a way without impediment, and out of the violent stream a green field:*

Just as Solomon prayed for wisdom and understanding and such came to him, Paul desires the same for believers in Ephesus. Once again, the use of the exact terminology "spirit of wisdom" being prayed for by both as well as revelation or understanding is very close indeed.

Ephesians 1:17 KJV
*That the God of our Lord Jesus Christ, the Father of glory, **may give unto you the spirit of wisdom and revelation in the knowledge of him:***
Wisdom of Solomon 7:7
*Wherefore **I prayed, and understanding was given me:** I called upon Elohim, and the spirit of wisdom came to me.*

Many scholars would claim the origin of the next verses in Isaiah 59:17 and no doubt there is synergy. However, King Solomon lived and wrote his books before Isaiah, and it is also Isaiah who quotes Wisdom of Solomon there as that is the chronological origin of this concept.

Ephesians 6:14 KJV
*Stand therefore, having your loins girt about with truth, and having on **the breastplate of righteousness;***
1 Thessalonians 5:8 KJV
*But let us, who are of the day, be sober, putting on **the breastplate of faith and love;** and for an helmet, the hope of salvation.*
Wisdom of Solomon 5:18
*He shall put on **righteousness as a breastplate,** and true judgment instead of an helmet.*

Continuing with the armor analogies of Ephesians, a full view demonstrates this source again as Wisdom of Solomon which denotes the complete or whole armor as the breastplate of righteousness, true judgment or salvation as a helmet, holiness or faith as a shield, and His wrath or spirit as a sword. Yahuah's creature is His weapon against His enemies, the unwise. Again, Solomon preceded Isaiah as the origin here. Isaiah 59:17 is missing the shield of faith or holiness, and the sword of the spirit or His wrath which are extracted from Wisdom of Solomon.

> *Ephesians 6:13-17 KJV*
> *Wherefore take unto you the **whole armour of God**, that ye may be able to withstand in the evil day, and having done all, to stand. Stand therefore, having your **loins girt about with truth**, and having on **the breastplate of righteousness**; And your **feet shod** with the preparation of the **gospel of peace**; Above all, taking the **shield of faith**, wherewith ye shall be able to quench all the fiery darts of the wicked. And take the **helmet of salvation**, and the **sword of the Spirit**, which is the word of God:*
> *Wisdom of Solomon 5:17-20*
> *He shall take to him His jealousy **for complete armor**, and **make the creature His weapon** for the revenge of his enemies. He shall put on **righteousness as a breastplate**, and **true judgment instead of an helmet**. He shall take **holiness for an invincible shield**. His severe **wrath shall He sharpen for a sword**, and the world shall fight with Him against the unwise.*

Where does Paul obtain the idea of a "crown of righteousness" given to the righteous on the Day of Judgment? The term is not used in the Old Testament nor by Yahusha except for Proverbs 16:31 which is not as direct, nor is the timing the same, but still Solomon writing. Of course, the scoffer would attribute the origin to only Proverbs because that is what is in their Pharisee Bible. However, regardless, both Proverbs and Wisdom were written by the same Solomon and this passage is far more like Wisdom than Proverbs especially the context of the Day of Judgment that appears in both 2 Timothy and Wisdom, but not specifically in Proverbs. Notice Solomon's references as well to Yahuah's hand just as Paul's to the Lord or Yahusha who is the Right Hand of Yahuah indeed which also, has no placement in the verse in Proverbs. This is surely Paul quoting Wisdom of Solomon.

> *2 Timothy 4:8 KJV*
> *Henceforth there is laid up for me a **crown of righteousness**, which the Lord, the **righteous judge**, shall give me at that day: and not to me only, but **unto all them** also that love his appearing.*
> *Wisdom of Solomon 5:16*
> *Therefore **shall they receive a glorious kingdom**, and a **beautiful crown from Yahuah's hand**: for with **His right hand shall He cover them**, and with **His arm shall He protect them**.*

Though Wisdom does not mention a sword specifically, the compatibility between Hebrews and Wisdom here is close. The Word is powerful, sharper than a sword thus not a sword but even more powerful. It leapt down from heaven from the throne of Yahuah as a fierce man of war. This integrates as Wisdom as the root of this concept as well.

Hebrews 4:12 KJV
For the word of God is quick, and powerful, and sharper than any two-edged sword, piercing even to the dividing asunder of soul and spirit, and of the joints and marrow, and is a discerner of the thoughts and intents of the heart.
Wisdom of Solomon 18:15
Your almighty word leapt down from heaven, out of your royal throne, as a fierce man of war into the midst of a land of destruction

Peter also seemed to be familiar with the Wisdom of Solomon when he speaks of a trial of our faith by fire. Much of this verse is a match such as being tried as gold in the furnace or fire. However, the end of both these are that we are as a burnt offering to Him and unto praise, honor and glory at the appearing of Yahusha in His return. This is the same timeframe even and coalesces as Wisdom as the origin.

1 Peter 1:6-7 KJV
Wherein ye greatly rejoice, though now for a season, if need be, ye are in heaviness through manifold temptations: That the trial of your faith, being much more precious than of gold that perisheth, though it be tried with fire, might be found unto praise and honour and glory at the appearing of Jesus Christ:
Wisdom of Solomon 3:5-6
And having been a little chastised, they shall be greatly rewarded: for Elohim proved them, and found them worthy for Himself. As gold in the furnace has He tried them, and received them as a burnt offering. (Cf. Sirach 2:5 which is quoting Wisdom of Solomon as well as it was written after)

In Revelation, Yahusha Himself is speaking of a sharp sword which later in Revelation he uses to consume the wicked. 2nd Esdras, a far later writing than Wisdom, mentions this is a sword of fire in fact. However, we do not find any Old Testament verses in the modern Pharisee canon which appear to fit this in inception. This appears to extract from the Wisdom of Solomon, and this is Yahusha speaking once again quoting our book. Solomon indeed saw the End Times prophetically.

Revelation 2:12 KJV
And to the angel of the church in Pergamos write; These things saith he which hath the sharp sword with two edges; (Cf. Rev. 19:15)
Wisdom of Solomon 18:16
And brought your unfained commandment as a sharp sword, and standing up filled all things with death, and it touched the heaven, but it stood upon the earth.

Another concept in Revelation appears to glean from Solomon's prophecy in Wisdom. There is no such event in his time nor before and this is the End Times.

Snow and ice were mixed with fire but did not melt. Fire burning the hail and sparkling in the rain destroyed the fruits or spirits of the enemies of Yahuah. This occurs on the Day of Judgment, and both agree as they had a vision of the same.

> ***Revelation 8:7 KJV***
> *The first angel sounded, and there followed **hail and fire mingled with blood**, and they were **cast upon the earth**: and the third part of trees was **burnt up**, and all green grass was **burnt up**.*
> ***Wisdom of Solomon 16:22***
> *But snow and ice endured the fire and melted not, that they might know that fire burning the hail, and sparkling in the rain, did destroy the fruits of the enemies.*
> *(Cf. Sirach 39:29 is quoting Wisdom of Solomon as well as it was written after)*

1611 KJV ANCHORS NEW TESTAMENT ORIGINS TO WISDOM OF SOLOMON:

With all this overwhelming evidence in a firm position proving Wisdom of Solomon was quoted in the New Testament, it is simply not enough for most scoffers. This renders this meaningless as there is no Biblical logic behind such opposition. However, even the Original 1611 Authorized King James Version anchors numerous New Testament passages as originating in Wisdom of Solomon. This is no surprise to those of us who have truly researched this book.

Wisdom of Solomon:	*New Testament: 1611 KJVA Anchor to NT*
1:6	*Gal. 5:22*
2:14	*John 7:7; Eph. 5:13, 14*
3:4	*Rom. 8:24; 1Cor. 5:1; 1Pet. 1:13*
3:7	*Matt. 13:43*
3:8	*Matt. 19:28. 1Cor. 6:2*
3:10	*Matt. 25:41*
4:4	*Matt.7:19*
6:3	*Rom. 13:1, 2*
7:26	*Heb. 1:3*
12:12	*Rom. 9:20*
12:13	*1Pet. 5:7*
12:24	*Rom. 1:23*
13:7	*Rom. 1:21*

WISDOM OF SOLOMON: 74-570: AFTER THE APOSTLES:

Appeared in the Septuagint, Syriac, Arabic, etc.

74: Barnabas, the companion of Paul the Apostle: Epistle of Barnabas, 6, quoted Wisdom 2:12. [91]

80: Clement of Rome: To the Corinthians, 27:5 quotes Wisdom 12:12, and 11:22. [81]

90: Josephus: War, 2, 8, 11 uses Wisdom of Solomon's concept derived from 1:4, 1:15-16, 2:13, 3:4, 3:8, 6:18-19, 8:17, 20, 9:15 without attribution. [96]

177: Melito of Sardes: Fragment in Eusebius' Ecclesiatical History, 4:26 defines Melito used Wisdom and Esdras as canon. [81]

197-200: Tertullian: On the Soul, 15 quotes Wisdom 1:6. Prescription Against the Heretics, 7 quotes Wisdom 1:1. [81] De Praescr. Haeres. c. 7; Adv. Valent. c. 2. [96]

198: Clement of Alexandria: The Instructor 2.1 quotes Wisdom 16:26 [89] And Wisdom 6:17-18. [90] And The Instructor, 1:8 quotes Wisdom 11:24 and Sirach 21:6. [81]

200: Muratorian Canon: On p. 11, line 8, notes the book of the Wisdom of Solomon. [81]

230: Origen: Fundamental Principles, 2:2 quotes Wisdom 11:17. [81]

235: Hippolytus: Against the Jews ,65 quotes Wisdom 2:1,12,13,15,16. [81][84][96]

252: Cyprian: Epistle 51/55:22 quotes Wisdom 1:13. [81] Exhortatf. Alart., 12. [96]

265: Dionysius the Great: To Dionsyius of Rome, 4 quotes Wisdom 7:25. [81]

305-384: Pope Damasus I: Divine Scriptures included Wisdom (of Solomon). [84]

311 (Before): Methodius of Olympus: Discourse on the Resurrection 8 quotes Wisdom 1:14. [84] This Bishop of Lycia quotes without reserve from Sirach, Wisdom, and Baruch, treating them all as 'Scripture.' [81]

315-403: Epiphanius of Salamis: Adversus Haereses, Haeres 76.5 cited "...the books of Wisdom, that of Solomon and the Son of Sirach as inspired scripture." [84]

337-397 St. Ambrose of Milan: Ibid. Bk. 1.7.49 quotes Wisdom 7:26. [84]

350: Cyril of Jerusalem: Catechetical Lectures, 9:2,3 quotes Wisdom 13:5. [81]

359: Hilary of Poitiers: On the Trinity, 1:7 quotes Wisdom 13:5. [81] Prol. in libr. Psalm (368 A.D.) "cites Ecclesiasticus and Wisdom as prophets, 'an expression which seems to imply his belief in their canonicity." [81]

371: Gregory of Nyssa: On Virginity, 15 writes: "[T]he Scripture tells us, 'into the malicious soul Wisdom cannot come'[Wisdom 1:4]." Wisdom of Solomon is Scripture. [81]

375: Basil: To Clergy of Samosata, Epistle 219:1 quotes Wisdom 11:20. [81]

378: Ambrose: Concerning Virginity, 7:35 quotes Wisdom 3:13. [81]

380: Gregory of Nazianzen: Oration 28, 2nd Theological 8 quotes Wisdom 1:7. [81]

382: Council of Rome: Decree of Pope Damasus listed the Old Testament to include Wisdom... Ecclesiasticus [Sirach]... Jeremias one book (with Baruch 1-6)... Daniel one book (with Susanna, Bel, and Azaryah)... Tobit... [81]

387-493: St. Patrick of Ireland: Letter to Coroticus 19 cites Wisdom 5:15. [84]

391: John Chrysostom: Homilies on John, 41 quotes Wisdom 1:5. [81]

393: Council of Hippo: Canon 36 included Wisdom. [81]

395: Jerome: To Paulinus, Epistle 58 quotes Wisdom 4:9. [81]

*397: Council of Carthage: the 'five books of Solomon', i.e. Proverbs, Ecclesiastes, Canticles, **Wisdom**,*

*and **Sirach**, are reckoned among the canonical Scriptures. [81]*
***419: Council of Carthage:** Affirmed 397 canon including Wisdom of Solomon. [81]*
***420: Jerome:** First to use the term "apocrypha" it appears including Sirach as such. In his Commentary on Isaiah (2:3) he prefaces quotations from Sirach and Wisdom with 'sicut scriptum est,' [81]*
***428: John Cassian:** Third Conference of Abbot Chaermon, 7 quotes Wisdom 1:13. [81][84]*
***430: Augustine:** De Doctr. Christiana, 2:8 and Speculum included Wisdom as canonical. [81]*
***461: Pope Leo the Great:** Sermon 78:2 quotes Wisdom 2:24. [81]*
***466: Theodoret of Cyrus:** To Cyrus Magistrianus, Epistle 136 cites Wisdom 4:11. [81]*
***483-565: Justinian the Emperor:** The Edict on the True Faith quotes Wisdom 14:9. [84]*
***550: Pseudo-Gelasian:** His list of canon includes Sirach and Wisdom... [81]*
***570: Cassiodorus:** "...in his enumeration of the books of the Bible {De inst. Div. litt. 14) also includes Sirach and Wisdom among the books of Solomon, and therefore regards them as canonical; so also Tobit..." [81]*

There is a proven track for Wisdom of Solomon as Bible Canon from Qumran to the New Testament to the Early Ekklesia. The Protestant Church today allows Pharisees and those who follow them to determine what is clearly a Pharisee Bible Canon. With all of this evidence and scripture accounting for far more wisdom from Solomon than exists in our modern Canon, there is truly no debating this book's inspiration, not Canonicity by those who matter. The impertinent scholars since who follow Pharisees have no opinion.

Vintage line drawing or engraving of the biblical story of King Solomon wisely judging two women about a baby. 1 Kings 3. Biblische Geschichte des alten und neuen Testaments, Germany 1859.

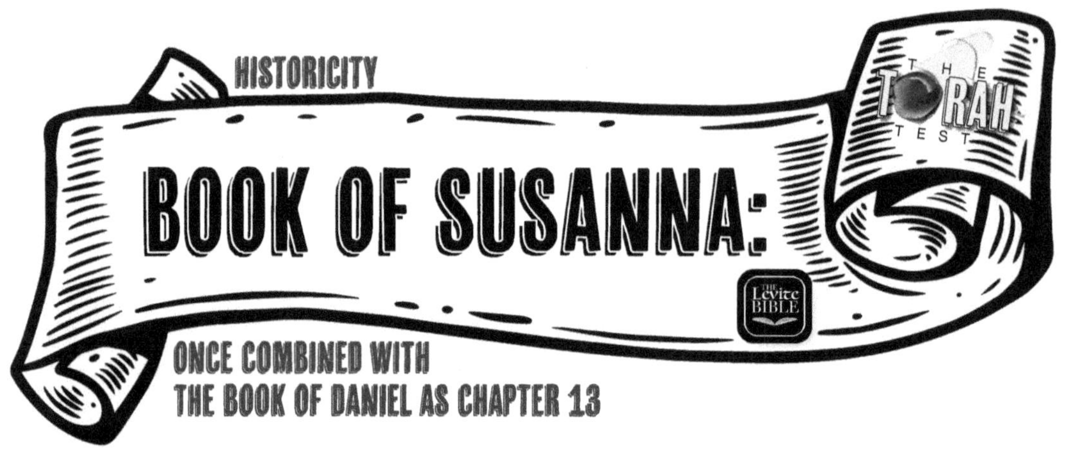

THE B.C. ERA:

The Book of Susanna was once part of the Book of Daniel either as an addendum after Chapter 12 as Chapter 13 or at the beginning of Daniel historically. In either event, it was considered in ancient times as Daniel by many. However, whether scholars wish to split hairs over which version places it where, the point is it was there in the Bible as Canon since early times. The Book of Daniel was certainly found in Qumran thus, by association as part of it, Susanna remains affiliated really.

However, though the scholarly language continues to refrain from commitment, there is a fragment identified even in Geza Vermes as: *"551=DanSus? Susannah episode in Daniel? [22]"* The question marks are since Susanna fragments evidently match its content on points, scholars still refrain from concluding it found there. They admitted at first there was a match and then, cowered into the background in the usual illiterate ignorance. What they did, however, is open a can of worms and leave them squirming without bothering to pick them up and organize them accordingly. They are not motivated to do so on this text likely because they do not wish to declare Susanna found in Qumran in most cases, even though they did initially. This same community is far too well documented even at this point in this book, as committing propaganda against the truth and these are not Bible scholars. For instance, one of the modern rockstar scholars James VanderKam notes:

> *"It is true that there are a few points of contact between the opening of Susanna and the general scene in 4Q551, but it is clear that, however the text may relate to Susanna, it is not from a manuscript of that story."*
> *– VanderKam [105]*

In our view, a "few points of contact" to Susanna's one chapter in fragments this small is solid in being able to affirm it found there. Fragments are all we have of most of the scripture found there and they had no problem trying to stretch the Proto-Esther Fragments belonging to 1st Esdras over to Esther in fraud. The question raised by D.S.S. scholars is whether this speaks of Susanna or Judges 19 *[Milik, 106]*. Initially, J.T. Milik suggested this fragment as belonging to the story of Susanna. He changed his view in the end but likely due to pressure.

> *4Q551 4QDanieTSuzanna (?) J.T. Milik, 'Daniel et Susanne a Qumran?',*
> *in: De la Torah au Messie, 337-359. Minute fragments which the editor*
> *connects with the story of Suzannah.*
> *– Martinez, The Dead Sea Scrolls Translated, p. 507 [107]*

In his attempted dismissal of this 4Q551 fragment as part of Susanna, VanderKam then, admits the historic pattern of addendums to the Book of Daniel, he calls *"a cycle of Daniel stories is well represented"* as firmly being present in Qumran in the Prayer of Nabonidus *[4Q242, 100 B.C., Vermes, p. 614, 22]*. Nabonidus is identified in the Babylonian exile in the days of Daniel and Daniel is mentioned in these fragments. Thus, the view that Daniel had addendums and extensions is not a new view in 200 A.D. as most scholars assert in ignorance, but consistent with the Dead Sea Scrolls and the Greek Septuagint in the B.C. era affirmed as early as 150 A.D. in Theodotion's Greek Version which included Susanna as part of Daniel in the same tradition and as Canon. It is not scholarship to then, dismiss that and claim that we should throw out Susanna, Bel & The Dragon, nor Prayer of Azaryah on such a false paradigm. They once again, build this supposition of an archetype on a house of cards lacking the backbone to commit to something obvious to us normal folk.

> *These meager data exhaust what the Qumran texts contain, so it has been*
> *thought, from the rather sizable corpus of literature called the apocrypha.*
> *It has appeared to be the case that none of the additions to Daniel such*
> *as Susanna figured there, even though a cycle of Daniel stories is well*
> *represented (e.g., the Prayer of Nabonidus).– VanderKam [105]*

The real question is what the text says and are these scholars really trying to reconcile it or due to pressure common in their circles, just backing off an initial position that this was in fact Susanna as is the case. This becomes rather embarrassing for these even rockstar scholars who seem to be incapable of a simple comparison. There are certain similarities in Judges 19 but anyone with a brain can quickly rule it out. What they are doing is trying to leave the false narrative in an unproven standard. They are not saying this fragment is not Susanna. Instead, they leave it as a question and fail to research which a child could conduct. They will not, but they will leave it vague so that no one can claim Susanna was found in Qumran. Let us not settle for such dubious models. An examination of the fragments reveals which is true and which is obvious propaganda.

4QDaniel-Suzanna (?) (4Q551)
"Frags. 1 + 3: 1 [...] knowledge [...]...
2 [.. . t]hen an old man[. . .] it is from
3 [...] son of Jonathan, son of Jeshua, son of Ishmael, son of [...] After this
4 [...] and all the men of the city gathered in front of the house and said to
him: «Make [...] come out [...] God». And they said:
5 [...] ... He [said] to them: «My brothers, do not do evil [. . .] here
6 for them 7 [...] which 8 [...] my spirit..."
– Martinez, The Dead Sea Scrolls Translated, p. 289-290 [107]

Let us break this down fragment by fragment as scholars should have already yet seem incapable. Does this adapt to the Story of Susanna or not? One can see how a scholar would begin to question if this were Judges 19 which is a fair inquiry and line of investigation, but even a little analysis would audit that as dishonest.

4Q551 TEST:

1. Knowledge:
Susanna: [1:48] "...without examination or knowledge of the truth..."
*Judges 19: This word **does not even appear**.*

2. Old man:
*Susanna: [1:52] Daniel said of the one judge: "you that are **waxen old** in wickedness;" [1:5] "...appointed two of the **ancients of the people** to be judges;" [1:61] The judges are referred to as: "the two **elders**."*
Judges 19: "old man" does occur 4 times [16, 17,20, 22].

3. "...son of Jonathan, son of Jeshua, son of Ishmael..." This lineage rings of the Tribe of Judah and the Levites embedded within.
*Susanna: **Daniel's lineage** is not listed in the Book of Daniel other than he is of royal or noble lineage (**Dan. 1:3**) meaning from David likely though there are several kings of Judah after David and before Daniel's time. It is definitive that Daniel is from the Tribe of Judah (**Dan. 1:6**) He also had two parents as all other children, and they could have been mixed between the Tribes of Judah and Levi even, and Daniel abided by the priestly oath indeed. Since we don't have Daniel's lineage, there is no connection to these three generations, but the names are certainly used by the Tribes of Judah and Levi in Yahudaea even in the time of the Babylonian captivity. One cannot test further because there is no recorded Biblical lineage that matches these three names which only serves as evidence that it is someone like Daniel who has an unknown family tree. However, Susanna is a probable match.*

*– **Jonathan**: As King David's best friend and the son of King Saul in antiquity. This name is very popular in the Tribe of Judah. During the Babylonian Captivity era, the name is mentioned by: **Ezra (2 times)**, **Nehemiah (3 times)**, **Jeremiah (3 times)**.*

*– **Jeshua**: Babylonian Captivity Era: Families in **Ezra (4 times)**, **Nehemiah (11 times)**.*

*– **Ishmael**: Not to be confused with Ishmaelites as his name was used in Judaea as well. Babylonian Captivity Era: **Ezra (1 time)**, **Jeremiah (19 times)**.*

*This is very **likely Daniel's lineage** and Susanna, to which this fragment appears to coalesce far better than any other book, appeared at times in history at the beginning of the Book of Daniel where such lineage would most likely appear. Of course, Daniel is also introduced as a young man in this story and the lineage may have been there in ancient versions as well.*

*Regarding her family, Susanna is only known as daughter of Chelcias whose descendancy may include these names as a possibility as well, though unlikely. McClintock and Strong Biblical Cyclopedia connects Chelcias as "Hilkiah of Neh. 12:7, or of Neh. 8:4" which fits linguistically. If so, there is no affinity with these three names and that lineage that we find. This lineage does not connect to anyone else in Bible history which only demonstrates this may very well be Daniel's missing family tree. Therefore, there are no alternatives that this defines anyone else, and it certainly does not fit **Judges**.*

Milik adds "Yap'an" at the end with space in between but that name does not exist in the Bible that we find either. Nothing firm can be connected with this but it leaves a possibility with a match to Daniel from Susanna.

Judges 19 has neither name and fails on this point.

4a. All the men of the city gathered in front of the house:
*__Susanna__: The narrative occurs in the garden of and **in front of Joacim's house**: [1:60] "With that all **the assembly cried out**..." [1:28] "...the next day, when the **people were assembled to her husband Joacim**, the two elders came..." [1:41] "Then **the assembly** believed them..." [1:34] Then the two elders **stood up in the midst of the people**..."*

*__Judges 19__: There is a house indeed and the sons of Belial surround the house: **"the men of the city**, certain sons of Belial, **beset the house round about**, and beat at the door [22]" but are not specifically in front of it. The **concubine falls down at the door to the house** [26-27] but most of the narrative is about what happens **inside the house**.*

4b. Come out:
Susanna: [1:28] "...the next day, when the people were assembled to her husband Joacim, the two elders came..." [1:14] "... when they were gone out, they parted the one from the other, and turning back again they came to the same place.." [1:60] "...cried out..." [1:24] "...cried out against her..."

Judges 19: "And the man, the master of the house, went out unto them... [23]" "... Bring forth the man that came into thine house... [22]"

5. Do not do evil:
Susanna: [1:57] "... would not abide your wickedness..."
[1:52] Daniel "...said unto him, O you that are waxen old in wickedness, now your sins which you have committed aforetime are come to light."
Judges 19: "... my brethren, nay, I pray you, do not so wickedly... [23]"

6-7. Too fragmented to connect to either narrative.

8. My spirit:
Susanna: [1:45] "Yahuah raised up the holy spirit of a young youth whose name was Daniel..."
Judges 19 does not even use the word spirit. It does use heart but so does Susanna.

In the commentary attributed to Milik by VanderKam [105], he cites some extra interpretation adding Line 1 to accompany these fragments which also helps to identify this fragment firmly and completely discounting Judges 19.

Line 1 of our fragment would contain a long title that explains the principal subject of the work: "Book of the words of X..., who, full of the Spirit...] of discernment ... [confounded] false witnesses."
– VanderKam quoting Milik. [105]

1a: Book of the words of:
Susanna: No match to either except Susanna used to be placed historically at the beginning of Daniel where such a line would make sense.
Judges 19: No connection even by association as this is the middle of the book.

1b: Full of Spirit... of discernment:
Susanna: [1:45] "Yahuah raised up the holy spirit of a young youth whose

*name was **Daniel**...." Daniel's discernment is the theme of the narrative from 45-64. [1:64] From that day forth was **Daniel had in great reputation in the sight of the people**..."*

*[1:2] Susanna, the daughter of Chelcias, a very fair woman, and **one that feared Yahuah**. (The fear of Yahuah is the beginning of wisdom/ discernment/understanding, Psa 111:10, Pro 9:10)*

*   **Judges 19:** There is **no connection**. It does not include the words discernment, wisdom, understanding, judgment, or similar which one could connect to a spirit of discernment. It also has no mention of spirit or the Holy Spirit as Susanna does. This is not a match for Judges and one would think VanderKam and Milik would know better. This should be embarrassing.*

*   **1c: False Witnesses:** This is the final nail for Judges 19 which never mentions such.*

*   **Susanna:** "...false witness..." [1:43, 49, 61 – 3 times] such as: [1:61] "And they arose against the two elders, for Daniel had convicted them of false witness..." [1:53] "For thou hast pronounced false judgment..."*

*   **Judges 19: does not include** the word **false** even once, **nor witness**. That is a huge miss for scholars.*

Basically, the math is simple. Out of 10 criteria, Susanna passes on 8 of 10 with an 80 percent score. The two criteria in which it doesn't agree, also do not correspond to Judges. However, Judges 19 fails miserably with a 50 percent score fitting 5 of 10 criteria. What kind of scholar cannot conduct such a simple test to decide? The kind that does not wish to perhaps due to pressure. This is gross negligence. This Qumran fragment squares to Susanna in content as Susanna was found there.

To further agitate the situation like a communist with no commitment to the truth, Milik not only equates a 50-percentile failure with an 80 percent suit, but he suggests perhaps there is even a third option which he exclaims could be totally lost, or maybe not. He does not know, and he cannot because the notion is illiterate. Perhaps a spaceship landed and took it because that is about as logical as such ignorance. There is nothing scholarly about the equation, which is proven uneducated based on a simple test, and to open the door to a third option without a single suggestion as to what that would even be, is saying nothing except the admission of being a propagandist. That is shameful scoffing, not scholarship.

"The Qumran fragment could as well belong to the first as to the second or even to a third composition, totally lost."– VanderKam citing Milik [105]

NEW TESTAMENT ORIGINS FROM THE BOOK OF SUSANNA:

As it is only one chapter long, the account of Susanna does not appear to be quoted in the New Testament. That should not be a surprise. However, Yahusha follows Daniel's example from Susanna in wisdom in John 8:1-11 in the account of The Adulterous Woman. The Pharisees claim the woman is caught in adultery like the story of Susanna, as she was falsely accused. With no drama involved, Yahusha bends down and begins writing on the ground. What did He write? No one knows except He, and those Pharisees. He proclaims: "He that is without sin among you, let him first cast a stone at her *(v. 7)*." Then, he bends down again and writes on the ground with His finger. It appears he wrote their sin or very likely, they may have been falsely accusing her as Pharisees are famous for such. Did He, as Daniel, see through their lies and call them out? The passage says they were "...convicted by their own conscience... *(v. 9)*" Yahusha does say to the woman after everyone left without stoning or further condemning her: "Neither do I condemn thee: go, and sin no more *(v. 11)*." Perhaps she sinned with some of those Pharisees in fact. It sure would make sense. However, the similarities in this and the story of Susanna are very interesting and certainly appear to connect even if not in their entirety.

> *Papias, 110 A.D.:*
> *"But concerning Matthew he (Papias) writes as follows: "So then **Matthew** **wrote the oracles in the Hebrew language**, and every one interpreted them as he was able." And **the same writer uses testimonies from the first Epistle of John and from that of Peter likewise. And he relates another story of a woman, who was accused of many sins before the Lord, which is contained in the Gospel according to the Hebrews."***
> *– Church History of Eusebius quoting Papias, 3:39:16. [108]*

In response, many scoffers, calling themselves scholars would cite the academic illiteracy that this account was added to the Gospel of John based on these words. The problem once again is those are incapable of credible analysis. Even when they do, they ignore what it says and reframe it. In 110 A.D., extremely close to the time of John within decades, Papias as recorded by Eusebius (300) as citing this account of The Adulterous Woman from John. He cites that it is contained in the "Gospel according to the Hebrews." The assumption of many illiterates then, is that must be either the Book of Hebrews which is wrong or some other unknown Gospel perhaps. Is John not a Gospel? Is Hebrews a Gospel? Is this really hard? This is yet another example of an extreme disability on the part of certain scholars.

However, we know it occurs in John and John was a Hebrew who wrote a Gospel as his father was Zebedee or Zebedaios (Ζεβεδαῖος) in Greek, which originates in the Hebrew name, Zebadyah *(Strong's 2199)*. John's Gospel is a Gospel of the Hebrews as is Matthew's and Peter's in Papias' mindset which is all that matters in interpreting what he said. He, first, defines this over two sentences here telling us Matthew wrote in Hebrew, not Greek, and ties that to John and Peter as the same. Deduction leads us to Papias quoting the Book of John here as he was not quoting Matthew, and Peter is not a Gospel and does not have this account. This is obvious.

Then, many scholars forget those two sentences and parse out the third sentence as a standalone fragment as if the other two did not exist. This is also how they read the Bible too often and no wonder their understanding is so poor on so many topics. If one thinks about it, Luke was Greek, not Hebrew so his Gospel is not that of the Hebrews. No one appears to know what Mark's nationality was and it is likely his text was Greek in origin. His name is Latin or Roman in origin *(Strong's G3138)* and he may well have been a Roman and not Hebrew either. Thus, this designation of the "Gospel according to the Hebrews" appears a clear reference to Matthew, John or Peter who were Hebrews. Note, also Peter's brother and fellow disciple, Andrew, was originally a Hebrew disciple of John the Baptist in Qumran/Bethabara where he met Yahusha when He was baptized there. Andrew followed Him from there. He was likely a Levite even as that was a community of such. One can see how tainted this paradigm of scholarship has become when quoting the Book of John must be justified that it is scripture, a Gospel and written by John, a Hebrew.

BOOK OF SUSANNA: 150-500: AFTER THE APOSTLES:

In ancient history, the canonicity of Susanna was not in question because it was not even treated as a separate publication. That is a newer development especially in the Protestant Church today. They have no precedence for separating it out from Daniel where it belongs as it was there in Qumran as Bible Canon and in the Greek Septuagint in the B.C. era [91], in documented tradition as early as 150 A.D. in Theodotion's Greek Version, and treated as Bible Canon by the early church fathers such as Irenaeus of Lyons *(180)*, Hippolytus *(204)*, and Origen *(230)* who still carried the tradition of Susanna as part of Daniel as Chapter 13 or before Daniel 1 as part of Daniel still *[91]*. This tradition continued with solid basis because Susanna has always been inspired scripture. When one reads this account showcasing the wisdom and discernment of a young Daniel, this provides background as another witness and perfect addendum to Daniel at the least. This text was clearly written by Daniel who also offers the first portions of his book in the third person in the very same way Susanna is written.

Origen *(230)* defends Susanna against Julius Africanus citing Susanna "as an authentic part of the Book of Daniel." It was originally part of Daniel as fact, not as speculation. He is referring to the time long before him as the original tradition, not a new one. How is it so many scholars cannot seem to even read.

230: Origen:

"Origen argues that the Story of Susanna is to be considered as an authentic part of the Book of Daniel." – Origen's Letter to Africanus [74]

"Your letter, from which I learn what you think of the Susanna in the Book of Daniel, which is used in the Churches. This, then, is my defense. I might, especially after all these accusations, speak in praise of this history of Susanna, dwelling on it word by word, and expounding the exquisite nature of the thoughts."
– Origen's Letter to Africanus [75]

Hippolytus (*204*) is specific that Susanna was placed *"at the beginning of the book [of Daniel]"* as *"a custom"* meaning it did not start in his time. However, one will find many scholars who try to claim this was new in the second to third centuries.

204: Hippolytus:

"What is narrated here, happened at a later time, although it is placed before the first book at the beginning of the book [of Daniel]. For it was a custom with the writers to narrate many things in an inverted order in their writings...To all these things, therefore, we ought to give heed, beloved, fearing lest any one be overtaken in any transgression, and risk the loss of his soul, knowing as we do that God is the Judge of all; and the Word Himself is the Eye which nothing that is done in the world escapes. Therefore, always watchful in heart and pure in life, let us imitate Susannah." Hippolytus, Commentary on Daniel, 6:1,61 (A.D. 204). [91]

200 A.D.: Archaeology: Papyrus 967 with Susanna:

In addition to the Dead Sea Scrolls in the B.C. era, the next oldest copy of a large portion of Susanna was found dated to about 175-200 A.D. In this find in Egypt, Susanna is only missing about 15 verses. This is very significant as Susanna and Bel & The Dragon appear with Daniel as the historic tradition records. There is no separating them. It would not matter if one did unless their agenda is to then, censor the inspired scripture of Susanna which is the communist tactic.

Circa 200 A.D.: Part of the Septuagint text of the Susanna story as preserved in Papyrus 967. Wikimedia Commons. Public Domain.

This particular papyrus is dated from the late 2nd to early 3rd century CE, and therefore pre-hexaplaric (Johnson in Johnson et al., 1938, p. 5). The main body of the papyrus was discovered in the early 1930s, and is considered Egyptian in origin; however, the origin of its parent text is uncertain. 967 originally contained (in order) Ezekiel, Daniel, Susanna and Bel, Esther (Johnson in Johnson et al., 1938, p. 3).

"We now have the text of 967 for most of Susanna, Daniel, and Bel and the Dragon..." – McLay [111]

THE HISTORIC RECORD AFTER THE APOSTLES:

The Book of Susanna was Bible Canon and in following the tradition of the Pharisee scribes, Jerome misplaced the book as "Apocrypha." Origen and Justin Martyr note this dynamic of the Pharisee scribes removing the Book of Susanna and other books from the Hebrew tradition. This is evident with Qumran Susanna.

"Origen received the story as part of the 'divine books' and censured 'wicked presbyters' who did not recognize its authenticity (Hom Lev 1.3.), remarking that the story was commonly read in the early Church (Letter to Africanus); and claimed the two Elders who had accused Susanna were Ahab ben Kolaiah and Zedekiah ben Masseiah, (Jeremiah 29:21); he also noted the story's absence in the Hebrew text, observing (in Epistola ad Africanum) that it was "hidden" by the Jews in some fashion. Origen's claim is reminiscent of Justin Martyr's charge that Jewish scribes 'removed' certain verses from their Scriptures (Dialogue with Trypho: C.71-3). Although omitted from current Jewish scripture, the story of Susanna is acknowledged to have been part of Jewish tradition in the Second Temple period [141]."
– "Susanna, Book of Daniel," Wikipedia (Sourced)

150: Theodotion: Greek Version placed Susanna at the opening chapter of Daniel. [81]
180: Irenaeus of Lyons: Against Heresies, 4:26:3 quotes Daniel 13:52-53, 56 (which is Susanna, Daniel ends at 12) also demonstrating Susanna was part of Daniel. [81]
200 A.D.: Archaeology of Papyrus 967 Septuagint: Most of Susanna found. 62a-62b. [P. Köln Theol. 37v].
204: Hippolytus: Commentary on Daniel, 6:1,61 quotes Susanna as part of the Book of Daniel. Commentary on Daniel, 6:55 also references the story of Susanna. [81]
230: Origen: Origen's Letter to Africanus "...praise of this history of Susanna, dwelling on it word by word, and expounding the exquisite nature of the thoughts." [75] Origen's Letter to Africanus, 5 defended the canonicity of Susanna [Daniel 13], Bel and the Dragon [Daniel 14], the prayers of Azarias, and the hymn of praise of the three youths in the fiery furnace [Daniel 3]. [81]
243: Latin Version of Theodotian's Greek: DePascha computus included Susanna as part of Daniel. [81]

*305-384: **Pope Damasus I:** "Divine Scriptures included... Daniel, one book..." (included Susanna, Bel & The Dragon, and Prayer of Azaryah). [84]*

*350: **Cyril of Jerusalem:** Catechetical Lectures, 16:31 quotes Daniel 13:45 which is Susanna. [81]*

*359: **Hilary of Poitiers:** On the Trinity, 4:8 quotes Daniel 13:42 that is Susanna. [81]*

*362: **Athanasius:** Discourses Against the Arians, 1:4 quotes Daniel 13:42 or Susanna. [81]*

*362: **Gregory of Nazianzen:** Oration 2, Flight to Pontus 64 quotes: "Passing by the elders in the book of Daniel [Daniel 13:5-Susanna]; for it is better to pass them by, together with the Lord's righteous sentence and declaration concerning them..." [81]*

*379: **Gregory of Nyssa:** Against Making of Man, 16 quotes Daniel 13:42 or Susanna as "The prophetical writing..." [81]*

*381: **Ambrose:** On the Holy Spirit, 3:6:39 quoted Daniel 13:44,45 or Susanna. [81]*

*382: **Council of Rome:** Decree of Pope Damasus listed the Old Testament to include Wisdom... Ecclesiasticus [Sirach]... Jeremias one book (with Baruch 1-6)... Daniel one book (with Susanna, Bel, and Azaryah)... Tobit... [81]*

*382: **Jerome:** Latin "Vulgate places Daniel between Ezekiel and Hosea as 'propheteia Danielis', Susanna being ch. 13." [81]*

*391: **John Chrysostom:** Homilies on First Corinthians, 15.10 quotes **Daniel 13:52 when Daniel ends at chapter 12. This is historically Susannah demonstrating it was part of Daniel** even quoted as such by title as the Book of Daniel Chapter 13. [84][81]*

*461: **Pope Leo the Great:** Sermon 49:6 quotes Daniel 13:56 or Susanna. [81]*

*500: **Cod. Wirceburgensis Palim:** Susanna verses 2-10 survive. [81]*

Understanding that there are one-off examples, Susanna as inspired scripture and Bible Canon is conclusive and not a matter for debate. The pattern is observed from Qumran fragments and the Greek Septuagint from the B.C. era, it appears Messiah follows Daniel's example from Susanna in John 8, canonicity is continued as attached to Daniel from 150-500 A.D., and that continues in some Bibles to this day. The new, strange doctrine is that which attempts to separate Susanna to attack it as a standalone book which it was not intended historically. Whether one finds an example here or there is of no consequence and not a debate point but obvious "willing ignorance" *(2 Peter 3)*. The Temple Priests settle such arguments with their authority to establish and keep Bible Canon ordained by Moses and Jacob.

In archaeology, we have fragments from 4Q551-Susanna (no question mark remains) in Qumran which vet as a match and Judges 19 fails. A supposed third option that never existed in a strawman suggestion by Milik was gross negligence and a poor attempt to offer confusion instead of facts which he shared no rapport it appears. That is followed by a large portion of Susanna represented in Papyrus 967 dated about 200 A.D., not as a new paradigm, but the continuation of the ancient tradition well-recorded from the B.C. era to 500 A.D. at least in affirmation. History and archaeology align demonstrating Susanna as inspired Bible Canon. This ancient records is preserved and all that matters in this determination.

THE B.C. ERA:

In light of the ancient association of Daniel and its addendum of Susanna, which was found in Qumran, it is more than reasonable to connect both Bel & The Dragon as well as Prayer of Azaryah as all three small books were once considered part of, and attached to, the Book of Daniel.

Though no direct Qumran fragments exist for this one chapter, the association is firm as demonstrated by the Greek Septuagint *(LXX)* from the B.C. era, Theodotion's Greek Version *(150) [81]*, and the Egyptian find of Papyrus 967 *(200)* especially *(McLay [108])*. Bel & The Dragon was also found in manuscript form in Cod. Ambrosianus *(313) [81]*. Cyprian *(257)* quoted Daniel 14:5 which is Bel & The Dragon published as the Book of Daniel *[84][81]*. Origen *(254)* defended it as canon *[81]*. Pope Damasus I *(305-384)* included Daniel as *"one book"* incorporating Susanna, Bel & The Dragon, and Prayer of Azaryah *[84]*. The tradition is well established. It does not matter that there may be some publishing from the ancient era which separated these books. What matters is that they were together in some form published within Daniel.

If this did not have the historic precedence of the Greek Septuagint in the B.C. era as well as the Qumran Scrolls where Susanna was found and the concrete evidence of early manuscripts found from 200-300 A.D., this may be a bit more difficult to connect. The other Qumran record of this tradition of Daniel's addendums included in the Book of Daniel is also preserved in *the Prayer of Nabonidus*, 4Q242 *[4QPrNab ar]* found in Cave 4 *(VanderKam: [105]; Vermes, p. 614: [22]; Martinez, p. 289: [107])*. It is fact that the true Bible paradigm kept these additions to Daniel as part of Daniel and this continued. For a scholar to seize on a find here or there that may treat them differently is meaningless. The Temple Priests already document this and any change is altering the Bible that was already established in canonicity for the Old Testament. Any scholar manipulating that record, daring to vote on something already resolved, is a propagandist who changes the Bible, and they are a cursed lot to which we should not be listening. It is sad that those within the

Catholic Church and the Pharisees disrespected the Word and the authenticity it holds. However, none of them had such right.

In fact, Bel & The Dragon is the story of Daniel, affirming the content of his book. He remains the main character which provides more background as to the elevation of the hatred Daniel's enemies garnered for him due to even more miraculous events. Removing this is a slap in the face to the Prophet Daniel who also likely authored it. One will also find Bel Marduk *(Ba'al)* is documented in archaeological history on the walls of the Palace of Assyria *(pictured on the cover of the full text)* and in written history as having a famous dragon. The photo of the relief demonstrates what we could call a dragon and this one was real, even centuries before Daniel, whether an exact likeness or not. We cover this at the end of this publishing.

There is also a Syriac version *(463)*, for one, which splits this book of one chapter into two parts as *"'Bel the idol', that of the Dragon having at its beginning the words, 'Then follows the Dragon. [81]"* However, that in no way challenges that Bel & The Dragon was part of Daniel and together as one book. There is nothing wrong with that treatmenr as the full book is still there.

NEW TESTAMENT ORIGINS FROM BEL & THE DRAGON:

We do not find any New Testament quotations of this one chapter of Daniel 14 which indicates nothing. Every time the Book of Daniel is quoted, it is included in association just as the Qumran finds of Daniel and Susanna bring in Bel & The Dragon by association.

BEL & THE DRAGON: 150-500: AFTER THE APOSTLES:

The Book of Daniel ends with Chapter 12. We saw Susanna was Chapter 13 of Daniel in ancient times. Bel & The Dragon is documented as Chapter 14 of Daniel by many. One cannot authentically isolate this book on its own as that is not how history treated it.

> *"In the Greek and Latin texts the three Additions to Daniel constitute an integral part of the canonical Book of Daniel, and were recognized as such, and therefore as themselves canonical, by the Council of Trent." – R.H. Charles, p. 652. [81]*

Even in Jerome's setting aside books then called "Apocrypha," Bel & The Dragon was still treated as part of the Book of Daniel as Chapter 14.

> *"In the Vulgate [382 A.D.] Bel and the Dragon forms ch. 14 of Daniel."*
> *– R.H. Charles, p. 652. [81]*

150: *Theodotion:* *Greek Version included Bel & The Dragon as part of Daniel. [81]*

180: *Irenaeus of Lyons:* *Adversus Haereses (Against Heresies) 4.5.2 quoted Bel and the Dragon 1:4-5. [84]*

200 A.D.: *Papyrus 967 Septuagint:* Bel & The Dragon found. *[P. Köln Theol. 37v].*

254: *Origen:* *Origen's Letter to Africanus, 5 defended the canonicity of Susanna [Daniel 13], Bel and the Dragon [Daniel 14], the prayers of Azarias [Daniel 3], and the hymn of praise of the three youths in the fiery furnace [Daniel 3]. [81]*

257: *Cyprian:* *Treatises, 11:11 quotes Dan. 14:5 which is Bel & The Dragon. [81]*

313: *Cod. Ambrosianus:* *"...exists in manuscript form" and includes Bel & The Dragon. Origin of Hexapla's Syriac version (617). [81]*

305-384: *Pope Damasus I:* *"Divine Scriptures included... Daniel, one book..." (included Susanna, Bel & The Dragon, and Prayer of Azaryah). [84]*

350: *Cyril of Jerusalem:* *Catechetical Lectures 14.25 quotes Bel and the Dragon. [84] Catechetical Lectures, 16:31 quotes Daniel 14 or Bel & the Dragon. [81]*

362: *Athanasius:* *Discourses Against the Arians, 3:30 quotes Daniel 14:5 (Bel & the Dragon). [81]*

374: *Gregory of Nazianzen:* *Oration 18, On the Death of his Father 30 quotes Daniel 14:33,34 which is Bel & The Dragon. [81]*

375: *Basil:* *On the Holy Spirit, 23:54 quotes Daniel 14:35 or Bel & the Dragon. [81]*

382: *Council of Rome:* *Decree of Pope Damasus listed the Old Testament to include Wisdom... Ecclesiasticus [Sirach]... Jeremias one book (with Baruch 1-6)... Daniel one book (with Susanna, Bel, and Azaryah)... Tobit... [81]*

382: *Jerome:* *"In the Vulgate Bel and the Dragon forms ch. 14 of Daniel." [81]*

463 A.D.: *Judaic-Syriac Corpus:* *Copy of Bel & The Dragon found in archaeology. [109]*

500: *The Peshitta:* *"...best preserved in the Cod. Ambrosianus B 21 (sixth century), reproduced in Walton's Polyglot and critically edited by Lagarde (Leipzic, 1 86 1). In Bel and the Dragon this version follows very closely..." [81]*

Though the footing is not as definitive as Susanna, we strongly assert that Bel & The Dragon is Bible Canon by association. It is a critical text in fully understanding the life of the Prophet Daniel and serves as affirmation of his exploits with additional detail we all need. There is nothing harmful in absorbing this one chapter of content and it certainly does not change Daniel, but confirms it.

Daniel's Answer to the King (1890). Oil on canvas, 120.5 x 187.9 cm (47.4 x 73.9 in). Manchester Art Gallery. Public Domain.

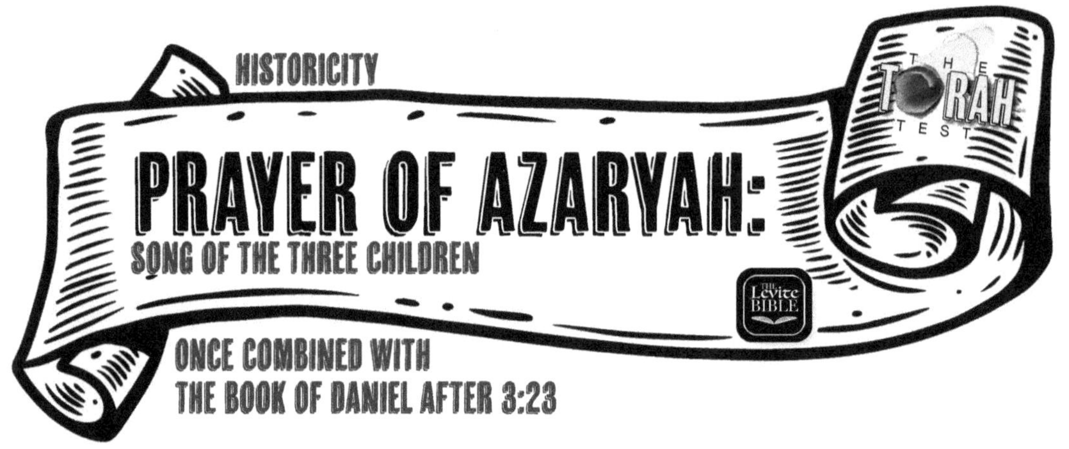

THE B.C. ERA:

In antiquity, the Prayer of Azaryah *(accurate rendering with "Yah")* is attested as included in the Book of Daniel with specific insertion after Daniel 3:23 as we even see historically in Cyprian *(258)*, Cyril of Jerusalem *(350)*, Athanasius *(362)* and the Council of Rome *(382)*. This is within the story of Daniel's three best friends and fellow prophets – Shadrach, Meshach and Abednego. These were the three who were thrown into the fiery furnace for refusing to bow to the mega statue. Azaryah is the Hebrew name for Abednego, and this was his prayer for deliverance which is monumental by all accounts. The notion that Daniel would not have included this one-chapter prayer as part of his book is unthinkable really. The thinking someone needed to make it up to complete Daniel is equally nonsensical. That position is merely ridicule and scoffing, not scholarship.

One such illiterate position comes from R.H. Charles *[Charles, p. 629, 81]*. He believed this book could not have been written by Azaryah because Hananiah or Shadrach is always listed first among the three. Thus, he was more significant which says nothing. It escapes us how this is called reason in scholarship. How is it that Charles could not deduce that Hananiah was listed first because he was likely older which has nothing to do with who said the prayer and wrote it down. Yahuah can use the youngest just as well and this is a lack of understanding as to whom He is.

The prayer was performed and written by Azaryah *(Abednego)* according to the text and who was Charles to claim he could not have written it in such ignorance? Charles then, using such reason deduces, also, that since the account mentions there were no Priests, Prophets, etc. in that age, that as usual, this must have been written in the Maccabean era about 168 B.C. *[Charles, p. 629, 81]*. The only term that could characterize such poor thinking is propaganda. For in the era of the Babylonian captivity, there were certainly dark times in which there appeared to be no Priests, Prophets, etc. Furthermore, when the sons of Zadok were exiled from the Temple around 165 B.C. by the Maccabees and Pharisees, they were still Priests and still writing prophecy even. We have their writings and that is a fact. Charles was not privy to that find, but such thinking is now obliterated in our age.

> ***300-200 B.C.: LXX (Septuagint) | 150 A.D. Theodotion | 383 A.D.: Vulgate:*** *The subject of this introduction is not really a 'book'; and it is **sometimes known as the 'First Addition' to the canonical Book of Daniel.** It is an illustrative interpolation inserted in that book after 3:23 (story of the fiery furnace); and is found there, forming an integral part of the book, in Theodotion, the LXX (Greek Septuagint), Vulgate, and some other versions dependent on the LXX.*
> *– R. H. Charles, p. 625 [81]*

We find one scholar after another attempting to ridicule this account when the Prophet Daniel included it and their illiterate paradigm tried to isolate it forgetting the tradition Daniel established. Again, specifically Daniel included this after 3:23 in placement even. The Septuagint tradition included it in the B.C. era and though it is not found in Qumran it is connected in association through Susanna and the Book of Daniel's established precedence including these addendums. It continued in 150 A.D. in Theodotion's Greek Version and about 382 A.D. in the Vulgate. Thus, there has never been a debate on this really.

As this is such a short prayer, it is no surprise the 1611 King James produces no cross-references here but, a simple reading of the prayer finds all kinds of Biblical references even to Genesis, whether the KJV included them or not. It continued to be quoted by so-called "Early Church Fathers" which again is not something needed, but secondary support that they continued to read it and apply it as scripture. The precedence that it was included in the Book of Daniel is too well attested to ignore. It continued as canon in as early as 150 A.D. not long after the Apostles *[81]*. Origen *(254)* also defended its canonicity *[81]* and he was not alone in the early church.

PRAYER OF AZARYAH: 150-500: AFTER THE APOSTLES:

*150: **Theodotion:** "The LXX (Septuagint) version of Daniel was almost universally displaced at an early date by that of Theodotion, made in the first half of the second century A.D. The English versions are made from Theodotion." [81]*

*254: **Origen:** Origen's Letter to Africanus, 5 defended the canonicity of Susanna [Daniel 13], Bel and the Dragon [Daniel 14], the prayers of Azarias [Daniel 3], and the hymn of praise of the three youths in the fiery furnace [Daniel 3]. [81]*

*258: **Cyprian of Carthage:** Treatises 4.8 quotes Song of the Three Children 1:27 known then as Daniel 3:51 (This confirms Azaryah was inserted into Daniel after 3:23). [84][81] Testimonies, 20 (ante A.D. 258) also quotes 3 Youths (Azaryah) as Daniel 3:37-43. [81]*

*305-384: **Pope Damasus I:** "Divine Scriptures included... Daniel, one book..." (included Susanna, Bel & The Dragon, and Prayer of Azaryah). [84]*

*350: **Cyril of Jerusalem:** Catechetical Lectures, 9:2,3 quotes Daniel 3:55-Three Youths. [81]*

*350: **Codex Vaticanus:** Prayer of Azaryah included as part of Daniel. [81]*

*362: **Athanasius:** Discourses Against the Arians, 2:71 quotes Daniel 3:57-Three Youths (Azaryah). [81]*

*382: **Latin Vulgate, Jerome:** "The Vulgate of Daniel is made from Theodotion, and includes the additions (Susanna, Bel & The Dragon, and Prayer of Azaryah)." [81]*

*382: **Council of Rome:** Decree of Pope Damasus listed the Old Testament to include Wisdom... Ecclesiasticus [Sirach]... Jeremias one book (with Baruch 1-6)... Daniel one book (with Susanna, Bel, and Azaryah)... Tobit... [81]*

*392: **John Chrysostom:** Homilies on 1st Corinthians, 18 quotes Daniel 3:29,33-Three Youths (Azaryah). [81]*

*400: **Codex Alexandrinus:** contains the whole 'Addition' as part of Daniel. [81]*

*440: **Theodoret of Cyrus:** Ecclesiastical History, 3:11 quotes Daniel 3:32-Three Youths (Azaryah). [81]*

*500: **Codex Marchalianus:** Daniel with additions including Prayer of Azaryah. [81]*

*500: **Psalterium Graeco-Latimim Veronense:** Daniel with additions including Azaryah. [81]*

The "Egyptian Versions," "The Ethiopic Version," "The Arabic Version," The Armenian Version are all "based on Theodotion." This means Susanna, Bel & The Dragon, and Azaryah were included as part of the Book of Daniel. [81]

Just as with Bel & The Dragon, even without fragments in Qumran, we find the association strong enough that Daniel did include these addendums as his practice. When one reviews this powerful prayer, it certainly rings true in content as well. There is nothing to be afraid in perusing this small book. At the end of the full publishing of this book, we will vet the plausibility of the details.

The symbolic story of tribulation and redemption is represented in this early Christian painting of the biblical story of "The Three Hebrews in the Fiery Furnace". From the Catacombs of Priscilla, Rome, Italy. Late 3rd century / Early 4th century. Public Domain.

3. ACCEPTANCE

For more on 1ˢᵗ and 2ⁿᵈ Esdras, please see our extensive Torah Test published in 2ⁿᵈ Esdras: The Hidden Book of Prophecy With First Esdras available free in eBook at 2Esdras.org. See Vol. 1 for first half of this examination.

As they all represent Old Testament times, all eleven of the mislabeled "Apocrypha" books fit well into the Biblical paradigm in the identity of Israel especially. One cannot get more Israelite than these books.

IDENTITY OF BIBLICAL ISRAEL:

Wisdom of Solomon:
Much like Ecclesiastes also written by King Solomon, this book of wisdom strings pearls of sagacity that are steeped in the Biblical view of Israel and its righteous lot while rebuking sin and idol worship throughout. This is the Bible message affirmed.

Book of Tobit:
Representing the Northern Tribes in Assyrian captivity, Tobit's view of Israel is consistent with that of the whole of scripture. When taken captive, he continued to give to his people in many ways. Unlike much of the North, Tobit remained holy even while in Israel continuing to visit the Temple in Jerusalem during the Feasts and even giving to the Temple Priests. He blurs the separation of the North and South with his actions as he saw the true Biblical Israel continued. He interceded for his people and his message coalesces. We cover the elements that have been attacked and ridiculed in this story at the end of the full publishing.

Book of Susanna:
Susanna, herself, is known as a righteous Israelite following the Law of Moses who is defended by the Prophet Daniel. Biblical Israel is at the forefront of this story.

Bel and the Dragon:
This text further defines the Prophet Daniel and defends Biblical Israel against the Priests of Bel Marduk *(Ba'al)*. Daniel, also, kills Marduk's famous sacred dragon demonstrating Yahuah is far more powerful than the pagan gods of Babylon. Biblical Israel is defended throughout.

Prayer of Azariah:
Also, an extension of the Book of Daniel, this short account is specific to the prayer issued by Abednego *(Azaryah)* while in the fiery furnace. He and his fellow prophets were cast into the fire for defending Biblical Israel and its Elohim. He represents the people of Israel in his prayer confessing their sins and affirming

Elohim's judgment. Azaryah also laments and intercedes for Biblical Israel asking forgiveness on their behalf and praying for deliverance.

YAHUSHA AND THE APOSTLES TO COME:

Of course, not all Old Testament books contain prophecy of the coming Messiah. One can force archetypes or types of Christs as some attempt, but there is never a need to do so and we will not in this testing in which all eleven of these texts already pass as identifying with Biblical Israel. It is notable, however, that some of these have strong prophesies of Yahusha coming in the flesh as well as His Second Coming and the Day of Judgment.

Wisdom of Solomon:
In 2:12-20, Solomon clearly identifies the holy Son of Yahuah. Even the Pharisees knew this to be a prophecy of Messiah when they ridicule Yahusha on the cross. They were clueless that Yahuah did help and would deliver Him and was about to do far greater. As usual Pharisees are incapable of reading in paragraphs and passages as Solomon clearly continues to identify that Messiah would be tortured and suffer a shameful death. That is absolutely Yahusha in accurate prophecy.

Book of Tobit:
Tobit predicted the destruction of the Temple still standing in his days as well as the desolation of Jerusalem *(14:4)*. In 14:5, he already knew the Southern Kingdom would return before they were even taken and that the Second Temple would be built before the First was even destroyed. He foretold of the return of the Lost Tribes in the very End Times as well as the Day of Judgment when the righteous would inherit the Earth. This is all part of Yahusha's story.

The rest of the eleven books labeled apocrypha are truly Old Testament in orientation and do not require prophesies of Yahusha. These include 1st Esdras (though found in 2nd Esdras), Susanna, Bel and the Dragon, Prayer of Azariah, and Prayer of Manasseh. These are Old Testament stories, and it is no surprise they do not possess direct prophesies of Messiah.

APOCRYPHA BOOKS THAT FAIL TO IDENTIFY WITH BIBLICAL ISRAEL AND MESSIAH:

Book Of Esther & Additions:
However, this becomes a major problem for Esther who failed to return to Israel with Ezra's last wave of returnees who left Babylon before Esther even entered the Palace. She is in the wrong place and time to be a part of Biblical Israel. There is no

credible reference to Yahusha either or even YHWH once for that matter. Esther fails this criterion as she is not even likely Hebrew, certainly does not represent the Biblical relationship with Yahauh, and she gains influence through adultery as a consort to the king initially. See the full test for details. This proves to offer a fake history of a story that could not possibly have happened to a righteous Judaean who should have been in Judaea at this point with the rest of her people. This appears a contrived story with the mission to confuse those who claimed to be Israel in Persia and Babylon who Ezra and the Priests sorted out and exposed in the return from Babylon. Esther's very occult representation cannot be overlooked as well.

1st & 2nd Maccabees:

The Maccabees *(Hasmoneans)* invaded Judaea as foreigners from Modi'in which is in Samaria in the territory of Dan. They not only do not represent Biblical Israel, but the opposite. They are the very enemies of Israel, and they are the Pharisees and Sanhedrin in origin which is their priestly caste who also opposed Yahusha and His Apostles. This book fails this criterion. See the full test for details.

Book of Judith:

The Book of Judith propagates a false history that could not possibly occur in the time she lived. It fabricates characters that could not exist such as a general Judith supposedly killed which at that time would be Nebuchadnezzar himself and this is illiterate. This book confuses Biblical Israel as Samaritans. In this time, the Samaritans were the replacements of the Northern Tribes of Israel who had ALL been taken captive into Assyria. This is a major problem for this book which we test in full. There is nothing worse than a book which identifies the synagogue of satan *(Rev. 2:9 and 3:9)* as Israel in confusion when they are the opposite.

4. IN AGREEMENT WITH THE WHOLE OF SCRIPTURE (OUR ADDITION)

For more on 1ˢᵗ and 2ⁿᵈ Esdras, please see our extensive Torah Test published in 2ⁿᵈ Esdras: The Hidden Book of Prophecy With First Esdras available free in eBook at 2Esdras.org. See Vol. 1 for first half of this examination.

We find most of these books quoted in content in the New Testament several times each. Messiah and the Apostles generally read them and taught them. Anyone claiming that Yahusha taught scripture with which He did not agree, is not a scholar of anything Biblical.

Wisdom of Solomon:

The writings of Solomon include very similar concepts as Wisdom which we have detailed, and it is often quoted in the New Testament.

Book of Tobit:

Though some attempt to ridicule the account due to their own ignorance on a host of topics we vet at the end of this full publishing of Tobit, Tobit not only matches scripture but provides an example of giving, contains accurate prophecy especially of the End Times, engages Raphael as the Angel of Healing he is documented in First Enoch to embody, introduces an ancient remedy that was used in history over thousands of years to the last century even, and exposes the prince demon Asmodeus who is celebrated in occult circles. Nothing in this book serves as a discrepancy to the Biblical record and all can be easily reconciled to scripture.

Book of Susanna:

This account affirms the Book of Daniel further detailing background of Daniel's early years in ministry. Nothing in the story vets as anything but credible and a match to similar accounts in the way Yahuah operates.

Bel and the Dragon:

In scoffing, some uneducated on the history of dragons and especially the famous dragon of Bel Marduk found in archaeology even, attempt to attack this book in ignorance. That is their shortcoming, however. This book leaves nothing to ridicule and vets as factual, credible and inspired.

Prayer of Azaryah:

Of course, one of the three in the fiery furnace said a prayer. It turns out that was Abednego *(Azaryah)*, and Daniel published it. There is nothing in this prayer that serves as anything but inspired in content.

BOOKS NOT IN AGREEMENT WITH THE WHOLE OF SCRIPTURE:

Book Of Esther:

Esther has a problematic history and an affinity to the occult over the Bible. In our full test in the back of this book, we will detail this overwhelmingly. It fails on this point as well especially since it places Esther and Mordecai in Persia after the final migration with Ezra. The story is at odds with scripture.

1st & 2nd Maccabees:

This history is false, and the Dead Sea Scrolls as well as Tacitus contain a true account that proves this was written by the enemies of Judaea not Hebrews and those of a different infused religion. We will provide a full testing of this book in the back.

Book of Judith:

Categorized as fiction even by Martin Luther, the Book of Judith fails because it disagrees with scripture in whole. It not only represents geographic and historic confusion but is a retelling of the opposite story confusing the synagogue of satan as Lost Tribes of Israel. It fails the test of secular and Biblical history, and there is nothing to be gained from this Nephilim account in allegory even.

With Vol. 1, this complete Torah Test offers a comprehensive view of each individual book labeled "Apocrypha" in the Original 1611 Authorized King James Version. Ultimately, this examination proves eleven of the fifteen books survey as inspired scripture. Four books fail, not only the challenge of inspired scripture, but these prove to be occult manipulations that never should have been titled "Apocrypha" in the first place. The entire category is a sham. This includes Esther whose Additions are included as "Apocrypha" and the book as Bible Canon when it never was, and should be removed from Bibles. This leaves us with a category of nothing as the term "Apocrypha" always has been fraud and never should be used as a paradigm of assessing the Bible. The fact that scholars throw the term out, proves those have never researched the topic adequately and they are not experts. If a book is not inspired, it does not belong. There is no such category as almost scripture in any credible ancient Bible library of the Temple Priests who treated eleven of these books as inspired scripture. The four that fail, are never referenced nor kept in their ordination.

It is time to restore the credible books which size up as inspired and Bible Canon. It is, also, time to eliminate Esther from our Bibles and end any discussion of all the Books of Maccabees, and the Book of Judith from any possible list of Bible Canon. In whole, our Torah Test thus far has restored The Books of Jubilees, First Enoch, 1st and 2nd Esdras, and nine books labeled "Apocrypha" *(eleven with 1st and 2nd Esdras)* as inspired scripture. Essentially, the modern Canon should be 65 books *(less Esther)* with at least thirteen books once part of the Bible Canon of the Temple Priests ordained to curate scripture. If one was to add those back in where they always should have been placed, this is really a total of 78 books thus far that were once included as Bible Canon by the only office of the keepers of Bible Canon. We are not suggesting to add to scripture but to restore what it has always been as the Pharisees and the Catholic Church are guilty of adding Esther and removing or separating these thirteen texts from our modern Bibles. Indeed, there are even more we will research in our next books. However, we are well on our way to restoring our Bibles and we will do our best to continue this vein of testing until we have exhausted the topic. The following chart will summarize our research on these books once "Apocrypha" in the 1611 King James, but neither belong in such a category and that has always been a fraudulent realm of scoffing.

1611 King James Version
APOCRYPHA
THE TORAH TEST CONCLUSION

See also, 2nd Esdras: The Hidden Book of
Prophecy, free in eBook at 2Esdras.org.
See Vol. 1 for first half of this examination.

CONCLUSION:

11 Texts Are Inspired Scripture
At Least By Historic Association.
Thus, Not Apocrypha!

4 Are Not Scripture At All
And Never Were.
There Is No Category
Of Apocrypha!

A Book That Is Not
Pharisee Is The Wrong
Measure To Begin With.
A Pharisee Canon Is
No Way To Determine
What Is Inspired!

Criteria set forth by Blue Letter
Bible with our additions. [1]

THE
TORAH
TEST

BOOK	1. Prophetic Authorship	2. Witness Historicity	3. Acceptance	4. Agreement w/ Scripture
FOUND IN QUMRAN:				
1st Esdras	✓ *Prophet Ezra*	✓	✓	✓
2nd Esdras	✓ *Prophet Ezra*	✓	✓	✓
Wisdom of Sirach *(Ecclesiasticus)*	✓ *Family of Sages*	✓	✓	✓
Wisdom of Solomon	✓ *King Solomon*	✓	✓	✓
Book of Tobit	✓ *Tobit Sage*	✓	✓	✓
Book of Susanna *(Once Part of Daniel)*	✓ *Daniel Prophet*	✓	✓	✓
Prayer of Manasseh *(Addendum to 2 Chronicles)*	✓ *Likely Jeremiah*	✓	✓	✓
Letter of Jeremiah *(Baruch 6 Historically)*	✓ *Baruch For Jeremiah*	✓	✓	✓
BY ASSOCIATION:				
Once Part of Jeremiah: **Baruch** *(Addendum to Jeremiah. Ch. 6 found)*	✓ *Baruch W/ Jeremiah*	✓	✓	✓
Once Part of Daniel: **Prayer of Azariah** *(Abednego - The Song of the Three Young Men)*	✓ *Azaryah Prophet*	✓	✓	✓
Bel and the Dragon *(Daniel's exploits)*	✓ *Daniel Prophet*	✓	✓	✓
NOT FOUND IN D.S.S.:				
Judith	✗ *Unknown*	✗ *Qumran-No!*	✗ *Qumran + Luther-No!*	✗ *Adds to Word*
Book Of Esther *& Additions*	✗ *Consort*	✗ *Qumran-No!*	✗ *Qumran + Luther-No!*	✗ *Adds to Word*
1st & 2nd Maccabees *& Additions*	✗ *Samaritans*	✗ *Qumran-No!*	✗ *Qumran + Luther-No!*	✗ *Adds to Word*

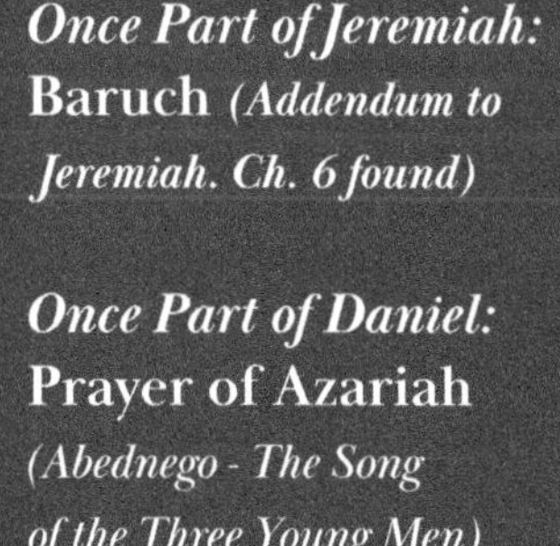

See Deconstructing The Book of Judith, Testing The Book of Esther & Purim, and Examining 1st & 2nd Maccabees & Hanukkah in the Back of This Book.

THE Levite BIBLE
LeviteBible.com

One of the saddest forms of scholarship is giving an answer in which the scholar has not remotely researched and clearly has no foundation in knowledge of the text, nor the actual paradigm. We have seen this on most of the topics we have researched, but especially with Jubilees, 1st Enoch, 1st and 2nd Esdras and now, with the Apocrypha books *(which include 1st and 2nd Esdras)*. The fact that most scholars have not even bothered to truly prove out this false label of Apocrypha demonstrates they are stuck in a blind box unqualified to even render such an opinion. They are uneducated in this regard and their initials do not somehow elevate them as experts, which is evident by the illiterate points they attempt. It is time to smash that enclosure and get to the truth. We find one false paradigm after the other in terms of the Apocrypha and one will observe, this is gross negligence.

For instance, the scholar will take one Apocryphal book that does not even test as inspired and apply its failure to all books in the category, which is simply stupid. They treat it as if there was ever a book called "Apocrypha" in origin which is false as the term did not exist in Bible scholarship until the Catholic Jerome in 382 A.D., which is far too late to be the origin of anything Bible. It is extremely laughable that many of these dunderheads then look for Messiah to have mentioned a term "Apocrypha," that did not even exist in His time in this application. His not mentioning it really serves as firm evidence the entire paradigm never had His endorsement to set aside any books, nor does He ever reference a category for "almost" or "maybe" scripture, with the suggestion to hide them. Again, this category is illiterate and never a Biblical manner of treating books. If they are not inspired scripture, why would they be in the Bible at all? They should not. However, as we have demonstrated in our Torah Test, many of these books were Bible Canon.

The notion is unthinkable, yet we will address one scholar who did exactly that in willing ignorance. He offers a vast assault on some books which vet as scripture. This is why we test these individually and we find some do fail indeed. One does not take those failures and apply their false doctrines to the inspired texts as they were never written together and the four books that fail are obvious Pharisee and occult infusions that never belong in any discussion about Bible Canon. Unfortunately, one of our favorite tools, BlueLetterBible.org, has a prominent scholar guilty of this.

In this section, we will respond addressing his shallow, even false allegations, regarding the Old Testament Apocrypha *[114]*. We are not attacking him personally, but the scholarly positions he upholds, that attack the Word. We are answering his charges, and we will call out falsehoods, false paradigms and misrepresentations. We wish we could not do this, but it must be addressed. He makes a plethora of insinuations, yet few of these are even positions at all. Some are outright untrue, and most are set in false paradigms. It is clear this scoffer has likely never even read these books, at least not seriously. His ramblings prove he certainly does not know them even a little and he should not be attempting to coach others until he grows up and learns how to research. He is not representing a scriptural position, nor an educated one, but a paradigm found in scholarship lined with a whole lot of leaven he seizes without any real testing. Jeremiah addressed those like this who attack the Word.

Jeremiah 8:8 KJV
How can you say, 'We are wise, and the law of the Lord is with us'? But behold, the lying pen of the scribes has made it into a lie.

Jeremiah is not referring to the holy scribes who kept Bible Canon as the sons of Zadok, who in that same era, are recorded as holy still three times in Ezekiel *(40:46, 44:15, 48:11)*. They continued to keep accurate Bible Canon to at least the First Century *(Deut. 31:9-11)*. We have found that Bible Canon in archaeology in Qumran/Bethabara. He refers to an unholy lot of Samaritan scribes and Jeremiah even rebukes pastors in Israel especially as bearing the responsibility for leading Israel astray *(Jer. 23:1-2, 2:8, 10:21, 12:10, 22:22)*. The sons of Zadok did not. One would be surprised how many times we have heard the accusation that Jeremiah was referring to the holy Priesthood from the Temple before the Maccabees, which requires a complete lapse in reason. The Maccabees and their paradigm are the corrupt scribes.

Origen and Justin Martyr further identify the scribes of manipulation as the

Pharisee Scribes who changed even the Hebrew Bible in their time *[140]*. This was merely a continuation of the Samaritan replacement imposters who defiled all things Bible. They still do. Their infused religion of Pharisaism, called Rabbinic Judaism today, has never been the Bible relationship in which we are to follow. History does not confuse this. A church who does not know their history does.

We will not name this scholar though the source information is there because what he is really doing is speaking for the scholarly paradigm. All of these points are found in scholarship and notice the excessive onslaught of words here in which every single point is either outright false or a false paradigm. We will address every one of his fallacious objections obliterating these lame arguments once and for all. In today's world, we would call this kind of thinking "fake news."

1A. THE APOCRYPHA HAS DIFFERENT DOCTRINE AND PRACTICES THAN HOLY SCRIPTURE? FALSE!

"For almsgiving saves from death and purges away every sin. Those who give alms will enjoy a full life (Tobit 12:9).
So now, my children see what almsgiving accomplishes, and what injustice does it brings death! (Tobit 14:11).
Was not Abraham found faithful when tested, and it was reckoned to him as righteousness (First Maccabees 2:52).

"The Bible, on the other hand, says that a person is saved by grace through faith. It is not based upon our good works. For by grace you are saved through faith, and this is not your own doing; it is the gift of God - not the result of works, so that no one may boast (Ephesians 2:8,9)." [114]

Notice how this scholar used three references not even about salvation from the Apocrypha to inject the polarizing salvation debate of faith verses works, which is a different topic altogether. Is his comprehension of sentences so poor? He does this to capture the Christian world especially scholars and pastors who read this to shock them from the start setting a false tone, causing them to dismiss the Apocrypha immediately from his first point which is not even a point at all. This can only be defined as ignorance. It is a dishonest tactic, and it is flawed!

He also cuts off the passage ignoring the next verse in which Paul's complete words here tell us faith requires good works and we are to walk in them which is the way scripture in context always teaches. It better, when the origin of the definition of salvation comes from Messiah in John 15 and Matthew 7, not Paul. It is ridiculous that they argue against men as responsiblc and walking in His ways, but instead, we are to operate as reckless and rebellious children in lawlessness which is defined as sin *(1 John 3:4)*. They are teaching a doctrine of sin which happens when one teaches in fragments out of context. This context is established inclusive of the next verse.

Ephesians 2:10 KJV
For we are his workmanship, created in Christ Jesus unto good works, which God
hath before ordained that we should walk in them.

Yes, Paul says we are to exhibit good works. He read and knew Messiah's teaching in John 15 or this scholar represents the strange doctrine Paul never taught. There is never an argument over this even between Paul and James, as illiterate scholars accuse, which is a false paradigm as well. They agree.

However, Ephesians is not addressing what Tobit is. Does Tobit say almsgiving is salvation? Does he represent that we are not saved by grace? Not even remotely. He says doing so leads to a long physical life just as the Commandment to love our parents leads to the same *(Ex. 20:12, Matt. 15:4-6)*. Neither are salvation, and this scholar addresses the wrong point trying to inject polarizing debate deceptively. Did Tobit say almsgiving overcomes spiritual death and replaces Yahusha whom he predicted to come as well as His role in the Last Days? No, he does not. Tobit refers to physical death in which he elaborates, if this scholar could read, in the next sentence. He, then, affirms his previous words in 14:11 again clearly speaking of physical death, not spiritual death, and definitively not replacing Messiah. These passages are not even about salvation, but living long on the Earth and they are not the only ones to do so. There is no conflict and nothing wrong with Tobit's words.

This is a misrepresentation of what is good doctrine corruptly injecting a completely different doctrine, not even addressed in the text in fraud. Notice, this scoffer lumps in Maccabees next which is not scripture and a false book. He equates it to Tobit which is inspired because he has never researched this topic. However, that passage in Maccabees is really a quote from James and/or Genesis and does not even represent salvation, nor is it in conflict. The book still fails, but there is nothing wrong with the affirmed New Testament doctrine of that passage and this scholar should know better.

James 2:23 KJV
And the scripture was fulfilled which saith, Abraham believed God, and it was
imputed unto him for righteousness: and he was called the Friend of God.

One could say James derived this in part from Genesis, but that would be incomplete. This is really a mixed reference of two books. What James is quoting directly in the other half of this is the Book of Jubilees which the Bible paradigm treated as Torah and inspired Bible Canon *(see The Book of Jubilees: The Torah Calendar, free in eBook at BookOfJubilees.org).*

Genesis 15:6 KJV (Cf. Romans 4:3)
And he believed in the LORD; and he counted it to him for righteousness.
Jubilees 19:9
...for he was found faithful, and was recorded on the heavenly tablets as the friend of Elohim.

How can this New Testament scholar not know James says that same thing? He is unqualified to render an opinion which is why he is so far off base. Again, we are addressing his article, but this is found across the board in much of scholarship.

1B. THE NON-BIBLICAL DOCTRINE OF PURGATORY IS TAUGHT IN THE APOCRYPHA: FALSE!

In regard to purgatory, this scholar only quotes the fraud book of 2nd Maccabees 12:41-45 which is the only place this doctrine appears in the books mislabeled "Apocrypha." We agree Maccabees espouses this false doctrine. However, BLB blames all of Apocrypha for this false book's doctrines when most of what is termed "Apocrypha" does not even belong in the same category, but vets as inspired scripture. This is not just false, it is a poorly positioned, overt lie. Maccabees fails, and this is another false narrative. Though Maccabees is wrong to teach such false doctrine indeed, this scholar does not find this doctrine in any of the Apocrypha texts which vet as inspired, nor will he. This is not a position except against the Book of Maccabees in which we agree is not scripture even for this very reason.

1C. ACCORDING TO THE APOCRYPHA GOD HEARS THE PRAYERS OF THE DEAD: FALSE READING!

"We find the Book of Baruch teaching that God hears the prayers of those who have died.

O Lord Almighty, God of Israel, hear now the prayer of the dead of Israel, the children of those who sinned before you, who did not heed the voice of the Lord their God, so that calamities have clung to us (Baruch 3:4).
The dead do not pray for the living. Only the living upon the earth pray for the other living ones on the earth." [114]

In this instance, Blue Letter Bible's scholar proves he cannot read English. This is a poor hatchet job of the English language. Baruch is referring to the prayers of those of Israel who are dead now, but their prayers were made while they were alive. Dead people don't pray such prayers, and Baruch never says they do. That is ridiculous. He assumes because he is stretching that Baruch may be against scripture based on his inability to read basic sentences. He is likely getting this from some other scholar, but regardless, this is inept and not even a point. To read this in the manner of this scoffer, one also has to forget that the sentence is formed in the past tense as these are those who "sinned" before and "did not heed" His voice before, when they were alive which is also when they said their prayers before they were dead which is the tense of the entire passage. An elementary school child could do a better job of reading. This is pathetic!

1D. THE APOCRYPHA TEACHES THE PRE-EXISTENCE OF SOULS: FALSE PARADIGM!

In this case, this scholar demonstrates he does not even know what scripture says. He provides no scripture that says the Bible does not teach the pre-existence of souls, which should be a requirement for even attempting the point. This is exactly the kind of poor scholarship that has mislead so many.

> *"The doctrine of the pre-existence of souls is found in the Apocrypha.*
> *As a child I was naturally gifted, and a good soul fell to my lot; or rather, being good, I entered an undefiled body (Wisdom 8:19,20).*
> *Scripture does not teach that souls have any existence before they are united into a body." [114]*

Again, he quotes one fragment from Wisdom of Solomon, that's it, and claims that forms a doctrine against scripture and also blames all of Apocrypha in ignorance. However, this scoffer does not even know scripture on this topic. First, how is it he has never read Jeremiah?

> *Jeremiah 1:5 KJV*
> *Before I formed thee in the belly I knew thee; and before thou camest forth out of the womb I sanctified thee, and I ordained thee a prophet unto the nations.*

How could Yahuah have known Jeremiah prior to his being conceived in the belly of his mother? In other words, before his physical existence, Jeremiah pre-existed in some form. What is that? His soul or spirit, which scripture uses interchangeably, pre-existed prior to his physical conception. How does this work? It is actually very simple and logical, and any scholar should know better. Jubilees 2 tells us all the spirits or souls of all of mankind who would ever live were all formed the First Day of Creation, thus pre-existed since the First Day of Creation. Indeed, even before Adam was formed physically, Yahuah knew him just as Jeremiah. This is Bible doctrine. Why is it not Blue Letter Bible's?

> *Jubilees 2:2*
> *For on the first day He created the heavens which are above and the earth and the waters and... of all the spirits of His creatures which are in the heavens and on the earth...*

That is how scripture operates. Human conception is physical, and our spirits enter our bodies at conception, but there is never a single scripture which says that the sperm and egg procreate a spirit. They equal only flesh, and the spirit enters the child in the womb. Why is it that this scholar does not know scripture?

For those scholars who would, then, respond with Genesis 2:7, perhaps they should consider courses on how to read. For Yahuah breathed the breath of life, His spirit into man, and then, man became a living soul. The body is not living until its spirit enters it, established since Creation. That is exactly what scripture teaches throughout. To use verses about man's conception and ignore this fact is simply ignorance and not a position. Even Zechariah documents this dynamic, and they will use that scripture to say the opposite, yet, how can their reading be so illiterate? The spirit is formed within the body as a separate process. Without that spirit, that man would never live.

> *Zechariah 12:1KJV*
> *The burden of the word of the LORD for Israel, saith the LORD, which stretcheth forth the heavens, and layeth the foundation of the earth, and formeth the spirit of man within him.*

Passages such as Psalm 139 do not even address this process at all. In the case of Lazarus, his body was dead in the grave, still there without a spirit which we all well know is how this operates throughout scripture.

1E. IT TEACHES CREATION OUT OF PRE-EXISTENT MATTER: FALSE READING!

Once again, this assumption is lousy. What a horrible way to read a sentence misleading many. Does the Wisdom of Solomon even disagree with Hebrews here?

> *"The doctrine of creation out of pre-existent matter is taught in the Apocrypha.*
> *For your all-powerful hand, which created the world out of formless matter, did not lack the means to send upon them a multitude of bears, or bold lions (Wisdom 11:17).*
> *The Bible says that God's creation was out of nothing.*
>
> *By faith we understand that the worlds were prepared by the word of God, so that what is seen was not made out of things which are visible (Hebrews 11:3)."*
> *[114]*

How is it that this scholar is supposed to know the Bible, but has not read Genesis 1:2 as creation was most certainly inclusive of matter that was void and without form? This should be so easily understood. Creation was already underway in Genesis

1:2, and it tells us the earth, which represents matter, was without form and void, the same language as Solomon here. However, the assumption that Solomon was referring to matter before matter was even created is utterly negligent. He never says that. The passage in Genesis is clear there is a great deep or abyss that requires matter as that was created on Day One first. Jubilees 2:2 affirms *"(He created) the abysses"* which were matter as they held the waters, the same as Genesis 1:2. Elohim, then, used that formless, created matter, the same language as Solomon, to create the world. This is so obvious especially by Solomon's wording of "formless matter." Why should we even have to correct something so oblivious to the Word based on a supposed Bible scholar who cannot even read and does not even have a basic understanding of Genesis 1. This is sad.

However, even worse, this scholar cannot even read Hebrews from just two verse earlier. How is it he does not know that Hebrews also defines this faith as "the substance of things hoped for" and "the evidence of things not seen *(Heb. 11:1)*." In other words, Hebrews and Wisdom agree with Genesis regarding things created from *"formless matter."* Wisdom of Solomon is solid doctrine. This scholar's is not.

1F. THE APOCRYPHA SAYS THE BODY WEIGHS DOWN THE SOUL: FALSE READING!

> *"The idea of the body as a weight upon the soul is found in the Apocrypha.*
> *For a perishable body weighs down the soul, and this earthy tent burdens the thoughtful mind (Wisdom 9:15).*
> *The idea that the body weighs down the soul is not biblical - the body is not evil.*
> *All of these doctrines are contrary to the teaching of Holy Scripture." [114]*

Where is the scripture that says the opposite, that the body does not weigh upon the soul? There is none. How is it that Blue Letter Bible is not aware that our bodies return to dust? They are temporary and corrupt in the whole of scripture from Genesis, since the fall of man, to Revelation on the Day of Judgment. Our flesh's corruptness logically weighs on the souls of men. This is not any sort of extreme, nor strange doctrine or declaration, in any way. The body is corrupt, thus, evil indeed. To say otherwise, again, demonstrates this scholar does not know scripture on yet another topic. How can he not be aware of the many passages that refer to the body or flesh as corrupt? How can he not know that after the Day of Judgment, we receive new glorified bodies as we never return to the old ones which become dust because they are corrupt?

> *Galatians 6:8 KJV*
> *For he that soweth to his flesh shall of the flesh reap corruption; but he that soweth to the Spirit shall of the Spirit reap life everlasting.*

Romans 8:21 KJV
Because the creature itself also shall be delivered from the bondage of corruption into the glorious liberty of the children of God.
2 Corinthians 5:4 KJV
For we that are in this tabernacle do groan, being burdened: not for that we would be unclothed, but clothed upon, that mortality might be swallowed up of life.
1 Corinthians 15:42 KJV
So also is the resurrection of the dead. It is sown in corruption; it is raised in incorruption:
2 Peter 2:19 KJV
While they promise them liberty, they themselves are the servants of corruption: for of whom a man is overcome, of the same is he brought in bondage.

How many times did Paul have to demonstrate there is a Law at work which is an opposite Law of the Flesh referred to as that of sin and death? The Flesh only leads to sin and death as it must return to dust. Our new glorified bodies will endure forever, not this one we live in. The same scholars accuse Yahuah of writing the Law of Moses, which He did with His very finger in part, as that being the Law of Sin and Death that Paul rebukes? What nonsense. Paul very clearly defines in Romans 7 and 8, whole chapters, that there are two opposite Laws at work. The first is the Law of Life which he calls the Law of Moses as do valid books in the Apocrypha such as Sirach 17:11 which is the origin of Paul's title for the Law. Paul also equates this as the Law of Life in Yahusha Messiah, contrasted with the second from which we are redeemed – the Law of Sin and Death. Imagine the number of supposed Bible scholars who accuse Yahuah of writing a Law of Sin and Death as His Law. How ridiculous. The Law of the Flesh is that it is corrupt period and leads to sin and death. This is found so many times in scripture, yet this scholar has failed us all with incomplete research providing a false answer and accusation he better prove. This is not scholarship on any level.

2. THE APOCRYPHA IS NEVER CITED IN THE NEW TESTAMENT AS SCRIPTURE: FALSE STATEMENT!

"Though the New Testament cites directly, or alludes to, almost every book of the Old Testament as Scripture, it never cites the Apocrypha as being God's Word. The Apocrypha was not the Bible of Jesus or His apostles. While Jesus and H(i)s apostles often quoted from the Septuagint, they never quoted from the Apocrypha.

Allusions Are Not The Same As Scripture
While there may be some allusions to the apocryphal books by New Testament writers there is no direct quote from them. An allusion is not the same as a direct quote." [114]

Before we enter this false paradigm, let us understand this scholar is not consistent as this is his reasoning in his article, "Does the New Testament Quote the Old Testament as Authoritative Scripture?" [115] He writes about Old Testament Books not quoted in the New Testament, as he admits four are not. That is not an accurate count, however, as he stretches some into claiming they are being quoted, yet the name of that prophet is not there such as Malachi. Malachi is scripture indeed, but he is applying a different rule in testing Apocrypha books from that of Malachi. That is a false test, and not honest.

He also treats the Apocrypha as if it is its own publication which is stupid. Apocrypha is a group of "hidden" books that were removed from Bible Canon and four false books also thrown into the category to deceive, but it is not a separate Bible, nor translation. He should know better. He compares it to the Septuagint, a Greek translation of the Hebrew Bible, which requires an obtuse view especially when the Septuagint includes many of these Apocrypha books. This is fundamentally retarded. He says, the other four not quoted in the New Testament, do not need to be. We have no problem with that if he were consistent in testing the Apocrypha with the same criteria. He does not. He, then, applies that rule he dismissed of those books against the Apocrypha as a negative because he claims they do need to be cited by the name of the author or they must be thrown out. How illiterate and dishonest. That is not a test, it is the mentality that hides scripture. Again, his number is also embellished. This is a false litmus test in his own words.

A perfect example of the hypocrisy of this scholar is his mistreatment of his application of criteria. For instance, Exodus would fail by the standard that he uses for Apocrypha, as would Malachi as we mentioned. Those are scripture and this is not an accurate way to test. He cites Ephesians, yet Paul does not credit Exodus nor Moses with this writing. We know that is where it comes from, and it is a direct quote. However, when the Apocryphal books have the same exact situation, he calls them a failure, because Paul, or whomever, did not attribute the author or book. That is insane hypocrisy, yet very common in scholarship. He, also, denies First Enoch which is quoted directly in Jude 1:14 with attribution of Enoch the Prophet writing in a book. We have that book, First Enoch, from which it proves a direct quote even and yet, Blue Letter Bible would apply a different standard to First Enoch claiming it fails when it does not. They do. This is not scholarship. It is the rambling of a "double-minded" man who is unstable in all his ways *(Jas. 1:8, 4:8)*.

> *"Children, obey your parents in the Lord, for this is right. Honor your father and mother-- this is the first commandment with a promise: so that it may be well with you and you may live long on the earth. (Ephesians 6:1-3 NRSV)" [115]*

Moses is not attributed here, nor is Exodus. It says commandment but since when did a modern scholar even understand what a commandment is? He claims

Matthew 4:10 is quoting Deuteronomy, and indeed it is. However, it is quoting the words of the book without attribution to Moses, nor the name of the book. He treats this as if that is a practice that is not accurate at all and it is the standard Bible practice as they did not always offer attribution for every scripture they quoted, nor did they ever have to. He cites Hebrews 13:5 as quoting Joshua and indeed, it does. However, it does not say that Joshua wrote that in his book, nor is there attribution. This is inconsistent nonsense. He admits that Judges and Ruth are not directly quoted as authoritative scripture which should not be a problem for any scholar as many books are not. They do not have to be, including the Apocrypha. However, this scoffer cites Hebrews 11:32 as mentioning people from those books which is fine, but he would never allow the same criteria in testing Apocrypha. Again, that is true and his criteria against the Apocrypha proves false in his own words yet again. He applies a stricter rule to Apocrypha than he does with the modern Bible Canon. That is dishonest, and his structure for testing proven false.

In his treatment of Kings, he lumps 1st and 2nd Kings into one book which we have no issue. However, the same scholar will forget that Baruch was published within the Book of Jeremiah as an addendum as was Letter of Jeremiah, also known as Baruch 6, and the same dynamic existed with Daniel as Susanna, Bel & The Dragon, and Prayer of Azaryah, were once published within the Book of Daniel as Chapters 13 and 14, with the other inserted at 3:23. He dismissed this in the case of Kings which again, we have no issue, but then, he fraudulently applies a stricter standard to the Apocrypha. That is fallacious and he does the same with 1st and 2nd Chronicles. The same criteria he applies to these books, would render portions of the Apocrypha as Bible Canon still, if he were consistent. He is not as most scholars are not on this topic.

Paul quotes Job 5:12-13 in 1 Corinthians 3:19-20. That is indisputable fact indeed. However, Job is not attributed as the author and the title of his book is not there. It is not called scripture in this case, but any quote from Yahusha and His Apostles is scripture whether the passage says so, or not. Otherwise, they would not quote it.

Matthew 27:30 quotes Lamentations 3:30, but once again, there is no attribution, it is not labeled as scripture, it does not even say it is written or was spoken by, nor any such language. We agree that would be a false litmus test to claim Lamentations not scripture and this scholar would not say that. However, he discounts Apocrypha books which are very directly quoted because he claims they must rise to a higher standard changing the criteria in a false paradigm. He even admits this is not a direct quote of Lamentations, but that is OK for him if it is not an Apocryphal book. Then, his standard is tightened which is not a fair, nor honest, assessment. We have no problem with Lamentations as scripture in this example as it is. However, this same scholar will throw out an Apocryphal book based on that same double standard. That makes his assessment worthless.

Paul quotes Habakkuk 2:4 in Galatians 3:11 yet again, fails to attribute the prophet and the book from where the quote originates. This is normal in the Bible practice and the oddity is the extreme criteria set by stupid scholars who change the test for the Apocrypha claiming it fails, when it meets the same standard as Habakkuk in being quoted. 2nd Esdras 1:30 is directly quoted practically word for word by Yahusha Himself in Matthew 23:37, even according to the 1611 KJV, and this scholar tells us to ignore that while claiming it is acceptable for Habakkuk, which he admits is not even a direct quote and falls even shorter. It is a clear double standard. These examples demonstrate the hypocrisy of scholars claiming to test the Apocrypha, who simply are not honest in their handling of the texts. They discount themselves from our listening to their impertinent pontifications.

As we have already demonstrated in the Torah Test for each book in Vol. 1 and 2, the Apocryphal books which vet as inspired scripture are in fact quoted numerous times by Yahusha and the Apostles. This point is a false statement and paradigm. However, then, this scoffer fully proves he is incapable of reading. Having already proven to apply stricter rules in testing Apocrypha from that of the modern Bible Canon, he, once again, forgets that in his other article testing Old Testament books quoted in the New Testament that some are not quoted, some are not attributed, and some are not direct quotes. In those cases, they are most certainly not defined as "authoritative" in those passages by his criteria he applies for "Apocrypha" which he does not for modern Bible Canon. They are authoritative indeed, and by the same standard so are several Apocrypha books. He admitted this already but then, forgot that some of the modern Bible Canon is not cited as authoritative and does not need to be. In fact, for Messiah or the Apostles to quote it in doctrine, it is authoritative period. We have no issue with that in applying the standard to Lamentations, but we take major issue when this scholar changes to a stricter criteria in assessing Apocrypha dishonestly.

"No Statement Introduced By "It Is Written"
In addition, no New Testament writer ever refers to any of these books as authoritative. Quotes from the accepted books are usually introduced by the phrase, "It is written," or the passage is quoted to prove a point. But never do the New Testament writers quote the Apocrypha in this way.
Furthermore no book of the Apocrypha is mentioned by name in the New Testament." [114]

Why does it need to be mentioned by name? In fact, many books bear different names and did not even have titles often. This is an example of a scholar who does not even know how the Bible paradigm operates on a basic level. Let us not forget as well, Manasseh's Prayer, or Apocrypha, is cited as written material in the days of Chronicles by Jeremiah, its writer. However, this scoffer would discount it even still though it fits his criteria, just as he does First Enoch which is a perfect fit to his criteria. There is no commitment to the truth. This prayer is recorded as written and published in the Book of Kings/Chronicles, yet it is missing from our modern Bibles. Where is his protest in consistency?

> *2nd Chronicles 33:18 KJV*
> *Now the rest of the acts of **Manasseh**, and his prayer unto his God, and the words of the seers that spake to him in the name of the LORD God of Israel, behold, they are written in the book of the kings of Israel. His prayer also, and how God was intreated of him, and all his sin, and his trespass, and the places wherein he built high places, and set up groves and graven images, before he was humbled: behold, they are written among the sayings of the seers.*

This supplication was found in the Dead Sea Scrolls kept as Bible Canon by the true Temple Priests. Thus, archaeology proves Prayer of Manasseh as Bible Canon. It was there. No, it's not quoted in the New Testament as it is a one-chapter prayer, but it is even better. It is recorded in the Old Testament. There is no need for anyone in the New Testament to cite or quote Manasseh's short prayer, the Old Testament does. They would likely then respond that Manasseh in the Dead Sea Scrolls in Hebrew does not read exactly the same as the one that came to us through the Greek paradigm and into the 1611 King James. It appears they cannot even hear themselves when they make illiterate points like this. Of course, from one language to another it would read a little different. The problem is we test the content in Vol. 1 line by line and yes, it is a match.

3. THE APOCRYPHA HAS ALWAYS BEEN REJECTED BY THE JEWS AS SCRIPTURE: FALSE STATEMENT AND PARADIGM!

Pharisees *(modern Jews)* do not get to select Bible Canon. The Old Testament was determined before they conquered Jerusalem in 165 B.C. as foreigners usurping the priesthood. Indeed, none of the Apocrypha books were included in Josephus' admission of the Pharisee Bible Canon which changed scripture. However, that is a false paradigm to begin with. Having said this, even the Pharisees quote some of Apocrypha using the texts regardless of whether they were termed Canon. That very Pharisee practice is exactly what Jerome followed, not the true keepers of Bible Canon, who had no such books catalogued as lesser or not quite scripture. However, even with this in mind, they used and quoted some of the Apocrypha such as the Wisdom of Sirach.

With the last-named work it has many points in common; and it is frequently quoted in the Talmud; passages from it are introduced by the formula reserved for the Biblical writings (Hag. 12a; Niddah 16b; Yer. Ber. 11c); and one verse is even referred to as if it belonged to the Hagiographa (B. K. 92a). It is cited by name in Sanh. 100b (= Yeb. 63c), where also a series of verses from it is given; and single verses appear in the following treatises and other works: Yer. Ber. 11b; Yer. Hag. 77c; Yer. Ta'an. 66d; Hag. 13a; Niddah 16b; Gen. R. viii., x., lxxiii.; Lev. R. xxxiii.; Tan., Wayishlah, 8; ib. Mikkez, 10; ib. Hukkat, 1; a midrashic passage preserved in the "Shibbole ha-Leket," ed. Buber, p. 23a; "Pirke de-Rabbenu ha-kadosh," ed. Schönblum, 14a; Baraita Kallah (ed. Coronel, 7c, and in the Wilna edition of the Talmud). It is cited also by R. Nissim ("Sefer Ma'asiyyot ha-Hakamim wehu Hibbur Yafeh meha-Yeshu ah"), and especially by Saadia in the preface to his "Sefer ha-Galui" (Harkavy, l.c.). In his commentary on the "Sefer Yezirah" the latter author quotes verbatim two verses of Ben Sira, although he attributes them to one Eleazar b. Irai, of whom nothing is known. In another part of this work (p. 178) he cites the same text, again attributing it to that author. This is the more remarkable since Saadia speaks of Ben Sira in his introduction, and cites no less than seven of his maxims.
– Jewish Encyclopedia [116]

If this scholar understood that modern Jews are not even Hebrew and was referring to the Yahudim *(the actually Hebrew word, never Jew)*, this is blatantly false as the Dead Sea Scrolls included most of these Apocryphal books either in fragments, very direct quotes or in documented historical association we have already proven. The New Testament also quotes these inspired books. This scoffer is unaware that 2nd Esdras is quoted in the Qumran Scrolls twice in great significance and there is no other origin of those passages. As we proved in Vol. 1, it dates to at least 100 B.C. which is 200 years earlier than his conclusion that it cannot be scripture. Most of these scrolls were found in part in Qumran and dated prior to the New Testament. This is a false statement, and not factual.

Then, this scholar keeps injecting what the Pharisees thought which is illiterate of what Pharisees represent. Their Canon, which is the origin of his Canon, the Pharisee Canon, is not the Bible Canon. That was found in Qumran/Bethabara as we have produced such track with abundant evidence especially in Vol. 1. Josephus' list of books is now proven by that archaeology as a manipulated, fraudulent list as is Jerome's or any Catholic Counsel which changed the Old Testament. One cannot go backwards when the bible set the authority to keep scripture with the Sons of Zadok who lived in Qumran/Bethabara in the time of Messiah. He was baptized there and visited there because that is where scripture was kept. He launched His ministry there as an endorsement of their practices and He exposed the Jerusalem Temple as defiled.

4. THE BOOKS OF THE APOCRYPHA WERE WRITTEN DURING THE SILENT YEARS: FALSE STATEMENT AND PARADIGM!

There were no "silent years" for the Bible paradigm necessarily. The exiled Temple Priests continued to write and keep scripture throughout this period and included most of these books mislabeled as Apocrypha in 382 A.D. by Jerome. That is a false paradigm never mentioned in scripture, and those priests continued to write even commentaries, songs, prophecy, etc. that entire time. Also, this is a lie. Baruch was written at the same time as Jeremiah in 500 or so B.C., not in the 400 "silent years." Ezra wrote 1st and 2nd Esdras in about 400 B.C. at the same time he wrote Ezra and Nehemiah. Susanna and Bel & The Dragon were written by Daniel as part of his book of Daniel 13-14 in his time long before. Tobit was written in 700 B.C. Prayer of Manasseh was written at the time of the Books of Chronicles. Really, only the completion of Sirach was written during the so-called 'silent years," but even that book was written over three generations of sages and only completed then. The four books that fail are impertinent as they are not scripture. What an incredibly ignorant statement this becomes. These were not silent, and scripture never references such. That is a Pharisee paradigm that fails.

5. THE SEPTUAGINT TRANSLATION PROVES NOTHING: FALSE PARADIGM!

> *"The fact that the **Apocrypha is found in the Septuagint translation** does not prove anything. It merely testifies that the Alexandrian Jews translated other religious material into Greek apart from the Old Testament Scripture. **A Greek translation is not the same thing as a book being part of the Hebrew canon.**" [114]*

The original Septuagint is not found yet in archaeology. Thus, it is true that we do not know when these books first appeared in the Septuagint. However, we do not need to know that as the precedence is well established by those he and other scholars have mischaracterized and shoved aside in ignorance. What we know is these are mostly found in Qumran where the true Temple Priests lived, and that is what established the precedence of Old Testament Bible Canon, not the Septuagint. The Greek Septuagint is a useful tool but was not translated by the sons of Zadok who were in the Temple at that time soon to be exiled to Qumran/Bethabara. They were not in Egypt.

There is no edict in scripture that books had to be preserved in the Hebrew language either. That is not even a statement of pertinence.

6. THERE IS NO EVIDENCE THE APOCRYPHA WAS IN SEPTUAGINT AT THE TIME OF CHRIST: FALSE PARADIGM!

This is a strawman argument which ignores the Qumran Scrolls which matter far more than the Septuagint. The fact these were mostly found there proves they most certainly were included in the Greek Septuagint in the B.C. era. The precedence is established and there is no need to prove they were definitively published in the Septuagint though there are very early church fathers even Polycarp, disciple of John the Apostle, who endorsed some of these books as Bible canon. In the early record, we find many of these, and this is not a scholarly position. They were already Bible Canon before there even was a Greek Septuagint.

7. THERE IS NO EVIDENCE OF A GREATER ALEXANDRIAN CANON: FALSE PARADIGM!

As we have proven, no one needs this Greater Alexandrian Canon to prove many of these so-termed "Apocrypha" books were inspired Bible Canon as that is the wrong measure. The Qumran Scrolls are the definitive Bible Canon of those ordained by Moses to establish, keep and teach Bible Canon. This is not up for debate.

8. THEY ARE NOT ON THE EARLY CANONICAL LISTS: FALSE STATEMENT AND PARADIGM!

Somehow, this scoffer is not aware of the Qumran Scrolls which is a listing and manifestation of Bible Canon in archaeology he cannot dispute dated to the B.C. era. He fails to realize that is before 170 A.D. He also slips to understand there are numerous church fathers who listed Canon prior to 170 A.D. of which we have covered, and some do include these books. Aside from that, there are those whose writings survive such as Polycarp long before that date and he was using some of these Apocrypha books as Bible Canon still. He treats this 170 A.D. list as the first and only listing of Canon at that time and that is simply false.

> *"The earliest existing list of the Old Testament canon comes from a man named Melito, a bishop of Sardis. In approximately A.D. 170 he wrote the following.*
>
> *When I came to the east and reached the place where these things were preached and done, and learned accurately the books of the Old Testament, I set down the facts and sent them to you. These are their names: the five books of Moses, Genesis, Exodus, Leviticus, Numbers, Deuteronomy, Joshua the son of Nun, Judges, Ruth, four books of the Kingdom, two books of Chronicles, the Psalms of David, the Proverbs of Solomon and his wisdom, Ecclesiastes, the Song of Songs, Job, the prophets Isaiah, Jeremiah, The Twelve in a single book, Daniel, Ezekiel, Ezra."* [114]

He, then, commits fraud claiming that Wisdom is a title for Proverbs when Proverbs of Solomon is already mentioned on the list. No, it is the Wisdom of Solomon well known even in that time as Wisdom in title. It was also found in the Qumran Bible Canon which we have covered. He also, misrecollects the established historical pattern that Daniel included Susanna *(13)*, Bel & The Dragon *(14)* and Prayer of Azaryah *(inserted after 3:23)* as well as Jeremiah included Baruch and Letter of Jeremiah within their books. So, yes, Melito does mention some of the Apocrypha, but this scoffer writes in ignorance not knowing the tradition, nor the value of the Qumran Scrolls. Notice, Esther is not there on Melito's list either, yet this scholar dismisses that and calls Esther Bible Canon claiming that Apocrypha fails falsely, in the same criteria that Esther fails in his own words, yet he will not admit that. If he were honest, he would petition to remove Esther from Bible Canon based on this criterion he set, which would be reasonable.

Finally, though a sincere man, who did Melito follow as supposed Hebrews? Oops! He went to Palestine in the days after the Lost Tribes were gone in 170 A.D. and who was left? The Pharisees. Melito is repeating the Pharisee Canon and so is this scholar using that as supposed pertinent data when it is nonsense and meaningless.

9. THEY WERE REJECTED BY MOST CHURCH LEADERS: FALSE STATEMENT AND PARADIGM!

Even if this were true, this remains far too late for the church to execute Counsels to determine what the Temple Priests already established long before there was a Pharisee in Jerusalem, nor a Catholic Church. This is their tactic as they even forget this is the Old Testament which no Catholic, nor Pharisee ever had jurisdiction. They weave in and out of history misusing it, and they lose sight of the track of the Biblically ordained keepers of scripture in Qumran/Bethabara which matters most. Any scholar who does not know that basic, is no Bible scholar. He time warps to 367 A.D. and who cares. It is far too late. There is no point to be made there. He needed to go back to the B.C. era first when the Old Testament was written and maintained to follow the actual evidence as we have. He neglects to do so and has nothing of value to offer on this topic.

However, this is about the same time that Jerome set aside these books as "Apocrypha" in 382 A.D. This means they were Bible Canon prior and set aside but still published within the Vulgate. Otherwise, why would Jerome add books into the Bible from a separate category? It makes no sense. Sure, he added four occult texts to the lot proving he was an occult agitator and no curator of scripture. As we have proven, some of these books were already in circulation as Bible Canon long before, and Jerome was attacking the Bible by creating this category of "hidden" books. He still published them within the Bible though which is key. He would not if all of them had no history or precedence prior. His listing was fraud from the beginning of his changing scripture adding and taking away in falsehood.

Then, this scholar is looking for the term prior to that as if Apocrypha is a book unto itself which is brainless. Jerome is the origin of the term according to R.H. Charles and that is the origin of the setting aside of these books. He did not stop there as he added other false books such as Maccabees into the mix that do not belong with the Bible. It is a big mess, and a Bible academic should know better.

10. THERE ARE OTHER BOOKS APART FROM THE APOCRYPHA THAT ARE CITED AS SCRIPTURE BY SOME CHURCH FATHERS: FALSE PARADIGM!

"The Church Fathers do not restrict themselves to the books that now make up the Apocrypha. Authors such as Justin, Tertullian, and Clement of Alexandria occasionally use books outside the present Apocrypha - especially the Book of Enoch and First Esdras (Third Esdras).

Clement of Alexandria accepted Second Esdras (Fourth Esdras). Origen believed that the books of First and Second Maccabees, as well as the Letter to Jeremiah, were part of Holy Scripture. Irenaeus cited the Book of Wisdom as being divinely inspired. Therefore appeal to the church fathers cannot settle the matter, seeing that they give conflicting evidence." [114]

1st and 2nd Esdras, Letter of Jeremiah, Wisdom of Solomon, and First Enoch all test as inspired scripture. Maccabees does not. That is research this simpleminded scholar has never conducted. Let us remember however, this is the Catholic Church who disconnected from most Bible practices and traditions early on. They lost the name of Yahuah, His Feasts, His Sabbath, His Commandments, etc. which is New Testament doctrine. It was never His church or ekklesia, and it never will be. They then, pick up on what the Pharisees practiced because they did not even know that Pharisees are the opposite of the Bible. In other words, the manner in which this scholar approaches this topic is already foreign to the Bible model. If he cannot get these elementary basics correct, he will never offer useful data. Also, it is bewildering neglect that this scholar does not know who kept Bible Canon to the first century ordained in scripture.

Worse, this scoffer erred as he seems to be unaware that 1st Esdras *(3rd Esdras)* is part of the Apocrypha in the 1611 King James. What an oversight. We agree it should not be as it is just simply Bible Canon when tested properly. The Book of Enoch indeed has nothing to do with the Apocrypha but requires a separate test on its own which we have conducted and this scoffer has not. Apocrypha, though he does not seem to know this, is a term for a group of books set aside by Jerome and they are not a book, nor a publishing, nor an accurate grouping in any measure. Most of them, were inspired Bible Canon in the days of the Qumran Temple Priests. Some of them are occult lies. The grouping is impertinent, and he continues to treat it as if it is a separate publication, which is inept. We agree the so-called "church fathers" offer conflicting evidence which is why they are not the measure for Bible Canon and he positions himself against a straw man argument once again in falsehood.

11. THE EARLY GREEK MANUSCRIPTS ARE NOT DECISIVE: FALSE PARADIGM!

This remains another empty suit argument as anyone thinking the Greek manuscripts would settle this debate, is ignorant of the most important element here. Again, it is the Qumran Temple Priests who were the ordained keepers of Bible Canon, and they set the precedent which they included most of these texts in their Bible. We should too.

12. THE APOCRYPHA IS NOT A WELL-DEFINED UNIT: FALSE PARADIGM!

Why would the "Apocrypha," a false term for a grouping of books by Jerome in 382 A.D. represent a well-defined unit? Again, this scholar is attempting to treat the Apocrypha as a book separate from Bible Canon. He has already decided it is not Canon before testing. One can do so and offer a genuine test, but he does not, nor have we seen a single scholar really do so. They would be swimming upstream in their paradigm, which is why we have no affiliation with any denomination. What he is observing in the more recent historical record is the actual changing of scripture. A redefining of Old Testament Bible Canon by those with no such authority long after. They were going backwards and changing the Bible. They do not get a ballot. The Temple Priests already determined Old Testament Canon and that is documented in archaeology indisputably where the only Biblically ordained keepers of scripture resided.

13-18. THE COUNCILS AT HIPPO AND CARTHAGE ARE NOT DEFINITIVE, THE AMBIGUOUS TESTIMONY OF SAINT AUGUSTINE, THE CLEAR REJECTION BY A REAL AUTHORITY - JEROME, EARLY CHRISTIAN ART IS NOT A TEST OF DIVINE TRUTH, & THEY WERE REJECTED BY MANY CATHOLIC SCHOLARS THROUGH THE PROTESTANT REFORMATION: COMPLETELY FALSE PARADIGM!

None of these Catholic Councels, nor Catholics in whole have any say in what is or is not Old Testament Canon. This would be laughable, if it were not so maddening. All these points are meaningless. The true test of Old Testament Bible Canon lies with the Temple Priests long before there was a Catholic Church. Archaeology proves, they changed the Bible, and this scoffer is trying to justify their fraud perhaps unknowingly. For a Protestant to declare that the Catholic Jerome was the "real authority" on the Old Testament demonstrates this scoffer is oblivious.

18. THEY WERE NOT OFFICIALLY ACCEPTED BY THE ROMAN CATHOLIC CHURCH UNTIL THE 16TH CENTURY: FALSE PARADIGM!

This too, is impertinent. This is the Old Testament, and this scoffer wishes to discuss how far off all of these paradigms were in the 1500s. We now have the archaeology which proves Old Testament Bible Canon in the First Century, and it cannot change after that. The Old Tesament was already complete.

19. THERE ARE OTHER BOOKS, APART FROM SCRIPTURE, FOUND AMONG THE DEAD SEA SCROLLS: FALSE STATEMENT AND FALSE PARADIGM!

We have been testing book by book from the Dead Sea Scrolls and so far, our findings are this is a completely false statement. Thus far, every test we have completed vets as inspired Bible Canon except the four fraudulent Apocryphal books we address in this book. Those, however, were not found in Qumran. We have a way to go, but there is a strong possibility there is much more inspired scripture there. For a Bible Scholar to have not actually read the Dead Sea Scrolls yet pretend to know something about them is gross negligence. This scoffer thinks the Qumran Temple Priests were Essenes which is Pharisee nonsense of the most illiterate kind. If he cannot even research basics like that, his opinion is of no use.

We have tied most of these books mislabeled as "Apocrypha" to Qumran and that is the location of the Temple practice where Yahusha launched His ministry and John the Baptist and the Sons of Zadok exiled Temple Priests operated. How can he not know this? He is not reading the scrolls, but only commentaries from lunatics who will draw the conclusion of Essenes in Qumran when Pliny placed them in Ein Gedi, archaeology of "The Essene Find" occurred in Ein Gedi, and there is never a single mention of Essenes in the Qumran Scrolls, but they identify themselves over 100 times as the exiled Temple Priests, sons of Zadok, sons of Levi, Levites, sons of Aaron, sons of Light, etc. It requires a profound disability in the face of all that evidence to attempt to claim they were Essenes, and a scholar of this claimed caliber should know better.

Finally, he is concerned with "Jewish thinking" or in other words, Pharisees or modern Jews. These are not Hebrews and rebuked by Yahusha as not knowing the Word and changing it *(Mark 7:9)*. He has tons to learn it appears.

20. THE PROTESTANTS HAVE ALWAYS REJECTED THE DIVINE AUTHORITY OF THE APOCRYPHA: FALSE PARADIGM!

However, it was the Temple Priests who established the Old Testament, not Protestants. They do not get to alter the Bible 1,500 years later. That is illiterate!

It does not matter who came along centuries later and tried to change the Bible. It matters even less that an offshoot branch of the Catholic Church, protesting it, decided to further attack the Bible Canon already establish in the B.C. era and now found in archaeology. This is another meaningless point of no consequence.

21. THERE ARE DEMONSTRABLE HISTORICAL ERRORS IN THE APOCRYPHA: FALSE STATEMENT!

He continues with a timeline contradiction in Tobit which he has never truly charted very clearly. Tobit's timeline is perfect and reconciles to the whole of scripture on every point. We have curated that timeline for this scholar to review at the end of the Book of Tobit. It is accurate, he is not. He claims there are others but provides no detail. However, with Tobit, we already know this false expert is illiterate. He cites an error in the Book of Judith which is not scripture and fails the test of history and Bible. We cover this in Testing the Book of Judith. Indeed, Judith's history is way off and the book is an occult manipulation never scripture.

He only uses Tobit and Judith as examples, but Judith has far more problems than timelines. It proves not scripture as we have covered. Mixing up the two together diminishes Tobit unfairly to begin with. However, to make such a claim against fifteen or so books and fail to provide more examples is gross negligence. We then, have what must be a joke as no one so educated could be so stupid as to read this sentence in the way that this scoffer does.

> *"Errors In The Book Of Judith*
> *Another example can be found in the opening verse of the Book of Judith.*
> *"It was the twelfth year of the reign of Nebuchadnezzar, who ruled over the Assyrians in the great city of Nineveh. In those days Arphaxad ruled over the Medes in Ecbatana (Judith 1:1)."*
> *There are two historical errors in this verse. Nebuchadnezzar was the ruler of the Babylonians, not the Assyrians, and he ruled from Babylon, not Nineveh."*
> *[114]*

Once again, we have a scholar who cherry picks the translation very deceptively. Again, Judith is not even scripture but he can't even get it right. It is reckless to cite one version which interprets the 1611 KJV Nabuchodonozor as Nebuchadnezzar erroneously. This scholar does not know history and cites a translation that did not either. It was not Nebuchadnezzar that conquered Assyria but his father, Nabopolassar. Regardless, Judith has major issues with its timeline but he cannot even get his criticism to a point of accuracy. His misunderstanding is profoundly illiterate. Judith's failings have nothing to do with Tobit, nor any other book of Apocrypha which is a counterfeit category.

When a scholar is this uneducated on how to read a sentence, it is no wonder so many of them get so much backwards. Yes, both Babylonian kings ruled over the Assyrians and that most certainly included the Assyrians who lived in Nineveh. Though Judith is not scripture, to use this kind of uneducated wordplay as a position against it, is retarded.

He, then, sets off on a conclusion he has no right to draw as his only example is illiterate and false. He claims: "It is not possible to argue for the historical accuracy of the books of the Apocrypha..." How would he know? The two examples he used were one false and one fraud. He does not put forth a position and should remove this uneducated trash until he takes the time to research this topic.

22. THERE IS SUB-BIBLICAL CONTENT IN THE BOOKS OF THE APOCRYPHA

"The content of the books of the Apocrypha is below that of canonical Scripture. Several of the books including Judith, Tobit, Susanna, and Bel and the Dragon read like legends. When one reads these books alongside canonical Scripture the differences become obvious."

Is Daniel writing an account such as Bel & The Dragon, where he performed miracles and triumphed over evil "sub-Biblical?" That is consistent with his other writings really. The Book of Tobit records the history of the Northern Tribes in captivity and certainly does not read as anything one would call "sub-Biblical." If Angels are a problem to this scholar, we would have to throw out Genesis and many other books. If miracles are his problem, then, throw out the Gospels especially. If demons make him uncomfortable, the Gospels would definitely have to be discarded, but even Psalm, Genesis, etc. Are the Gospels now sub-Biblical? Does this word even have meaning? This is ignorance.

This scholar thinks that Bible books can only be written in a certain genre which is ridiculous. He cites the story of Judith which is not scripture and impertinent. However, then, he mentions "Tobit, Susanna, and Bel and the Dragon read like legends." The Book of Jonah also reads like a legend in the same manner, and many have issues with his being swallowed by a great fish, not to mention most cannot seem to read the geography involved. However, we do not see consistency here with this scoffer once again. He is not advocating to throw out Jonah which would fail by his own stupid criteria. So, his criticism has no value. Yes, the Bible does include other books that appear to be written in this same genre he claims doesn't exist. It is dishonest.

23. THERE IS NO OBJECTIVE EVIDENCE OF DIVINE AUTHORITY IN THE APOCRYPHA: FALSE PARADIGM!

He, then, demonstrates he has never read these books in which he is commenting.

"The books of the Apocrypha do not contain anything like predictive prophecy, or the firsthand testimony of miracles, that would give evidence of their divine authority. If God divinely inspired these books, then we should expect to see some internal evidence confirming it. But there is none." [114]

No predictive prophecy in all the Apocrypha? What an outrageous lie. How can a Bible scholar be such a liar? The Book of 2nd Esdras is full of predictive prophecy including predicting Messiah's birth around 1 B.C. and even His name. It prophesies over chapters, Daniel's fourth beast in detail over thousands of years and then, into the End Times where it serves as the origin of many portions of Revelation. Clearly, this scoffer has a reading disability in declaring something so ignorant.

Sirach has multiple chapters of predictive prophecy, Tobit even predicts the Last Days and describes New Jerusalem on the Day of Judgment, and Baruch, just as Jeremiah, offers major prophesies to the Southern Kingdom in captivity. The real question is, can this scholar read? What negligence to express something so uneducated and pretend to be an expert on the topic.

No miracles in the Apocrypha? How can he claim to have read Tobit which has firsthand miracles where Tobit was blinded and then, healed and Sarah was being harassed by a Nephilim and through a miracle, rid of the oppression for good. Bel & The Dragon has Daniel killing a dragon as well as the Priests of Bel Marduk which is rather miraculous and certainly of Bible magnitude even consistent with Daniel. Susanna is sentenced to death and then, saved by the miracle of Daniel's coming to her rescue in wisdom. Manasseh is released from prison which was a miraculous answer to his prayer. However, it was very miraculous that he repented of having led Israel astray to becoming an example for them. Since when was the survival of the fiery furnace from Daniel and the Prayer of Azaryah not considered a miracle anymore? This is stupid, certainly not scholarship.

24. NONE OF THE BOOKS OF THE APOCRYPHA CLAIM DIVINE AUTHORITY: FALSE PARADIGM!

"From the documents themselves we find no claim of authority. This is in contrast to the books of the Old Testament that claim to record the words that God spoke and the deeds that He performed among the people. Therefore it is not logical to attribute God's authority to the books of the Apocrypha when they themselves make no claim to divine authority." [114]

This is outlandish. What is not logical is this guy writing as an expert on books he does not remotely know. Again, it is apparent that he is a scoffer and has not even read these books seriously. He is perhaps sharing thoughts of other scholars. Two of these books, Prayer of Manasseh and Azaryah are actual Bible accounts, and they were praying to Yahuah invoking His name. He answered and rescued both. If that was not by Yahuah's authority, whose was it? How is it that the accounts in 2nd Chronicles and Daniel are authoritative yet, someone these prayers included in those stories historically, are not? That is false. Prayer of Manasseh is documented in 2nd Chronicles 33:18-19 as being published in those days as inspired scripture. Fragments of this prayer were found in Qumran among the Temple Priests and they match the text we have today largely. Though only one-chapter, Manasseh uses the name of YHWH seven times. His authority is all over it.

Sirach, another book of wisdom like Solomon, begins with "All wisdom comes from Yahuah, and is with him forever." This scholar seems to be confused that wisdom that comes from Yahuah is authoritative. Sad. Chapter 17 is about Yahuah speaking to Israel. Is that not authoritative? Yahuah speaks in this text in 24:8 and 31 as well. It is a wisdom text all based on the wisdom of Yahuah from the beginning words and still has the words of Yahuah, but the entire book is His wisdom. We must have missed the passage that says His wisdom is almost or not quite authoritative. This scoffer is making things up having not read this book. It uses the name of YHWH about 225 times.

For Tobit, how can this scoffer be so blind? Tobit's sight was restored by Yahuah and hopefully his will too. Sarah was rid of the oppression of a Nephilim. It is a Biblical account quoted in the New Testament thus, authoritative. Yahuah is the center of the entire narrative and YHWH is there many times in the text. Yahuah speaks through His Archangel, Raphael, in a large portion of the book. Baruch uses YHWH 50 times in its six chapters representing His words many of those times.

25. THERE WAS NO HEBREW ORIGINAL FOR ALL OF THE BOOKS OF THE APOCRYPHA- FALSE STATEMENT AND OUTRIGHT LIE!

First, ancient history has no book called "Apocrypha" until 382 A.D. Second, this scholar has never even bothered to research the Dead Sea Scrolls in the slightest. Found in the Hebrew language dated to the B.C. era are fragments that prove that most of the Apocrypha was originally Hebrew. This is a completely outrageous lie of ignorance.

"It is clear that in the first century the Old Testament was complete. Jesus put His stamp of approval on the books of the Hebrew Old Testament but said nothing

concerning the Apocrypha. However, He did say that the Scriptures were the authoritative Word of God and they could not be broken. Any adding to that which God has revealed is denounced in the strongest of terms. Jesus asked the religious leaders a penetrating question." [114]

He very poorly uses Matthew 23:34-36 to make this point especially yet does not realize he is citing Messiah's quote of the Apocrypha to try to attack the Apocrypha as not authoritative as a result. That is pathetic.

"Therefore I send you prophets, sages, and scribes, some of whom you will kill and crucify, and some you will flog in your synagogues and pursue from town to town, so that upon you may come all the righteous blood shed on earth, from the blood of righteous Abel to the blood of Zechariah son of Barachiah, whom you murdered between the sanctuary and the altar. Truly I tell you, all this will come upon this generation (Matthew 23:34-36). . ."

It is incredible he is ignoring that the next verse, 37, is a direct quote of 2ⁿᵈ Esdras 1:30 by Messiah according to the 1611 KJV. That is where Messiah quoted a so-called "Apocryphal" book thus he leaves that out of course. To attack Apocrypha, a useless term, with a verse quoted from it, is an insane double standard. Not only did Yahusha quote 2ⁿᵈ Esdras, but we have found numerous such quotes from much of the Apocrypha which we cover in the Torah Test for each book.

However, how does this supposed scholar lack education realizing that Ezra who wrote 1ˢᵗ and 2ⁿᵈ Esdras was a prophet? The three writers of Sirach were sages of the same family. Baruch was a scribe and really, prophet even in Jeremiah as he was Jeremiah's mouthpiece as well. Solomon is Solomon and one could label him a sage but whatever his title, it was good enough for the modern Canon and Yahusha even cites him in Matthew 12:42 *(Luke 11:31)*. Jeremiah is still a prophet. Daniel who wrote Susanna and Bel & the Dragon remains a prophet, Azaryah *(Abednego)* was a fellow prophet with Daniel, and Tobit was a prophet prophesying New Jerusalem and the End Times. Every one of these credible books qualifies in this verse. These are the books he dismisses, yet all written by *"prophets, sages, and scribes"* sent by Yahusha. This is not a position. It is illiterate rambling, and it only gets worse.

"He mentions Abel and Zechariah as the first and last messengers of God that were murdered. Abel's murder is mentioned in Genesis while Zechariah's was in 2 Chronicles - the last Old Testament book in the Hebrew canonical order. The fact that these two are specifically mentioned is particularly significant. There are other murders of God's messengers recorded in the Apocrypha. Jesus does not mention them. This strongly suggests He did not consider the books of the Apocrypha as part of Old Testament Scripture as with the books from Genesis to 2 Chronicles." [114]

Though it goes without saying that Abel was the first martyr, where did Yahusha say Zechariah is the very last prophet? That is illiterate to Messiah's own words. This is Matthew 23, chronologically after John the Baptist was martyred whom Messiah called in Chapter 11, twelve chapters earlier, the last great prophet. How does a New Testament scholar not know that John was the last prophet, and not Zechariah? This is exactly how scholars bungle scripture which should be sacred to them, yet their treatment is very clearly one of disrespect.

Matthew 11:9-11 KJV
But what went ye out for to see? A prophet? yea, I say unto you, and more than a prophet. For this is he, of whom it is written, Behold, I send my messenger before thy face, which shall prepare thy way before thee. Verily I say unto you, Among them that are born of women there hath not risen a greater than John the Baptist: notwithstanding he that is least in the kingdom of heaven is greater than he.

He, then, tries to misuse Luke 24:25, 27 and 44, which he says does not cite a grouping called "Apocrypha" as scripture, yet it also does not mention Torah by name, but it certainly included Torah. Why would he expect such? It is rather idiotic to seek out a term from Yahusha in the First Century that was not even used regarding this set aside grouping of "hidden" books until Jerome in 382 A.D. Again, this demonstrates this is no scholar on this topic and he should be given no voice with such nonsensical answers. Also, the "Law of Moses, the Prophets and the Psalms" include most of what is termed Apocrypha when one assesses book by book. They were indeed written by prophets, sages and scribes.

26. THERE IS NOTHING NEW ADDED TO GOD'S TRUTH - FALSE STATEMENT!

If this were true, why is it that our Torah Test was able to find so many quotes in the New Testament that originate in these texts mislabeled "Apocrypha." Why does the 1611 KJV do the same? Why were they kept as Bible Canon by the Temple Priests? This is a lie.

2nd Esdras is full of prophecy predicting about 2,000 years as no other prophet ever has. If only this scholar could read... These prophesies become the origin of large portions of Revelation even. It also prophesies of Messiah's birth very closely in date. That is affirmation that Yahusha is indeed the only Messiah and Stewart calls that nothing new added? 1st Esdras documents the enemies of Israel in a way that connects the synagogue of satan like no other book. He would have to actually read these books to know these things and he clearly has not even bothered. That is just one example but most of these books are fraudulently classified as "Apocrypha."

Fragments from Wisdom of Sirach were found in Hebrew in Cave 2 in Qumran

2QSir/2Q18, Tobit was found in Hebrew in Cave 4 labeled 4Q196-200 *[Vermes, pp. 596-601] [22]*, Letter of Jeremiah *(Baruch 6)* was found in Cave 7, 7Q2, written in "Greek but closer to Hebrew tradition." *[Vermes, p. 472] [22]*, Prayer of Manasseh was discovered in Cave 4, 4Q381: 33, 8 *[Vermes, p. 319] [22]*, 1ˢᵗ Esdras was grossly mislabeled "Proto-Esther" which we have proven is all 1ˢᵗ Esdras and these were found in Cave 4 in Aramaic, not Greek *[Vermes, pp. 619-20] [22][88]*, and Susanna was found in Cave 4, 4Q551, in Aramaic, not Greek. *[Vermes, p. 651][22]*. 2ⁿᵈ Esdras *[22: Vermes, pp. 389-390] [22]* and Wisdom of Solomon *[4Q415–418, 423; 1Q26. Cave 4.][100][95]* are both quoted in Hebrew fragments. Prayer of Azaryah and Bel & The Dragon were both part of Daniel originally which comes to us originating in Hebrew. Frankly, none of these credible texts originate in Greek.

Not only is this a lie, but there is also no scripture which says Yahuah must preserve His Word in Hebrew on Earth. He does in Heaven but there are plenty of texts in the modern Canon for which the oldest copies we have are not necessarily Hebrew. This has never been a Bible command but a false paradigm.

27. JESUS' TESTIMONY IS DEFINITIVE: TRUE STATEMENT, FALSE PARADIGM!

"It is clear that in the first century the Old Testament was complete. Jesus put His stamp of approval on the books of the Hebrew Old Testament but said nothing concerning the Apocrypha. However, He did say that the Scriptures were the authoritative Word of God and they could not be broken. Any adding to that which God has revealed is denounced in the strongest of terms. Jesus asked the religious leaders a penetrating question." [114]

Indeed, the Old Testament was complete by the First Century, and we have it in archaeology from the Biblically ordained keepers of scripture in Qumran/ Bethabara. Most of these books removed and marginalized by Jerome in 382 A.D. are found in that Bible Canon which is the only scripture ever ordained. Yahusha endorsed this community where these books were found as Bible Canon. He quotes most of them which we have covered. He would never call them "Apocrypha" which is a half-witted term to use. No such category existed in His time and rejected the Pharisee Canon this scholar calls his Bible today. Let us not pretend he represents our Messiah's view on this.

As promised, we have demonstrated, this lengthy article on Blue Letter Bible is very poorly researched, full of lies and misrepresentations, and oblivious to the Word. This writer knows very little of the history of the Bible and that is sad. He does not put forth even one credible point in this entire smoke screen. There is no basis in which to test the "Apocrypha" this way, nor is there any truth in his stance against something he does not remotely understand.

THE NAME OF GOD IN "APOCRYPHA"

One revealing sign that portions of "apocrypha" may vet as legitimate is their use of the name of YHWH though more testing must be done. In a quick search of this book, we find over 450 uses of YHWH in what we will prove to be credible texts. However, the Book of Esther never addresses, prays to, fasts for, or even thanks or credits YHWH in the entire story which should raise many red flags. The Bible does not use an acrostic of the name of YHWH, it spells it out over 6,800 times directly in the Hebrew Old Testament. It is never hidden and always has been pronounced.

We learn from Jubilees Hebrew is the language of Creation thus it must be simple and somehow for thousands of years, it was written with just consonants and a couple of vowels *("A" and "U")* yet spoken without ever needing vowel points. Those were added in about 1000 A.D. by the Masoretes and at times serve to offer more confusion than clarity as they clearly were not honest about the name of Yahuah since it was their Pharisee practice to hide His name. Therefore, this must be a phonetic language requiring no vowels and no fancy rules especially those changing even within a word illogically. What we call Hebrew today is Yiddish-infused.

Phonetically, YH is simple. H is AH *(see chart to right)*. That's YAH. The next combination is HW which we know by the names of the prophets is HU. Thus, it's YAHU as with the prophets. Finally, we add the last H or AH for YAHUAH.

We recognize there is a whole church out there which stakes it's claim on the name Jehovah. Here's the largest problem with that word. It is not Ancient Hebrew, Aramaic, Greek, Latin, Old French, Old German nor Old English. In other words, every language in which the Bible has been interpreted through in origin cannot render" J" nor "V" until the Renaissance *(1500s or so)*. The Bible was already thousands of years old and never used "J" nor "V" in any ancient text. There is a Pharisee out there deceiving many by trying to make this fit, but we have the Dead Sea Scrolls dating to as early as 300 B.C. with even entire books such as the Isaiah scroll of about 25 feet in length which never renders a "J" nor a "V" even once.

This leads us to the name of Messiah as the same first 3 letters YHW or YAHU as set by Yahuah. Yes, He literally meant He came in His Father's name. His name ends with SH - SHIN, A - AYIN which is SHA. He is Yahusha with Yahushua also appearing as a variant in scripture. Joshua has this same name in Hebrew. His people are the YAHUdim never Jews but YAH's.

Finally, some focus on the one time in scripture that Yahuah says His name is HYH, HAYAH as His only name ignoring the 6,800 times it is recorded as YHWH, Yahuah. However, modern Yiddish renders this as EHYEH and similar in fraud. Ancient Hebrew is HA YAH or THE YAH. It is the same name. Yahuah is being specific in saying I am The Yah not to be confused with any other. He is still invoking His name Yahuah in that passage which matches. In fact, YAH is rendered in the Old Testament 45 times on a standalone basis. Scripture is clear and abundant on this.

FATHER YAHUAH

יהוה

HEY · WAW · HEY · YAD

HAU HAY

YAHUAH

Ancient Semitic/Hebrew

Early	Middle	Late	Name	Picture	Meaning	Sound
		א	El	Ox head	Strong, Power, Leader	ah, eh
		ב	Bet	Tent floorplan	Family, House, In	b, bh(v)
		ג	Gam	Foot	Gather, Walk	g
		ד	Dal	Door	Move, Hang, Entrance	d
		ה	Hey	Man with arms raised	Look, Reveal, Breath	h, ah
		ו	Waw	Tent peg	Add, Secure, Hook	w, o, u
		ז	Zan	Mattock	Food, Cut, Nourish	z
		ח	Hhet	Tent wall	Outside, Divide, Half	hh
		ט	Tet	Basket	Surround, Contain, Mud	t
		י	Yad	Arm and closed hand	Work, Throw, Worship	y, ee
		כ	Kaph	Open palm	Bend, Open, Allow, Tame	k, kh
		ל	Lam	Shepherd Staff	Teach, Yoke, To, Bind	l
		מ	Mem	Water	Chaos, Mighty, Blood	m
		נ	Nun	Seed	Continue, Heir, Son	n
		ס	Sin	Thorn	Grab, Hate, Protect	s
		ע	Ghah	Eye	Watch, Know, Shade	gh(ng)
		פ	Pey	Mouth	Blow, Scatter, Edge	p, ph(f)
		צ	Tsad	Trail	Journey, chase, hunt	ts
		ק	Quph	Sun on the horizon	Condense, Circle, Time	q
		ר	Resh	Head of a man	First, Top, Beginning	r
		ש	Shin	Two front teeth	Sharp, Press, Eat, Two	sh
		ת	Taw	Crossed sticks	Mark, Sign, Signal, Monument	t
			Ghah	Rope	Twist, Dark, Wicked	gh

AH U

Y

26

SON YAHUSHA

"YAHU IS SALVATION"

יהושע

AYIN · SHIN · WAW · HEY · YAD

NO "J"

NO "V"

NO VOWEL POINTS

Yeshua Is Missing Letters and of Pharisee Origin

AH S U HAY

YAHUSHA

YAHUdim יהודים
Yah's People (Never Jews, Yah's)

YAHUdah יהודה
"Yahu Be Praised" (Tribe of Judah)

Ha YAH היה
I AM or THE YAH

EliYAHU אליהו
"My God Is Yahu"

THE Levite BIBLE

YAHUAH TOLD US HIS NAME IS YHWH, YAHUAH MANY TIMES:

Isaiah 42:8: I am YHWH (יהוה): **that is my name**...

Exodus 20:2-4: I am YHWH (יהוה) thy God (Elohim)...

Exodus 6:6: I am YHWH (יהוה)

Leviticus 19:12: I am YHWH (יהוה)

Jeremiah 16:21: ...and they shall know that **my name is YHWH** (יהוה)

Exodus 3:15: And God (Elohim) said... **YHWH** (יהוה) God (Elohim) of your fathers, the God (Elohim) of Abraham, the God (Elohim) of Isaac, and the God (Elohim) of Jacob, hath sent me unto you: **this is my name for ever**, and this is my memorial unto all generations.

Zechariah 13:9: "**They will call on My name**, And I will answer them; I will say, 'They are My people,' And they will say, '**YHWH** (יהוה) **is my God** (Elohim).'"

Ezekiel 39:6: And I will send a fire on Magog, and among them that dwell carelessly in the isles: and they shall know that **I am YHWH** (יהוה)

YHWH PRONOUNCED IN THE BIBLE AS A PRACTICE:

Genesis 4:26: And to Seth, to him also there was born a son; and he called his name Enos: **then began men to call upon the name of YHWH** (יהוה)"

1 Samuel 7:5-9: Then Samuel said, "Gather all Israel to Mizpah and **I will pray to YHWH** (יהוה) for you."

1 Kings 18:36-37: At the time of the offering of the evening sacrifice, Elijah the prophet came near and said, "**O YHWH** (יהוה), **the God** (Elohim) **of Abraham**, Isaac and Israel..."

Jonah 2:2 and he said, "I **called out** of my distress **to YHWH** (יהוה)

Genesis 12:8: ...he built an altar **unto YHWH** (יהוה), and **called upon the name of YHWH** (יהוה)

Genesis 26:24-25: And **YHWH** (יהוה) **appeared** unto him the same night, and said, **I am** the Elohim of Abraham thy father: fear not, for I am with thee, and will bless thee, and multiply thy seed for my servant Abraham's sake. And he builded an altar there, and **called upon the name of YHWH** (יהוה)

1 Chronicles 16:8: Give **thanks unto YHWH** (יהוה), **call upon his name**...

Psalm 105:1: O give **thanks unto YHWH** (יהוה); **call upon his name**:

Zephaniah 3:9: For then will I turn to the people a pure language, that they may **all call upon the name of YHWH** (יהוה), to serve him with one consent.

Lamentations 3:55: I **called upon thy name**, O **YHWH** (יהוה)

2 Samuel 22:4: I **call upon YHWH** (יהוה), who is worthy to be praised...

Psalm 18:3: I **call upon YHWH** (יהוה), who is worthy to be praised...

1 Kings 18:24: "Then you call on the name of your god (Elohim), and **I will call on the name of YHWH** (יהוה)

2 Kings 5:11: ...Naaman was furious and went away and said, "Behold, I thought, 'Hewill surely come out to me and stand and **call on the name of YHWH (יהוה) his God** (Elohim)...

Psalm 18:6: In my distress **I called upon YHWH (יהוה)**

Psalm 28:1-2: To You, **O YHWH (יהוה), I call**...

Psalm 55:16: As for me, **I shall call upon God** (Elohim), **And YHWH (יהוה)** will save me.

Psalm 120:1: In my trouble **I cried to YHWH (יהוה)**, And **He answered me.**

Isaiah 58:9: Then **you will call, and YHWH (יהוה) will answer**...

Joel 1:19: To You, **O YHWH (יהוה), I cry**...

Joel 2:32: "And it will come about that **whoever calls on the name of YHWH (יהוה)**

Psalm 99:6: Moses and Aaron were among His priests, And Samuel was among those **who called on His name**; **They called upon YHWH (יהוה) and He answered**...

Numbers 21:7: So the people came to Moses and said, "We have sinned, because we have **spoken against YHWH (יהוה)** and you; **intercede with YHWH (יהוה)**

1 Samuel 12:19: Then all the people said to Samuel, "**Pray for your servants to YHWH (יהוה) your God** (Elohim)...

Genesis 13:4: ...to the place of the altar which he had made there formerly; and there **Abram called on the name of YIIWII (יהוה)**

Exodus 32:11-13: Then **Moses entreated YHWH (יהוה) his God** (Elohim), **and said**, "**O YHWH (יהוה)**

Deuteronomy 9:26-29: "**I prayed to YHWH (יהוה) and said, 'O YHWH (יהוה)**GOD (Elohim) do not destroy Your people...

Numbers 14:13-19: But **Moses said to YHWH (יהוה)**, "Then the Egyptians will hear of it, for by Your strength You brought up this people from their midst, and they will tell it to the inhabitants of this land. **They have heard that You, O YHWH (יהוה)**, are in the midst of this people, for **You, O YHWH (יהוה)**, are seen eye to eye... *(and there are many more as this name appears over 6,800 times)*

YHWH WILL BE RESTORED IN THE LAST DAYS SAYS YHWH:

Isaiah 52:6: Therefore **my people shall know my name**: therefore they shall know in that day that I am he that doth speak: behold, it is I.

Jeremiah 16:21: Therefore, behold, I will this once cause them to know, I will cause them to know mine hand and my might; and **they shall know that my name is YHWH (יהוה)**

Ezekiel 39:7: So **will I make my holy name known** in the midst of my people Israel; and I will **not let them pollute my holy name any more**: and the heathen **shall know that I am YHWH (יהוה)**, the Holy One in Israel.

All passages from the KJV.

THE WISDOM OF SOLOMON

BOOK OF WISDOM

WITH THE RESTORED NAME OF YAHUAH

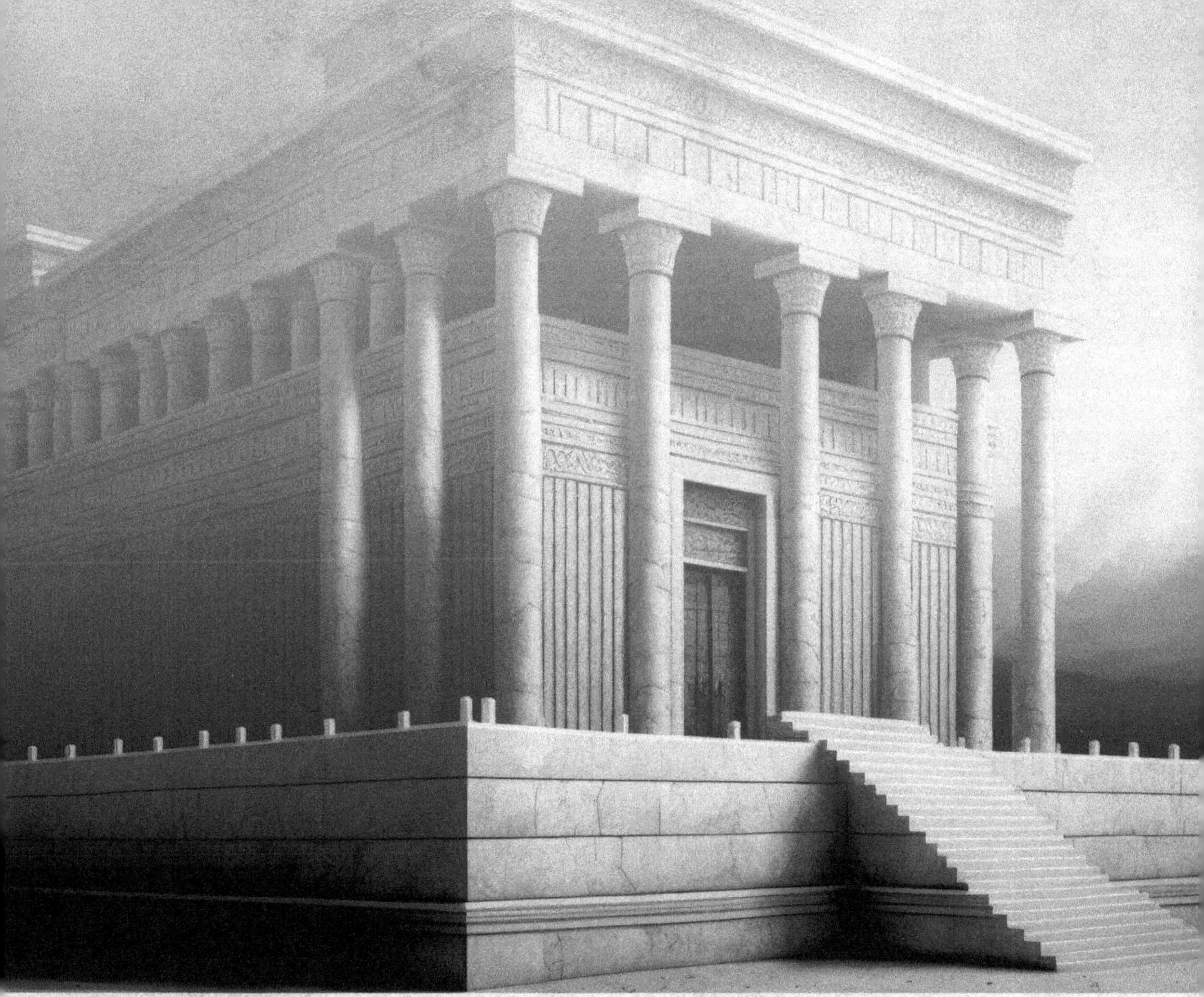

CHAPTER 1:

2 To whom Yahuah shows Himself, 4 and Wisdom herself. 6 An evil speaker cannot lie hid. 12 We procure our own destruction: 13 for Elohim created not death.

Cf. 1Ki. 3:3; Isa. 56:1, 13:4.

1-3: Cf. Jas. 1:6-8, 2:4, 4:3. [93]

Cf. Dt. 4:29.

Or, makes manifest.

Cf. Jer. 4:22. Or, is rebuked, or shows itself.

Cf. Gal. 5:22. Or, lips.

Or, upholds.

1 Love righteousness, you that be judges of the earth: think of Yahuah with a good (heart) and in simplicity of heart seek Him. 2 For He will be found of them that tempt Him not: and shows himself unto such as do not distrust Him. 3 For froward thoughts separate from Elohim: and His power when it is tried, reproves the unwise. 4 For into a malicious soul wisdom shall not enter: nor dwell in the body that is subject unto sin. 5 For the holy spirit of discipline will fly deceit, and remove from thoughts that are without understanding: and will not abide when unrighteousness comes in. 6 For wisdom is a loving spirit: and will not acquit a blasphemer of his words: for Elohim is witness of his reigns, and a true beholder of his heart, and a hearer of his tongue. 7 For the spirit of Yahuah fills the world: and that which contains all things has knowledge of the voice. 8 Therefore he that speaks unrighteous things, cannot be hid: neither shall vengeance, when it punishes pass by him. 9 For inquisition shall be made into the counsels of the ungodly: and the sound of his words, shall come unto Yahuah, for the manifestation of his wicked deeds. 10 For the ear of jealousy hears all things: and the noise of murmurings is not hidden. 11 Therefore beware of murmuring, which is unprofitable, and refrain your tongue from backbiting: for there is no word so secret that shall go for nought: and the mouth that bellies, slays the soul.

Or, reproving.

Cf. Jas. 4:11, 5:9 .[93]

Or, slanders.

12 Seek not death in the error of your life: and pull not upon yourselves destruction, with the works of your hands. 13 For Elohim made not death: neither has He pleasure in the destruction of the living. 14 For He created all things, that they might have their being: and the generations of the world were healthful: and there was no poison of destruction in them: nor the kingdom of death upon the earth. 15 For righteousness is immortal. 16 But ungodly men with their works, and words called it to them:

Cf. Dt. 4:23.

Cf. Rom. 8:20-21. [96]

for when they thought to have it their friend, they consumed to naught, and made a covenant with it, because they are worthy to take part with it.

CHAPTER 2:

1 The wicked think this life short, 5 and of no other after this.
6 Therefore they will take their pleasure in this, 10 and conspire against the just. 21 What that is which does blind them.

1 For the ungodly said, reasoning with themselves, but not aright: Our life is short and tedious, and in the death of a man there is no remedy: neither was there any man known to have returned from the grave. 2 For we are born at all adventure: and we shall be hereafter as though we had never been: for the breath in our nostrils is as smoke, and a little spark in the moving of our heart.

3 Which being extinguished, our body shall be turned into ashes, and our spirit shall vanish as the soft air: 4 And our name shall be forgotten in time, and no man shall have our works in remembrance, and our life shall pass away as the trace of a cloud: and shall be dispersed as a mist that is driven away with the beams of the sun, and overcome with the heat thereof. 5 For our time is a very shadow that passes away: and after our end there is no returning: for it is fast sealed, so that no man comes again. 6 Come on therefore, let us enjoy the good things that are present: and let us speedily use the creatures like as in youth. 7 Let us fill ourselves with costly wine, and ointments: and let no flower of the Spring pass by us. 8 Let us crown ourselves with rose buds, before they be withered. 9 Let none of us go without his part of our voluptuousness: let us leave tokens of our joyfulness in every place: for this is our portion, and our lot is this. 10 Let us oppress the poor righteous man, let us not spare the widow, nor reverence the ancient gray hairs of the aged. 11 Let our strength be the Law of justice: for that which is feeble is found to be nothing worth.

12 Therefore let us lie in wait for the righteous: because he is not for our turn, and he is clean contrary to our doings: he upbraids us with

Cf. Job 7:1; Matt. 22:23; 1Cor. 15:32.

Cf. Eccl. 2:23. [81]

Cf. Eccl. 3:19, 1:11, 2:6, 9:5. [81]

Or, moist.

Or, oppressed.

Cf. Jas. 4:14. [93]

Cf. 1Chr. 29:15.
Or, he.

Cf. Isa. 22:13, 56:12.
Or, earnestly.
1Cor. 15:32.

6-10: Cf. Eccl. 9:7-9. [81]

Or, jolity.
Cf. Eccl. 3:22, 5:18, 9:9.[81]

Cf. Jas. 2:6, 5:6. [93]

our offending the Law, and objects to our infamy the transgressing of our education. 13 He professes to have the knowledge of Elohim: and he calls himself the child of Yahuah. 14 He was made to reprove our thoughts. 15 He is grievous unto us even to behold: for his life is not like other men's, his ways are of another fashion.

Cf. Rom. 9:19-23.

Cf. John 7:7; Eph. 5:13,14.

Cf. Isa. 53:3, 55:8-9.

Cf. Rom. 8:20-21.

16 We are esteemed of him as counterfeits: he abstains from our ways as from filthiness: he pronounces the end of the just to be blessed, and makes his boast that Elohim is his father.

Or, false coin.

Cf. John 5:17-18.

17 Let us see if his words be true: and let us prove what shall happen in the end of him. 18 For if the just man be the son of Elohim, he will help him, and deliver

Cf. Ps. 22:8,9. Matt. 27:43.

him from the hand of his enemies. 19 Let us examine him with despitefulness and torture, that we may know his meekness, and prove his patience. 20 Let us condemn him with a shameful death: for by his own saying, he shall be respected. 21 Such things they did imagine, and were deceived: for their own wickedness has blinded them. 22 As for the mysteries of Elohim, they knew them not: neither hoped they for the wages of righteousness: nor discerned a reward for blameless souls. 23 For Elohim created man to be immortal, and made him to be an image of his own eternity. 24 Nevertheless through envy of the devil came death into the world: and they that do hold of his side do find it.

Cf. Jer. 11:19.

Greek: preferred or esteemed the reward.

Cf. Gen. 1:26-27, 5:1; Eccl. 17:3.

Cf. Gen. 3:12 interpreted later in John 8:44; Rev. 12:9; 20:2. Cf. Jas. 3:9. [93] [96]

CHAPTER 3:

1 The godly are happy in their death, 5 and in their troubles; 10 The wicked are not, nor their children:

15 But they that are pure, are happy, though they have no children:

16 For the adulterer and his seed shall perish.

1 But the souls of the righteous are in the hand of Elohim, and there shall no torment touch them.

Cf. Deut. 33. 3.

2 In the sight of the unwise they seemed to die: and their departure is taken for misery, 3 And their going from us to be utter destruction: but they are in peace. 4 For though they be punished in the sight of men: yet is their hope full of immortality. 5 And having been a little chastised, they shall be greatly rewarded:

Cf. 5.4.

Cf. Rom. 8:24; 1Cor. 5:1; 1Pet. 1:13.

4-6: Cf. Jas. 1:2-3, 12-13. [93]

Or, benefited. Ex. 16:4; Dt. 8:2. Or, meet.

5-6: Cf. 1Pet. 1:6-7.

for Elohim proved them, and found them worthy for Himself. 6 As gold in the furnace has He tried them, and received them as a burnt offering. 7 And in the time of their visitation, they shall shine and run to and fro, like sparks among

Cf. Matt.13:43.

the stubble. 8 They shall judge the nations, and have dominion over the people,

Cf. Matt. 19:28; 1Cor. 6:2.

and their Yahuah shall reign forever. 9 They that put their trust in Him, shall understand the truth: and such as be faithful in love, shall abide with Him: for

Or, and such as be faithful shall remain with Him in love.

grace and mercy is to his saints, and he has care for his elect. 10 But the ungodly shall be punished according to their own imaginations, which have neglected the righteous, and forsaken

Cf. Matt. 25:41.

Yahuah. 11 For who so despises wisdom, and nurture, he is miserable, and their hope is vain, their labors unfruitful, and their works unprofitable.

Or, light, or unchaste.

12 Their wives are foolish, and their children wicked.

13 Their offspring is cursed: wherefore blessed is the barren that is undefiled, which has not known the sinful bed: she shall have

Cf. Isa. 56:5.

fruit in the visitation of souls. 14 And blessed is the eunuch which with his hands has wrought no iniquity: nor imagined wicked things against Elohim: for unto him shall be given the

Cf. Isa. 56:4,5. Greek: the chosen, or amongst the people.

special gift of faith, and an inheritance in the Temple of Yahuah more acceptable to his mind. 15 For glorious is the fruit of good labors: and the root of wisdom shall never fall away. 16 As for the children of adulterers,

Or, be partakers of holy things.

they shall not come to their perfection, and the seed of an unrighteous bed shall be rooted out. 17 For though they live long, yet shall they be nothing regarded: and their last age shall be without honor. 18 Or if they die quickly, they have

Or, bearing.

no hope, neither comfort in the day of trial. 19 For horrible is the end of the unrighteous generation.

CHAPTER 4:

*1 The chaste man shall be crowned.
3 Bastard slips shall not thrive.
6 They shall witness against their
parents. 7 The just die young, and
are happy. 19 The miserable end of
the wicked.*

1 Better it is to have no children, and to have virtue: for the memorial thereof is immortal: because it is known with Elohim and with men. 2 When it is present, men take example at it, and when it is gone, they desire it: it wears a crown, and triumphs forever, having gotten the victory, striving for undefiled rewards. 3 But the multiplying brood of the ungodly shall not thrive, nor take deep rooting from bastard slips, nor lay any fast foundation. 4 For though they flourish in branches for a time: yet standing not fast, they shall be shaken with the wind: and through the force of winds, they shall be rooted out. 5 The imperfect branches shall be broken off, their fruit unprofitable, not ripe to eat: yes, meet for nothing. 6 For children begotten of unlawful beds, are witnesses of wickedness against their parents in their trial. 7 But though the righteous be prevented with death: yet shall he be in rest. 8 For honorable age is not that which stands in length of time, nor that is measured by number of years. 9 But wisdom is the gray hair unto men, and an unspotted life is old age. 10 He pleased Elohim and was beloved of Him: so that living amongst sinners, he was translated. 11 Yes, speedily was he taken away, lest that wickedness should alter his understanding, or deceit beguile his soul. 12 For the bewitching of naughtiness does obscure things that are honest: and the wandering of concupiscence, does undermine the simple mind. 13 He, being made perfect in a short time, fulfilled a long time. 14 For his soul pleased Yahuah: therefore, hasted he to take him away, from among the wicked.

15 This the people saw and understood it not: neither laid they up this in their minds, That His grace and mercy is with His Saints, and that He has respect unto His chosen. 16 Thus the righteous that is dead, shall condemn the ungodly, which are living, and youth that is soon perfected, the many years and old age of the unrighteous. 17 For they

Or, approved.

Cf. Matt. 7:19.

Cf. John 15:6.

Greek: sleeps.

Cf. Gen. 5:24; Heb. 11:5.

Greek: pervert.

Or, sanctified or consummated.

shall see the end of the wise and shall not understand what Elohim in his counsel has decreed of him, and to what end Yahuah has set him in safety. 18 They shall see him and despise him, but Elohim shall laugh them to scorn, and they shall hereafter be a vile carcass, and a reproach among the dead forevermore. 19 For He shall rend them, and cast them down headlong, that they shall be speechless: and He shall shake them from the foundation: and they shall be utterly laid waste and be in sorrow: and their memorial shall perish.

20 And when they cast up the accounts of their sins, they shall come with fear: and their own iniquities shall convince them to their face.

Or, to the casting up of the account.

CHAPTER 5:

1 The wicked shall wonder at the godly, 4 and confess their error, 5 and the vanity of their lives. 15 God will reward the just, 17 and war against the wicked.

1 Then shall the righteous man stand in great boldness, before the face of such as have afflicted him, and made no account of his labors. 2 When they see it, they shall be troubled with terrible fear, and shall be amazed at the strangeness of his salvation, so far beyond all that they looked for. 3 And they repenting, and groaning for anguish of spirit, shall say within themselves, This was he whom we had sometimes in derision, and a proverb of reproach. 4 We fools accounted his life madness, and his end to be without honor. 5 How is he numbered among the children of Elohim, and his lot is among the saints?

6 Therefore have we erred from the way of truth, and the light of righteousness has not shined unto us, and the sun of righteousness rose not upon us. 7 We wearied ourselves in the way of wickedness, and destruction: yes, we have gone through deserts, where there lay no way: but as for the way of Yahuah, we have not known it. 8 What has pride profited us? Or what good has riches with our boasting brought us?

9 All those things are passed away like a shadow, and as a post that hasted by. 10 And as a ship that

Or, parable.

Cf. 3.2.

Or, filled ourselves, or surfeited.

Cf. Jas. 4:6, 16, 1:10-12. [93]

Cf. 1Chr. 29:15, 2:5.

passes over the waves of the water, which when it is gone by, the trace thereof cannot be found: neither the pathway of the keel in the waves. 11 Or as when a bird has flown through the air, there is no token of her way to be found, but the light air being beaten with the stroke of her wings and parted with the violent noise and motion of them, is passed through, and therein afterwards no sign where she went, is to be found.

Cf. Prov. 30:19 Or, flies.

12 Or like as when an arrow is shot at a mark, it parts the air, which immediately comes together again: so that a man cannot know where it went through:

13 Even so we in like manner, as soon as we were born, began to draw to our end, and had no sign of virtue to show: but were consumed in our own wickedness. 14 For the hope of the ungodly is like dust that is blown away with the wind, like a thin froth that is driven away with the storm: like as the smoke which is dispersed here and there with a tempest, and passes away as the remembrance of a guest that tarries but a day. 15 But the righteous live forevermore, their reward also is with Yahuah, and the care of them is with the Most High. 16 Therefore shall they receive a glorious kingdom, and a beautiful crown from Yahuah's hand: for with His right hand shall He cover them, and with His arm shall He protect them. 17 He shall take to him His jealousy for complete armor, and make the creature His weapon for the revenge of his enemies. 18 He shall put on righteousness as a breastplate, and true judgment instead of an helmet. 19 He shall take holiness for an invincible shield. 20 His severe wrath shall He sharpen for a sword, and the world shall fight with Him against the unwise. 21 Then shall the right-aiming thunder bolts go abroad, and from the clouds, as from a well-drawn bow, shall they fly to the mark. 22 And hailstones full of wrath shall be cast as out of a stonebow, and the water of the sea shall rage against them, and the floods shall cruelly drown them. 23 Yes, a mighty wind shall

Cf. Job 8:9. Greek: thistle down. Or, chaffe. Ps. 2:4, 103:14; Prov. 10:25, 11:7; Jam. 1:10-11.

Cf. Jas. 4:6, 16, 1:10-12. [93] Cf. 2Tim. 4:8.

Or, palace.

Cf. Eph. 6:1.

Cf. Isa. 59:17; Eph. 6:13-17.

Or, equity.

stand up against them, and like a storm shall blow them away: thus iniquity shall lay was the whole earth, and ill dealing shall overthrow the thrones of the mighty.

CHAPTER 6:

1 Kings must give ear. 3 They have their power from Elohim, 5 Who will not spare them. 12 Wisdom is soon found. 21 Princes must seek for it: 24 For a wise Prince is the stay of his people.

1 Hear therefore, O kings, and understand, learn that you are judges of the ends of the earth. 2 Give ear you that rule the people, and glory in the multitude of nations. 3 For power is given you of Yahuah, and sovereignty from the Highest, who shall try your works; and search out your counsels. 4 Because being ministers of His kingdom, you have not judged aright, nor kept the Law, nor walked after the counsel of Elohim,

Cf. Rom. 13:1-2.

5 Horribly and speedily shall He come upon you: for a sharp judgment shall be to them that be in high places. 6 For mercy will soon pardon the meanest: but mighty men shall be mightily tormented. 7 For He which is Lord overall, shall fear no man's person: neither shall He stand in awe of any man's greatness: for he hath made the small and great, and cares for all alike. 8 But a sore trial shall come upon the mighty. 9 Unto you therefore, O kings, do I speak, that you may learn wisdom, and not fall away. 10 For they that keep holiness holily, shall be justified holy: and they that have learned such things, shall find a defense. 11 Wherefore set your affection upon my words, desire them, and you shall be instructed. 12 Wisdom is glorious and never fades away: yes, she is easily seen of them that love her, and found of such as seek her. 13 She prevents them that desire her, in making herself first known unto them.

Cf. 2Chr. 19:17; Dt. 10:17; Job. 34:19; Eccl. 35:12, 16; Acts 10:24; Rom. 2:11; Gal. 2:6; Eph. 6:9; Col. 3:25; 1Pet. 1:17.

14 Whoso seeks her early, shall have no great travail: for he shall find her sitting at his doors. 15 To think therefore upon her is perfection of wisdom: and who so watches for her, shall quickly be without care.

16 For she goes about seeking such as are worthy of her, shows herself favorably unto them in the ways, and meets them in every thought. 17 For the very true beginning of her, is the desire of discipline, and the care of discipline is love: 18 And love is the keeping of her Laws; and the giving heed unto her Laws, is the assurance of incorruption. 19 And incorruption makes us near unto Elohim. 20 Therefore the desire of wisdom brings to a kingdom. 21 If your delight be then in thrones and scepters, O you kings of the people, honor wisdom that you may reign forevermore. 22 As for wisdom what she is, and how she came up, I will tell you, and will not hide mysteries from you: but will seek her out from the beginning of her nativity, and bring the knowledge of her into light, and will not pass over the truth. 23 Neither will I go with consuming envy: for such a man shall have no fellowship with wisdom.

24 But the multitude of the wise is the welfare of the world: and a wise king is the upholding of the people. 25 Receive therefore instruction through my words, and it shall do you good.

Or, nurture.

CHAPTER 7:

1 All men have their beginning and end alike. 6 He preferred wisdom before all things else. 8 Elohim gave him all the knowledge, which he had. 22 The praise of wisdom.

1 I, myself also, am a mortal man, like to all, and the offspring of him that was first made of the earth,

2 And in my mother's womb was fashioned to be flesh in the time of ten months being compacted in blood, of the seed of man, and the pleasure that came with sleep. 3 And when I was born, I drew in the common air, and fell upon the earth which is of like nature, and the first voice which I uttered, was crying as all others do. 4 I was nursed in swaddling clothes, and that with cares. 5 For there is no king that had any other beginning of birth. 6 For all men have one entrance unto life, and the like going out. 7 Wherefore I prayed, and understanding was

Cf. Job 10:12.

Cf. Job 1:21; 1Tim. 6:7.

7-10: Cf. Jas. 1:5. [93] Cf. Eph. 1:17.

given me: I called upon Elohim, and the spirit of wisdom came to me. 8 I preferred her before scepters, and thrones, and esteemed riches nothing in comparison of her.

9 Neither compared I unto her any precious stone, because all gold in respect of her is as a little sand, and silver shall be counted as clay before her.

Greek: stone of inestimable price.

10 I loved her above health and beauty and chose to have her instead of light: for the light that comes from her never goes out. 11 All good things together came to me with her, and innumerable riches in her hands.

Cf. 1Ki. 3:13; Matt. 6:33.

12 And I rejoiced in them all, because wisdom goes before them: and I knew not that she was the mother of them.

Cf. Prov. 3 & 8, 13-20.

13 I learned diligently and do communicate her liberally: I do not hide her riches.

Greek: without guile. Greek: without envy.

14 For she is a treasure unto men that never fails: which they that use, become the friends of Elohim: being commended for the gifts that come from learning.

Or, enter friendship with God.

15 Elohim has granted me to speak as I would, and to conceive as is meet for the things that are given me: because it is He that leads

Or, Elohim grant. Or, are to be spoken of.

unto wisdom and directs the wise. 16 For in His hand are both we and our words: all wisdom also and knowledge of workmanship. 17 For He has given me certain knowledge of the things that are, namely to know how the world was made, and the operation of the elements: 18 The beginning, ending, and midst of the times: the alterations of the turning of the sun, and the change of seasons: 19 The circuits of years, and the positions of stars: 20 The natures of living creatures, and the furies of wild beasts: the violence of winds, and the reasonings of men: the diversities of plants, and the virtues of roots: 21 And all such things as are either secret or manifest: them I know. 22 For wisdom which is the worker of all things, taught me: for in her is an understanding spirit holy, one only, manifold, subtle, lively, clear, undefiled, plain, not subject to hurt, loving the thing that is good, quick, which cannot be allowed, ready to do good:

23 Kind to man, steadfast, sure, free from care, having all power, overseeing all things, and going through

Or, Elohim grant. Or, are to be spoken of.

Cf. 17-21: Ex. 31:3; 1Ki. 3:12, 4:29-34.

Cf. Jas. 1:17. [93]

Greek: only begotten.

Cf. Prov. 3:19, 8:22-26; Job 33:4; Eccl. 21:3.

all understanding, pure, and most subtle spirits.

24 For wisdom is more moving than any motion: she passes and goes through all things by reason of her pureness.

Or, vapor. Or, stream.

25 For she is the breath of the power of Elohim, and a pure influence flowing from the glory of the Almighty:

Cf. Job 32:8; Prov. 2:6; Eccl. 1:1.

therefore, can no undefiled thing fall into her. 26 For she is the brightness of the everlasting light: the unspotted mirror of the

Cf. Heb. 1:3.

power of Elohim, and the image of his goodness.

27 And being but one she can do all things: and remaining in herself, she makes all things new: and

Or, creates.

in all ages entering into holy souls, she makes them friends of Elohim, and Prophets. 28 For Elohim loves none but Him, that dwells with wisdom.

29 For she is more beautiful than the sun, and above all the order of stars, being compared with the light,

Cf. Jas. 1:17. [93]

she is found before it. 30 For after this comes night: but vice shall not prevail against wisdom.

CHAPTER 8:

2 He is in love with wisdom: 4 For he that has it, has every good thing. 21 It cannot be had, but from Elohim.

1 Wisdom reaches from one end to another mightily: and sweetly does she order

Or, profitably.

all things. 2 I loved her and sought her out, from my youth I desired to make her

Or, to marry her to myself.

my spouse, and I was a lover of her beauty. 3 In that she is conversant with Elohim, she magnifies her nobility: yes, Yahuah of all things himself loved her. 4 For she is privy to the mysteries of

the knowledge of Elohim,

Or, teacher. Or, chooser.

and a lover of His works.

5 If riches be a possession to be desired in this life: what is richer than wisdom that works all things? 6 And if prudence work; who of all that are, is a more cunning

Cf. Ex. 31:48, Prov. 3 & 8, 13-20; Gal. 4:3.

workman than she? 7 And if a man love righteousness, her labors are virtues: for she teaches temperance and prudence: justice and fortitude, which are such things as men can have nothing more profitable in their life. 8 If a man desire much experience:

she knows things of old, and conjectures aright what is to come: she knows the subtleties of speeches, and can expound dark sentences: she foresees signs and wonders, and the events of seasons and times. 9 Therefore I purposed to take her to me to live with me, knowing that she would be a counsellor of good things, and a comfort in cares and grief. 10 For her sake I shall have estimation among the multitude, and honor with the elders, though I be young. 11 I shall be found of a quick conceit in judgment, and shall be admired in the sight of great men. 12 When I hold my tongue they shall bide my leisure, and when I speak they shall give good ear unto me: if I talk much, they shall lay their hands upon their mouth. 13 Moreover, by the means of her, I shall obtain immortality, and leave behind me an everlasting memorial to them that come after me. 14 I shall set the people in order, and the nations shall be subject unto me. 15 Horrible tyrants shall be afraid when they do but hear of me, I shall be found good among the multitude, and valiant in war. 16 After I am come into mine house, I will repose myself with her: for her conversation has no bitterness, and to live with her, has no sorrow, but mirth and joy. 17 Now when I considered these things in myself, and pondered them in mine heart, how that to be allied unto wisdom, is immortality, 18 And great pleasure it is to have her friendship, and in the works of her hands are infinite riches, and in the exercise of conference with her, prudence: and in talking with her a good report: I went about seeking how to take her to me. 19 For I was a witty child, and had a good spirit. 20 Yes, rather being good, I came into a body undefiled. 21 Nevertheless when I perceived that I could not otherwise obtain her, except Elohim gave her me (and that was a point of wisdom also to know whose gift she was) I prayed unto Yahuah, and besought Him, and with my whole heart I said:

Cf. 17-21: Ex. 31:3; 1Ki. 3:12, 4:29-34.

Greek: will.

Cf. Job 29:8-11.

Or, govern.

Or, appear.

Or, being entered into mine house.

Cf. Prov. 7:3.

Or, fame.
Or, marry her.

Or, went.

CHAPTER 9:

1 A prayer unto Elohim for His wisdom, 6 without which the best man is nothing worth, 13 neither can he tell how to please Elohim.

1 O Elohim of my fathers, and Yahuah of mercy, who has made all things with your word, 2 And ordained man through your wisdom, that he should have dominion over the creatures, which you have made, 3 And order the world according to equity and righteousness, and execute judgment with an upright heart:

4 Give me wisdom that sits by your Throne and reject me not from among your children: 5 For I your servant and son of your handmaid, am a feeble person, and of a short time, and too young for the understanding of judgment and Laws. 6 For though a man be never so perfect among the children of men, yet if your wisdom be not with him, he shall be nothing regarded.

7 You have chosen me to be a king of your people, and a judge of your sons and daughters: 8 You have commanded me to build a Temple upon your holy mount, and an altar in the city wherein you dwell, a resemblance of the holy Tabernacle which you have prepared from the beginning: 9 And wisdom was with you: which knows your works, and was present when you made the world, and knew what was acceptable in your sight, and right in your Commandments. 10 O send her out of your holy heavens, and from the Throne of your glory, that being present she may labor with me, that I may know what is pleasing unto you. 11 For she knows and understands all things, and she shall lead me soberly in my doings, and preserve me in her power. 12 So shall my works be acceptable, and then shall I judge your people righteously, and be worthy to sit in my father's seat. 13 For what man is he that can know the counsel of Elohim? Or who can think what the will of Yahuah is? 14 For the thoughts of mortal men are miserable, and our devices are but uncertain. 15 For the corruptible body presses down the soul, and the earthly tabernacle weighs down the mind that muses upon many things. 16 And hardly do we guess aright at

Cf. Gen. 1. 28.

Cf. 1Ki. 3:5.

Cf. Ps. 116: 16.

Cf. Jas. 1:5.

[93]

Cf. 1Chr. 28:5; 2Chr. 1:9.

Cf. Prov. 3:19, 8:22-26; Job 33:4; Eccl. 21:3. John 1:2-3, 10.

Or, by her power or glory.

Cf. Isa. 40:13; Rom. 11:34; 1Cor. 2:16.

Or, fearful.

Cf. 2Cor. 5:1.

Greek: at hand.

Cf. Prov. 3:19, 8:22-26; Job 33:4; Eccl. 21:3. John 1:2-3, 10.

things that are upon earth, and with labor do we find the things that are before us: but the things that are in heaven, who has searched out? 17 And your counsel who has known, except you give wisdom, and send your holy spirit from above? 18 For so the ways of them which lived on the earth were reformed, and men were taught the things that are pleasing unto you, and were saved through wisdom.

Cf. Jas. 1:2-5, 3:15, 17. [93]

CHAPTER 10:

1 What wisdom did for Adam, 4 Noah, 5 Abraham, 6 Lot, and against the five cities, 10 for Jacob, 13 Joseph, 16 Moses, 17 and the Israelites.

Cf. Prov. 1, 7, 3

1 She preserved the first formed father of the world that was created alone, and brought him out of his fall,

Cf. Gen. 2:20.

2 And gave him power to rule all things. 3 But when the unrighteous went away from her in his anger, he perished also in the fury

Cf. Gen. 4:8.

wherewith he murdered his brother. 4 For whose cause the earth being drowned with the flood, Wisdom again preserved it, and directed the course of the

Cf. Gen. 7:21.

righteous, in a piece of wood, of small value.

5 Moreover, the nations in their wicked conspiracy being confounded, she found out the righteous, and preserved him blameless unto Elohim, and kept him strong against his tender compassion towards his son. 6 When the ungodly perished, she delivered the righteous man, who fled from the fire which fell down upon the five cities.

Cf. Gen. 11:9. Or, in.

Cf. Gen. 22:10, 19:16. Greek: Pentapolis.

7 Of whose wickedness even to this day the waste land that smokes, is a testimony, and plants bearing fruit that never come to ripeness: and a standing pillar of salt is a monument of an unbelieving soul. 8 For regarding not wisdom, they got not only this hurt, that they knew not the things which were good: but also left behind them to the world a memorial of their foolishness: so that in the things wherein they offended, they could not so much as be hidden. 9 But wisdom delivered from pain those that attended upon her. 10 When the righteous fled from his brother's wrath, she guided him in right paths: showed him the

kingdom of Elohim: and gave him knowledge of holy things, made him rich in his travails, and multiplied the fruit of his labors. 11 In the covetousness of such as oppressed him, she stood by him, and made him rich. 12 She defended him from his enemies and kept him safe from those that lay in wait, and in a sore conflict she gave him the victory, that he might know that godliness is stronger than all. 13 When the righteous was sold, she forsook him not, but delivered him from sin: she went down with him into the pit, 14 And left him not in bonds til she brought him the scepter of the kingdom and power against those that oppressed him: as for them that had accused him, she showed them to be liars, and gave them perpetual glory. 15 She delivered the righteous people, and blameless seed from the nation that oppressed them. 16 She entered into the soul of the servant of Yahuah, and withstood dreadful kings in wonders and signs, 17 Rendered to the righteous a reward of their labors, guided them in a marvelous way, and was unto them for a cover by day, and a light of stars in the night season: 18 Brought them through the Red Sea, and led them through much water. 19 But she drowned their enemies, and cast them up out of the bottom of the deep. 20 Therefore the righteous spoiled the ungodly, and praised your holy Name, O Yahuah, and magnified with one accord your hand that fought for them. 21 For wisdom opened the mouth of the dumb, and made the tongues of them that cannot speak, eloquent.

CHAPTER 11:

5 The Egyptians were punished, and the Israelites reserved in the same thing. 15 They were plagued by the same things, wherein they sinned. 20 Elohim could have destroyed them otherwise, 23 but he is merciful to all.

1 She prospered their works in the hand of the holy Prophet. 2 They went through the wilderness that was not inhabited, and pitched tents in places where there lay no way. 3 They stood against their enemies and were avenged of their adversaries. 4 When they were thirsty,

they called upon you, and water was given them out of the flinty rock, and their thirst was quenched out of the hard stone. 5 For by what things their enemies were punished, by the same they in their need were benefited. 6 For instead of a fountain of a perpetual running river, troubled with foul blood, 7 For a manifest reproof of that commandment, whereby the infants were slain, you gave unto them abundance of water by a means which they hoped not for,

8 Declaring by that thirst then, how you had punished their adversaries. 9 For when they were tried, albeit but in mercy chastised, they knew how the ungodly were judged in wrath and tormented thirsting in another manner than the just. 10 For these you did admonish and try as a father: but the other as a severe king you did condemn and punish.

11 Whether they were absent, or present, they were vexed alike. 12 For a double grief came upon them, and a groaning for the remembrance of things past. 13 For when they heard by their own punishments the other to be benefited, they had some feeling of Yahuah. 14 For whom they rejected with scorn when he was long before thrown out at the casting forth of the infants, him in the end, when they saw what came to pass, they admired. 15 But for the foolish devises of their wickedness, wherewith being deceived, they worshipped serpents void of reason, and vile beasts: you did send a multitude of unreasonable beasts upon them for vengeance,

16 That they might know that wherewithal a man sins, by the same also shall he be punished. 17 For your Almighty hand that made the world of matter without form, wanted not means to send among them a multitude of bears, or fierce lions, 18 Or unknown wild beasts full of rage newly created, breathing out either a fiery vapor, or filthy scents of scattered smoke, or shooting horrible sparkles out of their eyes: 19 Whereof not only the harm might dispatch them at once: but also, the terrible sight utterly destroy them.

20 Yes, and without these

Cf. Ex. 7:20.

Cf. Jas. 1:2-3, 12. [93]

Or, perceived.

Cf. Rom. 1:23.

might they have fallen down with one blast, being persecuted of vengeance, and scattered abroad through the breath of your power, but you have ordered all things in measure, and number, and weight. 21 For you can show your great strength at all times when you will, and who may withstand the power of your arm? 22 For the whole world before you is as a little grain of the balance, yes, as a drop of the morning dew that falls

Or, little weight.

down upon the earth. 23 But you have mercy upon all: for you can do all things, and wink at the sins of men: because they should amend. 24 For you love all the things that are, and abhor nothing which you have made: for never would you have made any thing, if you had hated it. 25 And how could any thing have endured if it had not been your will? Or been preserved, if not called by you? 26 But you spare all: for they are yours, O Yahuah, you lover of souls.

Cf. Rom. 2:4.

Cf. Rom. 8:20-21. [96]

CHAPTER 12:

2 Elohim did not destroy those of Canaan all at once. 12 If He had done so, who could control him? 19 but by sparing them He taught us; 27 they were punished with their gods.

1 For your incorruptible spirit is in all things.
2 Therefore you chasten them by little, and little, that offend, and warns them by putting them in remembrance, wherein they have offended, that leaving their wickedness they may believe on you O Yahuah. 3 For it was your will to destroy by the hands of our fathers, both those

old inhabitants of your holy land, 4 Whom you hated for doing most odious works of witchcraft, and wicked sacrifices; 5 And also those merciless murderers of children, and devourers of man's flesh, and the feasts of blood; 6 With their Priests out of the midst of their idolatrous crew, and the parents that killed with their own hands, souls destitute of help: 7 That the land which you esteemed above all other, might receive a worthy colony of Elohim's children. 8 Nevertheless, even those you spared as men, and did send wasps

Or, ancient.

Or, sorceries.

Or, new inhabitance.

forerunners of thine host, to destroy them by little and little.

9 Not that you were unable to bring the ungodly under the hand of the righteous in battle, or to destroy them at once with cruel beasts, or with one rough word: 10 But executing your judgments upon them by little and little, you gave them place of repentance, not being ignorant that they were a naughty generation, and that their malice, was bred in them, and that their cogitation would never be changed. 11 For it was a cursed seed, from the beginning, neither did you for fear of any man give them pardon for those things wherein they sinned. 12 For who shall say, what have you done? Or who shall withstand your judgment, or who shall accuse you for the nations that perish whom you have made? Or who shall come to stand against you, to be revenged for the unrighteous men? 13 For neither is there any Elohim but you, that cares for all, to whom you might show that your judgment is not wrong. 14 Neither shall king or tyrant be able to set his face against you, for any whom you have punished. 15 For so much then as you are righteous yourself, you order all things righteously: thinking it not agreeable with your power to condemn him but has not deserved to be punished. 16 For your power is the beginning of righteousness, and because you are the Lord of all, it makes you to be gracious unto all. 17 For when men will not believe, that you are of a full power, you show your strength, and among them that know it, you make their boldness manifest. 18 But you, mastering your power, judge with equity, and order us with great favor: for you may use power when you will. 19 But by such works have you taught your people, that the just man should be merciful, and have made your children to be of a good hope, that you give repentance for sins.

20 For if you did punish the enemies of your children, and the condemned to death with such deliberation, giving them time and place, whereby they might be delivered from their malice. 21 With how great circumspection did you

Cf. Ex. 33:2; Dt. 2:22.

Cf. Gen. 9:25.

Cf. Rom. 9:20. Or, in your presence. Or, a revenger.

Cf. 1Pet. 5:7.

Cf. Job 10:2.

Or, perfect.

judge your own sons, unto whose fathers you had sworn, and made covenants of good promises?

22 Therefore whereas you do chasten us, you scourge our enemies a thousand times more, to the intent that when we judge, we should carefully think of your goodness, and when we ourselves are judged, we should look for mercy. 23 Wherefore, whereas men have lived dissolutely and unrighteous, you have tormented them with their *Or, abominable idols.* own abominations. 24 For they went astray very far in the ways of error and held them for gods (which even amongst the beasts of their enemies were despised)

being deceived as children of no understanding. *Cf. 11:13; Rom. 1:23.*
25 Therefore unto them, as to children without the use of reason, you did send a judgment to mock them.
26 But they that would not be reformed by that correction wherein he tarried with them, shall feel a judgment worthy of Elohim. 27 For look, for what things they grudged when they were punished, (that is) for them whom they thought to be gods, [now] being punished in them; when they saw it, they acknowledged Him to be the true Elohim, whom before they denied to know: and therefore came extreme damnation upon them.

CHAPTER 13:

1 They were not excused that worshipped any of Elohim's works: 10 But most wretched are they that worship the works of men's hands.

1 Surely vain are all men by nature, who are ignorant of Elohim, and could not out of the good things that are seen, know Him that is: neither by *Cf. Rom. 1:20.* considering the works, did they acknowledge the

work-master; 2 But deemed either fire, or wind, or the swift air, or the circle of the stars, or the violent water, or the lights of heaven to be *Cf. Rom. 1:9; Dt. 4:19, 17:3.* the gods which govern the world: 3 With whose beauty, if they being delighted, took them to be gods: let them know how much better Yahuah of them is; for the *Cf. 1Cor. 8:5-6.* first Author of beauty has created them. 4 But if they were astonished at their power and virtue, let them understand by them, how much mightier He is that made them. 5 For by the greatness and beauty of the creatures, proportionably the Maker of them is seen.

6 But yet for this they are the less to be blamed: for they peradventure err seeking Elohim, and desirous to find Him.

7 For being conversant in his works, they search him diligently, and believe their sight: because the things are beautiful that are seen. 8 Howbeit, neither are they to be pardoned. 9 For if they were able to know so much, that they could aim at the world; how did they not sooner find out Yahuah thereof? 10 But miserable are they, and in dead things is their hope, who called them gods which are the works of men's hands, gold and silver, to show art in, and resemblances of beasts, or a stone good for nothing, the work of an ancient hand. 11 Now a carpenter that cuts timber, after he has sawed down a tree meet for the purpose, and taken off all the bark skillfully round about, and

Cf. Rom. 1:21. Or, seek.

Cf. Rom. 1:23.

has wrought it handsomely, and made a vessel thereof fit for the service of man's life: 12 And after spending the refuse of his work to dress his meat, has filled himself: 13 And taking the very refuse among those which served to no use (being a crooked piece of wood, and full of knots) has carved it diligently when he had nothing else to do, and formed it by the skill of his understanding, and fashioned it to the image of a man: 14 Or made it like some vile beast, laying it over with vermilion, and with paint, coloring it red, and covering every spot therein: 15 And when he had made a convenient room for it, set it in a wall, and made it fast with iron: 16 For he provided for it, that it might not fall: knowing that it was unable to help itself, (for it is an image and has need of help:) 17 Then, he makes prayer for his goods, for his wife and children, and is not ashamed to speak to that which has no life.

18 For health, he calls upon that which is weak: for life, prays to that which is dead: for aid, humbly beseeches that which has least means

Cf. Isa. 44:13. Or, timber-wright.

Or, chips.

i.e. a vivid reddish orange.

Greek: that has no experience at all.

to help: and for a good journey, he asks of that which cannot set a foot forward: 19 And for gaining and getting, and for good success of his hands, asks ability to do, of him that is most unable to do anything.

CHAPTER 14:

1 Though men do not pray to their ships, 5 Yet are they saved rather by them than by their idols. 8 Idols are accursed, and so are the makers of them. 14 The beginning of idolatry, 23 And the effects thereof. 30 Elohim will punish them that swear falsely by their idols.

1 Again, one preparing himself to sail, and about to pass through the raging waves, calls upon a piece of wood rottener than the vessel that carries him. 2 For verily desire of gain devised that, and the workman built it by his skill: 3 But your providence, O Father, governs it: for you have made a way in the sea, and a safe path in the waves: 4 Showing that you can save from all danger: yes, though a man went to sea without art. 5 Nevertheless you would not that the works of your wisdom should be idle, and therefore do men commit their lives to a small piece of wood, and passing the rough sea in a weak vessel, are saved. 6 For in the old time also when the proud giants perished, the hope of the world governed by your hand, escaped in a weak vessel, and left to all ages a seed of generation. 7 For blessed is the wood, whereby righteousness comes. 8 But that which is made with hands, is cursed, as well it, as he that made it: he, because he made it, and it, because being corruptible it was called Elohim. 9 For the ungodly and his ungodliness are both alike hateful unto Elohim. 10 For that which is made, shall be punished together with him that made it. 11 Therefore even upon the idols of the Gentiles shall there be a visitation: because in the creature of Elohim they are become an abomination and stumbling blocks to the souls of men, and a snare to the feet of the unwise. 12 For the devising of idols was the beginning of spiritual fornication, and the invention of them the corruption of life. 13 For

Or, ship.

Or, vessel or ship.

Cf. Ex. 14:22.

Cf. Gen. 6:4, 7:10.

Cf. Ps. 115:8; Bar. 6:3; Rom. 1:23.

Cf. Psal.5.5.

Or, to or by. Jer. 10:8; Hab. 2:18. Greek: scandals. Or, trap.

Cf. Rom. 1:24-27.

neither were they from the beginning, neither shall they be forever. 14 For by the vain glory of men they entered into the world, and therefore shall they come shortly to an end.

15 For a father afflicted with untimely mourning, when he has made an image of his child soon taken away, now honored him as a god, which was then a dead man, and delivered to those that were under him, ceremonies and sacrifices. 16 Thus in process of time an ungodly custom grown strong, was kept as a law, and graven images were worshipped by the commandments of kings, 17 Whom men could not honor in presence, because they dwelt far off, they took the counterfeit of his visage from far, and made an express image of a king whom they honored, to the end that by this their forwardness, they might flatter him that was absent, as if he were present.

18 Also the singular diligence of the artificer did help to set forward the ignorant to more superstition. 19 For he peradventure willing to please one in authority, forced all his skill to make the resemblance of the best fashion. 20 And so the multitude allured by the grace of the work, took him now for a god, which a little before was but honored as a man. 21 And this was an occasion to deceive the world: for men serving either calamity or tyranny, did ascribe unto stones, and stocks, the incommunicable Name. 22 Moreover this was not enough for them, that they erred in the knowledge of Elohim, but whereas they lived in the great war of ignorance, those so great plagues called they peace. 23 For while they slew their children in sacrifices, or used secret ceremonies, or made reveling of strange rites. 24 They kept neither lives nor marriages any longer undefiled: but either one slew another traitorously, or grieved him by adultery: 25 So that there reigned in all men without exception, blood, manslaughter, theft, and dissimulation, corruption, unfaithfulness, tumults, perjury, 26 Disquieting of good men, forgetfulness of good turns, defiling of souls, changing of kind, disorder in marriages, adultery, and

Greek: in timo.

Or, tyrants.

Or, in sight.

Greek: to the better.

Of Elohim.

Cf. Dt. 18:10; Jer. 7:9, 19:4.

Or, confusedly.

shameless uncleanness. 27 For the worshipping of idols not to be named, is the beginning, the cause, and the end of all evil. 28 For either they are mad when they be merry, or prophesy lies, or live unjustly, or else lightly forswear themselves. 29 For insomuch as their trust is in idols which have no life, though they swear falsely, yet they look not to be hurt. 30 Howbeit for both causes shall they be justly punished: both because they thought not well of Elohim, giving heed unto idols, and also unjustly swore in deceit, despising holiness. 31 For it is not the power of them by whom they swear: but it is the just vengeance of sinners, that punishes always the offense of the ungodly.

Greek: nameless.

Or, devoted.

CHAPTER 15:

1 We do acknowledge the true Elohim. 7 The folly of idol-makers, 14 and of the enemies of Yahuah's people: 15 because besides the idols of the Gentiles, 18 they worshipped vile beasts.

1 But you O Elohim, are gracious and true: long suffering, and in mercy ordering all things. 2 For if we sin, we are yours, knowing your power: but we will not sin, knowing that we are counted yours. 3 For to know you is perfect righteousness: yes, to know your power is the root of immortality. 4 For neither did the mischievous invention of men deceive us: nor an image spotted with diverse colors, the painter's fruitless labor. 5 The sight whereof entices fools to lust after it, and so they desire the form of a dead image that has no breath. 6 Both they that make them, they that desire them, and they that worship them, are lovers of evil things, and are worthy to have such things to trust upon. 7 For the potter tempering soft earth fashions, every vessel with much labor for our service: yes, of the same clay he makes both the vessels that serve for clean uses: and likewise, also all such as serve to the contrary: but what is the use of either sort, the potter himself is the judge. 8 And employing his labors lewdly, he makes a vain god of the same clay,

Cf. John 17:3.

Or, turns a reproach to the foolish.

Cf. Rom. 9:21.

even he which a little before was made of earth himself, and within a little while after returns to the same out of the which he was taken: when his life which was lent him shall be demanded.

Cf. Luke 12:20.

9 Notwithstanding his care is, not that he shall have much labor, nor that his life is short: but strives to excel goldsmiths, and silversmiths, and endeavors to do like the workers in brass, and counts it his glory to make counterfeit things. 10 His heart is ashes, his hope is viler than earth, and his life of less value than clay: 11 Forasmuch as he knew not his maker, and him that inspired into him an active soul, and breathed in a living spirit. 12 But they counted our life a pastime, and our time here a market for gain: for, say they, we must be getting every way, though it be by evil means. 13 For this man that of earthly matter makes brittle vessels, and graven images, knows himself to offend above all others. 14 And all

Or, be sick or die.

the enemies of your people, that hold them in subjection are most foolish and are more miserable than very babes. 15 For they counted all the idols of the heathen to be gods: which neither have the use of eyes to see, nor noses to draw breath, nor ears to hear, nor fingers of hands to handle, and as for their feet they are slow to go. 16 For man made them, and he that borrowed his own spirit fashioned them, but no man can make a god like unto himself.

Or, so.

Cf. Jas. 2:6, 5:6. [93]

Or, air.

17 For being mortal he works a dead thing with wicked hands: for he himself is better than the things which he worships: whereas he lived once, but they never. 18 Yes, they worshipped those beasts also that are most hateful: for being compared together, some are worse than others.

19 Neither are they beautiful, so much, as to be desired in respect of beasts, but they went without the praise of Elohim and his blessing.

CHAPTER 16:

2 God gave strange meat to his people, to stir up their appetite, and vile beasts to their enemies to take it from them. 5 He stung with his serpents, 12 but soon healed them by his word only. 17 The creatures altered their nature to pleasure Yahuah's people, and to offend their enemies.

1 Therefore by the like were they punished worthily, and by the multitude of beasts tormented. 2 Instead of which punishment, dealing graciously with your own people you prepared for them meat of a strange taste: even quail to stir up their appetite: 3 To the end that they desiring food, might for the ugly sight of the beasts sent among them, loath even that which they need to desire: but these suffering poverty for a short space, might be made partakers of a strange taste. 4 For it was requisite, that upon them exercising tyranny should come poverty which they could not avoid: but to these it should only be showed how their enemies were tormented.

5 For when the horrible fierceness of beasts came upon these, and they perished with the stings of crooked serpents, your wrath endured not forever. 6 But they were troubled for a small season that they might be admonished, having a sign of salvation, to put them in remembrance of the commandment of your Law. 7 For he that turned himself towards it, was not saved by the thing that he saw: but by you that are the savior of all. 8 And in this you made your enemies confess, that it is you who delivers from all evil: 9 For them the biting of grasshoppers and flies killed, neither was there found any remedy for their life: for they were worthy to be punished by such.

10 But your sons, not the very teeth of venomous dragons overcame: for your mercy was ever by them, and healed them. 11 For they were pricked, that they should remember your words, and were quickly saved, that not falling into deep forgetfulness, they might be continually mindful of your goodness. 12 For it was neither herb, nor mollifying plaster that restored them to health: but your word, O Yahuah, which heals all things.

Cf. 11:15-16; Num. 21:6.

Cf. Num.11:31.

Or, your people. Num. 21:6; 1Cor. 10:9.

Cf. Num. 21:9.

Cf. Ex. 8:24, 10:4. Rev. 9:7.

Hebrew: stung. Or, never drawn from.

Cf.
Ps. 105;
Dt. 32:39;
1Sam. 2,
6; Matt.
16:18; Rev.
6:8, 20:13,
20:14.
Note: Hell
is Sheol in
Hebrew or
Hades in
Greek. It is
the Inner
Earth where
all souls of
the dead,
good and
bad, go to
rest in all of
scripture.
Those
spirits rise
on the
Day of
Judgment.

13 For you have power of life and death: you lead to the gates of hell and bring up again. 14 A man indeed kills through his malice: and the spirit when it is gone forth returns not; neither the soul received up, comes again. 15 But it is not possible to escape your hand. 16 For the ungodly that denied knowing you, were scourged by the strength of your arm: with strange rains, hails, and showers were they persecuted, that they could not avoid, and through fire were they consumed. 17 For, which is most to be wondered at, the fire had more force in the water that quenches all things: for the world fights for the righteous. 18 For sometimes the flame was mitigated, that it might not burn up the beasts that were sent against the ungodly: but themselves might see and perceive that they were persecuted with the judgment of Elohim. 19 And at another time it burns even in the midst of water, above the power of fire, that it might destroy the fruits of an unjust land. 20 Instead whereof you fed your own people, with

Cf.
Ex. 9:23.

Cf.
Judg.5:20.

Angel's food, and did send them from heaven bread prepared without their labor, able to content every man's delight, and agreeing to every taste. 21 For your sustenance declared your sweetness unto your children and serving to the appetite of the eater tempered itself to every man's liking. 22 But snow and ice endured the fire and melted not, that they might know that fire burning the hail, and sparkling in the rain, did destroy the fruits of the enemies. 23 But this again did even forget his own strength, that the righteous might be nourished. 24 For the creature that serves you who are the maker, increases his strength against the unrighteous for their punishment, and abates his strength for the benefit of such as put their trust in you. 25 Therefore even then was it altered into all fashions, and was obedient to your grace that nourishes all things, according to the desire of them that had need: 26 That your children, O Yahuah, whom you love, might know that it is not the growing of fruits that nourishes man: but that it is

Cf.
Ex. 16:14;
Num.11:7;
Ps. 78:25;
2Esd. 1:19
John 6:31.

Cf.
Judg. 6:4.
Or, Manna.
Or, was
tempered.

Cf.
Rev. 8:7.

Cf. 19:20.

Or, things.
Or, of
them that
prayed.

Cf. Dt. 8:3; Matt. 4:4.

your word which preserves them that put their trust in you.

27 For that which was not destroyed of the fire, being warmed with a little sun beam, soon melted away, 28 That it might be known, that we must prevent the sun, to give you thanks, and at the day-spring pray unto you. 29 For the hope of the unfaithful, shall melt away as the Winter's hoarfrost, and shall run away as unprofitable water.

CHAPTER 17:

1 Why the Egyptians were punished with darkness. 4 The terrors of that darkness. 12 The terrors of an ill conscience.

Or, souls that will not be reformed.

1 For great are your judgments, and cannot be expressed: therefore, unnurtured souls have erred. 2 For when unrighteous men thought to oppress the holy nation:

Or, under their roofs. Or, fugitives.

they, being shut up in their houses, the prisoners of darkness, and fettered with the bonds of a long night,

Cf. Jas. 2:6, 5:6. [93]

lay [there] exiled from the eternal providence. 3 For while they supposed to lie hid in their secret sins, they were scattered under a dark veil of forgetfulness, being horribly astonished, and

Or, in. Or, sights.

troubled with (strange) apparitions. 4 For neither might the corner that held them keep them from fear: but noises (as of waters) falling down, sounded about them, and sad visions appeared unto them with heavy countenances. 5 No power of the fire might give them light: neither could the bright flames of the stars endure to lighten that horrible night. 6 Only there appeared unto them a fire kindled of itself, very dreadful: for being much terrified, they thought the things which they saw to be worse than the sight they saw not. 7 As for the illusions of art magic, they were put down, and their boasting in wisdom was reproved with disgrace. 8 For they that promised to drive away terrors, and troubles from a sick soul, were sick themselves of fear worthy to be laughed at. 9 For though no terrible thing did fear them: yet being scared with beasts that passed by, and hissing of serpents,

Cf. Ex. 7:12, 8:7,19.

Or refusing to look upon.

10 They died for fear, denying that they saw the air, which could of no side be avoided.

11 For wickedness condemned by her own witness, is very timorous, and being pressed with conscience, always forecasts grievous things. 12 For fear is nothing else, but a betraying of the succors which reason offers.

13 And the expectation from within being less, counts the ignorance more than the cause which brings the torment. 14 But they, sleeping the same sleep that night which was indeed *Or, wherein they could do nothing.* intolerable, and which came upon them out of the bottoms of inevitable hell: 15 Were partly vexed with monstrous apparitions, and partly fainted, their heart failing them: for a sudden fear and not looked for, came upon them. 16 So then, whosoever there fell down, was straitly kept, shut up in a prison without iron bars. 17 For whether he were husbandman, or shepherd, or a laborer in *Or, desert.* the field, he was overtaken, and endured that necessity, which could not be avoided: for they were all bound with one chain of darkness.

18 Whether it was a whistling wind, or a melodious noise of birds among the spreading branches, or a pleasing fall of water running violently: 19 Or a terrible sound of stones cast down, or a running that could not be seen of skipping beasts, or a roaring voice of most savage *Or, hideous.* wild beasts, or a rebounding echo from the hollow mountains: these things made them to swoon for fear. 20 For the whole world shined with clear light, and none were hindered in their labor. 21 Over them only was spread an heavy night, an image of that darkness which should afterwards receive them: but yet were they unto themselves more grievous than the darkness.

CHAPTER 18:

4 Why Egypt was punished with darkness, 5 and with the death of their children, 18 They themselves saw the cause thereof. 20 Elohim also plagued his own people. 11 By what means that plague was stayed.

1 Nevertheless, your Saints had a very great light, whose voice they, hearing and not seeing their shape, because they also had not suffered the same things, they counted them happy. 2 But for that they did not hurt them now, of whom they had been wronged before, they thanked them, and besought them pardon, for that they had been enemies. 3 Instead whereof you gave them a burning pillar of fire, both to be a guide of the unknown journey, and a harmless sun to entertain them honorably. 4 For they were worthy to be deprived of light, and imprisoned in darkness, who had kept your sons shut up, by whom the uncorrupt light of the law was to be given unto the world. 5 And when they had determined to slay the babes of the Saints, one child being cast forth, and saved: to reprove them, you took away the multitude of their children, and destroyed them altogether in a mighty water. 6 Of that night were our fathers certified afore, that assuredly knowing unto what oaths they had given credence, they might afterwards be of good cheer.

7 So of your people was accepted both the salvation of the righteous, and destruction of the enemies. 8 For wherewith you did punish our adversaries, by the same you did glorify us whom you had called.

9 For the righteous children of good men did sacrifice secretly, and with one consent made a holy Law, that the Saints should be alike partakers of the same good and evil, the fathers now singing out the songs of praise. 10 But on the other side there sounded an ill-according cry of the enemies, and a lamentable noise was carried abroad for children that were bewailed. 11 The master and the servant were punished after one manner, and like as the king, so suffered the common person. 12 So they altogether had innumerable dead with one kind of death, neither were the living sufficient to bury them: for

Cf. Ex. 10:23.

Or, incorrupt-ible.

Cf. Ex. 13:21, 14:24; Ps. 78:14, 105:29.

Cf. Ex. 14:24-25.

Cf. Ex. 11:4.

Cf. Ex. 12. Or, a covenant of Elohim, or league, see Ps. 50:5.

Cf. Ex. 11:5, 12:29.

in one moment the noblest offspring of them was destroyed. 13 For whereas they would not believe anything by reason of the enchantments, upon the destruction of the firstborn, they acknowledged this people to be the sons of Elohim. 14 For while all things were in quiet silence, and that night was during her swift course, 15 Your almighty word leapt down from heaven, out of your royal throne, as a fierce man of war into the midst of a land of destruction,

16 And brought your unfeigned commandment as a sharp sword, and standing up filled all things with death, and it touched the heaven, but it stood upon the earth. 17 Then suddenly visions of horrible dreams troubled them sore, and terrors came upon them unlooked for. 18 And one thrown here, another there half dead, showed the cause of his death. 19 For the dreams that troubled them, did foreshow this, lest they should perish, and not know why they were afflicted.

20 Yes, the tasting of death touched the righteous also, and there was a destruction of the multitude in the wilderness: but the wrath endured not long. 21 For then the blameless man made haste, and stood forth to defend them, and bringing the shield of his proper ministry, even prayer and the propitiation of incense, set himself against the wrath, and so brought the calamity to an end, declaring that he was your servant. 22 So he overcame the destroyer, not with strength of body, nor force of arms, but with a word subdued he him that punished, alleging the oaths and covenants made with the fathers. 23 For when the dead were now fallen down by heaps one upon another, standing between, he stayed the wrath, and parted the way to the living. 24 For in the long garment was the whole world, and in the four rows of the stones was the glory of the fathers graven, and your majesty upon the crown of his head. 25 Unto these the destroyer gave place, and was afraid of them: for it was enough that they only tasted of the wrath.

CHAPTER 19:

1 Why Elohim showed no mercy to the Egyptians. 5 And how wonderfully he dealt with his people. 14 The Egyptians were worse than the Sodomites. 18 The wonderful agreement of the creatures to serve Yahuah's people.

1 As for the ungodly, wrath came upon them without mercy unto the end: for he knew before what they would do; 2 How that having given them leave to depart, and sent them hastily away, they would repent and pursue them. 3 For while they were yet mourning, and making lamentation at the graves of the dead, they added another foolish device, and pursued them as fugitives, whom they had entreated to be gone. 4 For the destiny, whereof they were worthy, drew them unto this end, and made them forget the things that had already happened, that they might fulfill the punishment, which was wanting to their torments, 5 And that your people might pass a wonderful way: but they might find a strange death. 6 For the whole creature in his proper kind was fashioned again anew, serving the peculiar commandments that were given unto them, that your children might be kept without hurt. 7 As namely, a cloud shadowing the camp, and where water stood before dry land appeared, and out of the Red Sea, a way without impediment, and out of the violent stream a green field: 8 Where-through all the people went that were defended with your hand, seeing your marvelous, strange wonders. 9 For they went at large like horses, and leaped like lambs, praising you O Yahuah, who had delivered them.

10 For they were yet mindful of the things that were done while they sojourned in the strange land, how the ground brought forth flies instead of cattle, and how the river cast up a multitude of frogs instead of fishes. 11 But afterwards they saw a new generation of fouls, when being led with their appetite they asked delicate meats. 12 For quail came up unto them from the sea, for their contentment. 13 And punishments came upon

Or, cast out by entreaty.

Or, turns a reproach to the foolish.

Cf. 1Cor. 10:1.

Or, lice.

Or, comfort.

the sinners not without former signs by the force of thunders: for they suffered justly, according to their own wickedness, insomuch as they used a more hard and hateful behavior towards strangers: 14 For the Sodomites did not receive those whom they knew not when they came: but these brought friends into bondage, that had well deserved of them. 15 And not only so: but peradventure some respect shall be had of those, because they used strangers not friendly.

16 But these very grievously afflicted them, whom they had received with feastings, and were already made partakers of the same laws with them. 17 Therefore even with blindness were these stricken, as those were at the doors of the righteous man: when being compassed about with horrible great darkness, everyone sought the passage of his own doors. 18 For the elements were changed in themselves by a kind of harmony, like as in a psaltery notes change the name of the tune, and yet are always sounds, which may well be perceived by the sight of the things that have been done. 19 For earthly things were turned into water, and the things that before swam in the water, now went upon the ground. 20 The fire had power in the water, forgetting his own virtue: and the water forgot his own quenching nature. 21 On the other side, the flames wasted not the flesh of the corruptible living things, though they walked therein, neither melted they the icy kind of heavenly meat, that was of nature apt to melt. 22 For in all things, O Yahuah, you did magnify your people, and glorify them, neither did you lightly regard them: but did assist them in every time and place.

Gre. by themselves.

THE BOOK OF TOBIT

FACING THE GIANT

WITH THE RESTORED
NAME OF YAHUAH

THE
Levite
BIBLE
LeviteBible.com

CHAPTER 1:

1 Tobit his stock, and devotion in his youth, 9 His marriage, 10 And captivity, 13 His preferment, 16 Alms and charity in burying the dead, 19 For which he is accused and flees, 22 And after returns to Nineveh.

Or, acts.

One of the Northern Tribes of Israel.

Cf. 2Ki.17:3. Or, Kedes of Naphtali in Galilee, Judg.4.6.

1 The Book of the words of Tobit, son of Tobi'el, the son of Anani'el, the son of Adu'el, the son of Gaba'el, of the seed of Asa'el, of the Tribe of Naphtali, 2 Who in the time of Shalmaneser king of the Assyrians, was led captive out of This be which is at the right hand of that city, which is called properly Naphtali in Galilee above Asher. 3 I, Tobit, have walked all the days of my life in the way of truth, and justice, and I did many alms deeds to my brethren, and my nation, who came with me to Nineveh into the land of the Assyrians. 4 And when I was in my own country, in the land of Israel, being but young, all the tribe of Naphtali my father, fell from the house of Jerusalem, which was chosen out of all the tribes of Israel, that all the tribes should sacrifice there where the Temple of the habitation of the Most High was consecrated, and built for all ages. 5 Now all the tribes which together revolted, and the house of my father Naphtali sacrificed unto the heifer Ba'al. 6 But I alone went often to Jerusalem at the Feasts, as it was ordained unto all the people of Israel by an everlasting decree, having the first fruits, and tenths of increase, with that which was first shorn, and them, gave I at the Altar to the Priests the children of Aaron. 7 The first tenth part of all increase, I gave to the sons of Aaron, who ministered at Jerusalem: another tenth part I sold away, and went, and spent it every year at Jerusalem.

Cf. 1Ki. 12:30. Or, to the power of Ba'al, or the god Ba'al.

Cf. Dt. 14:28-29; Sir. 7:31.

Cf. Ex. 22:29; Dt.12:6. Leaders were Sons of Zadok since Solomon who remained holy. Cf. 1Chr. 16:39 Ez.44:24, 44:15, 48:11.

Or, Levites, specifically the sons of Zadok.

8 And the third, I gave unto them to whom it was meet, as Deborah my father's mother had commanded me, because I was left an orphan by my father.

9 Furthermore when I was come to the age of a man, I married Anna of mine own kindred, and of her I begat Tobias.

10 And when we were carried away captives to Nineveh, all my brethren, and those that were of my kindred, did eat

Cf. Num. 36:7.

TOBIT'S TITHE:

1/10TH OF INCREASE - FIRST FRUITS
Divided Into Three Categories

WHEN TOBIT LIVED IN NORTHERN ISRAEL:

TEMPLE PRIESTS
For Feasts/Sabbaths Operations & Their Needs

FEASTS EXPENSES
To, During and From Jerusalem For Feasts

DIRECT GIVING TO WIDOWS & ORPHANS
He Did Not Give That To The Priests To Disperse

Tobit was giving every year, not thirty percent it appears but ten percent which would be given one year to the Temple Priests as they have no inheritance by Law, the second was set aside to cover all the travel and expense to execute the Feasts and the third year, direct giving to the widows and orphans. The Law of Moses is very clear the Priests receive one-year's tenth only every three years, not annually. In 90 A.D., Pharisee Josephus taught error that the Priests receive annually. [73]

DEUTERONOMY 14:28-29 KJV
At the **end of three years** thou shalt bring forth **all the tithe** of **thine increase the same year**, and shalt lay it up within thy gates: And **the Levite** (#1), (because he hath no part nor inheritance with thee,) and **the stranger**, and the **fatherless**, and the **widow** (#3), which are within thy gates, shall come, and shall eat and be satisfied; that the LORD thy God may bless thee in all the work of thine hand which thou doest.

IN ASSYRIAN CAPTIVITY:

ALMS GIVING To Fellow Captives   **BREAD** to the Hungry
CLOTHES to the Needy   **BURIAL LABOR & EXPENSE** For the Needy

Note: When circumstances are financially overbearing, we give but to the degree that we can without condemnation. Tobit was righteous even so but was not able to continue this in much of captivity in the same manner. Churches not keeping the Feasts and Sabbaths are not qualified for a tithe generally.

Cf. Gen. 43:32.

Greek, my soul.

of the bread of the Gentiles. 11 But I kept myself from eating 12 Because I remembered Elohim with all my heart.

Greek: buyer. Tobit was a merchant, not a farmer.

13 And the Most High gave me grace, and favor before Shalmaneser, so that I was his purveyor. 14 And I went into Media, and left in trust with Gabael, the brother of

Or, in the land or country of Media.

Gabrias at Rages a city of Media, ten talents of silver. 15 Now when Shalmaneser was dead, Sennacherib his son reigned in his stead,

Greek: the ways of whom were unsettled.

whose estate was troubled, that I could not go into Media. 16 And in the time of Shalmaneser, I gave many alms to my brethren, and gave my bread to the hungry, 17 And my clothes to the naked: and if I saw any of my nation dead, or cast

Or, behind walls.

about the walls of Nineveh, I buried him. 18 And if the king Sennacherib had slain any, when he was come, and fled from Yahudea, I buried them privately, (for in his wrath he killed many) but the bodies were not found,

when they were sought for of the king. 19 And when one of the Ninevites went, and complained of me to the king that I buried them, and hid myself: understanding that I was sought for to be put to death, I withdrew myself for fear. 20 Then all my goods were forcibly taken away, neither was there anything left me, besides my wife Anna, and my son Tobias. 21 And there passed not five and fifty days before two of his sons killed him, and they fled into the mountains of Ararath, and Esar-Haddon his son reigned in his stead, who appointed over his father's accounts, and over all his affairs, Achiacharus my brother Anael's son. 22 And Achiacharus entreating for me, I returned to Nineveh: now Achiacharus was Cup-bearer, and keeper of the Signet, and Steward, and overseer of the accounts: and Esar-Haddon appointed him next unto him: and he was my brother's son.

Cf. 2 Ki. 19:35,36; Isa. 37:36-37; Ecclus. 48:18, 12:1.

Cf. 2Ki. 19:37; 2Chr. 32:21.

CHAPTER 2:

1 Tobit leaves his meat to bury the dead, 10 and becomes blind. 11 His wife takes in work to make a living. 14 Her husband and she fall out.

1 Now when I was come home again, and my wife Anna was restored unto me, with my son Tobias, in the Feast of Pentecost, which is

the holy Feast of the seven weeks, there was a good dinner prepared me, in which I sat down to eat. 2 And when I saw abundance of meat, I said to my son, Go and bring what poor man soever you shall find out of our brethren, who is mindful of Yahuah, and lo, I tarry for you. 3 But he came again and said, Father, one of our nation is strangled, and is cast out in the market place. 4 Then before I had tasted of any meat, I start up and took him up into a room, until the going down of the sun.

5 Then I returned and washed myself, and ate my meat in heaviness, 6 Remembering that prophesy of Amos, as he said; Your feasts shall be turned into mourning, and all your mirth into lamentation. 7 Therefore I wept: and after the going down of the sun, I went and made a grave, and buried him. 8 But my neighbors mocked me, and said, This man is not yet afraid to be put to death for this matter, who fled away, and yet lo, he buries the dead again. 9 The same night also I returned from the burial, and slept by the wall of my courtyard, being polluted, and my face was uncovered: 10 And I knew not that there were sparrows in the wall, and my eyes being open, the sparrows muted warm dung into my eyes, and a whiteness came in my eyes, and I went to the physicians, but they helped me not: moreover Achiacharus did nourish me, until I went into Elymais. 11 And my wife Anna did take women's works to do. 12 And when she had sent them home to the owners, they paid her wages, and gave her also besides a kid. 13 And when it was in my house, and began to cry, I said unto her, From whence is this kid? Is it not stolen? Render it to the owners, for it is not lawful to eat anything that is stolen. 14 But she replied upon me, It was given for a gift more than the wages: Howbeit I did not believe her, but bade her render it to the owners: and I was abashed at her. But she replied upon me, Where are your alms, and your righteous deeds? Behold, you and all your works are known.

Cf. Amos 8:10.

Cf. 1:19.

Approx. modern Khūzestān, Iran.

Or, was hired to spin in the women's rooms.

Young goat.

Cf. Dt. 22:1.

Cf. Job 2:9. Or, lo all things are known to you.

CHAPTER 3:

1 Tobit grieved with his wife's taunts, prays. 11 Sarah reproached by her father's maid, prays also. 17 An Angel is sent to help them both.

1 Then, I being grieved, did weep, and in my sorrow prayed, saying, 2 O Yahuah, you are just and all your works, and all your ways are mercy and truth, and you judge truly and justly forever. 3 Remember me, and look on me, punish me not for my sin and ignorance, and the sins of my fathers, who have sinned before you. 4 For they obeyed not your Commandments, wherefore you have delivered us for a spoil, and unto captivity, and unto death, and for a proverb of reproach to all the nations among whom we are dispersed. 5 And now your judgments are many and true: Deal with me according to my sins, and my fathers: because we have not kept your Commandments, neither have walked in truth before you. 6 Now therefore deal with me as seems best unto you, and command my spirit to be taken from me, that I may be dissolved, and become earth: for it is profitable for me to die, rather than to live, because I have heard false reproaches, and have much sorrow: command therefore that I may now be delivered out of this distress, and go into the everlasting place: turn not your face away from me. 7 It came to pass the same day, that in Ecbatana a city of Media, Sarah the daughter of Raguel, was also reproached by her father's maids, 8 Because that she had been married to seven husbands; whom Asmodeus the evil spirit had killed, before they had lied with her. Do you not know, said they, that you have strangled your husbands? You have had already seven husbands, neither were you named after any of them.

9 Wherefore do you beat us for them? If they be dead, go your way after them, let us never see of you either son or daughter. 10 When she heard these things, she was very sorrowful, so that she thought to have strangled herself, and she said, I am the only daughter of my father, and if I do this,

Cf. Dt. 28:15, 37.

Or, dismissed, or delivered.

Demons cannot kill directly. This was a living Nephilim giant whose spirit is a demon but he must be alive.

it shall be a reproach unto him, and I shall bring his old age with sorrow unto the grave.

11 Then she prayed toward the window, and said, Blessed are you, O Yahuah my Elohim, and your holy and glorious Name is blessed, and honorable forever, let all your works praise you forever. 12 And now, O Yahuah, I set my eyes and my face toward you,

13 And say, take me out of the earth, that I may hear the reproach no more.

14 You know, Yahuah, that I am pure from all sin with man. 15 And that I never polluted my name, nor the name of my father in the land of my captivity: I am the only daughter of my father, neither has he any child to be his heir, neither any near kinsman, nor any son of his

Or, brother.

alive, to whom I may keep myself for a wife: my seven husbands are already dead, and why should I live? But if it please not you that I should die, command some regard to be had of me, and pity taken of me, that I hear no more reproach. 16 So the prayers of them both were heard before the majesty of the great Elohim. 17 And Raphael was sent to heal them both, that is, to scale away the whiteness of Tobit's eyes, and to give Sarah the daughter of Raguel, for a wife to Tobias the son of Tobit, and to bind Asmodeus the evil spirit, because she belongs to Tobias by right of inheritance. The selfsame time came Tobit home, and entered into his house, and Sarah, the daughter of Raguel came down from her upper chamber.

CHAPTER 4:

3 Tobit gives instructions to his son Tobias, 20 and tells him of money left with Gabael in Media.

1 In that day Tobit remembered the money, which he had committed to Gabael in Rages of Media,

2 And said with himself, I have wished for death, wherefore do I not call for my son Tobias, that I may signify to him of the money before I die. 3 And when he had called him, he said; My son, when I am dead, bury me, and despise not your

mother, but honor her all the days of your life, and do that which shall please her, and grieve her not.

4 Remember, my son, that she saw many dangers for you, when you were in her womb, and when she is dead, bury her by me in one grave. 5 My son, be mindful of Yahuah our Elohim all your days, and let not your will be set to sin, or to transgress His Commandments: do uprightly all your life long and follow not the ways of unrighteousness. 6 For if you deal truly, your doings shall prosperously succeed to you, and to all of them that live justly. 7 Give alms of your substance, and when you give alms, let not your eye be envious, neither turn your face from any poor, and the face of Elohim shall not be turned away from you. 8 If you have abundance, give alms accordingly: if you have but a little, be not afraid to give according to that little. 9 For you lay up a good treasure for yourself against the day of necessity. 10 Because that alms do deliver from death and suffer not to come into darkness. 11 For alms is a good gift unto all that give it, in the sight of the Most High. 12 Beware of all whoredom, my son, and chiefly take a wife of the seed of your fathers, and take not a strange woman to wife, which is not of your father's tribe: for we are the children of the Prophets, Noah, Abraham, Isaac, and Jacob: remember, my son, that our fathers from the beginning, even that they all married wives of their own kindred, and were blessed in their children, and their seed shall inherit the land. 13 Now therefore my son, love your brethren, and despise not in your heart your brethren, the sons and daughters of your people, in not taking a wife of them: for in pride is destruction and much trouble, and in lewdness is decay, and great want: for lewdness is the mother of famine.

14 Let not the wages of any man, which has wrought for you, tarry with you, but give him it out of hand: for if you serve Elohim, He will also repay you: be circumspect, my son, in all things you do, and be wise in all your conversation.

15 Do that to no man which you hate: drink not wine to make you drunk; neither let drunkenness go with you in your journey. 16 Give of your bread to the hungry, and of your garments to them that are naked, and according to your abundance give alms, and let not your eye be envious, when you giue alms. 17 Pour out your bread on the burial of the just but give nothing to the wicked.

18 Ask counsel of all that are wise and despise not any counsel that is profitable.

19 Blesse Yahuah your Elohim always, and desire of Him that your ways may be directed, and that all your paths, and counsels may prosper: for every nation has not counsel, but Yahuah Himself gives all good things, and He humbles whom He will, as He will; now therefore my son, remember my commandments, neither let them be put out of your mind. 20 And now I signify this to you, that I committed ten talents to Gabael the son of Gabrias at Rages in Media. 21 And fear not my son, that we are made poor, for you have much wealth, if you fear Elohim, and depart from all sin, and do that which is pleasing in His sight.

*Cf.
Matt. 7:12;
Luke 6:31.*

*Cf.
Luke 14:13;
Matt. 6:1.*

"The uncommon Greek phrase occurs in Tob. 13:6 and 1Tim. 1:17, in both cases in an ascription of praise. With 4:9 Cf. 1 Tim. 6:19; Tob. 4:21 Cf. 1Tim. 6:6.Charles, p. 199 [81]

CHAPTER 5:

4 Young Tobias seeks a guide into Media. 6 The Angel will go with him, 12 and says he is his kinsman. 16 Tobias and the Angel depart together. 17 But his mother is grieved for her son's departing.

1 Tobias then answered and said, Father, I will do all things, which you have commanded me. 2 But how can I receive the money, seeing, I know him not? 3 Then he gave him the handwriting, and said unto him, seek you a man which may go with you while I yet live, and I will give him wages, and go, and receive the money. 4 Therefore when he went to seek a man, he found Raphael that was an Angel. 5 But he knew not; and he said unto him, can you go with me to Rages? And do you know those places well? 6 To whom the Angel said, I will go with you, and I know the

way well: for I have lodged with our brother Gabael.

7 Then Tobias said unto him, Tarry for me till I tell my father. 8 Then he said unto him, Go and tarry not; so he went in, and said to his father; Behold, I have found one, which will go with me. Then he said, call him unto me, that I may know of what tribe he is, and whether he be a trustworthy man to go with you. 9 So he called him, and he came in, and they saluted one another.

10 Then Tobit said unto him, Brother, show me of what tribe and family you are.

11 To whom he said, do you seek for a tribe or family, or an hired man to go with your son? Then, Tobit said unto him, I would know, brother, your kindred, and name. 12 Then he said, I am Azariah, the son of Ananiah the great, and of your brethren. 13 Then Tobit said, You are welcome brother, be not now angry with me, because I have inquired to know your tribe, and your family, for you are my brother, of an honest and good stock: for I know Ananiah, and Yonathas sons of that great Samayas: as we went together to Jerusalem to worship, and offered the firstborn, and the tenths of the fruits, and they were not seduced with the error of our brethren: my brother, you are of a good stock.

14 But tell me, what wages shall I give you? Will you a drachma a day? And things necessary as to my own son? 15 Yes, moreover, if you return safe, I will add something to the wages.

16 So they were well pleased. Then said he to Tobias; Prepare yourself for the journey, and Elohim send you a good journey. And when his son had prepared all things for the journey, his father said; Go with this man, and Elohim which dwells in heaven prosper your journey, and the Angel of Elohim keep you company. So, they went forth both, and the young man's dog with them.

17 But Anna his mother wept, and said to Tobit, why have you sent away our son? Is he not the staff of our hand, in going in and out before us? 18 Be not greedy (to add) money to money: but let it be as refuse in

respect of our child.

19 For that which Yahuah has given us to live with, does suffice us.

20 Then said Tobit to her, Take no care my sister he shall return in safety, and

your eyes shall see him.

21 For the good Angel will keep him company, and his journey shall be prosperous, and he shall return safe.

22 Then she made an end of weeping.

CHAPTER 6:

4 The Angel bids Tobias to take the liver, heart and gall out of a fish, 10 And to marry Sarah the daughter of Raguel; 16 And teaches how to drive the wicked spirit away.

1 And as they went on their journey, they came in the evening to the river Tigris, and they lodged there.

2 And when the young man went down to wash himself, a fish leaped out of the river, and would have devoured him. 3 Then the Angel said unto him, Take the fish; and the young man laid hold of the fish, and drew it to land.

4 To whom the Angel said, Open the fish, and take the heart, and the liver and the gall, and put them up safely.

5 So the young man did as the Angel commanded him, and when they had roasted the fish, they did eat it: then, they both went on their way, till they drew

near to Ecbatana. 6 Then the young man said to the Angel; Brother Azariah, to what use is the heart, and the liver, and the gall of the fish? 7 And he said unto him, Touching the heart and the liver, if a devil, or an evil spirit trouble any, we must make a smoke thereof before the man or the woman, and the party shall be no more vexed. 8 As for the gall, it is good to anoint a man that has whiteness in his eyes, and he shall be healed. 9 And when they were come near to Rages;

10 The Angel said to the young man, Brother, today we shall lodge with Raguel, who is your cousin; he also has one only daughter, named Sarah, I will speak for her, that she may be given you for a wife. 11 For to you does the right of her appertain, seeing you only

i.e. tribe. are of her kindred. 12 And the maid is fair and wise, now therefore hear me, and I will speak to her father, and when we return from Rages, we will celebrate the marriage: for I know that Raguel cannot marry her to another according to the Law of Moses, but he shall be guilty of death, because the right of inheritance does rather appertain to you, than to any other. 13 Then the young man answered the Angel, I have heard, brother Azariah, that this maid has been given to seven men, who all died in the marriage chamber: 14 And now I am the only son of my father, and I am afraid, lest if I go in unto her, I die, as the other before; for a wicked spirit loves her, which hurts nobody, but those which come unto her; wherefore I also fear, lest I die, and bring my father's and my mother's life (because of me) to the grave with sorrow, for they have no other son to bury them.

15 Then the Angel said unto him, Do you not remember the precepts, which your father gave you, that you should marry a wife of your own kindred? Wherefore hear me, O my brother, for she shall be given you to wife, and make you no reckoning of the evil spirit, for this same night shall she be given you in marriage. 16 And when you shall come into the marriage chamber, *Or, embers.* you shall take the ashes of perfume, and shall lay upon them, some of the heart, and liver of the fish, and shall make a smoke with it. 17 And the devil shall smell it, and flee away, and never come again any more: but when you shall come to her, rise up both of you, and pray to Elohim, which is merciful, who will have pity on you, and save you: fear not, for she is appointed unto you from the beginning; and you shall preserve her, and she shall go with you. Moreover I suppose that she shall bear you children. Now when Tobias had heard these things, he loved her, and his heart was effectually *Or, vehemently.* joined to her.

CHAPTER 7:

11 Raguel tells Tobias what had happened to his daughter: 12 and gives her in marriage unto him. 17 She is conveyed to her chamber, and weeps. 18 Her mother comforts her.

1 And when they were come to Ecbatana, they came to the house of Raguel; and Sarah met them: and after that they had saluted one another, she brought them into the house. 2 Then said Raguel to Edna his wife, how like is this young man to Tobit my cousin? 3 And Raguel asked them, from whence are you, brethren? To whom they said, we are of the sons of Naphtali, which are captives in Nineveh. 4 Then he said to them, Do you know Tobit our kinsman? And they said, We know him. Then said he, Is he in good health? 5 And they said, He is both alive, and in good health: And Tobias said, He is my father. 6 Then Raguel leaped up, and kissed him, and wept, 7 And blessed him; and said unto him, you are the son of an honest and good man: but when he had heard that Tobit was blind, he was sorrowful, and wept.

8 And likewise Edna his wife, and Sarah his daughter wept. Moreover, they entertained them cheerfully, and after that they had killed a ram of the flock, they set store of meat on the table. Then, said Tobias to Raphael, Brother Azariah, speak of those things, of which you did talk on the way, and let this business be dispatched. 9 So he communicated the matter with Raguel, and Raguel said to Tobias, Eat and drink, and make merry: 10 For it is meet that you should marry my daughter: nevertheless, I will declare unto you the truth. 11 I have given my daughter in marriage to seven men, who died that night they came in unto her: nevertheless, for the present be merry: But Tobias said, I will eat nothing here, till we agree and swear one to another.

12 Raguel said, then take her from henceforth according to the manner, for you are her cousin, and she is yours, and the merciful Elohim give you good success in all things.

13 Then he called his daughter Sarah, and she came to her father, and

A sucking ram or lamb.

Or, Law

155

he took her by the hand, and gave her to be wife to Tobias, saying, Behold, take her after the Law of Moses, and lead her away to your father: And he blessed them, 14 And called Edna his wife, and took paper, and did write an instrument of covenants, and sealed it. 15 Then they began to eat. 16 After Raguel called his wife Edna, and said unto her, Sister, prepare another chamber, and bring her in thither. 17 Which when she had done as he had bidden her, she brought her thither, and she wept, and she received the tears of her daughter, and said unto her, 18 Be of good comfort, my daughter, Yahuah of heaven and earth give you joy for this your sorrow: be of good comfort, my daughter.

Cf. Num. 36:6.

Or, licked.

CHAPTER 8:

3 Tobias drives the wicked spirit away, as he was taught. 4 He and his wife rise to pray. 10 Raguel thought he was dead: 15 But finding him alive, praises Elohim, 12 and makes a wedding feast.

1 And when they had supped, they brought Tobias in unto her. 2 And as he went, he remembered the words of Raphael, and took the ashes of the perfumes, and put the heart, and the liver of the fish thereupon, and made a smoke therewith. 3 The which smell, when the evil spirit had smelled, he fled into the outmost parts of Egypt, and the Angel bound him. 4 And after that they were both shut in together, Tobias rose out of the bed and said, Sister, arise, and let us pray, that Elohim would have pity on us. 5 Then began Tobias to say, Blessed are you, O Elohim of our fathers, and blessed is your holy and glorious Name forever, let the heavens bless you, and all your creatures. 6 You made Adam, and gave him Eve his wife for a helper and stay: of them came mankind: you have said, It is not good that man should be alone, let us make unto him an aid like to himself. 7 And now, O Yahuah, I take not this my sister for lust, but uprightly: therefore, mercifully ordain, that we may become aged together. 8 And she said with him,

Or, embers.

Cf. Gen. 2:7, 18, 22.

Amen. 9 So they slept both that night, and Raguel arose, and went and made a grave 10 Saying, I fear lest he be dead. 11 But when Raguel was come into his house,

12 He said unto his wife Edna, send one of the maids, and let her see, whether he be alive: if he be not, that we may bury him, and no man know it. 13 So the maid opened the door and went in, and found them both asleep, 14 And came forth, and told them, that he was alive. 15 Then Raguel praised Elohim, and said, O Elohim, you are worthy to be praised with all pure and holy praise: therefore, let your Saints praise you with all your creatures, and let all your Angels and your elect praise you forever.

16 You are to be praised, for you have made me joyful, and that is not come to me, which I suspected: but you have dealt with us according to your great mercy. 17 You are to be praised, because you have had mercy of two, that were the only begotten children of their fathers, grant them mercy, O Yahuah, and finish their life in health, with joy and mercy. 18 Then Raguel bade his servants to fill the grave. 19 And he kept the wedding feast fourteen days.

20 For before the days of the marriage were finished, Raguel had said unto him by an oath, that he should not depart, till the fourteen days of the marriage were expired, 21 And then he should take the half of his goods, and go in safety to his father, and should have the rest when I and my wife be dead.

CHAPTER 9:

1 Tobias sends the Angel unto Gabael for the money. 6 The Angel brings it, and Gabael to the wedding.

1 Then Tobias called Raphael, and said unto him, 2 Brother Azariah, take with you a servant, and two camels, and go to Rages of Media to Gabael, and bring me the money, and bring him to the wedding. 3 For Raguel has sworn that I shall not depart. 4 But my father counts the days, and if I tarry long, he will be very sorry. 5 So Raphael went out and lodged with Gabael, and

gave him the handwriting, who brought forth bags, which were sealed up, and gave them to him. 6 And early in the morning they went forth both together, and came to the wedding, and Tobias blessed his wife.

Or, Gabael blessed Tobias and his wife, Junius.

CHAPTER 10:

1 Tobit and his wife long for their son. 7 She will not be comforted by her husband. 10 Raguel sends Tobias and his wife away, with half their goods, 12 and blessed them.

1 Now Tobit his father counted every day, and when the days of the journey were expired, and they came not: 2 Then, Tobit said, are they detained? Or is Gabael dead? And there is no man to give him the money? 3 Therefore he was very sorry. 4 Then his wife said to him, my son is dead, seeing he stays long, and she began to bewail him, and said, 5 Now I care for nothing, my son, since I have let you go, the light of my eyes. 6 To whom Tobit said, hold your peace, take no care; for he is safe. 7 But she said, Hold your peace, and deceive me not: my son is dead, and she went out every day into the way which they went, and did eat no meat on the day time, and ceased not whole nights, to bewail her son Tobias, until the fourteen days of the wedding were expired, which Raguel had sworn, that he should spend there: Then, Tobias said to Raguel, Let me go, for my father, and my mother look no more to see me.

8 But his father-in-law said unto him, Tarry with me, and I will send to your father, and they shall declare unto him, how things go with you. 9 But Tobias said, no: but let me go to my father. 10 Then Raguel arose and gave him Sarah his wife, and half his goods, servants, and cattle, and money.

11 And he blessed them, and sent them away, saying, The Elohim of heaven give you a prosperous journey, my children. 12 And he said to his daughter, Honor your father and your mother in law, which are now your parents, that I may hear good report of you: and he kissed her. Edna also said to Tobias, Yahuah of heaven restore you, my dear

brother, and grant that I may see your children of my daughter Sarah before I die, that I may rejoice before Yahuah: behold, I commit my daughter unto you of special trust, wherefore do not entreat her evil.

CHAPTER 11:

6 Tobias' mother spies her son coming. 10 His father meets him at the door and recovers his sight. 14 He praises Elohim, 17 And welcomes his daughter in Law.

1 After these things Tobias went his way, praising Elohim that he had given him a prosperous journey, and blessed Raguel, and Edna his wife, and went on his way till they drew near unto Nineveh. 2 Then Raphael said to Tobias, you know brother, how you did leave your father. 3 Let us haste before your wife and prepare the house. 4 And take in your hand the gall of the fish: so, they went their way, and the dog went after them. 5 Now Anna sat looking about towards the way for her son. 6 And when she spied him coming, she said to his father, Behold, your son comes, and the man that went with him. 7 Then said Raphael, I know, Tobias, that your father will open his eyes. 8 Therefore anoint you his eyes with the gall, and being pricked therewith he shall rub, and the whiteness shall fall away, and he shall see you. 9 Then Anna ran forth, and fell upon the neck of her son, and said unto him, seeing I have seen you my son, from henceforth, I am content to die, and they both wept.

10 Tobit also went forth toward the door, and stumbled: but his son ran unto him, 11 And took hold of his father, and he applied the gall on his father's eyes, saying, Be of good hope, my father. 12 And when his eyes began to smart, he rubbed them. 13 And the whiteness peeled away from the corners of his eyes, and when he saw his son, he fell upon his neck. 14 And he wept, and said, Blessed are you, O Elohim, and blessed is your Name forever, and blessed are all your holy Angels: 15 For you have scourged, and have taken pity on me: for behold, I

see my son Tobias. And his son went in rejoicing and told his father the great things that had happened to him in Media. 16 Then Tobit went out to meet his daughter in law at the gate of Nineveh, rejoicing and praising Elohim: and they which saw him go, marveled because he had received his sight.

17 But Tobit gave thanks before them: because Elohim had mercy on him.

And when he came near to Sarah his daughter in Law, he blessed her, saying, You are welcome daughter: Elohim be blessed which has brought you unto us, and blessed be your father and your mother; And there was joy amongst all his brethren which were at Nineveh. 18 And Achiacharus, and Nasbas his brother's son came. 19 And Tobias' wedding was kept seven days with great joy.

Junius, who is also called Nasbas.

CHAPTER 12:

5 Tobit offers half to the Angel for his pains; 6 But he called them both aside, and exhorted them, 15 and told them that he was an Angel, 21 and was seen no more.

1 Then Tobit called his son Tobias, and said unto him, my son, see that the man have his wages, which went with you, and you must give him more. 2 And Tobias said unto him, O father, it is no harm to me to give him half of those things which I have brought. 3 For he has brought me again to you in safety, and made whole my wife, and brought me the money, and likewise healed

you. 4 Then the old man said: It is due unto him. 5 So he called the Angel, and he said unto him, take half of all that you have brought, and go away in safety.

6 Then he took them both apart, and said unto them, Bless Elohim, praise Him, and magnify Him, and praise Him for the things which he has done unto you in the sight of all that live. It is good to praise Elohim and exalt His name, and honorably to show forth the works of Elohim, therefore be not slack to praise Him.

Or, with honor.

7 It is good to keep close the secret of a King, but it is honorable to reveal the

works of Elohim: do that which is good, and no evil shall touch you. 8 Prayer is good with fasting, and alms and righteousness: a little with righteousness is better than much with unrighteousness: it is better to give alms than to lay up gold. 9 For alms do deliver from death and shall purge away all sin. Those that exercise alms, and righteousness, shall be filled with life. 10 But they that sin are enemies to their own life. 11 Surely, I will keep close nothing from you. For I said, it was good to keep close the secret of a King, but that it was honorable to reveal the works of Elohim. 12 Now therefore, when you did pray, and Sarah your daughter in Law, I did bring the remembrance of your prayers before the holy one, and when you did bury the dead, I was with you likewise. 13 And when you did not delay rising up, and leave your dinner to go and cover the dead, your good deed was not hid from me:

Cf. Rom. 6:23. "Wages of sin is death."

Greek: to go and bury.

but I was with you. 14 And now Elohim has sent me to heal you, and Sarah your daughter in law. 15 I am Raphael one of the seven holy Angels, which present the prayers of the Saints, and which go in and out before the glory of the Holy One. 16 Then they were both troubled and fell upon their faces: for they feared. 17 But he said unto them, fear not, for it shall go well with you, praise Elohim, therefore. 18 For not of any favor of mine, but by the will of our Elohim I came, wherefore praise Him forever. 19 All these days I did appear unto you, but I did neither eat nor drink, but you did see a vision. 20 Now therefore give Elohim thanks: for I go up to Him that sent me, but write all things which are done, in a book. 21 And when they rose, they saw him no more. 22 Then they confessed the great and wonderful works of Elohim, and how the Angel of Yahuah had appeared unto them.

Cf. Gen. 18:8, 19:3; Judg. 13:16.

CHAPTER 13:

The thanksgiving unto Elohim, which Tobit wrote.

1 Then Tobit wrote a prayer of rejoicing, and said, Blessed be Elohim that lives forever, and blessed be His kingdom: 2 For He does scourge, and has mercy: He leads down to hell, and brings up again: neither is there any that can avoid His hand. 3 Confess Him before the Gentiles, you children of Israel: for He hath scattered us among them. 4 There declare His greatness, and extoll Him before all the living, for He is our Yahuah, and He is the Elohim our Father forever: 5 And He will scourge us for our iniquities, and will have mercy again, and will gather us out of all nations, among whom He has scattered us. 6 If you turn to Him with your whole heart, and with your whole mind, and deal uprightly before Him, then will He turn unto you, and will not hide His face from you: Therefore see what He will do with you, and confess Him with your whole mouth, and praise Yahuah of might, and extol the everlasting King: in the land of my captivity do I praise Him, and declare His might and majesty to a sinful nation: O you sinners turn, and do justice before Him: Who can tell if He will accept you, and have mercy on you? 7 I will extol my Elohim, and my soul shall praise the King of heaven, and shall rejoice in his greatness. 8 Let all men speak and let all praise Him for His righteousness. 9 O Jerusalem the holy city, He will scourge you for your children's works, and will have mercy again on the sons of the righteous.

10 Give praise to Yahuah, for He is good: and praise the everlasting King, that His Tabernacle may be built in you again with joy: and let him make joyful there in you, those that are captives, and love in you forever those that are miserable. 11 Many nations shall come from far to the Name of Yahuah Elohim, with gifts in their hands, even gifts to the King of heaven: all generations shall praise you with great joy. 12 Cursed are all they which hate you, and blessed shall all be, which

Cf. Dt. 32:39; 1Sam. 2:6; Wisd.16:13.

"The uncommon Greek phrase occurs in Tob. 13:6 and 1Tim. 1:17, in both cases in an ascription of praise. With 4:9 Cf. 1 Tim. 6:19; Tob. 4:21 Cf. 1Tim. 6:6.Charles, p. 199 [81].

Or, he will lay a scourge upon the works of your children.

Or, to make.

love you forever. 13 Rejoice and be glad for the children of the just: for they shall be gathered together and shall bless Yahuah of the just. 14 O blessed are they which love you, for they shall rejoice in your peace: *Or, prosperity.* blessed are they which have been sorrowful for all your scourges, for they shall rejoice for you, when they have seen all your glory, and shall be glad forever. 15 Let my soul bless Elohim the great King. 16 For Jerusalem shall be built up with sapphires, and emeralds, and precious stones: your walls and towers, and battlements with pure gold. 17 And **the streets of Jerusalem shall be paved** with beryl, and carbuncle, and **stones of Ophir.** 18 And all her streets shall say, Hallelujah, and they shall praise Him, saying, Blessed be Elohim which has extolled it forever.

CHAPTER 14:

3 Tobit gives instructions to his son, 8 Specially to leave Nineveh. 11 He and his wife die and are buried. 12 Tobias removes to Ecbatana, 14 and there died, after he had heard of the destruction of Nineveh.

1 So Tobit made an end of praising Elohim. 2 And he was eight and fifty years old when he lost his sight, which was restored to him after eight years, and he gave alms, and he increased *Or, did more and more fear.* in the fear of Yahuah Elohim, and praised Him. 3 And when he was very aged, he called his son, and the six sons of his son, and said to him, my son, take your children; for behold, I am aged, and am ready to depart out of this life. 4 Go into Media, my son, for I surely believe those things which Jonah the Prophet spoke of Nineveh, that it shall be overthrown, and that for a time peace shall rather be in Media, and that our brethren shall lie scattered in the earth from that good land, and Jerusalem shall be desolate, and the house of Elohim in it shall be burned, and shall be desolate for a time: 5 And that again Elohim will have mercy on them, and bring them again into the land where they shall build a Temple, but not

New Jerusalem, not Jerusalem, Israel.

Cf. Rev. 21:21. Streets of New Jersulam will be paved with gold.

As Ophir is the Philippines, New Jerusalem must include it in area. 1En. 90:28 places it South of Israel, not in Israel. Verse 21 also notes "every several gate was of one pearl." Unless it is a gate for ants, that is not the small pearls we envision today. It requires a giant pearl which the largest on earth originate in the Philippines. This is the same gold and pearl resources of Gen. 2 from the land of Havilah, where Adam and Eve dwelled, which is surrounded by the Pison River from Eden.

like to the first, until the time of that age be fulfilled, and afterward they shall return from all places of their captivity, and build up Jerusalem gloriously, and the House of Elohim shall be built in it forever, with a glorious building, as the prophets have spoken thereof.

Cf. Ezra 3:8, 6:14. Forever is not in the Rom. copy.

6 And all nations shall turn, and fear Yahuah Elohim truly, and shall bury their idols. 7 So shall all nations praise Yahuah, and His people shall confess Elohim, and Yahuah shall exalt His people, and all those which love Yahuah Elohim in truth and justice, shall rejoice, showing mercy to our brethren.

8 And now, my son, depart out of Nineveh, because that those things which the Prophet Jonah spoke, shall surely come to pass.

9 But keep the Law and the Commandments, and show yourself merciful and just, that it may go well with you. 10 And bury me decently, and your mother with me, but tarry no longer at Nineveh. Remember, my son, how Aman handled Achiacharus that brought him up, how out of light he brought him into darkness, and how he rewarded him again: yet Ahiacharus was saved, but the other had his reward, for he went down into darkness. Manasseh gave alms and escaped the snares of death which they had set for him: but Aman fell into the snare and perished. 11 Wherefore now, my son, consider what alms do, and how righteousness does deliver. When he had said these things, he gave up the ghost in the bed, being a hundred, and eight and fifty years old, and he buried him honorably.

Or, preserued. Junius reads Nasban. Rom. which he had set.

12 And when Anna his mother was dead, he buried her with his father: but Tobias departed with his wife and children to Ecbatana, to Raguel his father-in-law:

Or, they.

13 Where he became old with honor, and he buried his father and mother-in-law honorably, and he inherited their substance, and his father Tobit's.

14 And he died at Ecbatana in Media, being an hundred and seven and twenty years old. 15 But before he died, he heard of the destruction of Nineveh, which was taken by Nabuchodonosor and Ahasuerus: and before his death he rejoiced over Nineveh.

Or, possessed.

Tobit lived 127 years. Likely Nabopolassar, father of Nebuchadnezzar, with and Cyaraxes, who destroyed Nineveh (616 B.C.). (Herod. 1, 106. McClintock and Strong [117]). If Tobit died that year which appears the case, he was born in 743 B.C. which fits the story with no issues.

Tobit is one of the most ridiculed books out there. Many scholars scoff at the story of Tobit because they do not know where demons originate, cannot seem to conduct even a quick Google search on the medicinal uses of fish bile for the eyes especially historically established, nor a Tigris fish large enough to sustain Tobias for food for ten days, and are unaware of the heightened smell and makeup of a Nephilim giant whether alone his sacred gods whose worship included this same fish smell. Thus, they scoff away in their own ignorance because they are uneducated and unqualified to write a sentence on this topic.

No doubt this added to the debate to remove Tobit from scripture. However, the Temple Priests ordained to establish Old Testament Canon most certainly kept Tobit as Canon in Qumran/Bethabara. There is no Pharisee, nor Catholic Counsel, or any brazen scholar, that can go backwards and take a vote as to whether Tobit was and is inspired scripture Biblically. Only the true Temple Priests exiled to Qumran/Bethabara retain that official ordination and authority according to Moses *(Dt. 31:24-26)* and even Jacob *(Jub. 45:16)*. Follow the ordinations and one will discover the only Bible Canon of the Bible's definition. Ignore that and simply do not refer to oneself as a scholar, nor educated in Biblical terms on very basic principles. The tradition, even as apocrypha, continued to the 1611 King James Version as well as some modern Bibles still include it. As Tobit is the possible origin of the phrase, they need to remove the scales from their eyes.

We will now execute a thorough examination of what appear the large stumbling blocks of this account. It merely requires a little research and logic and has never been in question if one did so. Not only is Tobit a valuable work of knowledge, it vets as accurate factually as well as inspired. Even the sheer number of times Tobit, Tobias, and the other characters worship Yahuah by name is precious.

TOBIT BLINDED BY BIRD DROPPINGS:
Does This Really Happen?

2:10 ...my eyes being open, the sparrows muted warm
dung into my eyes, and a whiteness came in my eyes...

SCIENCE SAYS YES!

"The 'white film' *that* 'scaled off from the corners of his eyes' *corresponds to the exudate of a purulent* conjunctivitis. *In* ancient as well as recent times, *the* prevalent blinding conjunctivitis *in the* Middle East *was due to* Chlamydia trachomatis *(p. 30).*
– *Journal of the Royal Society of Medicine, Jan. 2005 [67]*

Chlamydia trachomatis, an obligate intraocular bacteria causing trachoma, adult and neonatal inclusion conjunctivitis, was the **leading cause of blindness in the last century worldwide** *(p. 97).*
Trachoma usually affects both the eyes *and symptoms include itching, irritation,* discharge, swelling of eyelids, *photophobia, and pain. During the initial stage,* follicles appear in the upper tarsal conjunctiva which contains white blood cells followed by papillae *(p. 98).*
In 1990, *the WHO reported that* 146 million *individuals* across the globe *had active* trachoma
In 1995, *about* 15.5% *of the* total blindness across the world *were* due to trachoma *and it was the* second major cause of global blindness.
In 2013, *the WHO reported that* trachoma *was a major public health problem in* 53 socioeconomically underdeveloped countries of the world *in Africa, Central and South America, Asia, Australia, and the* Middle East *(p. 98).* – *2017 Indian Journal of Ophthalmology [66]*

Chlamydia trachomatis:
The bacteria can infect people exposed to infected birds. *It is important to know that infected birds do not always show signs of disease or seem sick. Both* sick birds and infected birds *without signs of illness* shed the bacteria in their droppings *and respiratory secretions.* When the droppings *and secretions* dry, small dust particles (that include the bacteria) can get into the air.
 – *Centers for Disease Control and Prevention [65]*

TOBIT'S BLINDNESS HEALED BY FISH BILE:
Effective Treatment To The Ancients?

6:8 As for the gall, it is good to anoint a man that has whiteness in his eyes, and he shall be healed.

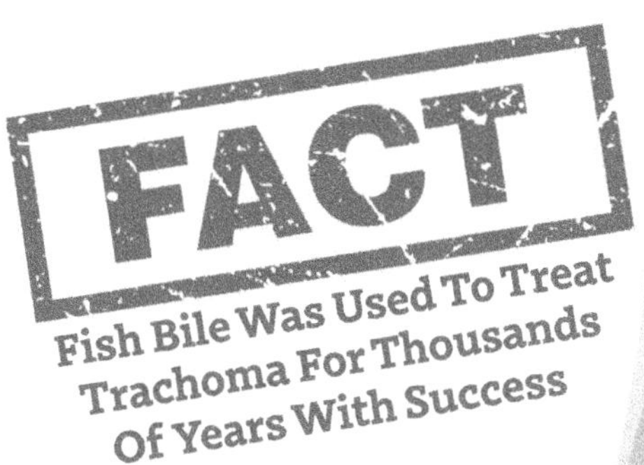

SCIENCE SAYS YES!

The gall of the callionymus *(dragonet fish) heals marks upon the* eyes *and cauterizes fleshy excrescences about those organs... (Ajasson: white rascasse fish; Hardouin: silurus fish; Schwab: mangar fish, see next page) The gall, too, of the coracinus (fish, Pliny, 5:10) has the effect of sharpening the eyesight. – Pliny's Natural History, Book 32. Chap. 24. AD 77–79.*

In the inflammatory stage of trachoma, blindness is due to pannus formation, the overgrowth of the cornea by vessels from the limbus. In the case of Tobit, the rapidity of the cure was miraculous, but the use of fish bile was probably based upon a common practice at the time—*a practice that may in fact have aided the* resolution of pannus and the restoration of vision *(p. 30)*.

Bile, *irritating as it is to the eye,* was evidently a traditional trachoma remedy that met with some success, *because it* remained in use for another two thousand years. *It was* recommended *in the* first century CE *by the* Roman encyclopaedist Celsus, *who wrote that* 'goat's bile...is suitable enough for the treatment of trachoma' *(he used the word aspritudo [ocularum] which, like the Greek trachoma, describes the Chlamydia psittaci is a type of bacteria that often* infects birds. *Less commonly, these bacteria* can infect people *and cause a disease called* psittacosis *(p. 30)* .

Even after Paracelsus had rejected most of Galenian Roman medicine *in the* 16th century, *his followers* still persisted in using bile for the treatment of trachoma. *In the* 17th century *the* Dutchman van Foreest, *the* German Sennert, *and the* Syrian Ibn Sallum all prescribed *for* trachomatous pannus *a* concoction that included eel bile and ox bile *(p. 30)*.

Until the discovery of the bacterial cause of trachoma and its treatment with antibiotics in the mid-20th century, the accepted treatment was little changed. *In* 1949, *one of the most widely used* textbooks of ophthalmology, May's Manual of the Diseases of the Eye, *directed that the inflammatory stage of trachoma, which was 'due to a filterable virus,' should be* treated with 'irritating applications'– *evidently following the* homeopathic principle of treating an inflammation with an inflammatory agent. *The text claimed that with the aid of such 'irritating applications' the* blinding pannus could regress completely, *making the* cornea transparent again.

In light of this, the story of Tobit becomes plausible *(p. 30-31)*.
– Journal of the Royal Society of Medicine, Jan. 2005 [67]

TIGRIS FISH TO FEED TOBIAS FOR TEN DAYS:
Do Such Large Fish Swim In The Tigris River?

Tigris River to Ecbatana = 594 km
Avg. Human Walking Pace = 4 km per hour
A 149-hour Journey = 10 or so days.
(All approx.)

Our Hypothesis: Mangar fish
Other possibilites exist. However, this appears the most likely.

They can grow over **seven feet long** and weigh over **300 pounds.** The largest fish in the **Euphrates River** are endemic only to that and the **Tigris River**... mangars are present only in Iraq, Iran, Turkey, and Syria. [71]

Tobias would not even need the largest mangar for this to be plausible.

Mentioned as early as 2,600 BC, the **mangar,** or, at least, its skin, seems to have served a religious purpose. Depictions of **Assyrian holy men wearing the skin of the mangar** have been uncovered, dating back to between 1,000–1,500 BC. That's right—the mangar is big enough that people can actually climb inside their skins. [71]

The Old Bridge, also known as the Old Tigris Bridge.

Mangar is a clean fish for Tobias to eat on the Biblical diet. It has both scales and fins.

THE LARGEST FISH IN THE EUPHRATES RIVER

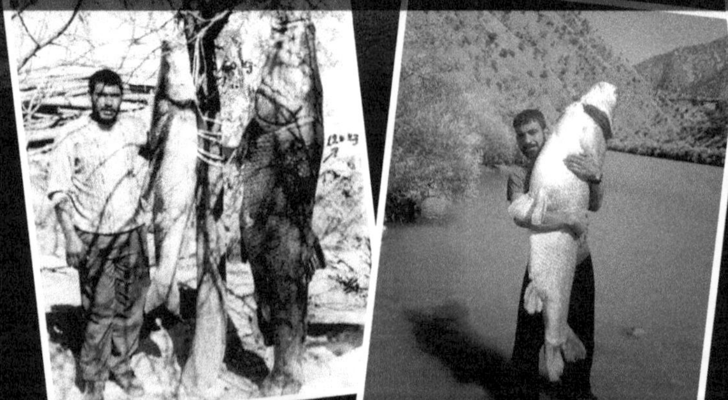

120 kg./265 lbs.

Photos Used Per Fair Use Act.

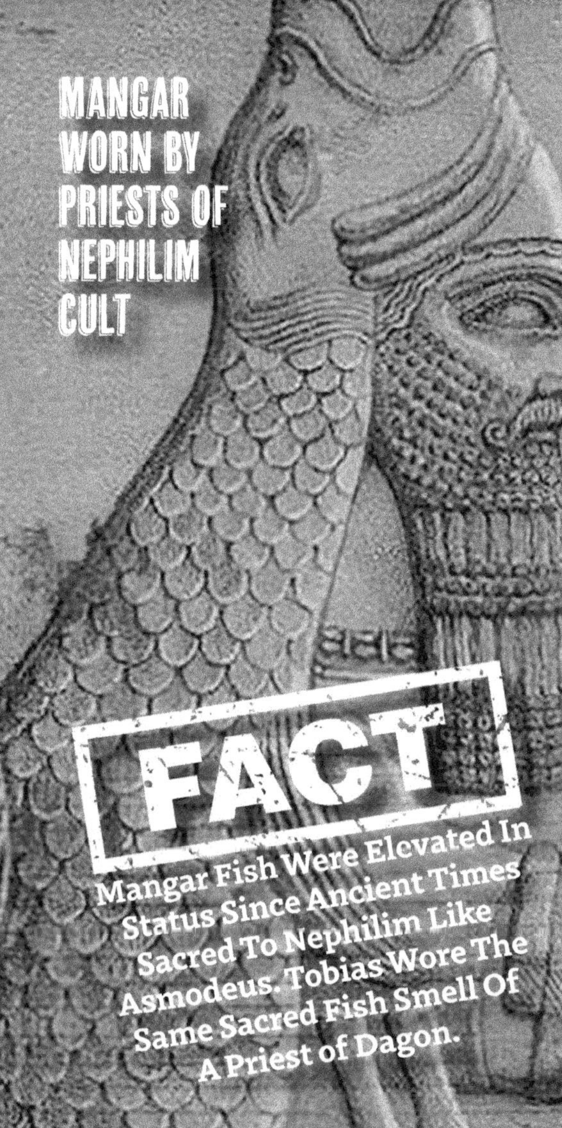

Judges 16:23 KJV
Then the lords of the Philistines gathered them together for to offer a great sacrifice unto **Dagon their god**...

1 Samuel 5:2-4 KJV
When the Philistines took the ark of God, they brought it into the **house of Dagon**, and set it by Dagon. And when they of Ashdod arose early on the morrow, behold, **Dagon was fallen** upon his face to the earth before the ark of the LORD. And they took Dagon, and set him in his place again. And when they arose early on the morrow morning, behold, **Dagon was fallen** upon his face to the ground before the ark of the LORD; and the head of Dagon and both the palms of his hands were cut off upon the threshold; only the stump of Dagon was left to him.

1 Chronicles 10:10 KJV
And they put his armour in the house of their gods, and fastened his head in the **temple of Dagon**.

"It was well-known even in ancient times and there are illustrations from 1500–1000 BC showing Assyrian priests or deities dressed in the skin of mangar."
– Proceedings of the 2nd International Congress on Applied Ichthyology & Aquatic Environment, 2016 [70]

"A plate *(6-cropped)* from the book "A second series of the monuments of Nineveh:" including bas-reliefs from the Palace of Sennacherib and bronzes from the ruins of Nimroud; from drawings made on the spot, during a second expedition to Assyria..."
– "Nineveh and Babylon." Austen Henry Layard. P. 168. London, 1853. [68]

RAPHA'EL:
Mighty Archangel of Healing

DO ANGELS CONCEAL THEIR IDENTITY FROM MEN?
CAN SCHOLARS READ?

Hebrews 13:2 KJV
Be not forgetful to entertain strangers: for thereby some have entertained angels unawares.

Who did? If Tobit is the only story in all of scripture where an angel hides his identity, then, Hebrews just quoted Tobit! However, it does appear Gen. 18 has the same practice, thus not new to scripture. Either way, scholars fail!

THE ARCHANGEL OF HEALING:

1 ENOCH 40:9 And the second (Archangel), who is in charge of all the diseases, and in charge of all the wounds of the sons of men, is Raphael...
Tobit 12:15 KJVA
"I am Raphael, one of the seven holy angels, which present the prayers of the saints, and which go in and out before the glory of the Holy One."
Tobit 3:17 KJVA
And Raphael was sent to heal them both, that is, to scale away the whiteness of Tobit's eyes, and to give Sarah the daughter of Raguel, for a wife to Tobias the son of Tobit, and to bind Asmodeus the evil spirit

ARCHANGEL OF THE CHAMBERS OF THE SOULS OF MEN INSIDE THE EARTH:

1 ENOCH 20:3 **Raphael**, one of the holy angels, who is over the *spirits of men*. (Chambers where the souls of the dead rest within the Earth).

HAS THE STRENGTH TO BIND FALLEN ANGELS AND NEPHILIM:

1 ENOCH 10:4 And further Yahuah said to Raphael: "Bind Azazel by his hands and his feet and throw him into the darkness. And split open the desert, which is in Dudael, and throw him there.
1 ENOCH 54:6 And Michael and Gabriel, Raphael and Phanuel - these will take hold of them on that great day. And throw them, on that day, into the furnace of burning fire...

And the fourth (Archangel), Raphael...
–War Scroll, Vermes, p. 174 & 4Q284, fr. 1

DO DEMONS SMELL & USE PHYSICAL FORCE:

Not in their current state which means Tobit is describing a demon spirit in its physical, Nephilim form.

6:7 And he said unto him, Touching the heart and the liver, if a devil, or an evil spirit trouble any, we must make a smoke thereof before the man or the woman, and the party shall be no more vexed.

NEPHILIM SPIRITS = DEMONS:

Jubilees 10

5 Thy Watchers, the fathers of these spirits (demons), acted in my day (procreating the Nephilim abomination, cf. Gen 6:1-4)*: and as for these spirits which are living, imprison them and hold them fast in the place of condemnation…*

11b …all the malignant evil ones we bound in the place of condemnation, and a tenth part of them we left that they might be subject before Satan on the earth.

12 And we (angels, likely Raphael) explained to Noah all the medicines of their diseases, together with their seductions, how he might heal them with herbs of the earth. 13 And Noah wrote down all things in a book as we instructed him concerning every kind of medicine. Thus the evil spirits were precluded from (hurting) the sons of Noah (Just as Tobias and Tobit).

DEMONS IN THEIR PHYSICAL NEPHILIM STATE:

…proclaim the majesty of his beauty to frighten and ter[rify] all the spirits of the destroying angels and the spirits of the bastards (Nephilim), the demons, *Lilith, the howlers…*

– 4Q510 & 4Q511, Fr. 35, Songs of the Sage, Vermes, p. 451

Lev 20:27 KJV: A man also or woman that hath a familiar spirit, or that is a wizard, shall surely be put to death: they shall stone them with stones: their blood shall be upon them.

Every man who preaches apostasy under the dominion of the spirits of Belial shall be judged according to the law relating to those possessed by a ghost or familiar spirit (Lev. 20:27). – The Damascus Document, Vermes, p. 143

FACT

Nephilim Spirits Are Demons In Any Stage Living or Dead. Asmodeus Was Living Still.

ASMODEUS:
Demon or Living Nephilim With A Demon Spirit?

Asmodeus was a physical Nephilim giant still alive in Tobit's time consistent with scripture and history. That is how he can physically smell and even strangle at least seven men *(6:13-14)*. Demons can do neither. His spirit is a demon, but he is alive at the time of Tobit and will die when imprisoned by Raphael *(8:3)* becoming a disembodied prince demon at that juncture. If he were already a roaming demon without a body, Raphael would have taken him to Tartarus as that is where Raphael himself imprisoned Azazel, the Watchers and Nephilim. *(1En. 10, Jub. 10)*

The lore surrounding Asmodeus, also known as Ashmedai for his region of Media even as such, is massive especially in the occult world. In texts not proven as inspired such as Testament of Solomon in verses 21–25, a 1st–3rd century occult text likely of Pharisee origin, the king invites Asmodeus to assist in the construction of the Temple. Once again, the dynamic there is that he was alive in physical form as a Nephilim giant who has a demon spirit. Demons can't build, physical Nephilim with their spirits being demons can. The demon appears and predicts Solomon's kingdom will one day be divided attributing powers to this Nephilim that may or may not be true as is the entire narrative unreliable in our opinion.

In Judaism, the embellished, occult Talmud claims Solomon captured Asmodeus as a slave during the construction project. Asmodeus claims the throne of Solomon even in the fictional Talmudic account *(Git. 68a–b; Num. R. 11:3)*. That fallacious tale includes Asmodeus gifting a worm, *shamir*, to Solomon whose touch cleaves rocks which one can only define as illiterate leaven. Solomon was to blame for dividing his own kingdom in scripture and that is a lie. In Kabbalistic lore, the very name of Asmodeus is invoked to cast spells and incantations *(Git. 68a–b)*.

Other unbiblical, unreliable Jewish *(Pharisee)* myth depicts Asmodeus as a more beneficent figure as the "king of the demons" which concurs with Tobit in scope *(Aggadah, Pes. 110a)*. He is, also, the Persian aesma daeva or aesmadiv, "the spirit of anger" sidekick to the god of evil, known as satan. A connection can also be made to the false god of the Samaritans, Ashima *(2 Ki. 17:24-41)*, which also serves as the true etymological origin of Hashem, the god of Judaism who is nothing like the Elohim of the Bible in any sense.

He may likely have been the Prince or Principality of Persia in Daniel's time who was strong enough to delay Gabriel from delivering his message to Daniel requiring the Archangel Michael's assistance to overcome him. This does not appear a minor Nephilim, nor demon. He would have died physically about a century or more before the days of Daniel, due to his being bound by Raphael with no escape (8:3). Giant tribes are still recorded in scripture in that era especially the Philistines.

In the area of Media in modern West Azerbaijan, Iran, there survives a legend of the Prison of Solomon *[72]* where he supposedly incarcerated evil demons which Solomon had no way to do so except in their physical Nephilim state. It is no coincidence that is the home region of this Asmodeus a few centuries later as there is no reason to believe Solomon could maintain a prison that far away. He would not be able to escape his demise in the end of Tobit when Raphael, the archangel bound the physical giant, Asmodeus, for good.

This is what happens to Nephilim spirits as they are destined to crawl the dry places *(Matt. 12:43; Luke 11:24)* of the Earth. They have no place to go when they die as men's spirits do. A demon is a disembodied spirit of a Nephilim, and they can possess a human or animal if invited but they do not replace the beings' spirit. In fact, the doctrine of reincarnation is literally something only a demon can do and never a man's spirit.

Thus, Asmodeus is documented even historically as a physical Nephilim and a demon principality.

No conflict exists.

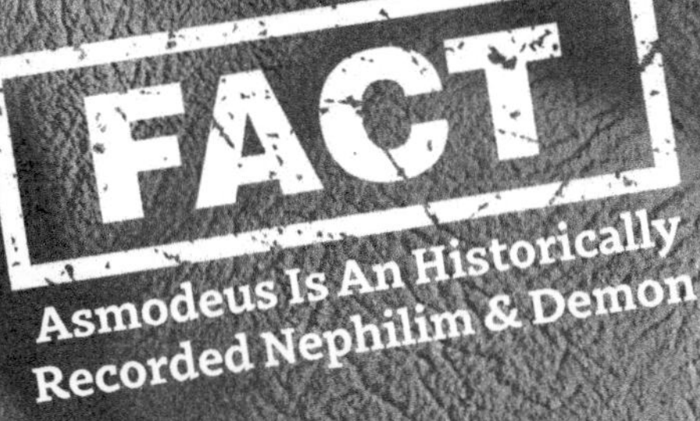

Prison of Solomon,
West Azerbaijan
Province, Iran

"HISTORICAL ERRORS" OF TOBIT?

LIE №1: *"Also, **Tobit implied he was alive during the reign of Jeroboam I (930 BC)**, but at his death he was noted as 117 years old." – Compelling Truth, a Ministry of GotQuestions.org*

Jeroboam is not found in the 1611 KJVA in Tobit 1:5. This is a Catholic corruption added to confuse and this scholar uses it in error. However, the Catholic GNT, NRSV, CEV, NAB, and DRB reference the idol that Jeroboam built in the past tense representing Tobit's ancestors had worshipped that same before. That language does not represent Tobit's era in origin even in the Catholic versions. This is a misreading and outright lie. It merely states that Tobit's family used to go to worship the idol established before his time on the hilltops, a practice Tobit discontinued. Jeroboam established the idol indeed, but Tobit never says that occurred in his time instead clearly noting it happened long before. This is an illiterate scholar who can't read. Also, the 1611 KJVA documents Tobit as 127 years of age when he died, not 117 *[14:14]*. This vets as accurate. Date corruptions in ancient texts are not rare, as a scholar should be aware. If he is not, he is no scholar on this topic.

LIE №2: *"Among the historical problems noted is that **Tobit 1:15 incorrectly notes that Sennacherib was Shalmaneser's son (rather than the son of Sargon II)."***
– Compelling Truth, a Ministry of GotQuestions.org

Gleason Archer well addresses this false paradigm with facts that seem to escape scholars who speak without researching. Son is not a term requiring bloodline association for kings of Assyria, Babylon, Persia, or even Egypt which examples he notes.

"This argument, however, overlooks the fact that by ancient usage the term son often referred to a successor in the same office whether or not there was a blood relationship."
"In Assyria a similar practice was reflected in the Black Obelisk of Shalmaneser III, which refers to King Jehu (the exterminator of the whole dynasty of Omri) as "the son of Omri." [118]

Additionally, because of the different dates especially from the Greek Septuagint and Catholic versions, this becomes confused. However, Tobit preserved a credible, valid timeline found in the King James Version since 1611, which perfectly fits history. There is essentially a 5-year period in which he was taken into Assyria. This ties with the time of Sennacherib's reign that is when Tobit lost everything in terms of possessions. There is no need for Tobit to record the king in between. Tobit was blinded at the affirmed age of 58, that ties to the first year of Esarhaddon's reign he also mentions accurately. He did, in fact, live to hear of the destruction of Assyria as that occurred in 616 B.C. before Nebuchadnezzar was king as it was his father's conquest, not his. The fact many scholars are unaware demonstrates they do not know history. There are no "historical errors" here. The Book of Tobit's timeline is as solid as most of the other books of the modern Bible Canon and this is not a valid criticism but one proven to be ignorant of the text and history.

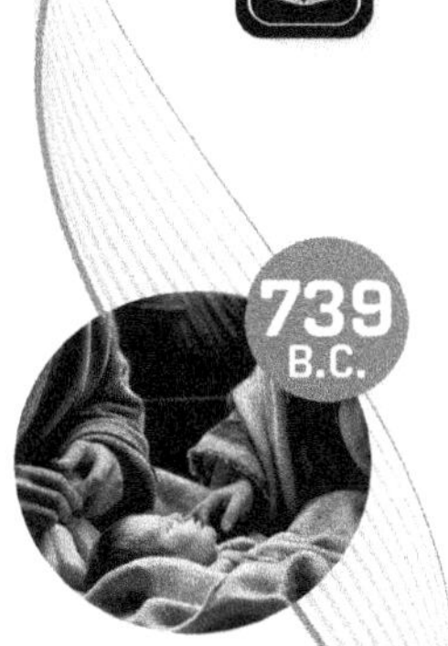

TIMELINE

TOBIT'S LIFE
127 YEARS

739 B.C.

Accurate!
Josh McDowell's review of a fraudulent Catholic text is impertinent, and not a position when the 1611 KJVA says nothing of Jeroboam.

TOBIT BORN
14:14. Tobit never says he lived during the reign of Jeroboam I and in the 1611 KJVA, never even mentions Jeroboam period. That is a false Catholic corruption. *1:5*

TOBIT 17 years old

722 B.C.

Accurate!
Tobit was from the Tribe of Naphtali. He does not represent which wave of captivity but was taken between 12-17 years of age.

TOBIT TAKEN
Captive By Shalmaneser V (727 – 722 B.C.) with the Northern Kingdom of Israel. *1:2*

TOBIT 34 years old

705 B.C.

Accurate!
Tobit properly records this king as son of Shalmaneser, not by blood, but as successor.

TOBIT ROBBED
By Sennacherib's administration (705 – 681 BC). *1:15-20*

TOBIT 58 years old

681 B.C.

Accurate!
This is even the *leading cause of blindness in the last century worldwide* today. [65-67] 58 years from the 1611 KJVA is affirmed by Dead Sea Scroll fragments *(Fitzmyer 318)*. 4Q196, fr. 18 + 4Q198, fr. 1 + 4Q200 Fr. 7 *[Vermes, p. 594-601. 22]*

TOBIT BLINDED
By Bird Droppings entering his eyes. Esarhaddon's reign dates this to about 681 B.C. when Tobit was 58 years old. *2:10, 14:2*

TOBIT 123 years old

616 B.C.

Accurate!
Scholars who are not aware it was Nebuchadnezzar's father, and not him, who first sacked Assyria are not educated on this topic.

ASSYRIA CONQUERED BY BABYLON
By Nabopolassar, father of Nebuchadnezzar. Tobit was alive. *14:15*

All Dates Are Approximations based on the 1611 KJVA.

TOBIT 127 years old

612 B.C.

Accurate!
All within Tobit's timeline vets as true historical fact. These are not errors.

TOBIT DIED
After Assyria was Conquered in 616 B.C. This entire timeline is firmly set on Esarhaddon's reign when Tobit was 58. *14:14-15*

WHY CAN'T SO MANY SCHOLARS READ, NOR COUNT?

FACT
PERFECTLY HISTORICAL

DANIEL'S
WITNESSES
DANIEL & HIS RIGHTEOUS FRIENDS

THE BOOK OF SUSANNA

DANIEL 13 IN ANCIENT HISTORY

WITH THE RESTORED NAME OF YAHUAH

THE Levite BIBLE
LeviteBible.com

CHAPTER 1:

16 Two judges hide themselves in the garden of Susanna to have their pleasure of her: 28 which when they could not obtain, they accuse and cause her to be condemned for adultery, 46 but Daniel examines the matter again, and finds the two judges false.

1 There dwelt a man in Babylon, called Yoacim.

2 And he took a wife, whose name was Susanna, the daughter of Chelcias, a very fair woman, and one that feared Yahuah. 3 Her parents also were righteous and taught their daughter according to the Law of Moses. 4 Now Yoacim was a great rich man, and had a fair garden joining unto his house, and to him resorted the Yahudim: because he was more honorable than all others. 5 The same year were appointed two of the ancients of the people to be judges, such as Yahuah spoke of, that wickedness came from Babylon from ancient judges, who seemed to govern the people. 6 These kept much at Yoacim's house: and all that had any suits in law, came unto them. 7 Now when the people departed away at noon, Susanna went into her husband's garden to walk. 8 And the two elders saw her going in every day and walking: so that their lust was inflamed toward her. 9 And they perverted their own mind, and turned away their eyes, that they might not look unto heaven, nor remember just judgments. 10 And albeit they both were wounded with her love: yet dare not one show another his grief. 11 For they were ashamed to declare their lust, that they desired to have to do with her. 12 Yet they watched diligently from day to day to see her. 13 And the one said to the other, Let us now go home: for it is dinner time. 14 So when they were gone out, they parted the one from the other, and turning back again they came to the same place, and after that they had asked one another the cause, they acknowledged their lust: then they appointed a time both together, when they might find her alone. 15 And it fell out as they watched a fit time, she went in as before, with two maids only, and she was desirous to

Greek: as yesterday and the day before.

wash herself in the garden: for it was hot. 16 And there was nobody there save the two elders, that had hid themselves, and watched her. 17 Then she said to her maids, bring me oil and washing balls, and shut the garden doors, that I may wash me. 18 And they did as she bade them, and shut the garden doors, and went out themselves at private doors to fetch the things that she had commanded them: but they saw not the elders, because they were hid.

Or, side doors.

19 Now when the maids were gone forth, the two elders rose up, and ran unto her, saying, 20 Behold, the garden doors are shut, that no man can see us, and we are in love with you: therefore, consent unto us, and lie with us. 21 If you will not, we will bear witness against you, that a young man was with you: and therefore, you did send away your maids from you. 22 Then Susanna sighed and said, I am straited on every side: for if I do this thing, it is death unto me: and if I do it not, I cannot escape your hands. 23 It is better for me to fall into your hands, and not do it: than to sin in the sight of Yahuah. 24 With that Susanna cried with a loud voice: and the two elders cried out against her. 25 Then ran the one and opened the garden door.

26 So when the servants of the house heard the cry in the garden, they rushed in at a private door to see what was done unto her. 27 But when the Elders had declared their matter, the servants were greatly ashamed: for there was never such a report made of Susanna. 28 And it came to pass the next day, when the people were assembled to her husband Yoacim, the two elders came also full of mischievous imagination against Susanna to put her to death, 29 And said before the people, Send for Susanna, the daughter of Chelcias, Yoacim's wife. And so, they sent. 30 So she came with her father and mother, her children and all her kindred. 31 Now Susanna was a very delicate woman and beautiful to behold. 32 And these wicked men commanded to uncover her face (for she was covered) that they might be filled with

Parallel this to Esther who was a consort to the king first and never prayed to YHWH nor worshipped Him, nor thanked Him.

her beauty. 33 Therefore her friends, and all that saw her, wept. 34 Then, the two elders stood up in the midst of the people and laid their hands upon her head.

35 And she weeping looked up towards heaven: for her heart trusted in Yahuah.

36 And the Elders said, as we walked in the garden alone, this woman came in, with two maids, and shut the garden doors, and sent the maids away. 37 Then, a young man who was hid there, came unto her and lay with her. 38 Then we that stood in a corner of the garden, seeing this wickedness, ran unto them. 39 And when we saw them together, the man we could not hold: for he was stronger than we, and opened the door, and leaped out. 40 But having taken this woman, we asked who the young man was: but she would not tell us: these things do we testify.

41 Then the assembly believed them, as those that were the elders and judges of the people: so they condemned her to death. 42 Then Susanna cried out with a loud voice and said:

O everlasting Elohim that knows the secrets and knows all things before they be:

43 You know that they have born false witness against me, and behold I must die: whereas I never did such things, as these men have maliciously invented against me. 44 And Yahuah heard her voice.

45 Therefore when she was led to be put to death: Yahuah raised up the holy spirit of a young youth, whose name was Daniel,

46 Who cried with a loud voice: I am clear from the blood of this woman.

47 Then all the people turned towards him, and said: what mean these words that you have spoken? 48 So he standing in the midst of them, said, are you such fools you sons of Israel, that without examination or knowledge of the truth, you have condemned a daughter of Israel? 49 Return again to the place of judgment: for they have born false witness against her.

50 Wherefore all the people turned again in haste, and the elders said unto him, come sit down among us, and show it us, seeing

Elohim has given you the honor of an elder. 51 Then said Daniel unto them, put these two aside one far from another, and I will examine them. 52 So when they were put asunder one from another, he called one of them, and said unto him, O you that are waxen old in wickedness: now your sins which you have committed aforetime, are come [to light.]

53 For you have pronounced false judgment, and have condemned the innocent, and have let the guilty go free, albeit Yahuah says, the innocent and righteous shall you not slay. 54 Now then if you have seen her: tell me, under what tree saw you them companying together? Who answered, Under a mastic tree.

Cf. Ex. 23:7.

Gr. lentisk tree, same as mastic.

55 And Daniel said, very well; You have lied against your own head: for even now the Angel of Elohim has received the sentence of Elohim, to cut you in two. 56 So he put him aside, and commanded to bring the other, and said unto him, O you seed of Canaan, and not of Yahudah, beauty has deceived you, and lust has perverted your heart.

57 Thus have you dealt with the daughters of Israel, and they for fear companied with you: but the daughter of Yahudah would not abide your wickedness. 58 Now therefore tell me, under what tree did you take them companying together? Who answered, Under a holme tree. 59 Then said Daniel unto him, well: you have also lied against your own head: for the Angel of Elohim waits with the sword to cut you in two, that he may destroy you. 60 With that all the assembly cried out with a loud voice, and praised Elohim who saves them that trust in Him.

Or, kind of oak.

61 And they arose against the two elders, (for Daniel had convicted them of false witness by their own mouth) 62 And according to the Law of Moses, they did unto them in such sort as they maliciously intended to do to their neighbor: And they put them to death. Thus, the innocent blood was saved the same day.

Cf. Dt. 19:19; Prov. 19:5.

63 Therefore Chelcias and his wife praised Elohim for their daughter Susanna, with Yoacim her husband,

and all the kindred: because there was no dishonesty found in her. 64 From that day forth was Daniel held in great reputation in the sight of the people.

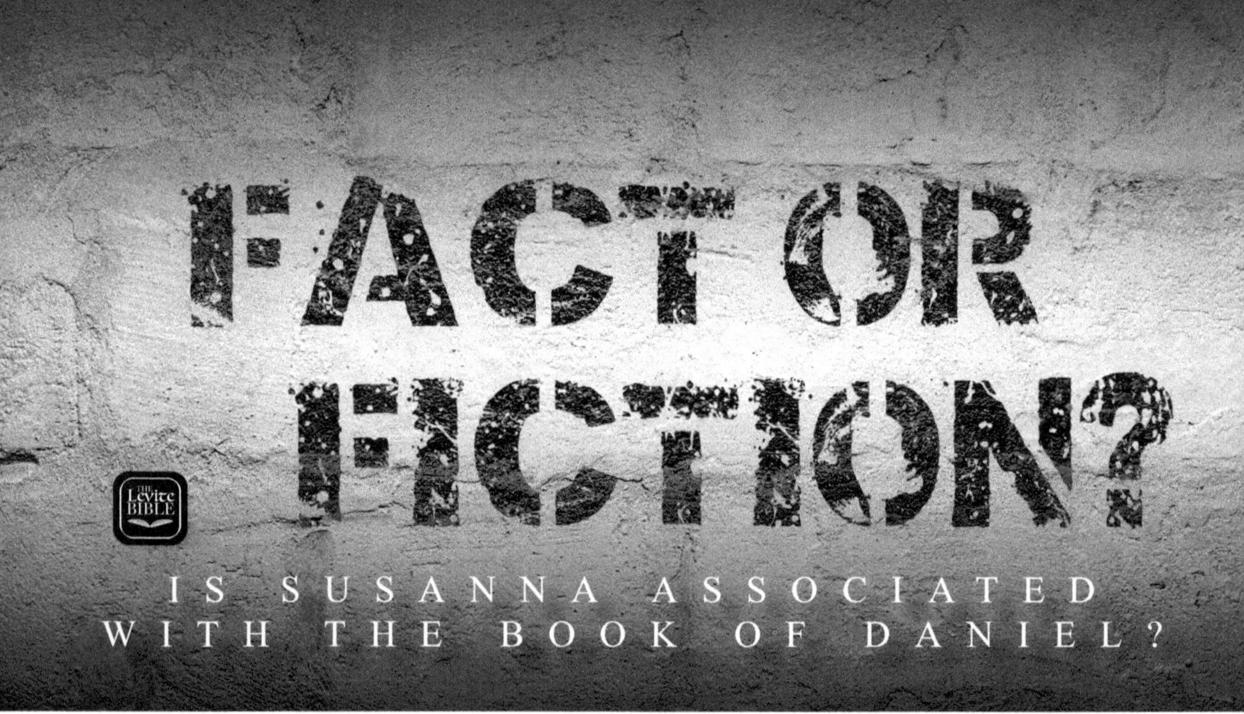

In the Introduction, we test the text of 4Q551 originally identified as a fragment from the Book of Susanna. This was found in the same cave as the Book of Daniel which is no coincidence. Those attempting to muddy the waters by trying to fit other stories fail. It is a content match to Susanna just as they identified first *(see Torah Test in the Introduction)*. This is a perfect example of the pressure applied in scholarship to offer dishonest conjecture to support a paradigm, rather than presenting the facts.

We, also, prove out the association of Susanna as essentially Chapter 13 of the Book of Daniel historically as well as Bel & The Dragon as Chapter 14 and Prayer of Azaryah as inserted at 3:23. This association of addendums to Daniel is well documented including the Prayer of Nabonidus also found in Qumran. The Torah Test in the Introduction details this much deeper.

However, what is the thinking of those scholars who continue to suppress and censor these addendums to Daniel? How could they draw conclusions against the evidence? They live in a box in which they are entrapped.

"The evidence supports the conclusion that the Prayer of Azariah, Suzannah, and Bel and the Dragon are Jewish additions from perhaps the second century or even the first century BC. These are not included in the Jewish Bible. They are not found in the Daniel manuscripts of the Dead Sea Scrolls. If we accept the Jews to be the ones chosen by God to determine the Old Testament canon, then, by definition, these additions are non-canonical. There is no evidence that the originals of these stories were in Hebrew or even in Aramaic. More likely, the original of these additions was in Greek, as the only ancient versions of them are in that language. The Greek "Apocrypha" (literally hidden books) of the Old Testament crept into use in the Septuagint, principally in the early Christian church, not among the Jews. It is doubtful that a consensus of Jews ever accepted these writings as canonical."

"In conclusion, I reject the additions to Daniel as not inspired or reliable for at least three reasons. 1. The Jews, the arbiters of the Old Testament canon do not include them. 2. The additions were most likely not even originally in Hebrew or Aramaic and 3. The actual content does not have the marks of inspired writing." – "Apocrypha, Bible Manuscripts and Textual Questions, Daniel, General, Reliability of the Bible." By John Oakes, [118]

Once again, we have a scholar who does not even know what was found in Qumran and what it represents. There is no "Jewish Bible" in scripture and there is no ordination of modern Jews or Rabbis as *"the arbiters of the Old Testament."* The Dead Sea Scrolls rebuke that faction employing negative titles such as the "Sons of Belial." What makes this and most scholars accept that the Sons of Belial are supposed to be the legitimate curators of scripture? This is dangerous as this scholar hands over an authority that belonged to the true Temple Priests exiled to Qumran/Bethabara transferred to their imposters who exiled them usurping the priesthood illegally. How is it this scholar does not know that Rabbinic Judaism is the continuation of Pharisaism and Pharisees were never ordained to keep Bible Canon, but rebuked as turning Torah against Torah by Yahusha Himself *(Mark 7:9)?* That is a basic that every scholar should have a mastery, and few even know. They live in paradigms, not facts, and they do not research adequately.

Most Old Testament Bible Canon books have this same date. Their oldest copies as well are principally found in Qumran/Bethabara. The argument he uses against these books as scripture, if applied consistently to the modern Old Testament Bible Canon, would cause much of scripture to fail. It is a false test setting up failure, not even realizing this scholar condemns what he calls inspired scripture with his double-minded logic. No wonder atheists have a field day with modern scholars who have no foundation. No, Pharisees are not the "arbiters" of anything Bible and this is why the modern church fails on so many topics in scholarship. Who cares what Pharisees included in their already censored, illegitimate Bible Canon and why does this supposed Bible scholar not know this?

When he notes: *"There is no evidence that the originals of these stories were in Hebrew or even in Aramaic,"* and *"2. The additions were most likely not even originally in Hebrew or Aramaic,"* he sets a paradigm in ignorance. Why did those in Babylon have to write in Hebrew first? There is no scripture that requires that as a litmus test of inspired scripture. However, he wrongly notes that none of these were found there in Hebrew or Aramaic. Susanna was found in Aramaic in Qumran *(4Q551)* which we test in the Introduction. However, some scholars have noted that the style of this fragment appears to be based on earlier Hebrew traditions, which we find probable. That is a realm of speculation, however, we will not enter. It does stand to reason that since Daniel was found with many of its chapters represented in Hebrew, that the origin of Susanna is also Hebrew. No one needs to prove such as that is a false test. It does not have to be found in Hebrew to be inspired. Scholars need to stop fabricating.

For his third point accusing these three books of not having *"the marks of inspired writing,"* this, as well, is a false standard. Azaryah is the prayer of the Bible character while in the fiery furnace praising Yahuah as the Creator of all things. The content of the prayer is not only Biblically accurate, but inspirational. How exactly does that not have the marks of inspired scripture especially when it is an account from the Book of Daniel 3 as well? Nonsense.

Bel & The Dragon, which reads like Daniel, sets up the entire Book of Daniel coalescing perfectly as to continued triumphs of Daniel over the priests of Bel Marduk (Ba'al), and his killing the historically documented idol dragon of Bel Marduk. That dragon is even found illustrated on the reliefs of the walls of the palace in Assyria as historical fact. Daniel was, then, cast into the lion's den, and if this scholar does not know that story from Daniel, shame on him. There is nothing uninspired about these accounts.

Finally, Susanna is rescued by Daniel who exercises righteous wisdom and judgment at a young age very consistent with the Book of Daniel. It also reads like the Book of Daniel as written by Daniel. If these three books do not have the marks of inspired writing, then, the Book of Daniel would fail based on the same criteria which of course, this scholar would not apply such in that case hypocritically. These affirm the Book of Daniel further proving scripture as inspired and all three are documented as addendums to Daniel. The real point is how dare this scholar continue the attempt to silence the witnesses of Daniel without any valid research. There is no merit to his rambling as neither of his three points is an accurate position. Of course, he does not stand alone in his textual criticism of ignorance.

"These manuscript fragments do not contain any of the additions that are in all the Greek manuscripts, such as the Prayer of Azariah, the Song of the Three Young Men, and the Story of Susanna."
"This means that we have at our disposal from the Dead Sea scrolls parts of all chapters, except Daniel 9 and 12." – Dr. Gerhard Hasel, Dean of the Seventh Day Adventist Theological Seminary

Notice how this scholar disagreed with himself here and also made an error confusing the two titles of Azaryah as separate books and forgetting Bel & The Dragon. Everyone makes such typos and blunders, but that demonstrates his lack of familiarity with this entire scenario. Frankly, he should not have written anything on this topic as he was uneducated. Perhaps he was unaware and had conducted no research on the placement of Susanna and Bel & The Dragon as Chapters 13 and 14 of the Book of Daniel. However, he admitted no Daniel fragments are found in Qumran beyond Daniel Chapter 11. That is already a lie even if one contested the Susanna fragment as a portion of Prayer of Nabonidus is most certainly there. That is an addendum to Daniel proving that was Daniel's practice. In his own box of logic, he is seeking something he should not necessarily expect to find. However, a fragment of the Book of Susanna *(Ch. 13)* was found at Qumran and that obliterates this false paradigm. In fact, based on Daniel fragments discovered in Qumran, Dr. Hasel drew an interesting conclusion to which we agree:

Subsequent to this, he stated that based on the Qumran manuscripts, "there can no longer be any possible reason for considering the book as a Maccabean product" (Harrison 1979:862). The most recent publications of Daniel manuscripts confirm this conclusion.
– Dr. Gerhard Hasel, Past Dean of the Seventh Day Adventist Theological Seminary [119]

Indeed, he understood the scribal tradition establishes these fragments as from copies, not originals. This should be no surprise to any scholar. However, most scholars, then, forget that the same tradition applies to the other books found in Qumran regardless of whether they may be published in the modern Pharisee Bible Canon. One can and must reach this same conclusion regarding these books as well. Otherwise, scholarship is not consistent and applying stricter criteria to the other books found in Qumran as if it is a different paradigm requiring such. Such scholars disqualify themselves from testing these books of Apocrypha and other texts found outside the modern Bible Canon as they are not honest, regardless of their intention which may not be nefarious.

These are not academic, nor scholarly charges. They are baseless accusations that these supposed experts fail to test their own theories. They offer hypocrisy as they would not apply such strict criteria to the modern Canon texts. They sow the seeds of doubt enough so that seminaries and pastors use their ignorance as supposed positions against these books. The problem is these are illiterate notions, and they seem incapable of conducting even a little research.

Mushkhusshu, the dragon
of Marduk, depicted as bas-
relief on the original Ishtar
gate, ancient Babylon, Iraq.
This was constructed circa
575 BCE by order of King
Nebuchadnezzar II There is
a rendering of this historic
dragon who can even be seen
here breathing fire.

BEL & THE DRAGON

DANIEL 14 IN ANCIENT HISTORY

WITH THE RESTORED
NAME OF YAHUAH

DANIEL SLAYS THE DRAGON,
SURVIVES PRIESTS OF BEL & LION'S DEN

CHAPTER 1:

19 The fraud of Bel's Priests, is discovered by Daniel, 27 and the Dragon slain, which was worshipped. 33 Daniel is preserved in the Lion's den. 42 The King does acknowledge the Elohim of Daniel and casts his enemies into the same den.

1 And King Astyages was gathered to his fathers, and Cyrus of Persia received his kingdom. 2 And Daniel conversed with the king and was honored above all his friends. 3 Now the Babylonians had an idol called Bel, and there were spent upon him every day twelve great measures of fine flour, and forty sheep, and six vessels of wine.

Or, lived with the King.

i.e. Marduk, Ba'al.

4 And the king worshipped it and went daily to adore it: but Daniel worshipped his own Elohim. And the king said unto him, why do you not worship Bel?

5 Who answered and said, Because I may not worship idols made with hands, but the living Elohim, who has created the heaven, and the earth, and has sovereignty over all flesh. 6 Then said the King unto him, think you not that Bel is a living god? See you not how much he eats and drinks every day? 7 Then Daniel smiled, and said, O king, be not deceived: for this is but clay within, and brass without, and did never eat or drink anything. 8 So the king was wroth, and called for his Priests, and said unto them, if you tell me not who this is that devours these expenses, you shall die.

Cf. Ecclus. 30:19.

9 But if you can certify me that Bel devours them, then Daniel shall die: for he has spoken blasphemy against Bel. And Daniel said unto the king, let it be according to your word.

10 (Now the Priests of Bel were threescore and ten, beside their wives and children) and the king went with Daniel into the temple of Bel. 11 So Bel's Priests said, lo, we go out: but you, O king, set on the meat, and make ready the wine, and shut the door fast, and seal it with your own signet:

12 And tomorrow, when you come in, if you find not that Bel has eaten up all, we will suffer death; or else Daniel, that speaks falsely against us. 13 And they little regarded it: for under the table, they had made a private entrance, whereby

they entered in continually, and consumed those things. 14 So when they were gone forth, the king set meats before Bel. Now Daniel had commanded his servants to bring ashes, and those they strewed throughout all the temple, in the presence of the king alone: then went they out and shut the door, and sealed it with the king's signet, and so departed. 15 Now in the night came the Priests with their wives and children (as they were wanting to do) and did eat and drink up all. 16 In the morning early the king arose, and Daniel with him. 17 And the king said, Daniel, are the seals whole? And he said, yes, O king, they be whole. 18 And as soon as he had opened the door, the king looked upon the table, and cried with a loud voice, Great are you, O Bel, and with you is no deceit at all. 19 Then laughed Daniel and held the king that he should not go in, and said, Behold now the pavement, and mark well whose footsteps are these. 20 And the king said, I see the footsteps of men, women and children: and then the king was angry,

21 And took the Priests, with their wives and children, who showed him the private doors, where they came in, and consumed such things as were upon the table.

22 Therefore the king slew them, and delivered Bel into Daniel's power, who destroyed him and his temple.

Of The Dragon.

23 And in that same place there was a great Dragon, which they of Babylon worshipped. 24 And the king said unto Daniel, Will you also say that this is of brass? Lo, he lives, he eats and drinks, you cannot say, that he is no living Elohim: therefore, worship him.

25 Then said Daniel unto the king, I will worship Yahuah my Elohim: for he is the living Elohim.

26 But give me leave, O king, and I shall slay this dragon without sword or staff. The king said, I give you leave.

27 Then Daniel took pitch, fat, and hair, and did boil them together, and made lumps thereof: this he put in the Dragon's mouth, and so the Dragon burst in sunder:

Or, Behold what you worship

and Daniel said, lo, these are the gods you worship. 28 When they of Babylon heard that, they took great indignation, and conspired against the king, saying, the king is become a Yahudim, and he has destroyed Bel, he has slain the Dragon, and put the Priests to death. 29 So they came to the king, and said, deliver us Daniel, or else we will destroy you and your house. 30 Now when the king saw that they pressed him sore, being constrained, he delivered Daniel unto them: 31 Who cast him into the lion's den, where he was six days.

Cf. Dan.6.16.

32 And in the den there were seven lions, and they had given them every day two carcasses, and two sheep: which then were not given to them, to the intent they might devour Daniel. 33 Now there was in jury a Prophet called Habakkuk, who had made pottage, and had broken bread in a bowl, and was going into the field, for to bring it to the reapers. 34 But the Angel of the Yahuah said unto Habakkuk, Go carry the dinner that you have into Babylon unto Daniel, who

Or, two slaves.

Lived the same time as Daniel.

Or, sod.

is in the lion's den. 35 And Habakkuk said, Yahuah, I never saw Babylon: neither do I know where the den is. 36 Then the Angel of Yahuah took him by the crown, and bare him by the hair of his head, and through the vehemency of his spirit, set him in Babylon over the den. 37 And Habakkuk cried, saying, O Daniel, Daniel, take the dinner which Elohim has sent you. 38 And Daniel said, You have remembered me, O Elohim: neither have you forsaken them that seek you, and love you. 39 So Daniel arose and did eat: and the Angel of Yahuah set Habakkuk in his own place again immediately. 40 Upon the seventh day the king went to bewail Daniel: and when he came to the den, he looked in, and behold, Daniel was sitting. 41 Then cried the king with a loud voice, saying, Great are you, O Yahuah Elohim of Daniel, and there is none other besides you. 42 And he drew him out: and cast those that were the cause of his destruction into the den: and they were devoured in a moment before his face.

Cf. Ez. 8:3.

Cf. 1Ki. 17:4.

Cf. Jer. 37:17.

One of the oddest fallacies in modern scholarship is the thinking that dragons are somehow fictional characters. This requires a disbelief of the Bible on a large scale. These are not students of the Bible, they are unbelievers. They also demonstrate a complete ignorance of history. The confusion begins with the term dragon. Up until the 1800s, there was no classification we call dinosaurs today which is a new designation known historically as dragons. The same scholar who believes dinosaurs were real many times, then, questions whether dragons once were without even realizing they are the same thing essentially. However, what other books are these hypocrites suggesting censoring because they mention dragons? If they were honest and consistent, they would have to discard many for such reason.

DRAGONS OF THE BIBLE:

The Bible has the word "dragon" as a translation 19 times. However, in the Hebrew it is the word, which is the same used for Leviathan who, by definition, is a fire-breathing sea dragon in Job.

תנין: *tannîyn, tan-neen'; or* תנים: *tannîym; (Ezekiel 29:3), intensive from the same as H8565; a marine or land monster, i.e. sea-serpent or jackal:—dragon, sea-monster, serpent, whale. (H8577)*

Genesis defines tannim as Yahuah's creation on the Fifth Day *(1:23)*. That is well affirmed in Jubilees, 2nd Esdras, and throughout scripture.

Genesis 1:21 KJV
*And **God created great whales**, (H8577) and every living creature that moveth, which the waters brought forth abundantly, after their kind, and every winged fowl after his kind: and God saw that it was good.*

"Great whales" is a misleading translation for what is the sea dragon known as the Leviathan species including the land dragons, Behemoth. This is consistent with the Book of Jubilees. These were the first creatures formed by the hands of Elohim and He boasts righteously about creating them in Job. They are not demons.

Jubilees 2:11a
And on the fifth day He created great sea monsters in the depths of the waters, for these were the first things of flesh that were created by His hands...

However, as Strong's Concordance rightly indicates, tannim *(dragons)* are not just sea creatures, but there is a land species as well. Leviathan, the sea dragon, was given residence in the Rivers from Eden that are at the bottom of the world ocean today, and Behemoth, the land dragon, dwelled upon the dry land.

2nd Esdras 6:47-52 KJVA
*Upon the fifth day, you said unto the seventh part, where the waters were gathered, that it should bring forth living creatures, fouls and fishes: and so it came to pass. For the dumb water, and without life, brought forth living things at the commandment of Elohim, that all people might praise your wondrous works. Then did you ordain **two living creatures**, the one you called **Enoch**, and the other **Leviathan**, And did **separate the one from the other**: for the seventh part (namely where the water was gathered together) might not hold them both. Unto **Enoch you gave** one part which was **dried up** the third day, that he should dwell in the same part, wherein are a thousand hills. But **unto Leviathan you gave the seventh part**, namely **the moist**, and has kept him to be devoured of whom you will, and when.*

These dragons are unique in that the sea variety was created first as female and the land species as male originally as counterparts separated in dwelling. They are one species. Yahuah did this so that these creatures would procreate. This would lead to a sea and land species both male and female each over time, but not in origin. Because they are a created animal, the land dragon would have been represented as a young, healthy pair on Noah's ark. This is unlike many dinosaurs, especially meat eaters, that were likely hybrid beings manipulated by Nephilim incursions with the animals as First Enoch and Jubilees so well define. A Noah fragment within First Enoch defines this species who were created in the Land of Creation.

1 Enoch 60:7-8 (A Book of Noah Fragment)
*And on that day were **two monsters parted**, a female monster named **Leviathan**, to dwell in the abysses of the oceans, over the fountains of the waters. But the **male is named Behemoth, who occupied with his breast a waste wilderness named Duidain**, on the east of the Garden where the elect and righteous dwell.*

This has always been detailed in the Book of Job who describes both Leviathan and Behemoth as giant dragons. The sea dragon, Leviathan, breathes fire from his mouth fitting to this story of Bel & The Dragon. Daniel used that against Bel's Dragon slaying him with wisdom and using science. We will address whether that specific dragon was also real, and even the science behind breathing fire.

Job 41:6-34 KJV (The Sea Dragon, Leviathan Species)
*Shall the companions make a banquet of him? shall they part him among the merchants? Canst thou fill his skin with barbed irons? or his head with fish spears? Lay thine hand upon him, remember the battle, do no more. Behold, the hope of him is in vain: shall not one be cast down even at the sight of him? None is so fierce that dare stir him up: who then is able to stand before me? Who hath prevented me, that I should repay him? whatsoever is under the whole heaven is mine. I will not conceal his parts, nor his power, nor **his comely proportion**. Who can discover the face of his garment? or who can come to him with his double bridle? Who can open the doors of his face? his **teeth are terrible** round about. His **scales are his pride**, shut up together as with a **close seal**. One is so near to another, that **no air can come between them**. They are joined one to another, they stick together, that they cannot be sundered. By his neesings a light doth shine, and his eyes are like the eyelids of the morning. **Out of his mouth go burning lamps, and sparks of fire leap out. Out of his nostrils goeth smoke, as out of a seething pot or caldron. His breath kindleth coals, and a flame goeth out of his mouth. In his neck remaineth strength**, and sorrow is turned into joy before him. **The flakes of his flesh** are joined together: they are firm in themselves; they cannot be moved. His heart is as firm as a stone; yea, as hard as a piece of the nether millstone. When he raiseth up himself, the mighty are afraid: by reason of breakings they purify themselves. The **sword** of him that layeth at him **cannot hold**: the **spear**, the **dart, nor** the **habergeon**. He esteemeth **iron as straw, and brass as rotten wood**. The **arrow cannot make him flee: slingstones** are turned with him **into stubble**. Darts are counted as stubble: he laugheth at the shaking of a spear. Sharp stones are under him: he spreadeth sharp pointed things upon the mire. He **maketh the deep to boil** like a pot: he maketh the sea like a pot of **ointment**. He maketh a path to shine after him; one would think the deep to be hoary. Upon earth there is not his like, who is made without fear. He beholdeth all high things: he is a king over all the children of pride.*

Then, Job details the land dragon known as behemoth in similar terms. Remember, these two creatures mate since creation and are really the same kind. They would have many similarities as a result. Both are creations from the Fifth Day of Creation, and neither are demons, mystical beings, nor magical in any sense.

Job 40:15-24 KJV (The Land Dragon, Behemoth Species)
*"Behold, [fn]Behemoth, which I made as well as you; He eats grass like an ox. "Behold, his **strength in his waist**, And his power in the **muscles of his belly**. "He hangs his tail like a cedar; The tendons of his **thighs are knit together**. "His **bones** are tubes of **bronze**; His limbs are like bars of iron. "He is the first of the ways of **God**; Let his Maker bring His sword near. "Indeed the **mountains bring him food**, And all the animals of the field play there. "He lies down under the lotus plants, "The lotus plants cover him with shade; "If a river rages, he is not alarmed; He is confident, though the Jordan rushes to his mouth. The willows of the brook surround him. In the **hiding place** of the reeds and the marsh. "Can anyone capture him when he is on watch, Can anyone **pierce his nose with barbs?***

BEL & THE DRAGON: FACT OR FICTION
SEA DRAGON
leviathan
Job 41
Origin at Creation:
Only Female
These are the same
kind as behemoth
procreating.
1 Enoch 60:7-8;
2nd Esdras 6:47-52
Comely in proportion
"...the first things of flesh that
were created by His hands..."
Jubilees 2:11, Genesis 1:21
Will go extinct.
Isaiah 27:1;
Psalm 74:14
Note: May be already.
Strong Neck
Impenetrable Scales
Breathes Fire
Can melt metals
Terrible Teeth
Lives in the Great Deep
THE Levite BIBLE

Origin at Creation: Only Male
These are the same kind as leviathan procreating.
Very tall
LAND DRAGON
b e h e m o t h
Job 40
Eats grass like an Ox
Hangs tail like a cedar
Strong Bones
like metal
Muscular Belly
Strong Waist
Thigh tendons
knit together
Lives on Dry Land

Mushkhusshu, the dragon-serpent depicted on the door of Ishtar. Reconstruction 1918 based on archaeology from 1904-1914. Originally constructed circa 575 B.C. by order of King Nebuchadnezzar II. Pergamon Museum, Berlin. Public Domain. Wikimedia Commons.

The Statue of Marduk depicted on a cylinder seal of the 9th century BC Babylonian king Marduk-zakir-shumi I. Detailed info, from Schaudig (2008), p. 559. Franz Heinrich Weißbach (1903). Public Domain.

THE HISTORIC DRAGON OF BEL MARDUK:

"And in that same place there was a great Dragon, which they of Babylon worshipped."
Bel & The Dragon 1:23 KJVA (A factual, historical dragon used in worship there)

"...he lives, he eats and drinks..."
Bel & The Dragon 1:24 KJVA (A living, breathing dragon)

However, imagine the shame of the many scholars who scoff at the inclusion of a dragon in this account, when they finally learn history records a specific dragon of Bel Marduk named Mushkhusshu *(above)*. His image is even documented in archaeology on a relief of the Ishtar Gate in ancient Babylon constructed about 575 B.C. by order of King Nebuchadnezzar II. Based on archaeology from 1904-1914, it was reconstructed for the Pergamon Museum in Berlin about 1918. He looks like what one would picture as a dragon indeed, though without wings. His features match that of Job's description of Leviathan as well, but this creature represents the land species, not the ones in the sea. Also, Mushkhusshu appears to be breathing fire in that illustration which is consistent with Daniel's account. Daniel did not carve this. The Babylonians did as they worshipped this beast. Because, we do not find these dragons today, scholars ridicule this, yet that merely demonstrates their own lack of knowledge. They have no true basis.

Also, we find Mushkhusshu documented as late as Daniel's time and then, he seems to disappear from the Babylonian paradigm. This is no surprise because Daniel killed him and he was no more. It serves as evidence Daniel's account is fact.

CAN AN ANIMAL SCIENTIFICALLY BREATH FIRE?

YES. There is a species who expels that like fire today even. In fact, this species serves to disprove the Theory of Evolution as well. If this reaction chamber within his apparatus were a fraction of a cm further inside, he would have exploded in his phase of evolution. There would be no species left to evolve.

*"The closest equivalent is probably the **Bombardier beetle (Brachinus species)**. These store hydroquinone and hydrogen peroxide in separate chambers in their abdomens. When threatened, the beetle can squirt these chemicals into a reaction chamber where they mix with a catalytic enzyme to undergo a violent exothermic reaction, expelling a boiling puff of acrid gas and vapour."*
– BBC Science Focus Magazine [120]

In the account of Jonah, he is swallowed by a "great fish." Many think that may have been a whale based on poor translation. Logically, science has debunked the notion that a human could survive inside a whale's belly, not to mention the acid would severely bleach the skin, among other issues. However, if one tests leviathan as this creature, there is room enough for Jonah as well as the mechanism for him to breath oxygen inside. That makes far more logical sense.

Bombardier beetle (Brachinus species) is known to expel
"a boiling puff of acrid gas and vapour." [120]

DRAGONS IN HISTORY?

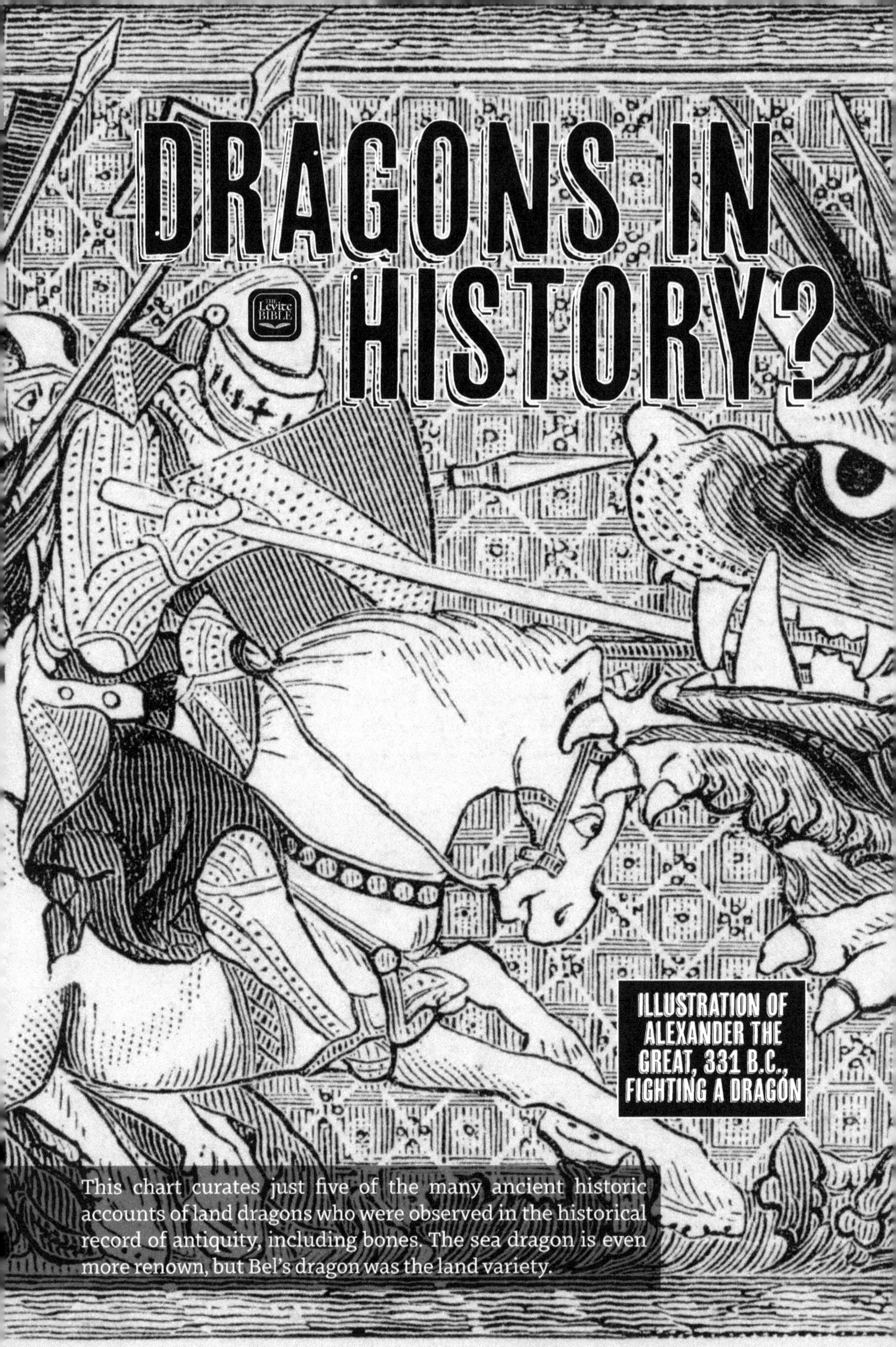

ILLUSTRATION OF ALEXANDER THE GREAT, 331 B.C., FIGHTING A DRAGON

This chart curates just five of the many ancient historic accounts of land dragons who were observed in the historical record of antiquity, including bones. The sea dragon is even more renown, but Bel's dragon was the land variety.

425 B.C.: HERODOTUS

"The History Of Herodotus" Vol. 1, Book 2.75. Tr: G. C. Macaulay
Saudi Arabia and Egypt: "winged serpents... I saw bones of serpents and spines in quantity so great... like that of the watersnake; and it has wings not feathered but most nearly resembling the wings of the bat." *Statue of Herodotus, Public Domain.*

331 B.C.: ALEXANDER THE GREAT

"On Animals," Claudius Aelianus, Book 15, Chapter 19-23, c.210-230.
India: "In 330 BC, after Alexander the Great invaded India, he brought back reports of seeing a great hissing dragon living in a cave, which people were worshiping as gods." *AdobeStock.*

90 A.D.: FLAVIUS JOSEPHUS

Antiquities of the Jews, Book II , 13.3
Mentions "dragons" in *Egypt.*
AdobeStock.

200 A.D.: GAIUS JULIUS SOLINUS

"Gaius Iulius Solinus and his Polyhistor," 30.15
Ethiopia: "Among these fires of continual heat there is a great abundance of dragons. True dragons have small mouths, which do not gape open to bite. They have a narrow tube, through which they drag breath and thrust out their tongues."
Photo: Hartmann Schedel, Nuremberg Chronicle, 1493. Public Domain.

1275 A.D.: MARCO POLO

The Travels of Marco Polo, Book 2, Chapter XL, pg. 185-186
China: "Here are seen huge serpents, ten paces in length (about 30 feet), and ten spans (about 8 feet) girt of the body. At the fore part, near the head, they have two short legs, having three claws like those of a tiger, with eyes larger than a forepenny loaf (pane da quattro denari) and very glaring.
"The jaws are wide enough to swallow a man, the teeth are large and sharp..." *AdobeStock.*

IS A LARGE FLYING DRAGON POSSIBLE?

YES. However, the Bible never attributes ancient dragons as flying, nor does the relief in Assyria of the actual dragon of Bel Marduk, Mushkhusshu, mentioned in this account. That does not mean there was not a variety that perhaps did. In the Bible, these are one kind in which one swims and the other lives on land. Neither have wings. The European dragon of legends is likely embellished though perhaps not. However, that is impertinent in the discussion of the existence of dragons.

We do know that there are bones to support the existence of dragons. We call them dinosaurs today and there are some with wings even. Nothing would survive of the skeleton to ascertain whether these breathed fire or not. Let us not treat those who demand such inerudite evidence as educated. They are not on this.

"The Late Cretaceous pterosaur Quetzlcoatlus northropi was one of the largest known flying animals. Estimates of its size vary, but even the most conservative estimates place its wingspan at 11 meters (36 feet), with a weight of around 200 to 250 kilograms (440 to 550 pounds)."– ThoughtCo [121]

Indeed, in modern times, it appears at least the land species is extinct at this point. However, how many of the dinosaur bones science has been finding, those not manufactured in China of course, are actually documenting Behemoth? It appears there are many. They will not likely ever find bones of Leviathan, the sea dragon, as that species lived, and perhaps still does, in the Great Deep where man has never conducted excavations, and cannot actually go. Even the entire ocean remains an enigma to modern science as they have not even explored 10% of the ocean floor especially the Great Deep.

However, these dragons are predicted to go extinct in Isaiah 27:1 and Psalm 74:14. It would be no surprise if they were already gone since we are not seeing them today. That is no excuse to scoff as a fool though. There is no need to set a false paradigm requiring one to find them in order to believe that Biblical and historic dragons existed. The evidence is already imperative enough. No one needs any more data to ascertain dragons are not fiction generally, whether any specific account may embellish or not. The Bible does not, and it represents historic fact.

Some have even ridiculed the Bible for many years because it mentions the unicorn. However, the Bible unicorn is the one-horned rhinoceros as opposed to the bicorn, or two-horned one. These are not the mythical occult creature who is likely fiction especially in the powers attributed. Certainly there are other hybrids mentioned in the Bible, but this is well explained by the presence of Nephilim who also procreated with animals manipulating their orders. That was the reason for the Flood. Those scholars who ignore that account in Genesis 6, First Enoch, Jubilees, etc. have no good explanation for the cause of the Flood. However, the origin of Bible dragons is Creation, and they are not hybrids originally even in Job when Yahuah boasts of forming them.

As far as the rest of this story, likely written by Daniel himself, it reads like the rest of Daniel's book. Bel Marduk is known as Ba'al in Canaan. That is the same god rebuked in scripture many, many times as the enemy of YHWH. Daniel exposed and overcame the priests or Bel (Ba'al). That should not be a surprising account from the great prophet who also defeated the trickery of the Chaldean magicians, etc. Without this account, Daniel is incomplete. With it, one begins to see a clearer picture as to why the enemies hated Daniel with such furver. He did not just expose their priests. He killed their living, prized dragon which they included in the worship of Bel Marduk. As the story continues, the account of Daniel in the lion's den has a second witness that scholars ignore. Scripture says it should.

DANIEL IN THE LION'S DEN:

Bel & The Dragon sets up the circumstances for Daniel's being cast into the lion's den lending it more credibility. We all know the story from Daniel where the officials conspired to entrap Daniel, now in Persia, with the Law of His Elohim. They would convince the king to decree that if one prayed to another God for that next thirty days, they would be cast into the lion's den. Though there were many reasons for these officials to be jealous of Daniel, none were as motivating as Daniel's killing their Dragon of Bel Marduk, whom they worshipped, as well as his exposing their priesthood as frauds also regarding the feeding of that same dragon. He proved their god was not a god at all. With Bel & The Dragon, this account makes much more sense. These officials were enraged that Daniel killed their god and this was their response in both accounts – Daniel 6 and Bel & The Dragon.

As of Chapter 6 in the Book of Daniel, Daniel had left Babylon and was now in the Palace of Susan in Persia. In fact, he was somewhere other than the palace in Babylon in Chapter 5 even as he had to be called to the palace. He no longer lived there. This fits the timeline of Bel & The Dragon which does not cover the Baylonian era, but begins in the days of King Cyrus of Persia taking over the entire kingdom. This is when Daniel exposed the fraud of the Priests of Bel Marduk and next, Daniel slayed their recorded dragon of Bel Marduk whom they worshipped as well. These are the circumstances that led to an extreme reaction to entrap Daniel.

Without Bel & The Dragon, Daniel in the lion's den almost reads as fiction because it is less believable. Jealousy alone, is not a compelling reason to drive such extreme measures. These were the new rulers of the land under King Darius, and they were endangering many of their own innocent people with such a decree. It was an act that they must have known the people, generally, would hate them for implementing. They did it anyway. The account in the Book of Daniel begs for more detail to explain this severe ordinance. In reading it, there must be a more apt reason for such a drastic, compulsory dictum. There was. We would not know this, however, if it were not for Bel & The Dragon, which is Chapter 14 of Daniel.

Any scholar who claims Bel & The Dragon is fiction because it has a dragon, they erroneously claim a fictional character, is truly ignorant. In order to be consistent and not liars, they would have to then, apply that rationale to every other book of the modern Bible Canon which mention dragons. They are undermining much of scripture without even realizing it. That is the worst of gross negligence. If they wish to discard this book for that reason, then, they must censor Job, Nehemiah, Psalm, Isaiah, Jeremiah, Ezekiel, and Revelation as well. Now that is stupid, not scholarship! When scholars are incapable of simple reason, we should not give them attention they do not deserve.

THE Levite BIBLE
LeviteBible.com

PRAYER OF AZARYAH

SURVIVING THE FIERY FURNACE
INSERTED AT DANIEL 3:24
IN ANCIENT HISTORY

WITH THE RESTORED
NAME OF YAHUAH

The Song of the
Three Children

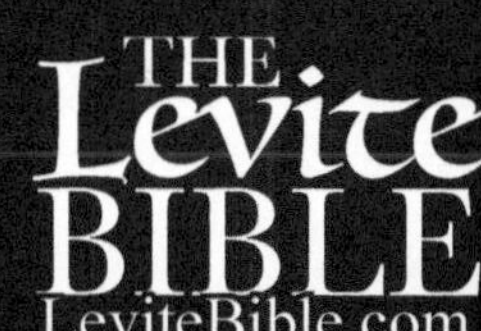

CHAPTER 1:

1 Azaryah his prayer and confession in the flame, 24 wherewith the Chaldeans about the oven were consumed, but the three young men within it were not hurt. 28 The Song of the three youths in the oven.

1 [And they walked amid the fire, praising Elohim, and blessing Yahuah.] Then Azaryah stood up and prayed on this manner and opening his mouth in the midst of the fire, said, 2 Blessed are you, O Yahuah Elohim of our fathers: your Name is worthy to be praised, and glorified for evermore. 3 For you are righteous in all the things that you have done to us: yes, true are all your works: your ways are right, and all your judgments truth. 4 In all the things that you have brought upon us, and upon the holy city of our fathers, even Jerusalem, you have executed true judgment: for according to truth and judgment, did you bring all these things upon us, because of our sins. 5 For we have sinned and committed iniquity, departing from you. 6 In all things have we trespassed, and not obeyed your Commandments, nor

kept them, neither done as you have commanded us, that it might go well with us. 7 Wherefore all that you have brought upon us, and everything that you have done to us, you have done in true judgment. 8 And you did deliver us into the hands of lawless enemies, most hateful forsakers [of Elohim] and to an unjust King, and the most wicked in all the world. 9 And now we cannot open our mouths, we are become a shame, and reproach to your servants, and to them that worship you. 10 Yet deliver us not up wholly for your Name's sake, neither disannul your Covenant:

11 And cause not your mercy to depart from us: for your beloved Abraham's sake: for your servant Isaac's sake, and for your holy Israel's sake. 12 To whom you have spoken and promised, that you would multiply their seed as the stars of heaven, and as the sand that lies upon the sea shore. 13 For we, O Yahuah, are become less than any nation, and be kept under this day in all the world, because of our sins. 14 Neither is there at this

time, Prince, or Prophet, or leader, or burnt offering, or sacrifice, or oblation, or incense, or place to sacrifice before you, and to find mercy.

15 Nevertheless in a contrite heart, and a humble spirit, let us be accepted. 16 Like as in the burnt offering of rams and bulls, and like as in ten thousands of fat lambs: so let our sacrifice be in your sight this day, and [grant] that we may wholly go after you: for they shall not be confounded that put their trust in you. 17 And now we follow you, with all our heart, we fear you, and seek your face. 18 Put us not to shame: but deal with us after your loving kindness, and according to the multitude of your mercies. 19 Deliver us also according to your marvelous works, and give glory to your Name, O Yahuah, and let all of them that do your servants hurt be ashamed. 20 And let them be confounded in all their power and might, and let their strength be broken. 21 And let them know that you are Yahuah, the only Elohim, and glorious over the whole

world. 22 And the king's servants that put them in, ceased not to make the oven hot with rosin, pitch, tow, and small wood. 23 So that the flame streamed forth above the furnace, forty and nine cubits: 24 And it passed through and burnt those Caldeans it found about the furnace. 25 But the Angel of Yahuah came down into the oven, together with Azaryah and his fellows, and smote the flame of the fire out of the oven: 26 And made the midst of the furnace, as it had been a moist whistling wind, so that the fire touched them not at all, neither hurt nor troubled them. 27 Then the three, as out of one mouth, praised, glorified, and blessed Elohim in the furnace, saying; 28 Blessed are you, O Yahuah Elohim of our fathers: and to be praised and exalted above all forever. 29 And blessed is your glorious and Holy Name: and to be praised and exalted above all forever. 30 Blessed are you in the Temple of your holy glory: and to be praised and glorified above all forever.

31 Blessed are you that beholds the depths, and sits

Or, by your power and might.

rosin: *solid form of resin obtained from pines and some other plants.*
tow: *fiber of flax or another material prepared for spinning.*

Dan. 3:1, the statue was 60 cubits tall. Azariah writes only of the flames another 49 cubits above that perhaps.

Or, coals.

upon the Cherubim, and to be praised and exalted above all forever. 32 Blessed are you on the glorious Throne of your kingdom: and to be praised and glorified above all forever. 33 Blessed are you in the firmament of heaven: and above all to be praised and glorified forever. 34 O all your works of Yahuah, bless you Yahuah: praise and exalt Him above all forever.

Or, highly exalt: and so in the rest.

35 O you heavens, bless Yahuah: praise and exalt Him above all forever.

Cf. Ps. 148:4.

36 O you Angels of Yahuah, bless Yahuah: praise and exalt Him above all forever. 37 O all you waters that be above the heaven, bless Yahuah: praise and exalt Him above all forever. 38 O all you powers of Yahuah, bless Yahuah: praise and exalt Him above all forever. 39 O you sun and moon, bless Yahuah: praise and exalt Him above all forever. 40 O you stars of heaven, bless Yahuah: praise and exalt Him above all forever. 41 O every shower and dew, bless Yahuah: praise and exalt Him above all forever. 42 O all you winds, bless Yahuah: praise and exalt Him above all forever.

43 O you fire and heat, bless Yahuah: praise and exalt Him above all forever.
44 O you Winter and Summer, bless Yahuah: praise and exalt Him above all forever. 45 O you dews and storms of snow, bless Yahuah: praise and exalt Him above all forever. 46 O you nights and days, bless Yahuah: praise and exalt Him above all forever.
47 O you light and darkness, bless Yahuah: praise and exalt Him above all forever.
48 O you ice and cold, bless Yahuah: praise and exalt Him above all forever. 49 O you frost and snow, bless Yahuah: praise and exalt Him above all forever. 50 O you lightnings and clouds, bless Yahuah: praise and exalt Him above all forever.
51 O let the earth bless Yahuah: praise and exalt Him above all forever. 52 O you mountains and little hills, bless Yahuah: praise and exalt Him above all forever. 53 O all you things that grow on the earth, bless Yahuah: praise and exalt Him above all forever.
54 O you fountains, bless Yahuah: praise and exalt Him above all forever.
55 O you seas and rivers,

bless Yahuah: praise and exalt Him above all forever. 56 O you leviathan and all that move in the waters, bless Yahuah: praise and exalt Him above all forever. 57 O all you fouls of the air, *Greek: heaven.* bless Yahuah: praise and exalt Him above all forever. 58 O all you beasts and cattle, bless Yahuah: praise and exalt Him above all forever. 59 O you children of men, bless Yahuah: praise and exalt Him above all forever. 60 O Israel bless Yahuah: praise and exalt Him above all forever. 61 O you priests of Yahuah, bless Yahuah: praise and exalt Him above all forever.

62 O you servants of Yahuah, bless Yahuah: praise and exalt Him above all forever. 63 O you spirits and souls of the righteous, bless Yahuah, praise and exalt Him above all forever. 64 O you holy and humble men of heart, *Or, Saints.* bless Yahuah: praise and exalt Him above all forever. 65 O Hananyah, Azaryah, and MishaEl, bless Yahuah, praise and exalt Him above all forever: for He has delivered us from hell, and saved us from the hand of death, and delivered us out of the midst of the furnace, [and] burning flame: even out of the midst of the fire has He delivered us. 66 O give thanks unto Yahuah, because He is gracious: for His mercy endures forever. 67 O all you that worship Yahuah, bless the Elohim of Elohim, praise Him, and give Him thanks: for His mercy endures forever.

Or, grave. Note: Sheol is not the burning hell of the Greeks and occult mythos. It is where all souls rest in chambers upon death including the righteous who are not judged yet. Azaryah knew this as the entire Bible does.

Was Azariah *(Babylonian name, Abednego)* not cast in the fiery furnace with his two fellow prophets, Shadrach and Meshach? We all know the Book of Daniel affirms that. Where scholars take issue is making claims based on things they do not even know. Some criticize that Shadrach is mentioned first so he would have to be the only possibility of one who prayed while surviving the ordeal. That is not logic, nor reason, it is ridiculous and unscholarly. Have these never read the story of Jacob, Joseph, Ephraim, Gideon, etc., etc., etc.? These were the oldest. Who could call themselves a Bible scholar and even suggest such? The point is fine to attempt, but to use it as a bully pulpit to censor this one-chapter book, is utter ignorance. Do they use such criteria to test the books of their modern Pharisee Canon? Of course not. They are inconsistent, uneducated on the topic, and unworthy of a platform to dispense such false paradigms they would never apply to other Biblical books.

The Bible does not say Shadrach was the oldest, nor that he said a prayer in the furnace, and there is no Prayer of Hananyah *(Shadrach)* on record. Their paradigm is set up to fail exactly as they desire. That is fraud. Age does not determine who is led to pray in the face of crisis in scripture either. That is a lie. All three of Daniel's co-ministers were prophets and could pray. Daniel included Azaryah's prayer.

That discipline makes such mistakes often even confusing things like the order of Noah's three sons when Shem is always the oldest in all scripture, at all times. He does not grow younger and older in different passages. The criteria of one listed first always having to represent the oldest is stupid. The claim only the oldest prays, is a fictional paradigm. Without the Book of Jubilees, they are missing the history book of Bible lineages which defines Shem as the oldest even demonstrating the year he and his brothers were born. It settles the debate, yet modern scholarship ignores that history book even for chronology when it is accurate.

Prayer of Azaryah was historically inserted within the Book of Daniel's third chapter at verse 23 *(see Torah Test in the Introduction)*. Daniel did not write it, Azaryah, the prophet, did and Daniel published it within accordingly. He was not inside the fiery furnace himself with his three fellow prophets. Azaryah *(Abednego)* wrote down his prayer from the encounter. This prayer is Biblical in content calling on the Creator to intervene in their potential demise. It accurately represents YHWH the same as all of scripture. Someone better have prayed, and why not Azaryah?

One sign of inspired scripture is the use of YHWH, Yahuah, written and, at times, pronounced over 40 times in this one-chapter prayer. That alone is the likely reason the Pharisees removed this portion of the Book of Daniel. They have several major problems with especially the prophesies of Messiah in Daniel which Yahusha, and only Yahusha, fulfilled. They also espouse the most illiterate doctrine ever in claiming we are to hide the name of our Yahuah. The problem is the patriarchs including Adam, pronounced and over 6,800 times in the Hebrew Old Testament, wrote the name of YHWH, Yahuah. This includes Yahuah pronouncing His own name for the prophets including Abraham who knew how to pronounce and write this name. He did so multiple times to his wife, his sons, his servants, and even to the King of Sodom. However, Bible scholarship is placating that despicable doctrine by continuing to hide the name of YHWH, Yahuah, in our modern Bibles replacing it most of the time with LORD, a generic title. It appears censoring or marginalizing this book also materializes as part of that plot to hide the name of YHWH, Yahuah.

The real challenge to scholars who reject this book, is what exactly does Azaryah pray that is inaccurate to the whole of scripture? There is nothing. This prayer in content passes the test of inspired, as does the historicity of this book *(see Torah Test)*.

DID DANIEL WRITE THAT THESE MEN PRAYED WHEN THROWN INTO THE FIERY FURNACE?

Also, Shadrach, Meshach and Abednego definitively bowed down and prayed when they were cast into the fiery furnace. They were not bowing to Nebuchadnezzar, but to Yahuah, who sends a Messenger – likely Yahusha in spirit form as He is described as *"the form of the fourth is like the Son of God (3:25)."* Daniel 3:23 is exactly where they bowed down and prayed in the text:

And these three men, Shadrach, Meshach, and Abednego, **fell down** (nᵉp̄al: נפל) *bound into the midst of the burning fiery furnace.*
Strong's H5308, Brown-Driver-Briggs Hebrew Lexicon: nᵉp̄al: נפל: fall down and do homage: Daniel 3:5, Daniel 3:6, Daniel 3:7, Daniel 3:10, Daniel 3:11, Daniel 3:15; ל location Daniel 3:23; of voice, אִימְשֻׁומ Daniel 4:28 [Daniel 4:31].

Daniel used this word interpreted "fell down" to refer to prayer indeed. This is where the Prayer of Azaryah was historically inserted in the Book of Daniel and now, it is removed and treated as a separate writing erroneously *(see Introduction)*.

Did These Ever
Belong In The Bible?

THE
Levite
BIBLE
LeviteBible.com

Martin Luther, 1483-1546:

"I am so great an enemy to the second book of the Maccabees, and to Esther, that I wish they had not come to us at all, for they have too many heathen unnaturalities. The Jews much more esteemed the book of Esther than any of the prophets; though they were forbidden to read it before they had attained the age of thirty, by reason of the mystic matters it contains."

"The Table Talk of Martin Luther." Ch. 24, pp. 27-28. [110]

TESTING THE BOOK OF ESTHER

& PURIM

IS ESTHER ISHTAR?

WAS ESTHER EVER SCRIPTURE?

1611 APOCRYPHA ADDITIONS TO ESTHER?

WHY DOES ESTHER MATCH AN OCCULT ACCOUNT?

THE Levite BIBLE
LeviteBible.com

One portion of the 1611 King James Apocrypha is titled "Additions to Esther." The Book of Esther ends at chapter 10:3 and these add new content from 10:4 through the end of chapter 16. The modern KJV still does not recognize these additions as it continues to culminate with 10:3. However, since they were attempting at some time to fix challenges with Esther it appears, this raises the much larger question: Is the Book of Esther inspired? Every scholar should research this and hardly any burden themselves with such truths. Martin Luther did on this book and many Protestant theologians and pastors are not even aware, or they ignore it.

Why would Martin Luther take such a strong stand against the Book of Esther? This is not mere rebuke, but he was *"so great an enemy"* to the Canonization of Esther. He accused the book of being occult having *"too many heathen unnaturalities."* Certainly, he was human and made many errors in which we do not agree with every position he ever held. Most of all, he attempted to reform an already rotten foundation of the Catholic Church which one cannot rehabilitate. It must be torn down completely, and a new foundation set on the solid rock. The Protestant generally has still accepted much leaven as a result. His position here is that Esther is an occult book and story. Yet, it is in our Bibles today, even Protestant. How did this happen especially when Esther is riddled with a dubious past? This debate will never go away until this book is removed from any consideration as Canon.

REJECTED AS INSPIRED SCRIPTURE IN THE B.C. ERA:

The Book of Esther was not found in the only historic Bible Canon curated by the ordained keepers of Old Testament scripture. She, Mordecai, Haman, nor any portion of her story, especially the new Feast Day of Purim, are not even known in the whole of the local Qumran community writings either. How could the true Temple Priests not even be aware of Esther, nor Purim? Purim does not appear on any of their years of calendars either. The story was likely not even written until the time of Josephus. For those such as Geza Vermes who claim this may be *"purely accidental [Vermes, p.11, 22],"* they appear to lack the ability to conduct simple research. When the book is not found there, its Feast not kept there on actual calendars over years, and it never mentioned in any of the local writings, there is no accident. It was not there. When will these quacks refrain from their witchcraft?

The attempt to stretch so-labeled "Proto-Esther" fragments as Esther is obvious fraud when they represent Priest Ezra and the narrative of 1st Esdras from the same time *(see Torah Test in the Introduction from Vol. 1)*. We also address more recent supposed interpretations of these same fragments which remain 1st Esdras, and not a single fragment refers to Esther, Mordecai, nor Purim.

In the last texts to be included, such as those with the title 'proto-Esther', the connection is even more tenuous and remote. It is really literature which is parallel to, earlier than, or simultaneous with, the biblical text, but with no direct connection to it. – Dead Sea Scrolls Translated, Martinez, p. 218 [107]

Though Esther began to be included in the Greek Septuagint, no one has an index from the B.C. era to know whether it was originally included back then. There is no evidence to suggest it was and the Qumran scrolls prove it was not considered scripture at that time by the ones who mattered most. They are the only authority on this topic of Old Testament canonization, not Pharisees, nor Catholics, nor modern scholars. Many commentaries will attribute those from about one thousand years later as if nothing was added. Of course, they will apply the opposite standard to a false testing of the Apocrypha in hypocrisy.

In recent news in 2021, modern Israel's National Library was celebrating the return of one of the oldest copies of the Book of Esther. Megillah Esther is dated to about 1465 in origin and that is one of the oldest they have. Somehow, they could afford a Carbon-14 dating of this far newer text, but cannot seem to afford to scientifically assess Jubilees, First Enoch and other major finds in Qumran. The hypocrisy is staggering. They just guess on those and forget the scribal tradition of copying scrolls to maintain them.

REJECTED AS INSPIRED SCRIPTURE IN THE FIRST CENTURY:

Where is Esther recorded in the New Testament? The New Testament writers knew nothing of Esther either as she is never mentioned once, even in allusion. There are no quotes from her story and even the 1611 KJV anchors no New Testament passages to Esther in origin. Her supposed new Feast Day of Purim was never observed in the New Testament in any passage either. If Esther were inspired scripture especially establishing a supposed new Bible Feast, it would be there, and it is missing because the story is suspect.

REJECTED BY SOME EARLY RABBIS/PHARISEES AS INSPIRED SCRIPTURE – FIRST TO FOURTH CENTURY:

Many scholars will begin their data point with the so-called "Early Church Fathers" to attempt to determine what the original Canon was in antiquity. Though we also catalogue these, we do not apply them as authoritative because when they disagree with the only librarians of Bible Canon appointed by Moses, their opinions are worthless. Others heavily weigh the Pharisee Canon kept by the usurpers of the Temple known as the Pharisees and Sanhedrin. Their Canon is a changing of scripture, even Torah, according to Yahusha *(Mark 7)*. They were never legitimate replacements for the actual Temple Priests whom they exiled to Qumran/Bethabara along with the only authoritative Bible Canon. That is now uncovered in archaeology affirming this since 1947 or so.

Having noted that, there are some such as Melito who did not include Esther as Canon even in the second century A.D. Melito traveled to Palestine to learn the Pharisee Canon. Lost Tribes had been displaced prior to that and none remained in Israel. Therefore, his listing is impertinent since we found the archaeology of the actual Bible Canon of the exiled Temple Priests in Qumran/Bethabara. However, it is important to understand that Melito documented even the Pharisee Canon did not include Esther at that time in his observation. He was an eyewitness that some Pharisees refused Esther as Bible Canon in the second century. We have the true Canon catalogued today in the time capsule discovered in Qumran/Bethabara among the sons of Zadok. Pharisees do not matter in this regard. However, notice, even some Pharisees did not view Esther as Bible Canon then and it was not present in the Qumran community.

> *"The fact that the exact names, number and order of the Jewish Scriptures was a matter of dispute by the second century A.D. is clearly evident in the tradition of Melito, who traveled to Palestine in order to ascertain "the exact truth" on the matter. Though the concept of a twenty-two-book canon was well known, there was no agreement concerning its actual structure. It is interesting to note that Melito omits the book of Esther in his curious list, which does not arrange the books into a canon of twenty-two."*
> *– Journal of the Evangelical Theological Society 29/1 (March 1986) [122]*

Of course, this supposed scholar of the Bible continues to then, justify Melito's observation claiming, *"the omission of Esther may be accidental."* Indeed, a spaceship may have landed and distracted him in his travels as that is just as believable. He does not understand there is already a debate even among the Pharisees who do not all agree on Esther at this point in the second century. All indications point to Melito as a humble man who became a martyr for his cause even. He may not have been correct on everything in an era of confusion, but doubting his sincerity and accuracy in what he observed because it does not fit one's paradigm, is not scholarship, it is useless scoffing.

This scoffer then, assails Melito further in propagating *"the restoration of Esther to Melito's list."* If Melito was not clear in omitting Esther, which is not there, why would this scholar claim to change his words? This is not scholarship. It is witchcraft when one tells us something does not read as it very clearly and simply does, changing those words into the opposite. This same pretender of intellect repeats Melito's sincere words demonstrating he has no right to then question the sincerity of the observation at all. This critic is choosing not to read what is before him, but instead changes it to say the opposite to fit his paradigm. That is evil. There is no capacity for ambiguity in Melito's account.

> *"This fact is all the more striking in light of Melito's very words as addressed to "Onesimus his brother":*
> *"Since you have often requested, through the earnest desire that you cherish for the word [of God], that you might have a selection made for you from the Law and the Prophets, which has respect to our Saviour and the whole of our faith; and since moreover you have been desirous to obtain an accurate account of the ancient books, both as to their number and their order; I have taken pains to accomplish this, .. . making a journey therefore into the east [Palestine], and having arrived at the place where these things [i.e. scriptural events] were proclaimed and transacted, I there learned accurately the books of the Old Testament, which I here arrange and transmit to you."*
> *– Journal of the Evangelical Theological Society 29/1 (March 1986) [122]*

There is no doubt that some other church fathers such as Origen did include Esther in their lists of Canon while also including books later set aside and hidden as Apocrypha. These charlatans calling themselves scholars forget they applied that reason to justify Esther while applying the opposite logic to the Apocrypha to render those books as failures in a false test. The confusion begins with the Pharisees as Melito observed. Neither of them was using the accurate measure to determine Bible Canon because they were not the Biblical custodians of scripture, but pretenders and religious tyrants who had the wrong answers and still do. One Pharisee faction included Esther, and another did not. That is all these accounts testify and they remain incongruous. Qumran/Bethabara settles this with archaeology of the only Bible Canon that no one can dispute.

One will read one commentary after another that focus on the math of twenty-two Old Testament books recounting Josephus and the Council of Jamnia from 90 A.D. They are attempting to match the Pharisee Canon which they also manipulate in understanding. Though they claim Josephus included Esther, his list in Against Apion does not even mention Esther. It notes the timeframe of the Old Testament inaccurately as ending with Artaxerxes. However, Ezra, Nehemiah, and 1st and 2nd Esdras were written during that time, and by a prophet. Those were found represented in Qumran in Bible Canon *(see Torah Test, Vol. 1).* Esther was not. Such era does not specify Esther as scripture and Josephus states these were the writings of the Prophets. Since when was Esther a prophet? Can scholars even read? Absurd!

> *"But as to the time from the death of Moses, till the reign of Artaxerxes, King of Persia, who reigned after Xerxes, the Prophets, who were after Moses, wrote down what was done in their times, in thirteen books."*
> *– Flavius Josephus, Against Apion, 1.8*

In fact, Josephus quotes 1st Esdras' account of the Three Bodyguards though a little differently. This does not exist anywhere else, but clearly, he was aware of Ezra likely including all four books as one. He also discusses Ezra the prophet as he was aware of his writings as that is where you learn of Ezra. He seems to quote 1st Esdras 2 in paraphrase extensively. This is the language of 1st Esdras which he recounts that account from chapter 5:1-5 in "Antiquities of the Jews."

"...his name was Esdras. He was very skilful in the laws of Moses;"
"...reader of the laws of God...,"
"When Esdras had received this epistle, he was very joyful; and began to worship
God, and confessed, that He had been the cause of the King's great favour to him,"
"... what kindness he had for Esdras.."
– Flavius Josephus, Antiquities of the Jews, Book 11.5.1-5

Josephus also seemed to be aware of 2nd Esdras 13 as he records the Northern Kingdom Lost Tribes are beyond the Euphrates even in his time using the language of 2nd Esdras appearing to quote it without attribution. He was definitely aware of 1st and 2nd Esdras and one cannot use that era as belonging only to Esther.

*"...while an **immense number of the ten tribes never returned**; but, as he believed,*
*continued then **beyond Euphrates**: Chap. 5. § 2, 3. Of which multitude of Jews*
***beyond Euphrates** he speaks frequently elsewhere.*
– Flavius Josephus, Antiquities of the Jews, Book 11.5.2-3

Therefore, the assumption that Esther is one of the 13 Prophets is not only ludicrous, but Ezra is also one of those and he mentions Artaxerxes. There is no foundational basis to think that Esther was even included in Josephus' listing of the Pharisee Canon. It would not matter if he did include Esther, however, as Josephus was no authority on Bible Canon. He was a Pharisee and still, he does not include Esther as Canon in 90 A.D. He is the first to publish the Book of Esther that we can find. He seems to treat it as history, though it is not, but he does not claim it to be Bible Canon, nor inspired scripture that we find. Again, it does matter if he did.

With the accurate understanding that some of these books included others such as Ezra and Nehemiah as one book, which may have included 1st and 2nd Esdras as well, one can arrive at a vacillating enumeration. That number can change with the wind as it depends on the criteria used and the speculation is vast. This is no measure by which to test. These hypocrites live in this grey area where they can manipulate the data however they wish. This remains a puzzling paradigm because they are not aware of the gravity of the find at Qumran/Bethabara where the only authoritative Bible Canon was cherished and preserved. That settles this. Esther was not among that library and is not inspired Bible Canon.

However, the Pharisees themselves document what Melito observed. They did not agree since early times that Esther was inspired and they debated its canonicity. Though "Maimonides *(1135-1204)* ranked Esther immediately after the Pentateuch in importance... *[123]*," Esther was debated among the Jews *(Pharisees)* according to the Talmud even.

> *Moreover, according to the Talmud, some Jews continued to reject the book as late as the third or fourth century A.D. (Megilla 7a; Sanhédrin II). – The Biblical Archaeologist, 1986. p. 63. [111]*
>
> *"That such things troubled the sages of blessed memory is indicated by a discussion in the Babylonian Talmud tractate Megillah 7a – a tractate dedicated to the rites and rituals of Purim. In the discussion, we find the vestiges of a debate about whether Megillat Ester even should be included in the Tanach."*
> *– Rabbi Engelmayer, Jewish Standard, 2014 [112]*

Scholars are dishonest in claiming the Pharisees embraced this work of fiction. Some did not. Regardless, they do not even have a say, and still some deserted.

> *"For which cause the Jews still keep the forementioned days, and call them days of Phurim [or purim]." – Josephus: Antiquities of the Jews, Book 11.6.13*

REJECTED BY THE EARLY EKKLESIA AS INSPIRED SCRIPTURE – FIRST TO FOURTH CENTURY:

Though some did embrace Esther as Canon, some of the Early Church Fathers rejected it.

> *"In the first five centuries of the Christian Church, Christians were even more sharply divided over the question of Esther's canonicity, as can be seen from an examination of the Lists of Canonical Books according to various Church Fathers."*
> *– The Biblical Archaeologist, 1986. p. 63. [111]*

Though it matters not how many scholars rejected or accepted Esther, their ballot does not count. As the Qumran Temple Priests were the curators of Old Testament Canon, it is very revealing that Esther has remained so controversial for thousands of years. The reason is there is no debating this is an occult book that never belonged in Bibles. If its position was not so weak, the debate would have been over long ago. Though it continues to be forced into Bibles, it has never been authoritative to anyone who honestly and thoroughly researches it.

The book of Esther has maintained an uncomfortable position within the Christian canon throughout the history of the Church. A number of Eastern Church Fathers denied Esther canonical status, including: Athanasius, Gregory of Nazianzus, Theodore of Mopsuestia, and more. Furthermore, only one quotation of Esther by Chysostom can be found among the Antiochian Church Fathers.
– John Anthony Dunne, PhD, University of St Andrews. [124]

REJECTED AS INSPIRED SCRIPTURE BY MARTIN LUTHER IN THE 1500S:

Martin Luther, 1483-1546:
"I am so great an enemy to the second book of the Maccabees, and to Esther, that I wish they had not come to us at all, for they have too many heathen unnaturalities. The Jews much more esteemed the book of Esther than any of the prophets; though they were forbidden to read it before they had attained the age of thirty, by reason of the mystic matters it contains."
– "The Table Talk of Martin Luther." Ch. 24, pp. 27-28. [110]

In addition to an outright rebuke of Esther, Luther wished the Book of Esther was never considered as scripture. The question remains how could anyone calling themselves an expert of the Bible, even suggest it? His reasons could not be more profound as he defines Esther as an occult story, not remotely of Bible caliber. He accused the Jews *(Pharisees)* of elevating Esther above the Prophets which remains true and is a ludicrous proposition. According to him, the Jews well knew that Esther was too mature for children under the age of thirty and contains *"mystic matters."* No wonder the book never mentions Yahuah as it is not His Word. Though Martin Luther was no prophet, and certainly not a replacement for the ordained Temple Priests to the first century, his condemnation is judicious regarding this book.

1611 KJV ANCHORS NO NEW TESTAMENT TO ESTHER, ONLY 2 OLD TESTAMENT AS HISTORY:

The very revealing state of Esther in the 1611 Authorized King James is it has no affinity to scripture. It is not inspired scripture and never was. Though Esther sets forth a new Feast for Israel supposedly, the entire New Testament never mentions it, nor Esther by name nor content. There is not a single passage in the New Testament that originates in Esther according to the 1611 KJV. In fact, over the ten chapters of Esther, there are only two margin notes linked to any scripture at all *(1: 1:14 to Ezra.7.14, and 2:6, to 2Ki.24 15l; 2: Jer.24:1; and 2Chr. 36:10).* The state of Esther in evidence is quite sad and far from what should be considered scripture, even in 1611 when it was erroneously included as Bible Canon.

The first cross-reference is to Ezra as the two share the same era and they only share a history Esther copies likely from one of Ezra's four books but gets wrong. Ezra is accurate to history, and Esther is not. However, Ezra already migrated to Israel with the last wave of Southern Kingdom returnees in which Esther and Mordecai were absent, and evidently stayed when their people did not. That identifies them as unholy pagans, not even Hebrew, never fitting the Bible paradigm as those righteous returned to Israel before Esther even entered the palace. Israelites were not even there in Persia at that time to be persecuted and this whole story falls apart. However, this tells us Esther is quoting Ezra and not the other way around. With these two books at the same exact time, there should be a large number of similarities, and this becomes a glaring complication for Esther which shares only this one historic reference to the time period of Ezra. Ezra was a prophet. Esther was a consort who became queen. Ezra restored scripture and the Law in Temple worship. Esther reads as an occult account of Ishtar matching her story. This will become obvious. These two accounts should match and they do not.

The second cross reference is merely to passages that offer the historical narrative of the Southern Kingdom being taken captive into Babylon which Esther is copying but that does not make Esther scripture. In both cases, Esther is using those histories and then, grossly distorting them or there would be tons of anchors to scripture in Esther. This is critical for a book of this size labeled as Bible Canon and yet, it is extremely weak and outright occult in nature, even according to Martin Luther. Protestant scholars defend it with lame language of the uneducated. This is one of the largest frauds in modern times. An old fraud is still fraud today, just more odious.

REJECTED AS INSPIRED SCRIPTURE IN RECENT CENTURIES:

The quandary amongst scholars regarding Esther is really one of how on earth can they be so ignorant of the troubles with this book? This is not "textual criticism." These are facts that few in the modern church are addressing.

> *"As early as the eighteenth century, scholars began to doubt the veracity of many facts described in Esther, as they seemed to be contradictory to the customs of the Persians recorded by Herodotus, and pronounced them unhistorical." – The Jewish Quarterly Review, 1918, University of Pennsylvania. [113]*

Unfortunately, scholarship has kept this book they well know is not scripture, in our modern Bibles. They are allowing occult indoctrination that even the Jews were aware according to Martin Luther. Of course, this is not surprising as today, even some Christian Schools are lined with occult teachings that are unbiblical. We have exposed many in our research.

*"In our skeptical age, we should expect such a story to be held the most credible
of al the narratives of the Old Testament. Just the contrary has happened. None
among them is more discredited by modern exegetes, except a few, than this story.
The narrative is by some partly doubted, partly denied, by others denied altogether.
– The Jewish Quarterly Review, 1918, University of Pennsylvania. [113]*

When the book fails as Biblically inspired and offers no credible history, what
exactly is its value? It has none. This is why Luther rebuked Esther as an occult tale
he wished was not even published. The Bible is only dragged down by the inclusion
of such a false story. It never needed this embellished account.

ESTHER FAILS AS BIBLE HISTORY:

Ezra's four books were written of the same exact timing of Esther. Ezra was a
Prophet. Esther and whomever wrote it were not. It is evident the author of Esther
was not familiar with Persian history, nor that of the Southern Kingdom. In a
comparison with Ezra's writings, Esther fails.

> *Esther 1:1-2 KJV*
> *Now it came to pass in the **days of Ahasuerus**, (this is Ahasuerus which reigned,
> from India even unto Ethiopia, over an hundred and seven and twenty provinces:)
> That in those days, when the king Ahasuerus sat on the throne of his kingdom,
> which was in Shushan the palace,*

In Esther as well as Ezra's books, Ahasuerus is Artaxerxes, grandson of Darius I.
It was King Darius who moved the capitol to Susan. Artaxerxes reigned from about
464-424 B.C. Some claim it was Xerxes, his father and it really does not matter
which, this is still a major obstacles for Esther.

> *Esther 2:16 KJV*
> *So Esther was taken unto king Ahasuerus into his house royal in the tenth month,
> which is the month Tebeth, in the seventh year of his reign.*

This would calculate to about 457 B.C. One enormous challenge for the setting
of the Book of Esther is earlier in this same year, the final wave of the Lost Tribes
of Israel returned to Jerusalem with the Prophet Ezra. Anyone not returning and
remaining in Persia, was not following the Bible. For those scholars who attempt to
claim some may have had health issues, perhaps some did. However, if they could
only read Mordecai and Esther were healthy and that is a false straw man argument
to justify ignorance.

> *1st Esdras 8:6-7 KJVA*
> ***In the seventh year of the reign of king Artaxerxes, in the fifth month, (this was
> the king's seventh year) for they went from Babylon in the first day of the first***

> *month, and came to Yerusalem, according to the prosperous journey which Yahuah gave them. For Ezra had very great skill, so that he omitted nothing of the Law and Commandments of Yahuah, but taught all Israel the Ordinances and Judgments.*

In the Southern Kingdom's final return to Jerusalem, Ezra and the mass migration left Babylon in the first day of the first month in the seventh year of Artaxerxes' reign. As supposedly healthy Hebrews, Mordecai and Esther should not be in Persia at that point. If they were, assuming the story of Esther even true, they were pagans who did not worship Yahauh. They were hearty and there is no excuse for one remaining in captivity. Was Yahuah setting up a story for Zionist propaganda? He does not do so. Esther did not enter the palace until the tenth month of this same exact year. That is about nine months after her supposed people returned to their homeland without her and her uncle. Yahuah does not promote disobedience and those in rebellion do not encounter his intervention. Of course, in all fairness, the Book of Esther never says Yahuah is even involved in her story at all. This is not a Bible account. So, why is it in our modern Bibles?

> *Esther 3:8-11 KJV*
> *And **Haman said unto king Ahasuerus**, There is a certain people scattered abroad and dispersed among the people in all the provinces of thy kingdom; and their laws are diverse from all people; neither keep they the king's laws: therefore it is not for the king's profit to suffer them. If it please the king, let it be written that they may be **destroyed**: and I will pay ten thousand talents of silver to the hands of those that have the charge of the business, to bring it **into the king's treasuries**. And **the king took his ring from his hand**, and gave it **unto Haman** the son of Hammedatha the **Agagite**, the Jews' enemy. And the king said unto Haman, The silver is given to thee, the people also, to **do with them as it seemeth good to thee**.*

The anonymous author of Esther proves to be a fraud in this. He is unaware or does not care in sharing his fiction, Artaxerxes was a friend to the Southern Kingdom and was already very invested in their freedom fearing the reaction of their Elohim. He well knew whom they were as a people and he supported their return, their newly rebuilt Temple, and did nothing to hinder their return to the worship of their Yahuah. How is it that the writer of Esther did not know this?

> *1st Esdras 8:1-4 KJVA*
> *And after these things, when **Artaxerxes the king of the Persians reigned**, came **Ezra** the son of Seraiah, the son of Azariah, the son of Hilkiah, the son of Shallum, The son of Zadok, the son of Ahitub, the son of Amariah, the son of Uzzi, the son of Memeroth, the son of Zaraias, the son of Sauias, the son of Bukki, the son of Abishua, the son of Phineas, the son of Eleazar, the son of Aaron the chief Priest. This **Ezra** went up from Babylon, as a Scribe being very ready in the Law of Moses, that was given by the Elohim of Israel, And **the king did honor him: for he found grace in his sight in all his requests**.*

In fact, by royal decree in writing, Artaxerxes even encouraged Ezra to teach Yahuah's law to his people and others in his kingdom. Oops! How can the fiction writer of Esther not be aware that Artaxerxes already knew and embraced the Law of Yahuah in writing. However, we are supposed to believe just months later, he forgot about his decree and promise? There is no Persian history of a persecution of the Hebrews. They freed them. He and his friends even gave gifts to Yahuah of Israel. He embraced this Elohim at least in respect and would not have fallen for Haman's ridicule of the Law of Yahuah this king supported publicly. We are supposed to believe the king forgot his commitment and financial investment completely acting as if he did not even know anything of the Law of Yahuah. The king even financed the Temple, the worship of Yahuah and the implementation of His Law. He told Ezra in writing to *"do according to the will of your Elohim."* This is not an ignorant king unaware of the Law of Yahuah. It is one who embraced and supported it in application even. He did not then, turn around just after that and disremember because Haman offered him a bribe especially not when he feared Yahuah's power in response to such an action. Esther's story unravels as false.

1st Esdras 8:8-22 KJVA
*Now the copy of the Commission which was written from Artaxerxes the King, and came to **Ezra the priest and reader of the Law of Yahuah**, is this that follows. **King Artaxerxes unto Ezra the Priest and reader of the Law of Yahuah, send greeting.** Having determined to **deal graciously**, I have **given order**, that such of the **nation of the Yahudim**, and of the **Priests and Levites being within our Realm, as are willing and desirous, should go with you unto Yerusalem.** As many therefore as have a mind thereunto, let them depart with you, as it has seemed good both to me, and my seven friends the counselors, That they may **look unto the affairs of Yahudea and Yerusalem, agreeably to that which is in the Law of Yahuah. And carry the gifts unto Yahuah of Israel to Yerusalem, which I and my friends have vowed,** and all the **gold and silver** that in the country of Babylon can be found, **to Yahuah in Yerusalem,** With that also which is **given of the people, for the Temple of Yahuah their Elohim at Yerusalem:** and that silver and **gold may be collected for bullocks, rams and lambs,** and things thereunto appertaining, To the end that **they may offer sacrifices unto Yahuah, upon the Altar of Yahuah their Elohim,** which is in Yerusalem. And whatsoever you and your brethren will do with the silver and gold, that **do according to the will of your Elohim.** And the holy vessels of Yahuah which are given to you, for the use of the Temple of your Elohim which is in Yerusalem, you shall set before your Elohim in Yerusalem. **And whatsoever thing else you shall remember for the use of the Temple of your Elohim, you shall give it out of the king's treasury.** And I, king Artaxerxes, have also **commanded the keepers of the treasures in Syria and Phoenicia, that whatsoever Ezra the priest, and the reader of the law of the Most High Elohim shall send for, they should give to him with speed,** To the sum of an hundred talents of silver: likewise also of wheat even to an hundred cors, and an hundred pieces of wine, and other things in abundance. **Let all things be performed after the law of Elohim diligently unto the Most High Elohim,** that wrath come not upon the kingdom of the King and his sons. I command you also that you **require no tax, nor any other imposition of any***

of the Priests or Levites, or holy singers, or porters, or ministers of the temple, or of any that have doings in this temple, and that no man have authority to impose anything upon them. And you, Ezra, according to the wisdom of Elohim, ordain judges, and justices, that they may judge in all Syria and Phoenicia, all those that know the law of your Elohim, and those that know it not you shall teach. And whosoever shall transgress the law of your Elohim, and of the king, shall be punished diligently, whether it be by death or other punishment, by penalty of money, or by imprisonment. Then said Ezra the Scribe, Blessed be the only Yahuah Elohim of my fathers, who has put these things into the heart of the king, to glorify his house that is in Yerusalem;

Artaxerxes even opened his treasury to support Ezra as well as the treasuries of Syria and Phoenicia to Ezra, the *"reader of the law of the Most High Elohim"* and commanded they *"give to him with speed."* No wonder the Samaritans hated Judaea so much as well. This king wrote *"Let all things be performed after the law of Elohim diligently unto the Most High Elohim"* and warned that wrath would come on those who disobey. This is the opposite of Esther's fraud. How does a king who decreed *"no man have authority to impose anything upon them"* referring to the Priests and ministers of Yahuah of the Yahudim, then, ammend his thinking to the opposite due to a bribe when he gave so generously in backing the teaching and implementing of the Law of Yahuah. Money was no motivator to this king over the fear of Yahuah.

Artaxerxes believed so passionately in allowing Ezra to teach the Law of Yahuah, that he not only commanded Ezra to teach his own people, but all those in the region who did not know it as well including Gentiles and enemies. He, then, takes it a step further and demands that anyone not obeying the Law of Yahuah, will be punished. We are to believe he bowed instead to a little ridicule and scoffing accompanied by a bribe as if he never even knew the Law to which Haman referred. That is illiterate and Esther fails.

Who wrote Esther? Very clearly it was an enemy of Israel such as these counterfeit priests who lied to try to infiltrate them. Perhaps, Josephus authored it since he was first to publish the account it appears. This cult of imposters will eventually join with the Samaritans and conquer the Temple in Jerusalem in 165 B.C. They are the Pharisees or Farsees. This is Persian Priesthood in Samaria which will eventually control the Sanhedrin in the time of Messiah. They are not Hebrew and unaware of the actual history of Israel. However, in modern times, these Pharisees are viewed as the authorities of a history they do not know and a Bible they ignore.

1st Esdras 5:37-39 KJVA
Neither could they show their families, nor their stock, how they were of Israel: the sons of Delaiah, the sons of Tobiah, the sons of Nekoda, six hundred fifty and two. And of the Priests that usurped the office of the Priesthood, and were not found, the sons of Habaiah: the sons of Hakkoz, the sons of Yaddus, who married Agia one of the daughters of Barzillai, and was named after his name. And when the description of the kindred of these men was sought in the Register, and was not found, they were removed from executing the office of the Priesthood.

Not only is the content an issue for Esther regarding the timeline, but 1st Esdras also directly defines that ALL of the Yahudim taken into captivity were commanded to return and gather at the Temple. Mordecai and Esther were not there because they were fictional characters who never existed or at least were not Hebrews.

1st Esdras 9:3 KJVA
And there was a proclamation in all Yahudea and Yerusalem, to all them that were of the captivity, that they should be gathered together at Yerusalem:

ESTHER FAILS AS SECULAR HISTORY:

There is no argument for Esther as historically accurate even in the secular realm. Most scholars have abandoned even defending this position in this regard. Though we believe the king at the time of her story and Ezra's seems to have been Artaxerxes I, there are conflicting opinions where some believe it was his father and some his son. It really does not matter which but we will vet the wives of all three kings just to be safe. Is there a match to Vashti or Esther?

"Some other books of the Hebrew Bible also fairly cry out for all the help that the archaeologist can provide; but such is not the case with the Book of Esther. At least, not at first glance. Even though the Book of Esther claims to be a strictly historical account, ever since the work of J. S. Semler in 1773, that claim has increasingly been rejected, to the point that in the twentieth century only a handful of critical scholars have strenuously argued for the book's historical accuracy."
– The Bible Archaeologist, Vol. 38, p. 63. Gettysburg College, 1975[111]

In a paradigm that is supposed to be protecting true scripture and testing that which is not, modern scholarship has really failed us all regarding Esther. They know it fails but simply will not come to terms with it in most cases.

"As to the historical value of the foregoing data, opinions differ. Comparatively few modern scholars of note consider the narrative of Esther to rest on an historical foundation."
"The vast majority of modern expositors have reached the conclusion that the book is a piece of pure fiction, although some writers qualify their criticism by an attempt to treat it as a historical romance." – Jewish Encyclopedia [125]

Not only is the accusation that Artaxerxes would stand against the very Law of Yahuah he endorsed, funded and feared with passion, but Haman would also never have been given an open, blanket authority to kill, steal from and destroy the Hebrews especially keeping the very Law the king commanded. There is nothing in the Persian era that agrees with Esther's fiction. Certainly, one can see this writer trying to borrow from Daniel, but very poorly. Daniel tests as scripture and he was a prophet. Especially with the restoration of Bel & The Dragon, one can see why the movement against Daniel was so motivated. He killed their god.

In his case, hundreds of regional presidents forced the hand of Darius. Whereas Haman was an impertinent Agagite, or Amalekite really, whose people were taken captive just as Judaea was. He was not Daniel and this is unbelievable. He was a foreigner to Persia as well and it is unlikely he would have risen to such a level of power that he alone could convince the king to abolish the king's own decree and command the opposite with an Empire-wide authority Haman never earned. Nothing of substance about this narrative even rings as true really.

Esther 3:13 KJV
And the letters were sent by posts into all the king's provinces, to destroy, to kill, and to cause to perish, all Jews, both young and old, little children and women, in one day, even upon the thirteenth day of the twelfth month, which is the month Adar, and to take the spoil of them for a prey.

Also, Judaea was no longer dispersed already about nine months before Esther entered the king's palace. The ones in Egypt who were left also returned to Judaea. The fact that the writer of Esther did not know that those abiding by Yahuah's Laws also keep the laws of their respective nations is a foolish blunder. The notion they were still scattered after they no longer were, is an oversight no Hebrew would have made. This was not written by a Yahudim, nor one seemingly familiar with the time, the way Persia operated, nor Israel's migrations. It is illiterate!

"Hardly less striking is the description of the Jews by Haman as being "dispersed among the people in all provinces of thy kingdom" and as disobedient "to the king's laws" (iii. 8). This certainly applies more to the Greek than to the Persian period, in which the Diaspora had not yet begun and during which there is no record of rebellious tendencies on the part of the Jews against the royal authority."
– Jewish Encyclopedia [125]

The bribe of 10,000 talents of silver offered by Haman is far to embellished to be true. Though calculations vary, some scholars quantify this would be as much as $200 million today. Even if they are only 10% accurate in their estimates, that is far too much money for one who was a captive at the same time as the Southern Kingdom to amass. Haman's family would have lost likely everything in the conquest and displacement into Babylon. Agag was from just South of Israel and they were also taken captive at the same time. Though the amount may be enticing to any king, the offering is ludicrous fiction from an Agagite former captive to gain permission to carry out an ethnic cleansing of Persian citizens especially empire wide. The writer forgot that Jerusalem remained inside of the Persian Empire which is described in his account from Ethiopia to India. After Darius saw the completion of the Jerusalem Temple with his support, his son and grandson continued to accommodate. However, we are led to believe they turned against the Temple, its Law and its people which simply never happened. If it did, Persian history would agree, and it does not.

In the end, Haman is exposed and then, hanged for his crime (7:10). If the account ended there, it would yet more credible. It did not and it goes way too far. Additionally, Esther and her people would not have been given the Empire-wide permission to massacre their enemies in one day either especially not from Ethiopia to India. No Persian records attest this, and they would if it were true. This is a fairy tale in scope. This is standard Pharisee to embellish in such an unimaginable way and think that people will accept it. Esther smells of another Jewish fable as Paul warned us against such leaven *(1 Tim. 1:4, 1:14)*. Paul never said not to learn of accurate lineages especially of the Bible. He spoke against the false Pharisee claims in bloodlines. Peter addressed the same as "cunningly devised fables *(2 Pet. 1:16)*." Esther is not even cunning as it is outrageous that any scholar could ever even consider it as remotely accurate.

Esther 8:11 KJV
Wherein the king granted the Jews which were in every city to gather themselves together, and to stand for their life, to destroy, to slay, and to cause to perish, all the power of the people and province that would assault them, both little ones and women, and to take the spoil of them for a prey,

Such a massacre would be a part of Persian record and there is nothing to support this in the historic annals. They have no need to cover it up because they did not do it. The Jews did supposedly killing 75,000 in one day *(9:16)*. So, the king traded one evil ethnic cleansing for another. This is a whopper of a prevarication.

There is no history to support that Persia ever had a Queen Esther in that era, certainly not one of Jewish lineage. Esther supposedly concealed her identity as a Jewess, yet was known to be from the household of Mordecai, a known Jew. She was a Queen and they check such things. There was no Queen Vashti whom was removed which never happened. During that time there was a Persian queen who remained all the way to her son's reign and this proves a work of stupid fabrication. It matters not whom has been gullible enough to buy this yarn of tales. Even the Jewish Encyclopedia admits this. There is no reconciling this text to the truth.

Finally, in this connection, the author's knowledge of Persian customs is not in keeping with contemporary records. The chief conflicting points are as follows: (a) Mordecai was permitted free access to his cousin in the harem, a state of affairs wholly at variance with Oriental usage, both ancient and modern. (b) The queen could not send a message to her own husband (!). (c) The division of the empire into 127 provinces contrasts strangely with the twenty historical Persian satrapies. (d) The fact that Haman tolerated for a long time Mordecai's refusal to do obeisance is hardly in accordance with the customs of the East. Any native venturing to stand in the presence of a Turkish grand vizier would certainly be severely dealt with without delay. (e) This very refusal of Mordecai to prostrate himself belongs rather to the Greek than to the earlier Oriental period, when such an act would have involved no personal degradation (compare Gen. xxiii. 7, xxxiii. 3; Herodotus, vii. 136). (f) Most of the proper names in Esther which are given as Persian appear to be rather of Semitic than of Iranian origin, in spite of Oppert's attempt to explain many of them from the Persian (compare, however, Scheftelowitz, "Arisches im Alten Testament," 1901, i.). – Jewish Encyclopedia [125]

Very close to the era of Esther, we have histories from Plutarch, Herodotus, etc. and neither leaves room for a Jewess to be Queen whether alone one who won a beauty contest. Even if Esther would someone become one of multiple wives, there is nothing in history to corroborate this. For those who believe Xerxes was the Ahasuerus of this story, this fails. He was married to the same woman who was still around in the days of his son's reign. That could not be Vashti, who was removed from the palace, nor Esther.

When thinking of kings, it would not be rare to find multiple wives as well as mistresses. However, when one enters that thinking in regard to Esther, they are ignoring the story to create a position the story does not allow. The king was married to Vashti who refused him, so he had her removed from the palace. This is already a major dilemma for Esther because neither of these three kings has any such history. Then, that king would have had to abolish the ritual of marrying Persian royalty, hosted a beauty contest which no history agrees, and then, choose a foreign wife from his concubines as Vashti's replacement. This would be affirmed.

Artaxerxes 1 was married to a native Persian named Damaspia. Though there is not a great abundance of information available on her, this was preserved by Ctesias *[130]*. She died, still Queen, on the same day as Artaxerxes I. If Ahasuerus was somehow his father, Xerxes I, this is even worse for Esther. Herodotus documents he was married to Amestris, the native Persian daughter of his commander *(Herodotus 7.61.2)*. She was the mother of Artaxerxes I and died at an old age, towards the end of Artaxerxes' reign *(Ctesias, fragment 14) [130]*. She remained in the palace the entire time and could not be Vashti, nor Esther. Finally, if Xerxes II, son of Artaxerxes I was Ahasuerus, this also fails for the Book of Esther. His Queen was also native Persian royalty as well. They were married before Xerxes II became king. Though there was some drama along the way, she was not removed from the palace as Vashti and cannot be Esther. Esther fails the test of history.

"Stateira, daughter of Hydarnes, descended from one of the men who had put Darius I on the throne (DB 4.84-85: Vidarna), and sister of (inter aliis) Tissaphernes and Terituchmes (Ctesias, 53-55)." [130]

Other unexplained issues render Esther erroneous such as a 180-day feast that appears in no Persian history *(1:1-3)*. Queen Vashti refused the king which did not and would not happen *(1:12)*. Not only did she never exist, someone else was Queen during that time and it was not Esther either. There is no record of a royal decree to the men of the empire to be *"master of his own home (1:22)."* That would not be necessary in the Middle Eastern culture in that age. Supposedly, these letters were sent out in ALL the languages of the empire which is incredibly inept *(1:22; 3:12; 8:9)*. They would write such a decree in the official language of the empire in either Persian or perhaps Aramaic and certainly not all languages. This fiction writer who authored this made up his own paradigm on many levels. He was very lax.

Persian kings did not hold beauty pageants to choose a Queen. They chose from royal families of Persian and not foreigners *(2:1-4, 2:17)*. This is nonsense. There is no evidence a concubine prepared for an entire year for one night with the king *(2:12)*. Though Daniel was an alien appointed a leader, he earned his position and he was one of many leaders. However, for Mordecai to be promoted from gate guard to prime minister is falsity *(3:1; 8:2; 10:3)*. In 5:14, they made new gallows of 50 cubits high. If Answers In Genesis is correct, a Babylonian cubit is 19.8 inches *(50.3 cm)*, which means these were over 80 feet tall *(25+ m)*. A child can write more believable fiction. If we are understanding this timeline correctly, Haman met with the king in the twelfth month, the decree was written and signed in the first month, and yet, people were given the order to kill all Jews on the thirteenth of the twelfth month. Does this not seem ridiculous that an ethnic cleansing was preplanned almost a year in advance to occur on only one day*(3:8-15)*? It really appears this idiot who wrote this did not even think through the details at all. The king allowed 500 murders by the hands of the Jews in his own palace with no hesitation *(9:11-15)*. Could this be any more amateur?

Finally, Mordecai was supposedly taken into captivity by Nebuchadnezzar with Jeconiah king of Judah *(2:5-6)*. That is a very specific date on March 15-16th, 597 B.C. Esther's story begins in 457 B.C. when Mordecai would be about 140 years old, yet not only was he still living, but he also worked as a guard at the gate at 140? Even if this were Xerxes instead of Artaxerxes, he would still be over 100. In their attempt to puff up the resume of Mordecai, they very stupidly made him over 100 years old at the time of Esther's story. Now, that is stupid, not scholarship. Many of the same scholars who defend Esther for this, attack Tobit which does not actually possess such conflicts. They just cannot read. This is hypocrisy.

These are just some of the irreconcilable conflicts in Esther. History and the Bible are not the only challenges as it matches neither. The story is saturated in Pharisee leaven as an obvious contrived narrative forced down our throats by dunderhead scholars who are incapable of simple testing. Textual criticism becomes so strict with the Apocrypha and other books found in Qumran but not in the modern Canon. However, with Esther, these scholars prove dishonest in their dealings, and they should not be handling scripture.

The different versions of Esther also vary significantly. Haman is an Agagite or Amalekite in one, a Macedonian in another, and Bougaion *(Greek?)* in another. This is not a minor difference, and all are foreigners who would not have had such a prominent position in the Persian government. Of course, there is also the outrageous embellishment of the insane amount of silver he supposedly gave.

THE OCCULT ROOTS OF THE BOOK OF ESTHER:

It is not a new observation that Esther has elements of the occult story of the goddess Ishtar. It is simply ignored by pastors and scholars who have failed to devote any research to this topic. First, the name of Esther is suspect.

> *"Name of the chief character in the Book of Esther, derived, according to some authorities, from the Persian "stara" (star); but regarded by others as a modification of "Ishtar," the name of the Babylonian goddess"* – Jewish Encyclopedia [125]

Ishtar, also known as Astarte, Ashtaroth and similar, is the goddess of fertility in the Persian and Babylonian regions. She is known for the Star of Ishtar, or East Star. The Persian reference is the same. In fact, Strong's Concordance defines this the same.

> אסתר *:'estēr, es-tare'; of Persian derivation; Esther = "star." (Strong's H635)*
> *Brown-Driver-Briggs: Esther (Persian: stâra, star)*

Notice how, though the spelling is different, this word has the same meaning as the false goddess, Ashtaroth *(Ashtar)* rebuked in scripture many times. Certainly, these names have the same derivative and lead to Esther being named after an occult goddess indeed. That is no coincidence. Esther was a consort to the king just as Ishtar was a consort to the gods. Esther won a beauty pageant, and Ishtar is known for great beauty as well. Esther used her looks to gain favor as did Ishtar. In the end, Esther becomes a catalyst for war ethnically cleansing her enemies just as Ishtar is the goddess of war as well. In Joshua 12:4 the remnant of the giants or Nephilim, gathered at a place named for the goddess Ashtaroth as this is part of their worship system, not the Bible's. The giant Og of Bashan dwelled in that same city likely naming it in his Nephilim lore.

> עשתרות: *'Ashtârôwth, ash-taw-roth'; or* עשתרת: *'Ashtârôth; plural of H6251; Ashtaroth, the name of a Sidonian deity (Strong's H6252)*

Some think that somehow because Esther had the name in origin of Hadassah mentioned one time, and never again in all of scripture, that this redeems her as Hebrew. The fact is this name is just as occult in origin as Esther is. Even if it was Hebrew, it would not redeem the fictional story. Hadassah is not a name of Hebrew origin. The story says she was a Jewish virgin but Ishtar/Isis also claimed to have a virgin pregnancy. It is close to the Babylonian Sumerogram of "aššatum" meaning "wife" or "bride" *[126]*. Strong's suggests this word originates in the Hebrew word for myrtle tree, hadas. However, these words are not Hebrew in origin and the myrtle is a known occult symbol tied to Ishtar. Hadas, or myrtle is of uncertain derivation. It is not likely Hebrew, but Babylonian in origin. It does not make her Hebrew regardless. Her customs would and they certainly do not. Her Elohim would and she never mentions Him in her entire narrative. In Yemeni Arabic, this is the word for *"springs"* as in *"growing rapidly"* [Gesenius], another expression for fertility.

הדסה: *Hădaççâh, hăḏasâ; feminine of H1918; Hadassah (or Esther):–Hadassah. Strong's H1919.*

הדס: *hădaç: hăḏas: of uncertain derivation; the myrtle:–myrtle (tree).: Strong's H1918.*

However, even in the context of the myrtle tree, this is not a good representation. In the occult realm, the myrtle tree is a symbol for *"fertility [127]"* or the fertility goddess Ishtar, has *"star-shaped flowers [127]"* or representing Ishtar's star, and *"...is often trimmed to look like a fuzzy bowling ball balancing on top of a long stem or a pyramid [127]"* or the eye of Horus/Tammuz in the same paradigm of Ishtar/Isis. This goes even deeper when one realizes that Esther and Hadassah were selected to embody that same occult paradigm. Esther was a *"virgin [127]"* and this plant symbolizes such. Also, continuing in the Ishtar paradigm as she is the goddess of *"love [127]"* as well, that is yet another meaning.

> *The plant has many, layered meanings—youth, virginity (before marriage), fertility, innocence, immortality, fidelity—but, above all, love. – Smithsonian [127]*

This plant represents the ancient goddess in other occult cultures. It is also the wedding flower just as it always has been in its Sumerian/Babylonian origin.

> *The Greeks and Romans knew the plant as Myrtos and Myrtus and it was closely associated with the goddesses Demeter and Aphrodite. Venus is described by Ovid as emerging from the sea on her half-shell holding a sprig of myrtle. The wonderfully scented plant was considered an aphrodisiac, known to appear in wedding crowns for either the bride or the groom. – Smithsonian [127]*

Thanks to the Catholic perversion of Mary, this symbol for female sexuality was transferred from Ishtar to Mary, the modern version of their ancient goddess. The mother of Yahusha would be disgusted. Yahuah always rejects such mixing. Long before this was rebranded as a tradition of the false Virgin Mary, rather than the righteous mother of Yahusha, it was the ancient goddess of fertility whose names and attributes the Catholics imprint onto Mary erroneously.

> *In Christianity, losing its Greco-Roman association with female sexuality, myrtle came to be an emblematic symbol of the purity of the Virgin Mary. – Smithsonian [127]*

When Martin Luther detected occult influences in the story of Esther, he unfortunately does not elaborate on which accounts may be sources. The scholarly paradigm generally demands that, and it is not necessary. They must first prove the story compared to scripture could even be considered Canon, and they cannot. Whomever compiled the Book of Esther appears to have included Babylonian lore indeed and Luther's point was accurate. Certainly, the names Esther and Hadassah both lead to Ishtar in association and Mordecai is too like the Sumerian god Marduk. The debate rages back and forth in scholarship when the real point is, Esther is not inspired scripture, and no one can prove it is. The fact that such a debate exists with such monumental conflicts in the text, is already problematic for the book's canonicity. The same argue against books of the Apocrypha in hypocrisy as they forget the same points they attempt, are even worse for this Book of Esther. It has never belonged in the Bible with any credibility.

When a fraudulent author borrows from Nephilim-inspired histories, it is no surprise they may not copy it in exactness. It would require profound stupidity to attempt to pass it off as Bible then. Of course, there are additions and changes but that as well is the definition of leaven that Pharisees add even to scripture. No one needs to prove the leaven is not there in order to notice this book is a contrived story loaded with what is clearly not a Bible message. The forced, polarizing focus on race sounds more like a modern lawyer for the ACLU manipulating what they call racism to justify an even worse racism. Esther's ethnic cleansing had no backing from Yahuah who is not even included in the story. For a Bible scholar to refer to it as Bible, requires blinders.

There are especially many similarities between the Enuma Elish which the author of Esther appears to have borrowed. It really does not matter whom agrees with that or not as there is much more evidence against this book as Canon. Esther is not the Occult Creation Myth as some demand to make such connection. The triumph of Marduk rings so familiar to the story of Mordecai, it is rather difficult to ignore especially the name even. However, Additions to Esther most certainly loans some of that content even adding to the story to round out its occult influence. Regardless, we know for certain, the writer of the Book of Esther was no prophet, nor even a Hebrew believer. The following chart is based on a scholarly compilation of this correlation. Of course, if one ignored this chart, Esther still fails miserably but this is a route that efficient analysis must consider.

BOOK OF ESTHER   vs.   ENUMA ELISH

THE EVIL SCHEME:

Haman irritated by "different rules" for the Jews. 3:8	Apsu must irradicate younger gods because their "way has become painful" 1:35
Haman must ethnically cleanse the innocent group. 3:6	Apsu must destroy the innocent group 1:39
Mordecai learns of Haman's plot against his people. 3:12	Apsu's scheme becomes known to his innocent victims. 1:55–7
Mordecai's refusal to bow before Haman leads to a response to eradicate his people. 3:2-15	The younger gods respond in rebellion killing Apsu. Tiamat decides to eradicate all. 1:69
Mordecai 'rent his clothes and puts on sackcloth and ashes.' 4:1	Anshar 'struck his thigh and bit his lip.' 2:49-50
The people of Susa, upon hearing Haman's plan expressed 'startled dismay.' 3:15	When learning the news, the gods 'were stunned, they sat down in silence.' 1:58

THE DEFENSE STRATEGY:

Fate of the Jews is reversed and they slay their enemies instead. 9:5	The gods slated to be eradicated turn the narrative and slay their enemies instead after first seeking peaceful resolution. 4:97
Mordecai sends Esther to plead for mercy before a dangerous king. 4:8	The Anunnaki plead before Tiamat. 2:72
Esther was concerned that approaching the king was considered too dangerous. 4:11-13	The intermediary complains that approaching Tiamat was too dangerous. 2:80–2, 2:90–1

THE TRIUMPH:

Haman and his 10 sons are hanged and killed. Eleven total. 7:10, 9:7-10, 9:14	Eleven evil monsters are captured, tied up and killed. 4:115–8, 4:120, 6:31
Mordecai was 'made great... and exalted, and set his seat above all princes.' 3:1	From obscurity, Qingu was 'exalted... in their midst, she made him great.' 1:147
The king 'removed his (signet) ring from his hand and gave it to Haman...' 3: 10	Tiamat presented Qingu with the 'tablet of destinies', saying 'Your command shall always be greatest, over all the Anunna-gods' 1:156–7
Shortly after being empowered, Haman resolves to destroy the Jews and famously casts lots to determine the timing. 3:6-7	When Qingu receives this power, he and Tiamat immediately 'ordained destinies for his divine children.' 1:160

Charting of the data from "The Book of Esther and the "Enūma Elish."– Silverstein. Bulletin of the School of Oriental and African Studies, University of London, Vol. 69, No. 2 (2006). [123]

ESTHER'S ABSENCE OF YHWH:

The Book of Esther has major protests as inspired when it fails to include the name of YHWH even once. She never mentions Yahuah and never prays to Him. She fasted, but that is a pagan custom and not to Yahuah, never worships Him, and never thanks Him in the entire narrative even once. Those claiming that the name of YHWH was suppressed in Persia are illiterate, not scholars. In 1st and 2nd Esdras, the Prophet Ezra used Yahuah's name hundreds of times. He still lived in the Persian Empire when he was in Babylon and when he and the final migration of Lost Tribes returned to Jerusalem.

Ezra was commissioned by this same king as Ether's story to teach the Law of Yahuah. This was written in the King's mandate in his words in which the King Artaxerxes himself wrote the name of YHWH nine times *(1 Esd. 8:8-15)*. It appears Ezra, also, spoke Yahuah's name to king Artaxerxes *(1 Esd. 8:25)*. Even in Esther's fairy tale, the Jews were vindicated and there remained no more reason to hide the name of YHWH. That is nonsense. Later record of the story would include it.

In addition, Artaxerxes' decree included the title *"Most High Elohim"* for Ezra's God twice *(1 Esd. 8:19, 21)*. He wrote that or at least certified it none-the-less. Again, this is the same period in which Esther entered the palace. There was no aversion towards pronouncing and writing the name of YHWH, nor His titles. What is evident, is the writer of Esther is a fraud who was not a prophet, nor even a believer, and they do not get to write something called inspired scripture. Wake up scholars and educate yourselves. This is very damning to Esther's canonization which should never have occurred. The fact the church has also lost the name of YHWH used over 6,800 times in the Hebrew Old Testament contributes to this ignorance.

> *"As to this whole book of Esther in the present Hebrew copy, it is so very imperfect, in a case where the providence of God was so very remarkable, and the Septuagint and Josephus have so much of religion, that it has not so much as the name of God once in it; and 'tis hard to say who made that epitome which the Masoretes have given us for the genuine book it self. No religious Jews could well be the authors of it: whose education obliged them to have a constant regard to God, and whatsoever related to his worship: nor do we know that there ever was so imperfect a copy of it in the world, till after the days of Barchocab, in the second century."*
> *– Flavius Josephus: Antiquities of the Jews, Book 11.6, Footnote 25*

ADDITIONS TO FIX ESTHER IN THE 1611 KING JAMES APOCRYPHA:

In order to attempt to redeem this fraudulent occult tale of Esther, someone at a later date, added to the already failed narrative. It becomes obvious by the first opening verse of what is termed to be, but never was historically, Esther 10:4. The KJV completes the canonized book of Esther at 10:3 and separates these out as

"Additions to Esther." Since the book never mentions Elohim or God, this addresses that shortcoming immediately with tailored leaven.

Additions To Esther 1:1 KJVA (1611) (Labeled as 10:4 in fraud)
Then Mardocheus saide, God hath done these things.

Marduk, as the 1611 laughably renders the name as *"Mardocheus"* failed to mention Elohim in any previous verse yet, miraculously this addition addresses what the entire story does not right from the first words. It is a clear attempt in fraud to pad the debate on the failed side demonstrating just how weak the position has always been. Elohim is not there in the first 10 Chapters of origin even once. Now, it becomes a theme. This is very simple to observe and expose. The translators of the KJV at least had the sense to keep it separate recognizing it is a later augmentation, and not part of the original work. It would not matter because Esther has no historicity as legitimate Old Testament Canon because it is the only book of that modern Canon not found in Qumran.

In symbolism, he has a dream in which Esther again matched the fertility goddess being identified as a *"river"* with much *"sun"* and *"light (Add. 1:3, or 10:6 in KJVA)."* That leads to a fertile environment. Haman, is now rendered as *"Aman"* which oddly is similar to the Hebrew spelling of Egypt's false god, Amun *(Jer. 46:25, Nah. 3:8)* which is never Amen in Hebrew, though some very stupid scholars have attempted such.

Haman and Mordecai are dragons in this dream. Oddly, dragons are never considered a good symbol in the bible. It is as if this writer, as well, never even read it. Even satan is identified as a dragon *(Rev. 12:3-17, 13:2, 4, 11, 16:13, 20:2)*. Essentially, the equation of the two supposed opposites as both dragons is also flawed writing though we find that Haman and Mordecai are both representatives of evil dragons indeed. Both wanted to ethnically cleanse a people. This is a story of mass murder that is not truly justified ethically. The day of Purim is so commanded, not by Yahuah, but by Mordecai and is missing from every Bible text during and after that era including Ezra written of the same time.

Very oddly, Chapter 2 of Additions *(11:1 KJVA)* attributes that one named Dositheus brought the Epistle of Purim to Ptolemy's son. It invokes Cleopatra who ruled in 51-30 B.C. proving these additions as centuries later and fraud. Even worse, this Dositheus is recorded as a Samaritan Gnostic from the synagogue of satan, who claimed to be a Levite priest erroneously. Oops! We do not believe that to be a coincidence. The timeline is mixed up very poorly in these characters and far later than the story of Esther. It is not the Bible practice to add to a story 500 years later. Those scholars that accuse the Temple Priests of that, are ignorant of whom they were, and apply Pharisee doctrine in place of Biblical fact.

It appears the author of this trash, had no idea even of the story of Esther as in 2:2, they tell us Mordecai served in the court of the Artaxerxes the great in his second year of reign. That did not happen for more than a decade in the narrative of Esther causing this "addition" to offer corrupt information. Esther did not even enter the palace until the seventh year of his reign *(2:16)*.

In 2:5 *(11:5 KJV)*, the dream unfolds as a further match to the Enuma Elish beginning with *"thunder and earthquakes and uproar." "Two great dragons came forth ready to fight (2:6 or 11:6 KJV)"* which is a match to Tiamat, the dragon of the sea. Marduk is noted to have a great dragon whom Daniel slayed. One could not fabricate any more of an obvious occult tale. In verse 7, it claims *"all nations"* would battle with the *"righteous people."* However, Israel is not known as righteous in this period. That is why they had to experience exile in captivity for about seventy years. All nations were not against them either. Right from the Tiamat legend of the Enuma Elish, verse 8 invokes *"day of darknesse and obscurity: tribulation, and anguish, affliction, and great vproare vpon the earth."* This is where many scholars have followed the Occult Creation Myth against the Bible and suggest the darkness in Genesis 1:2 was somehow evil and even the Pharisees *(modern Rabbis)* insert that doctrine in error.

Then, Esther is invoked as the *"little fountain"* from whom *"was made a great flood (2:10 or 11:10 KJVA)."* That is the Rivers from Eden from Job 28 and never Esther who did not even exist. Such an equation is blasphemy. It elevates her to a goddess status and infuses the Enuma Elish even further now including the Occult Creation Myth they left out in the original Esther. Somehow, they think we would never figure this out and modern scholars are too blinded to do so. Also, this chapter changes the story claiming Haman's motive for punishing Mordecai was different because he exposed the two Eunuchs who plotted against the king's life. That is an extraneous addition seen often in Pharisee leaven.

In the next chapter, the king's decree is also embellished. It appears at this point; he now claims the Jews were responsible for chaos disturbing the peace which he is renewing. That is new. Then, he goes way too far in praising Haman which is ridiculous. The Jews are now categorized as terrorists as *"malicious people."* That is a different story and a change that proves these additions as fraud. Hebrew believers do not despise the laws of governments either. The Jews are blamed in the same fashion as we read propaganda about Hitler, for impeding the *"uniting of our kingdoms (4:4 or 13:4 KJVA)."*

In 4:8 *(13:8 KJVA)*, Mordecai finally prays to YHWH and this is the first time that the name of Yahuah appears in Esther in additions attempting to salvage it. Then, in 5:1 *(14:1 KJVA)*, Esther then, seeks YHWH which she never did in the original story. She also puts on clothes of mourning also not found in the original narrative, but the Mordecai did. She prays to YHWH which never happened *(5:3 or 14:3 KJVA)*. Once again, in this comedy, Esther is claiming to be in captivity still *(5:8 or 14:8 KJVA)* after the final wave of Lost Tribes already returned to Jerusalem with Ezra. This writer was insanely ignorant of the Bible. She accuses Persians of wanting to *"quench the glory of thy house (the Temple), and of thine Altar (5:9 or 14:9 KJVA)."* Though construction was halted long before Esther, the Temple was reconstructed and operating by her time with Persia's overwhelming blessing. This is even more ludicrous as it is Persia who assisted financially and with full authority, the rebuilding of the Second Temple. The original Esther does not make such a claim, and this is fallacious.

It appears Esther then prays to Yahauh to kill Haman *(5:13 or 14:13 KJVA)* which never happened and is not a Biblical prayer. She claims to be righteous in this prayer *(5:15 or 14:15 KJVA)* but there is a massive obstacle with that claim. Righteous Hebrews returned to Jerusalem to worship Yahuah at His Temple. Esther did not and this is a lie. Esther was a concubine who slept with a *"heathen" (5:15 or 14:15 KJVA)* king whom she claimed to abhor now, yet she had the option to return to her homeland to worship Yahuah at His Temple. She chose the way of the heathen, and this is a lie. When one lies to Yahuah in a prayer, let us not call that inspired scripture. She claims in this prayer to hate being Queen *(5:16 or 14:16 KJVA)* yet she never had to be. She was not forced. She chose such position and power above relationship with Yahuah or she would have returned with the other Lost Tribes. This is fraud. Esther claims she does not wear her crown in private which is a very stupid way to frame her protest and uprightness. Yahuah's prophets and vessels don't just serve Him in private. That demonstrates again this writer has likely never even read the Bible and does not understand it. He also did not even understand that this is not even a point as many royals do not wear their crowns in private. They are uncomfortable to wear and the purpose is public. How stupid.

In further Pharisee embellishment, Esther now faints, and that act changes the heart of the king *(6:8 or 15:8 KJVA)*. She, then, tells him she saw a vision of the king as an Angel of Elohim which adds even more to the narrative and is a blasphemous lie of unbiblical nature.

Conflicting with the version of Esther in the 1611 KJV, Haman is now listed as Macedonian. Agagites are from South of Israel from the Amalekite peoples, not Macedonia in Europe. This author is illiterate of the Bible and history. In verse 14, the king accuses Haman of a conspiracy to translate *"the kingdom of the Persians to the Macedonians."* This is out of time and place written by one who clearly authored this after the Greek conquest who was to stupid to realize it. He now declares the Jews live by the laws of Persia, yet somehow was incapable of conducting a little research to determine such before condemning an entire race to death. He now, miraculously remembers the language he used with Ezra calling Yahuah the Most High and most mighty living Elohim *(6:16 or 6:16 KJVA)*. He not only decrees Purim, but now ramps up the language stating: *"You shall therefore among your solemne feasts keepe it an high day with all feasting."* Either way, Yahuah did not and it is not found anywhere in Persian history, nor in the Bible in this era nor beyond. These fraud additions end on this ludicrous note:

Additions to Esther, 1611 KJVA
"Therefore euery citie and countrey whatsoeuer, which shall not doe according to these things, shall bee destroyed without mercy, with fire and sword, and shall be made not onely vnpassable for men, but also most hatefull to wilde beasts and foules for euer."

Has there ever been a king so dull that they would issue an erroneous decree without bothering to research something they already knew committing to the opposite just before? They turn against the promise to Ezra and enter an agreement with Haman without bothering to verify anything? Then, after they realize they erred, and it is the king who is ultimately responsible here, they turn around again and change the story. That is bad enough and the original narrative of Esther is different. However, now this motley fool threatens entire cities and nations that he will ethnically cleanse them if they do not ethnically cleanse Haman's race to protect Esther's race who he had already decreed to ethnically cleanse prior. One would have to be insane to refer to themselves as academic on any level to embrace this rubbish as anything but the occult nonsense it is.

It is always laughable that Pharisee scholars attempt a dating of a text based on writing style as if anyone perpetrating fraud could not copy such style from earlier times. That is illiterate. Again, with other books labeled "Apocrypha" they demand one produce actual fragments dated to the Bible era which the Dead Sea Scrolls largely materialized for many such texts. However, they do not apply this to Additions to Esther, nor the Book of Esther. They ignore the failure of Esther and its additions as if that does not matter, while using the same to discount most of the Apocryphal books which were either present or present by historic association in Qumran/Bethabara. It is a double standard from a group of double-minded men who are not honest in this regard. Theirs is no test. It is gymnastics which lead to their foredrawn conclusion maintaining a paradigm of ignorance.

Also published in 1560, the Geneva Bible included the same books labeled Apocrypha as the 1611 King James Version. Baruch includes Letter of Jeremiah and these additions to Esther appear there as well. Esther is already considered Canon at that point as well but never should have been. Additions to Esther is separated. That is not scholarly treatment. Additions never belonged as they conflict with Esther even. Esther does not belong either as it disagrees with the Bible and is not endorsed as part of it in any credible way. It is time scholars do their job and remove this outlandish occult infiltration from our Bibles. Every Bible that is printed with Esther is tainted and marginalized. The rest of the modern Old Testament Canon vets as inspired scripture and other books are missing which must be tested and considered. Scholarship refuses to conduct such research. We must prove all things.

One would think we would not have to even enter this line of research for the Bible as in thousands of year, this should have already been tested and proven. It has not been by the paradigm of scholarship. These scoffers are as Stalin termed "useful idiots" to the occult Pharisee realm of Stoics. They not only rest on Esther as scripture without testing, they reject books that test as inspired scripture vehemently. They are easily offended by the truth and express outrage when they are too inept to research their own narratives and examine them for lies. We wish this were not so easy to unravel and so obvious in pure research. In these days of increasing knowledge, this will be restored.

Though attributed to Hitler, this deceptive doctrine has always been an anchor of the Pharisee party from whom this thinking really originates. Today, we call this Rabbinic Judaism, and it continues to attack Yahusha and His Word. Catholic scholars speak of hatred of all things Jewish yet, then, treat these Pharisees as credible regarding Bible Canon, which they have never been. The Protestant Church rails against Catholics yet, also follows their foundation as well as the Pharisees in this same paradigm. They will even argue with the Early Church Fathers who were early infiltrators into the Biblical ekklesia changing its Bible practices. It is as if they have never read the Bible and do not even know their enemy who is already within since their inception.

> *"If you tell a lie big enough and keep repeating it, people will eventually come to believe it. The lie can be maintained only for such time as the State can shield the people from the political, economic and/or military consequences of the lie. It thus becomes vitally important for the State to use all of its powers to repress dissent, for the truth is the mortal enemy of the lie, and thus by extension, the truth is the greatest enemy of the State." – "Mein Kampf," Adolf Hitler [129]*

The Book of Esther and Additions to Esther are the Big Lie indeed. It is inconceivable that Bible scholars would be so gullible as to not see this simple truth. They are trained to deny the facts and make up their own. They debate to win points even turning themselves into liars to succeed, yet failure is all they know on this. May we all place Esther where it belongs and stop the attempt at the corruption of our children and families with this propaganda. The Book of Esther fails every examination as an occult fraud which is no Bible account.

Martin Luther, 1483-1546:

"I am so great an enemy to the second book of the Maccabees, and to Esther, that I wish they had not come to us at all, for they have too many heathen unnaturalities."

– *"The Table Talk of Martin Luther." Ch. 24, pp. 27-28. [110]*

EXAMINING 1ST & 2ND
MACCABEES
& HANUKKAH

THE LEAVEN OF AN
8TH CANDLE?

WAS MACCABEES
EVER SCRIPTURE?

DOES IT RECORD
VALID HISTORY?

THE
Levite
BIBLE
LeviteBible.com

One of the greatest distortions in the modern church mindset, is the thinking that modern Rabbis represent anything other than Pharisees. Many place their doctrines even from the very occult Talmud above the Bible which is an insane proposition. In addition to Esther, Pharisees offer other contrived supposed scripture even rewriting history and it is extremely obvious upon examination. There is no better example of this than Maccabees. That includes all such books by that title. As usual, Pharisees continued to leaven their own propaganda to the point of making major errors they were too thick to realize. Liars are typically tripped up by such embellishment. You will find that theme prominent in the Talmudic paradigm and Yahusha exposed them.

There is no affirmation of this fiction in the Greek record and the Greeks really did not care whether the behavior of a king or leader offended other cultures. They would not have any motivation to rewrite such. However, the Dead Sea Scrolls record this history, and it proves the opposite of the Books of Maccabees. This is confirmed by Tacitus, the Roman historian. All these books are falsified history, and not credible as a true audit will uncover.

Even worse, Maccabees includes pagan doctrines such as praying for the dead which is against scripture and the festival of lights which has become known as Hanukkah in fraud is an occult event, never Bible. Oddly, they thought they could slip in two new Feasts claiming to leaven the seven into nine and get away with it. No one can change Yahuah's perfect number of seven as that is complete. As with Purim, there is no mention of the Hanukkah of Maccabees ever in scripture and that is impossible unless it is false. Some try to stretch the fallacious reading of Messiah being present in the Temple for the Feast of Dedication as somehow the December holiday. They forget that Hanukkah typically takes place in the Fall still in season which requires complete illiteracy.

Of course, Yahusha was there in the winter in about late February or early March for the Feast of Dedication commemorating the building of the Second Temple in the return from Babylon. Though they deceptively borrowed the word "Dedication" which is Hanukkah in Hebrew, there is nothing similar about the two events. We will expose this in full. The Qumran/Bethabara scrolls written before this false Maccabees account proves the opposite true. Hasmoneans were foreign conquerors who defiled the Temple and exiled the Temple Priests exactly as Daniel, David, and even Enoch predicted. They transgressed the Temple usurping the Priesthood with their foreign, criminal priests claiming to be Hebrews, while the Temple Priests were gone. They never relinquished that stolen authority.

REJECTED AS INSPIRED SCRIPTURE IN THE B.C. ERA:

Among the many texts found even in fragments in the Qumran Scrolls, not a single piece exists for either Maccabees. The Temple Priests tell us they were exiled there by the Maccabees and Pharisees and somehow, church scholars stupidly follow the Pharisee history and they have failed us all on this narrative. When one sets the synagogue of satan in a position of authority over scripture, they could not wax more illiterate. Modern scholarship relies heavily on these Pharisees especially regarding the Dead Sea Scrolls. They follow these Rockefeller-funded propagandists who lie as Messiah said they do. They claim Essenes lived in Qumran which is among one of the dumbest pretenses they have ever told. The Essene Find in archaeology is in Ein Gedi, not Qumran. The Qumran community identified as the sons of Zadok exiled there from the Temple, and Pliny the Elder even placed the Essene headquarters in the mountains just above Ein Gedi. It takes an incredibly illiterate scholar on this topic to claim Essenes lived in Qumran and ignore the Temple Priests who did. However, most of scholarship repeats that absurdity.

It is true that far later copies of the Greek Septuagint include Maccabees but there is no evidence it was even written in the B.C. era for that matter, and it was not included in the original translation. Flavius Josephus is the first to publish it in 90 A.D., but he does not label it as Bible Canon. He was a Pharisee and still did not include the book as scripture. That same year, the Council of Jamnia, an impertinent Pharisee Council of no consequence and with no authority, supposedly met and discussed Bible Canon. In their case, Maccabees was not included either. However, they left that history so loose that some even question if the council even met, others whether they even discussed Canon and really, who cares? They had no right to try to determine scripture which was already catalogued far prior. The fact they lost this information, proves they are not the Biblical ekklesia. Why does modern scholarship follow them on any subject?

REJECTED AS INSPIRED SCRIPTURE IN THE FIRST CENTURY EVEN BY PHARISEES:

Yahusha and the Apostles never quote either Book of Maccabees and neither ever mention the Jewish Hanukkah which is adding to the Bible Feasts in leaven. This December Festival of Lights is a satanic holy day in December from long before this event. There are many Winter Solstice Festivals, Sol Invictus Saturnalia, Yule, etc. which celebrate the victory of light over darkness in December for Dionysos, Hercules, Adonis, Mithras and even Tammuz, the ancient Mesopotamian god of fertility. Indeed, Christmas has this same origin and remains one of the most ludicrous of holidays when Yahusha was born on Shavuot in June *(Watch When Was Jesus Born Series)*. This is the Pharisee version of this same occult holy day which is never observed in the Bible paradigm in any Bible text at any time. One cannot find a better example of Pharisee leaven expanding the Word.

We will address the one-time Messiah observed the Feast of Dedication visiting the Second Temple in the Winter. It was not this holiday, but the actual Second Temple Dedication in late February to early March which is Winter, scholars. The Bible has no Holy Days in December period and many years the Jewish Hanukkah does not even take place in Winter. Adding to scripture with a false history is among one of the worst practices exposing modern Rabbinic Judaism as Pharisaism. They will suffer the consequences for that.

However, even the Pharisees did not treat Maccabees as inspired scripture generally in the First Century. Josephus published an account of the Maccabees but does not refer to it as Bible Canon in his listing of such, nor that a book by such title even existed still. Also, about 90 A.D., the Council of Jamnia (Yavneh) also did not recognize Maccabees as Bible Canon. Since the true Temple Priests did not keep it as scripture nor did the Pharisees, anyone changing that later is adding to the Word and that is rebuked throughout scripture. It really does not matter what Jerome, Origen and others included far later, nor that they claim to have seen a copy of Maccabees in Hebrew which is impertinent. These books were not scripture to the Biblically ordained keepers of Old Testament scripture, were not used by the New Testament writers, and even the Pharisees admit Maccabees was not Canon in the first century including Josephus and the Council of Jamnia. There is nothing to debate nor discuss on this matter.

In fact, to this day, the Rabbis focus on the miracle of the oil lamp in the Hanukkah story which is fiction added later as that account is not mentioned at all in either book of the Maccabees. That is ridiculous and an oversight of liars as one cannot miss that. They clearly are playing games of manipulation to force a new Bible Feast Day which never was a Bible practice, has no mention in any scripture anywhere, and this entire history propagated by Maccabees is grossly erroneous.

REJECTED AS INSPIRED SCRIPTURE BY MARTIN LUTHER IN THE 1500S:

> *Martin Luther, 1483-1546:*
> *"I am so great an enemy to the second book of the Maccabees, and to Esther, that I wish they had not come to us at all, for they have too many heathen unnaturalities."*
> *–"The Table Talk of Martin Luther." Ch. 24, pp. 27-28. [110]*

As with Esther, Luther was strongly opposed to especially 2nd Maccabees, as an occult account he wished had never been passed down as supposed scripture. It is ignorant that he would accept 1st Maccabees if so. He did not remove that from the Bible, however as some attempt to frame in fraud. The Temple Priests who originally curated Bible Canon, never included it and it was never part of the Bible Canon legitimately. This should be very basic understanding for a Bible scholar, yet we find a whole discipline that do not even know the Bible and are not scholars. Let us be clear, Luther was not either as he had no authority to change what the Temple Priests kept as Old Testament Canon. He just so happens to have been accurate on Esther and Maccabees defining them as occult which we will test.

1611 KJV ANCHORS NO NEW TESTAMENT QUOTES TO MACCABEES, BUT JOSEPHUS INSTEAD:

In the 1611 Authorized King James Version, unlike the larger books of Apocrypha it's size, there exist no attributions or a single anchor to the New Testament for 1st or 2nd Maccabees. Being 16 chapters in total, this is unthinkable if these events of Maccabees possessed even a little bit of truth. If the Maccabees were the bastions of truth they claim, their story would be referenced all over the New Testament. Not once do we find this. What we do find is Josephus, the Pharisee of Maccabean bloodline, is anchored to this book many times over in the 1611 Authorized King James Version as the root source. That speaks for itself. This is not Bible, it is a Pharisaical, Hasmonean exercise in disinformation and indoctrination.

1 Maccabees:	*Josephus: 1611 KJV Anchors:*
5:54	Antiq. 12.12
6:49	Add out of Josephus
7:1	Ant. Lib. 10, 12. Cap.16
9:35	Antiq. Lib. 13. Cap. 1
9:49	Ant. Lib. 13. Cap. 1
10:81	Antiq. Lib.13. Cap. 8
11:34	Antiq. Lib. 13. Cap. 8
12:7	Ant. Lib. 13. Cap. 8
12:28	Lib. Ant. 13, Cap. 9

2 Maccabees	*Josephus: 1611 KJV Anchors:*
6:2	Jos. Lib. 12. Cap. 7

The real question here is what are scholars doing since they clearly are not executing their calling to protect the flock? This is super obvious with even a little research on this topic which they refuse to conduct.

MACCABEES FAILS AS BIBLE AND SECULAR HISTORY:

The Maccabees, or a sect thereof, are documented to have existed in history indisputably. Judaea had been under the rule of the Babylonian, Medo-Persian, and Greek Empires in territory but something happened about 165 B.C. which changed that for a short period. There was a gap beginning with the end of the Greek empire until Rome absorbed it as part of its territory. However, did Judaea rule itself or was it conquered by a less significant power than the dominant Empires? Was the Temple also transgressed and defiled by someone other than Greece, which no history ever affirms? Was the Levitical Temple leadership from the sons of Zadok then, replaced with foreigners who were not even Levites, nor Hebrews? This is well documented in other sources proving Maccabees a false account of history. Rome would crush the ruling power from that period but was that power a foreign invader prior all the same? Or was it the Judaeans creating their own government? This is easily understood with a full view of history rather than narrow, Pharisaic propaganda found in the Books of Maccabees.

Josephus is the only ancient historian, however, to use this strange account from the Books of Maccabees claiming it as history, yet valid history affirms this story is told wrong in Maccabees as well as by Josephus. He knew this as he had to defend it and, in his defense, changes his position repurposing his argument exposing himself. Indeed, he cites six lost works as supporting that the Maccabees existed, yet that is not in question. That is all he says about those with no detail that proves either ever supported that Pharisaic view on the Hasmoneans or better said, on themselves as they are from that paradigm. They were the victors retelling and manipulating history and it does not require an expert to uncork these lies.

Josephus, as a Pharisee and Maccabee, is not credible on this topic. In his citing of six lost works oddly to support this history of Antiochus IV Epiphanes spoiling the Temple, he provides no detail of these sources and what they actually record. Let's be clear, he only says these suggest Antiochus took goods from the Temple which does not affirm he sacrificed a pig there, nor placed a statue of Zeus or whomever there, defiling it. His taking golden vessels, etc., if it did occur, does not represent a defiling of the Temple as Daniel's definition of the "Transgression of Desolation" Josephus lied about. Daniel is clear that defilement is the usurping of the priesthood taking over the daily sacrifice illegitimately. That happened.

Josephus only argues here that Antiochus IV Epiphanes is mentioned by others as a thief who stole from the Temple, but neither account affirms a defilement by Antiochus, nor does any. The defilement occurred under the Maccabees and did not happen at the hand of Epiphanes, nor the Greeks says valid history. He, then, admits, the Maccabees entered as foreigners representing their account as also not finding a golden calf there in his answering Apion. That merely proves Josephus was aware the Maccabees were not Temple Priests as they would have been eyewitnesses to that long before if they were. He would never attempt such a point if they were accustomed to the actual Temple practice as a son of Zadok would be. He exposes his own fraud.

However, not even one of those six lost works survives to confirm Josephus' account. Again, the Hasmoneans certainly existed, but nothing affirms his details proving his story and the Books of Maccabees false. However, Tacitus does survive and proves Josephus a liar as do the Dead Sea Scrolls, Daniel and Psalm 83. In fact, here Josephus even shifts the focus from the sacrifice to the spoiling of gold and silver, which is not a fulfillment of Daniel 8. It appears he was aware in this defensive response, that there was no evidence of a pig sacrifice in the Temple, and the Greeks never defiled the Temple. He now says Antiochus only entered the Temple to take gold, not to defile it with a pagan sacrifice. This is a retraction from his previous position and from the Maccabees claim which is left completely unsupported at that point.

*"But for Antiochus [Epiphanes], he had no just cause for that ravage in our temple that he made. **He only came to it when he wanted money;** without declaring himself*

*our enemy; and attacked us while we were his associates, and his friends. Nor did he find any thing there that was ridiculous. **This is attested by many worthy writers. Polybius of Megalopolis; Strabo of Cappadocia; Nicolaus of Damascus; Timagenes; Castor the Chronologer; and Apollodorus: (4)** who all say that it was out of Antiochus's want of money that he brake his league with the Jews, and despoiled their temple, when it was full of gold and silver."*
– Josephus, Against Apion 2.7
*Footnote (4): **"'Tis great pity that these six pagan authors, here mentioned to have described the famous profanation of the Jewish temple by Antiochus Epiphanes, should be all lost.** I mean so far of their writings as contained that description. Though 'tis plain Josephus perused them all; as extant in his time."*

Mentioning the Maccabees is not reserved for only those six lost works, it is detailed in the Dead Sea Scrolls by a different story as they were the foreign invaders stealing the Temple and the Priesthood. That is supported with affirming specifics from Tacitus as well as an accurate interpretation of Daniel 8 and Psalm 83 which the Pharisees forget a lot of detail Daniel did not. The dilemma for Josephus and his Pharisee faction remains as their story needs to be proven true. The problem is there is too much affirmation of a different story of this period for anyone to read the Books of Maccabees as anything but false propaganda. Is it really a mystery that those whom Yahusha called "the synagogue of satan who say they are Yahudim and are not, but do lie *(Rev. 2:9 and 3:9)*" would write a false history attempting to reposition themselves as Israel when they were foreigners who stole the Temple and its practices illegally? Let us examine the actual history of the era.

TACITUS AFFIRMS THE DEAD SEA SCROLL HISTORY AS WELL AS DANIEL AND PSALM 83:

We have observed some who claim Antiochus IV Epiphanes is mentioned in Tacitus' account which is illiterate. As a Roman pagan, Tacitus writes of the Roman era merely mentioning that a King Antiochus *"endeavored to abolish Jewish superstition and to introduce Greek civilization."* However, his aim was interrupted not being fulfilled, and there was no defiling of the Temple in Jerusalem by that Antiochus. Even if there were, this is the wrong Antiochus according to Tacitus. This was during the period of the Arsaces' Parthian revolt from Greece which occurred around 250 B.C. under Antiochus II, not IV, far too early. They seize on the language which seems to match the claim in Maccabees, but they fail to realize it is the wrong king in the wrong period over 80 years too soon and Tacitus mentions the Maccabean Revolt event later even condemning it.

He is clear this Antiochus never acted on any kind of crushing of the Jewish people, nor the Temple. What he clearly shows, which is no surprise for a Roman, is he does not know the difference between a Samaritan and a Judaean. This is because Samaritans were claiming to be Jews just as Messiah identified *(Rev. 2:9, 3:9)*.

That was not a new declaration but a pattern really since 2 Kings 17.

He, then, covers the next era where the Jews selected their own kings and that is the Hasmonean period indeed which occurs later, not during the Antiochus he mentions which is Antiochus II, not Antiochus IV Epiphanes. He confuses the Hasmoneans for Jews which they were foreigners which is very typical of the Roman paradigm. This is when Tacitus said they *"banished citizens, destroyed towns, killed brothers,"* etc. and *"committed every other kind of royal crime without hesitation."* That is the Hasmoneans/Maccabees in 165 B.C., and they have no record of being holy. Nothing credible affirms the Books of Maccabees.

"While the East was under the dominion of the Assyrians, Medes, and Persians, the Jews were regarded as the meanest of their subjects: but after the Macedonians gained supremacy, **King Antiochus endeavoured to abolish Jewish superstition and to introduce Greek civilization; the war with the Parthians, however, prevented his improving this basest of peoples; for it was exactly at that time that Arsaces had revolted. (about 250 B.C.)** *Later on, since the power of Macedon had waned, the Parthians were not yet come to their strength, and the Romans were far away, the Jews selected their own kings. These in turn were expelled by the fickle mob;* **but recovering their throne by force of arms, they banished citizens, destroyed towns, killed brothers, wives, and parents, and dared essay every other kind of royal crime without hesitation;** *but they fostered the national superstition, for* **they had assumed the priesthood** *to support their civil authority.*
– The Histories of Tacitus, Vol. 3, Book 5.8.1 [139]

Hasmonean coins demonstrate they were occultists and even Hellenists themselves, as did their actions. They usurped the priesthood themselves. Tacitus condemned them thinking they are Jews, but they were not. It was not actually a revolt but a conquest. This is easy to assume when both fell under Ptolemy's authority within the Greek infrastructure just as the entire area will remain united as a province under Rome largely. Tacitus was unaware of the origin of the Hebrews but seemed aware of the ancestral root of the Samaritans he thought were Jews as he cites Nephilim origins of the Samaritans unknowingly. "They had assumed the priesthood" is a condemnation of the usurping of the Temple by the Hasmoneans, Pharisees and Sanhedrin confirming they had no such right. The sons of Zadok, already in the priesthood in the Temple, could not assume it, they were already the priesthood. This is why one will find no Pharisee order nor Sanhedrin of such in the entire Old Testament in Jerusalem. They were installed with the Hasmonean Assault. In order to "assume the priesthood," one who is not a priest must take it over illegitimately. Tacitus outright condemns the Hasmoneans and affirms the Dead Sea Scrolls, Daniel and David. This account records the opposite of the Maccabees accounts, and no history affirms Maccabees. There is no dodging these facts. Maccabees lies.

DEAD SEA SCROLL HISTORY OF THE TEMPLE DEFILEMENT DISPROVES MACCABEES & JOSEPHUS:

The Books of Maccabees posit a completely falsified history never recorded anywhere but these books and the Pharisee paradigm. The Bible model of the exiled Temple Priests records the opposite as does Greek history. These prove Maccabees an outright lie.

First, the Dead Sea Scrolls valid history affirmed in archaeology, defines the city of Jerusalem was not delivered into the hands of or attacked by Greece period. They tell us the Greeks did not defile the Temple and they date that from the time of Antiochus I to the conquest of the Roman Empire. This is a massive challenge Maccabees cannot overcome as it proves it erroneous. This clarifies very specifically that Greece NEVER defiled the Temple even in the times of Antiochus IV Epiphanes (175-164 B.C.) as that era is covered in between Antiochus I and the coming of the Kittim (Rome) which expressed the entire era from 294-162 B.C. This is already recorded in prophecy in Daniel as well also as a power rising from within the Greek empire which is new and not Greece. It rises out of Ptolemy's Greek territory. It also cannot be the Seleucids from where Antiochus IV Epiphanes ruled.

> *"Whither the lion goes, there is the lion's cub, [with none to disturb it] (ii, 11b). [Interpreted, this concerns* **Deme]trius** *king of Greece who sought, on the counsel of those who seek smooth things, to enter Jerusalem. [But God did not permit the city to be delivered] into the hands of the kings of Greece, from the time of Antiochus until the coming of the rulers of the Kittim. But then she shall be trampled under their feet..."*
> – *Commentary on Nahum, Vermes, p. 505. [22]*

"Those who seek smooth things" in the Qumran scrolls are the Pharisees and Sanhedrin who controlled the religious system in Jerusalem at that time. Here, they are equated as the Hasmonean paradigm accurately as they are the Priests of such control system of conquerors. Notice, they were even prodding Alexander and previous Greeks to attack Judaea. However, Alexander did not attack Jerusalem but was welcomed with open arms by the Temple Priests. No defiling of the Temple occurred by the Greeks from the time of Alexander to the time of Antiochus I to the time of the coming of the Roman Empire, who are the Kittim. That includes and surpasses the entire reign of Antiochus IV Epiphanes whom Maccabees claims defiled the Temple when he did not. The Temple would be trampled under the feet of Rome in 70 A.D. This prophecy in that regard is exact proving this to be accurate history and Bible record. Maccabees is occult nonsense and a lie. Origen also records this Greek history which does not match Maccabees.

> *"The Jewish Nation was so preserved by the divine Power, that* **they did not undergo any Affliction, even under Alexander, the Macedonian, nor by**

him; altho' they would not take up Arms against Darius, on Account of certain Leagues and Oaths, [by which they were bound to him.] Then it was, they say, that the High Priest of the Jews, as he was clothed with his sacerdotal Garment, was adored by Alexander: Who said, that a Person was seen by him in that very Habit, who promised, in a Dream, to subdue Asia to him."
– *"Origen Contr. Cels.," Whiston. [132]*

Even in Alexander's time, it is the Samaritans who were the true enemies of Judaea, not the Greeks. In fact, you may have heard of an alternate Temple on Mt. Gerizim in Samaria. That is a vain effort to copy the Jerusalem Temple just as the Samaritans were the imposters of 2 Kings 17. They tried to infuse their Babylonian/Assyrian/Persian religions with the Bible in error. That became Rabbinic Judaism.

"Alexander the Great had required of the High Priest of the Jews, when he was at the Siege of Tyre, Auxiliaries, and Provisions, and the same Tribute which he had aforetime paid to the Persians. The High Priest returned Answer, that having taken an Oath to Darius, not to bear Arms against him, he never would do it while Darius lived. Upon which Alexander was very angry, and threatened, that after he had taken Tyre, he would lead his Army against the High Priest; and by his Punishment teach all Men, to whom they were to keep their Oaths. In which nice Juncture **Sanballat the Samaritan, sent Alexander 8000 Auxiliaries, and thereby obtained Leave to build a Temple upon Mount Gerizim.***"*
– *"Josephus, Antiq." Whiston. [132]*

Though displeased with the Temple Priests in this regard, Alexander's true enemy within was Judaea's enemy as well. The Samaritans were a problem, and it was they who attacked the Temple and exiled the Temple Priests, never Greece. They were a Greek territory, but they were not representing Greece. They moved against Jerusalem as soon as there was a vacuum of power that allowed them to do so. Greece was greatly weakened at that time, and the Hasmoneans seized the opportunity to attack the Temple which they opposed even its construction.

*"**Alexander, when he had taken Tyre, invaded Judea; where when he was favourably received, he offered Sacrifices to God, and paid great Honoours to the High Priest of the Temple:** Leaving Andromachus as Governor of those Parts, who was afterward* **slain by the Samaritans.** *Upon which Alexander, when he returned out of Egypt, inflicted great Punishments upon them and their City [**Samaria,**] and gave it to Macedonians to inhabit."*
– *"Eusebius' Chronicon as given us by his Translator Jerom," Whiston. [132]*

Valid history records that Alexander respected the Temple so much that he even offered spice sacrifices there. However, no Greek is ever recorded in credible history as changing this manner of respect for the Temple. In fact, Alexander was even told of Daniel's prophecy foretelling his conquest over Medo-Persia. It was the Samaritans who were at odds with Greece much of the time and they were also enemies of Judaea especially the Temple. Greece was not the adversary of Judaea and there is no evidence of the Greeks forcing their customs on the Yahudim as Maccabees claims.

*"It reached to a Place called Sapha; which name, translated into Greek, signifies a Prospect; for you have thence a **Prospect both of Jerusalem and of the Temple. And when the Phoenecians, and the Chaldeans [Citheans] that followed him, thought they should have Liberty to plunder the City and torment the High Priest to Death; which the King's Displeasure** fairly promised them; the very reverse of it happened. For Alexander, when he saw the Multitude at a Distance, in white Garments; while the Priests stood clothed with fine Linnen; and the High Priest in Purple and scarlet Clothing, with his Miter on his Head, having the golden Plate, whereon the name of GOD was engraved; **he approached by himself, and adored that Name, and first saluted the High Priest.** The Jews also did altogether, with one Voice, salute Alexander, and encompass him about: Whereupon the **Kings of Syria, and the Rest, were surprized at what Alexander had done, and supposed him disordered in his Mind.** However, Parmenio alone went up to him, and asked him, How it came to pass, that when all others adored him, he should adore the High Priest of the Jews?"*

*"And when he had said this to Parmenio, and had given the High Priest his right Hand; the Priests ran along by him, and he came into the City. And when **he went up into the Temple, he offered Sacrifice to God, according to the High Priest's Direction; and magnificently treated both the High Priest and the Priests.**" – Whiston. [132]*

By 165 B.C., Greece was distracted and otherwise engaged as they were in decline. Multiple battles with Rome for over five decades were taking a toll. Greek resources were shifted back to Greece to fight the Romans and it makes no sense for a Greek ruler to begin to act as a dictator. The entire narrative of Antiochus IV Epiphanes needing to enter the Temple to sacrifice a pig instigating another front of war with Judaea would not just be incredibly stupid timing, it never happened. It was the Samaritans who sensed the absence of Greek power and in that vacuum, they seized the opportunity to assault and capture the Temple never returning it to the Levites. They claim to be Levites yet all the sons of Zadok were in the Temple at that time managing worship and none lived in Samaria from where the Maccabees originated. The problem for Maccabees is they came from a foreign country, not Judaea. No sons of Zadok were there in Modi'in, and they were not Levites. They were foreign invaders conquering the Temple which they had desired for many centuries.

DANIEL'S "TRANSGRESSION OF DESOLATION" PROPHECY PROVES MACCABEES' AND JOSEPHUS' HISTORY OF THE MACCABEES FALSE:

Unfortunately, Josephus, whom many modern scholars follow in error, was incapable of reading. Daniel was extremely specific regarding the territory of Greece from which this Little Horn that would defile the Temple would rise. It was not to rise out of the Seleucids, but from Ptolemy. It is incredibly ignorant to forget Daniel's actual directions to place this in the Seleucid territory in such error in propaganda. That is a massive oversight of epic proportion and most modern scholars are guilty of blindly following along just as they do with much of Josephus' manipulated history. Daniel even places this territory belonging to Ptolemy's jurisdiction as to the North and West of Jerusalem. That is not difficult to locate and what is found there? Modi'in is. That is where the Maccabees commenced in Samaria as a foreign power conquering Judaea and the Temple. How can anyone call themselves a scholar and miss this?

"[An. 165.] When therefore the generals of Antiochus's armies had been beaten so often, Judas assembled the people together, and told them, that "After these many victories which God had given them, they ought to go up to Jerusalem, and purify the temple, and offer the appointed sacrifices." But as soon as he, with the whole multitude, was come to Jerusalem, and found the temple deserted, and its gates burnt down, and plants growing in the temple of their own accord, on account of its desertion, he and those that were with him began to lament, and were quite confounded at the sight of the temple. So he chose out some of his soldiers, and gave them order to fight against those guards that were in the citadel; until he should have purified the temple. When therefore he had carefully purged it; and had brought in new vessels; the candlestick; the table [of shew-bread,] and the altar [of incense;] which were made of gold; he hung up the veils at the gates, and added doors to them. He also took down the altar [of burnt-offering;] and built a new one of stones that he gathered together, and not of such as were hewn with iron tools. So on the five and twentieth day of the month Casleu, which the Macedonians call Apelleus, they lighted the lamps that were on the candlestick; and offered incense upon the altar [of incense;] and laid the loaves upon the table [of shewbread;] and offered burnt offerings upon the new altar [of burnt-offering.] Now it so fell out, that these things were done on the very same day on which their divine worship had fallen off, and was reduced to a profane and common use, after three years time. For so it was, that the temple was made desolate by Antiochus, and so continued for three years. For this desolation happened to the temple in the hundred forty and fifth year; on the twenty fifth day of the month Apelleus; and on the hundred fifty and third Olympiad. But it was dedicated anew, on the same day, the twenty fifth of the month Apelleus, on the hundred forty eighth year; and on the hundred fifty fourth Olympiad. And this desolation came to pass according to the prophecy of Daniel, which was given four hundred and eight years before. (30) For he declared

that the Macedonians would dissolve that worship, [for some time.26]"
– Flavius Josephus, Antiquities of the Jews, 90 A.D., Book 12.7.6

After Alexander the Great passed, known in Daniel's vision as the one large horn *(8:5)*, this one "notable horn" was then, broken into "four notable horns" which accurately describes the Greek Empire split into four after Alexander's death *(8.8)*. History well records Lysimachus, Cassander, Ptolemy, and Seleucis I Nicator shared this power after Alexander's demise. Daniel was perfect in his vision. Then, a Little Horn rises to attack Jerusalem and the Temple. However, Daniel tells us exactly from where it will ascend to power as well as the timing. It is not in power yet at this time, thus, cannot be an existing horn, but rises from within an existing horn of Greece, never Rome. Daniel's prophesy must come to pass while Greece is still considered in power before the Roman conquest, and that is exactly what happens in the attack of the Hasmoneans on Judaea. The obstacle for Maccabees and Josephus is, they prove they are incapable of reading very simple prophecy from one of scripture's greatest prophets. Pharisees are not huge fans of Daniel not because they cannot understand him, but because they do not wish to as he exposes them. Not only does he reveal their false Messiah and foretell of Yahusha so accurately leaving them no room to ignore Him, but Daniel also called them out as the enemy of Jerusalem long before they even attacked it.

Daniel 8:9 KJV
*And **out of one of them came forth a little horn**, which waxed exceeding great, **toward the south, and toward the east, and toward the pleasant land.***

Now, this Little Horn rises from where? "And out of one of them" means this new power would rise from inside of one of the four horns. That cannot be Rome which has always been illiterate. It must be a lesser power rising out of one of the four territories. To clarify, it is not one of the four powers themselves, but a power from within. It must be smaller than that territory representing only a portion of it. Where is this located? How can scholars not read what Daniel identifies here? If this power comes into Jerusalem, which is the pleasant land, by heading toward the South and East, we can trace this territory backwards as being located Northwest of Jerusalem.

This passage also identifies that this Little Horn rises from inside of the same horn in which Jerusalem is located. Thus, this is not a mystery in the slightest. Jerusalem is in Ptolemy and this enemy, which is not Greece though part of its conquest, are just to the Northwest of Jerusalem which must still be Ptolemy. They cannot be the Seleucids who are already an identified horn and this one is new rising out of Ptolemy which narrows this down. The area there falls outside of Judaea in Samaria but Southern Samaria at this time was still part of Ptolemy's region still. The locals still observed the separation of Judaea from Samaria but Greece and even Rome later, never really did. The Seleucid area begins just North of that which would no longer be Ptolemy and cannot conform to Daniel's prophecy. It is a complete lie that Antiochus IV Epiphanes, a Seleucid, defiled the Temple according to Daniel.

This must be a power within Ptolemy, smaller than all of Ptolemy, that rises, thus was not risen as a power yet in those days. It cannot be a full horn of four, but a Little Horn rising as a portion of one of the four, and it attacks Ptolemy's portion of Jerusalem including the Temple especially. This means Daniel defines Josephus and Maccabees as a false history as both fail to even understand the geography of those days. The Seleucid Antiochus IV Epiphanes was not from Ptolemy, is not a new power, and cannot rise out of Ptolemy when the horn of his authority was already in power since Alexander's death, and not new. That traditional interpretation has always been harebrained and uneducated. The Dead Sea Scrolls fully reveal this.

[For the violence done to Lebanon shall overwhelm you, and the destruction of the beasts] XII shall terrify you, because of the blood of men and the vio-lence done to the land, the city, and all its inhabitants (ii, 17).

*Interpreted, this saying concerns **the Wicked Priest**, inasmuch as he shall be paid the reward which he himself tendered to the Poor. For Lebanon is the Council of the Community; and **the beasts are the simple of Judah who keep the Law**. As he himself plotted the destruction of the Poor, so will God condemn him to destruction. And as for that which He said, Because of the blood of the city and the violence done to the land: interpreted, the city is **Jerusalem where the Wicked Priest committed abominable deeds and defiled the Temple of God**. The violence done to the land: these are the **cities of Judah** where he robbed the **Poor** of their possessions.*
– Commentary on Habakkuk, Vermes, p. 515. [22]

The "Wicked Priest" is not one man but the Hasmoneans and Pharisees who attacked the Temple in the Hasmonean Revolt which was an assault. Those who keep the Law who are the poor are the Temple Priests. These factions exiled the sons of Zadok from the Temple when they "committed abominable deeds and defiled the Temple of Elohim." How can language be any clearer? They sacked the cities of Judaea and controlled the Temple from 165 B.C. to 70 A.D. It was defiled all along which is why Yahusha did not launch His ministry there but did where the true Temple Priests then resided. The Qumran community understood how to read Daniel, and anyone can do so without a degree in stupid required of Bible scholars who cannot seem to see this. There is no other way to view it.

This horn does not just defile the Temple and leave which is a lousy reading. It takes over the Temple and the daily sacrifice as its own. It usurps the priesthood becoming the Temple Priests illegally continuing the sacrifices replacing the legitimate Priesthood. Daniel could not express more precision. This only fits the Maccabees/Hasmoneans as the defilers of the Temple. However, this narrative is exposed and repeated in the Qumran local historic texts. Maccabees is the opposite of this story proving it false.

4Q163: First Century B.C.:
Thus said the Lord, the Holy One of Israel', You shall be saved by returning and resting; your strength shall be in silence and trust. ' But you would not. You [said], 'No. We will flee upon horses and will ride on swift steeds.' Therefore 5 your pursuers shall be speedy also. A thousand shall flee at the threat of one; at the threat of five you shall flee [till] you are left like a flagstaff on top of a mountain and like a signal on top of a hill. Therefore the Lord waits to be [gra-cious to] you; therefore He exalts Himself to have mercy on you. For the Lord is a God of justice. How blessed are all those who wait for him! (xxx, 15-18).
*This saying, referring to the **last days**, concerns the **congregation of** 10 those who seek smooth things in Jerusalem ... [who despise the] Law and do not [trust in God] ... As robbers lie in wait for a man ... they have despised [the words of] the Law... – Commentary on Isaiah, Vermes, p. 499. [22]*

First Century B.C.:
*These are the **Scoffers in Jerusalem** who have **despised the Law of the Lord** and **scorned the word** of the Holy One of Israel. Therefore the wrath of the Lord was kindled against His people. He stretched out His hand against them and smote them; the mountains trembled and their corpses were like sweepings in the middle of the streets. And [His wrath] has not relented for all these things [and His hand is stretched out still] (v, 24-5). This is the **congregation of Scoffers in Jerusalem** ... – Commentary on Isaiah, Vermes, p. 499. [22]*

Daniel provides even more detail which most scholars read and then ignore in their lacking theological positions. This event is not to be confused with the Last Days' "Abomination of Desolation." It occurred in 165 B.C. when the Hasmoneans defiled the Temple, never the Greeks.

Daniel 8:10-14 KJV
*And it waxed great, even to the host of heaven; and it cast down some of the host and of the stars to the ground, and stamped upon them. Yea, he magnified himself even to the prince of the host, and **by him the daily sacrifice was taken away, and the place of his sanctuary was cast down**. And an host was **given him against the daily sacrifice by reason of transgression, and it cast down the truth to the ground**; and it practised, and prospered. Then I heard one saint speaking, and another saint said unto that certain saint which spake, How long shall be the vision concerning the daily sacrifice, and the **transgression of desolation**, to give **both the sanctuary and the host to be trodden** under foot? And he said unto me, Unto **two thousand and three hundred days; then shall the sanctuary be cleansed.***

Transgression is trespassing or continuing the very sacrifices of the Temple in which one is intruding illegally. It is not about bringing an end to, but a usurping of such practice. Even the land was being trespassed, not by the Greeks who controlled it until that point with the blessing of the Temple Priests. That would not be a trespassing. The foreign Samaritans had no right to be there even to defend Judaea with their military if that were even true. If it were, they would have left after helping to free their neighbor. That is not the story even in Maccabees. The problem is they stole the Temple and the Priesthood never returning that authority back to the Temple Priests.

A perfect example is the entire synagogue worship system which was new in that time installed by these Pharisees and the like. We do not find those in the Old Testament. Oops! Rabbis were now in charge, yet the Old Testament never refers to the Bible worship leadership in such title and Messiah condemned that title and office. How did so many scholars miss this? The daily sacrifice is "taken away" by "transgression" or in other words, they steal the daily sacrifice and continue it trespassing the Temple and its worship. They take it over and continue it which is exactly what the Hasmoneans and Pharisees did. It is rather funny they even call it a revolt when it was a conquest because Hasmoneans were not Hebrews, nor Temple Priests, but foreign invaders. Sure, they claimed to be with no accurate track which is typical of the synagogue of satan. If they were practicing and holy Temple Priests, they never would have resided in Samaria. That is ridiculous.

Notice how Strong's manipulates the definition of a revolt to make room for the Hasmonean Revolt. A foreign power does not enter a neighboring land and conquer it in a revolt and if they do, they leave afterwards. This is fraud.

פשע: pesha', peh'-shah; from H6586; a revolt (national, moral or religious): rebellion, sin, transgression, trespass. H6588.

When will the sanctuary be cleansed? This does not happen until the Day of Judgment and never before then. Yes, the Bible identifies there will be a Third Temple where the Beast will declare he is God in spiritual *"Sodom and Egypt (Rev. 11:8),"* as modern Jerusalem is known in scripture. These same Pharisees have returned to defile the land and they will build a Temple and reinstitute their false sacrifices in their false worship.

The Pharisees derive a false history from Maccabees which is not supported by any valid history and certainly not the Bible paradigm. They are guilty of the same attempt to infuse the synagogue of satan, whom they embody, as the Lost Tribes of Israel which they never were, and still are not. After the fake Hasmonean Revolt which was a foreign power attacking and conquering Judaea and the Temple, they installed their rulers and their control religion even displacing the priesthood and taking over the Temple practice. What a stupid lie. They conquered the Hebrews of Judaea and replaced their religion, yet that is somehow framed as "autonomy" for the Hebrews, who are never Jews in any credible etymology which is fraud as well. For the Jewish Virtual Library who is clearly too inept to understand the definition of simple English, this is slavery, not autonomy! When someone from a foreign country enters yours, conquers it, takes over the worship exiling the Temple Priesthood, that is called evil conquest and does not leave one in "autonomy."

"142-129 B.C.E.: Jewish autonomy under Hasmoneans."
– Jewish Virtual Library [138]

They do the same with Gamaliel whom they forgot was a Pharisee from the Hasmonean paradigm, never the Bible one. He was a Jewish leader-scholar around 40 C.E. Indeed, Paul writes of this same Gamaliel as a prominent Pharisee whom he studied under when he was a Pharisee before his conversion *(Acts 5:34, 22:3)*. They mix in the Bar Kochba Revolt which occurred after the Lost Tribes were gone from Judaea and that was an impertinent Pharisee rebellion as was the First such rebellion. You can see the shift in the synagogue of satan claiming to be Yahudim as Yahusha warned in Revelation 2:9 and 3:9. However, this was not new as they did so in Samaria all along.

Notice this as well was the 25th day of Kislev *(correlates to December)*, a Babylonian designation. It is no coincidence that Christmas, which is Saturnalia in origin in Rome, also takes place on the 25th Day of December. Both are worship of occult and never included as Bible worship in any context. This demonstrates that the church has followed Pharisees who are occultists into introducing the occult practice to their parishioners in either Hanukkah or Christmas.

PSALM 83 WAR PROVES MACCABEES AND JOSEPHUS FALSE:

Just as Daniel, King David foresaw this same conquest of the Temple where he even lists enemies involved including Samaria especially. He predicted the house of Elohim would be taken by neighboring enemies in the same fashion as Daniel predicted and the Qumran scrolls' history records. These enemies wish to see Israel cut off as a nation and they entered and stole the Temple in 165 B.C.

Psalm 83:1-12 KJV
*[[A Song or Psalm of Asaph.]] Keep not thou silence, O God: hold not thy peace, and be not still, O God. For, lo, thine enemies make a tumult: and they that hate thee have lifted up the head. They have **taken crafty counsel against thy people, and consulted against thy hidden ones.** They have said, Come, and **let us cut them off from being a nation**; that the name of Israel may be no more in remembrance. For they have **consulted together with one consent:** they are **confederate against thee:** The tabernacles of **Edom,** and the **Ishmaelites;** of **Moab,** and the **Hagarenes; Gebal,** and **Ammon,** and **Amalek;** the **Philistines** with the inhabitants of **Tyre; Assur** also is joined with them: they have holpen the **children of Lot.** Selah. Do unto them as unto the Midianites; as to Sisera, as to Jabin, at the brook of Kison: Which perished at Endor: they became as dung for the earth. Make their nobles like*

Oreb, and like Zeeb: yea, all their princes as Zebah, and as Zalmunna: **Who said, Let us take to ourselves the houses of God in possession.**

Many scholars have noted this word interpreted "hidden ones" is a reference to the Temple. The Holy of Holies is the hidden one there, it is a "secret place" which Yahuah treasured indeed. The later reference to the "houses of Elohim" is just house and very clear.

> צפן *: tsâphan, tsaw-fan'; a primitive root;* **to hide** *(by covering over); by implication, to hoard or* **reserve;** *figuratively to deny; specifically (favorably) to protect, (unfavorably) to lurk:—esteem, hide(-den one, self), lay up, lurk (be set) privily, (keep) secret(-ly,* **place***). Biblical Usage: to hide, treasure, treasure or store up.*

Notice the Samaritans are here definitively as the conquering power as Gebal and Tyre *(Both in Samaria)* as well as in multiple tribes such as Philistines, Amalekites, and even some Ishmaelites lived in Samaria. They were joined on the Eastern border of Judaea by the sons of Lot – Ammon and Moab, on the Southern border by the sons of Esau – Edomites, and the Hagarenes – a sect of Egypt. Ptolemy's seat of power was Egypt, and this is that territory indeed further entrenched matching Daniel's prophecy and the Qumran scroll's valid history. This has never actually been in question. The history of Maccabees is false written by the victors who rewrote themselves in as the good guys saving Judaea when they conquered it and the Temple which is evidenced by the fact that the false Sanhedrin remained in power in the time of Messiah in the First Century. If it were not a conquest even of the religion, there would be no Pharisees nor Sanhedrin and that is not even the same religion. The Bible sets forth the sons of Zadok to lead Temple Worship and they were exiled to Qumran/Bethabara in the Wilderness of Judaea. There, their prophesies even tell us they would prepare the way in the wilderness for Messiah just as John the Baptist is credited as he was one of those sons of Zadok continuing the Temple practice.

An actual true reading of Maccabees proves it affirms this Psalm 83 alliance with these exact foreign powers of the Hasmoneans. Indeed, Judas Maccabeus went into Edom *(Idumea)* and fought the Edomites *(5:3)*, but among them were his people he labels as Israel *(5:2)* but none of Israel was in Edom at this time. You will observe the pattern in these conquests where Judah and his brothers are joined by those within these powers who are Samaritans, not Israel. It is often mentioned he then brings them into Jerusalem. They would do so as a conquering foreign powers just as Psalm 83 identifies.

He rescued those of his allies which would be foreigners, not Hebrews, from Gilead which includes Zees Nephilim territory of Ammon outlined as an ally of the invaders *(5:6-16)*. There were no Lost Tribes of Israel in Ammon, nor Gilead to rescue. Hagerites or Hagerenes, as in Psalm 83, also occupied portions of Gilead.

This continues as Judas discovers his people in Galilee, Ptolemais, Tyrus, and Sidon are being attacked by Greeks in response to his aggression *(5:17-23)*. He sends his brother Simon with a force to rescue his people living there, but the problem is, there were no Lost Tribes of Israel in those areas. That is Samaria and Simon was rescuing Samaritan imposters representing them as Israelites when they were not just as Yahusha identifies in Revelation 2:9 and 3:9. He, then, brings those from Galilee to Judaea to occupy territory not theirs as foreign conquerors. This is a major obstacle for Maccabees as Judas just brought Samaritans misrepresenting them as Israelites into Judaea where they did not belong. This is a further completion of David's prophecy in Psalm 83 also adhering to Daniel 8.

1 Maccabees 5:23 KJVA 1611:
And those that were in Galilee and in Arbattis, with their wiues and their children, and all that they had, tooke he away with him and brought them into Iudea, with great ioy.

Judas follows these actions by sending his brother, Jonathan, over the Jordan River to ally with the Nabataeans, who are Ishmaelites from Kedar, the second son of Ishmael *(Genesis 25:13)*. That fulfills the Psalm 83 War prophecy.

In other words, as Psalm 83 identifies, the Maccabees indeed had the exact allies of the invaders and defilers of the Temple. That is right out of the Book of Maccabees itself and cannot be debated. They rescued those who lived in tents within Edom exactly as Psalm 83 revealed *(5:6-16)* who were not Israel, allied with the Nabataeans of Kedar from Ishmael *(5:24-30)*, freed his Samaritan brothers, not Israelites, from all the areas of Galilee, Tyre, and Sidon *(5:17-23)* which would include Gebal, Amalek, and Judas went into Gilead and Ammon which included Hagarenes, which would include Moab where he rescued his Samaritan bloodline who were not Israelites *(5:6-16)*. Judas entered the land of the Philistines and conquered there as well *(5:66)*. The Hasmoneans also conquered Ephron *(5:46)* and Bethsan *(5:52)* which are in Samaria, not Judaea and not part of Israel in those days since the Northern Lost Tribes were taken captive and never returned. The Samaritans were also originally Assyrians *(2 Kings 17)*, thus even Assyrians did join them in this overthrow of the Temple and Judaea exactly as David and Daniel identified. Of course, after Antiochus IV Epiphanes death in Persia, the host of his forces returned from Persia and Media *(Assyria)*. Once again, Judas freed Samaritans and relocated them into Judaea where they did not belong.

1 Maccabees 5:53 KJVA 1611:
And Iudas gathered together those that came behind, and exhorted the people all the way through, till they came into the land of Iudea.

Judas then, allies with Rome *(8:20-21)*. This will lead to Rome's acquiring Judaea over time and oddly, Herod and his sons even married royal Hasmoneans under Rome keeping them in power. Josephus admits he was a royal Hasmonean (Maccabee) and he even infiltrated the Roman Emperor family of the Flavian Dynasty being adopted into their family. It is no surprise his would represent a falsified history to benefit his bloodline.

In addition, Maccabees confirms again that the Hasmonean leadership melted together parts of Samaria into Judaea which was not the case prior. Only Samaritans would do this, and it proves the Samaritans conquered Judaea.

> *1 Maccabees 10:38-39 KJVA 1611:*
> *And concerning the three gouernments that are added to Iudea from the countrey of Samaria, let them be ioyned with Iudea, that they may be reckoned to be vnder one, nor bound to obey other authoritie then þe high priests As for Ptolemais and the land pertaining thereto, I giue it as a free gift to the Sanctuary at Ierusalem, for the necessary expences of the Sanctuary.*

About a decade later around 153 B.C., the Hasmonean rulers would appoint themselves as kings and High Priests of the Temple illegally. This was against scripture also solidifying Daniel's prophecy of the Transgression of Desolation as they were trespassers who stole the Temple, usurped the priesthood and never gave it back as Daniel foresaw. The act reveals Hasmoneans were never holy, nor Levites, but were the defilers of the Temple affirmed by the Dead Sea Scrolls, Psalm 83, and ancient historians Tacitus and Origen.

In fact, the High Priest Jason who served from 175-172 B.C. is known as the last of the Zadokite dynasty. His successor Menelaus was evidently not a son of Zadok, thus already illegitimate as a Temple High Priest. It was under his reign that Judas Maccabeus was then, installed as the Temple High Priest. In reading Maccabees, Judas was characteristically a Nephilim in behavior and certainly no Temple Priest. However, as the last Zadokite High Priest was Jason, this proves Judas, and his family were never sons of Zadok as Maccabees claims.

After the death of Judas Maccabeus, his brother, Jonathan, executed the office of High Priest dressed in the holy robe of the High Priest. This, too, was illegitimate. It also was a lousy interpretation of Tabernacles by a foreigner who clearly did not understand that the Feast of Tabernacles, especially its Sabbath, was not a time to hype war. This is evidencing this foreign power usurped the priesthood and misapplied even the Biblical Feasts they did not understand. This mindset remains with us today in the continuation of the Hasmonean paradigm with their priesthood called Pharisees who became Rabbinic Judaism after the destruction of the Second Temple. Handing out armor for battles is not a custom of Tabernacles and is forbidden on the Feast Sabbath in fact which forbids war activities on the day of rest. A son of Zadok and any Levite would know this. The fact that this Maccabee did not, proves he was not a Temple Priest and did not know how Yahuah operated. Maccabees even records the defiling of the Feast of Tabernacles by the Maccabees.

1 Maccabees 10:21 KJVA 1611:
*So in the seuenth moneth of the hundreth and sixtieth yere, **at the feast of the Tabernacles, Ionathan put on the holy robe, and gathered together forces, and prouided much armour.***

This is affirmed again in 1 Maccabees 11:27 when the King of Greece confirmed Jonathan Maccabeus as High Priest. This was illegitimate and a fulfillment of Daniel 8 and Psalm 83.

1 Maccabees 11:26-28 KJVA 1611:
*Yet the king entreated him as his predecessors had done before, & promoted him in the sight of all his friends, And **confirmed him in the high priesthood, and in all the honours that hee had before**, and gaue him preeminence among his chiefe friends. Then **Ionathan** desired the king, that hee would make Iudea free from tribute, as also the **three gouernments with the countrey of Samaria**, & he promised him three hundred talents*

Notice as well, the emphasis by Jonathan to tie together Judaea and Samaria who are not the same race and Samaritans were never Yahudim prior, but the imposters of 2 Kings 17 who tried to replace Israel. Some worry of Replacement Theology typically with little understanding that modern Jews are those replacements of true Israel, and this continues to this day.

We are then given a listing of the three Samaritan governments that are then, joined to Judaea illegally. They are "Apherema, and Lidda, and Ramathem *(11:34)*."

1 Maccabees 11:34 KJVA 1611:
*Wherefore we haue ratified vnto them **the borders of Iudea, with the three gouernments of Apherema, and Lidda, and Ramathem, that are added vnto Iudea**, from the countrie of Samaria, and all things appertaining vnto them, for all such...*

Therefore, Maccabees is a false history to Greek history, it fails the test of the Qumran scrolls which tell the opposite story, its story is the Transgression of Desolation of Daniel 8 as the enemies of the Temple and Judaea, and their account matches the defiling of the Temple predicted in Psalm 83 with the Hasmoneans and their priestly factions as the trespassers. They came from a foreign land, invaded Judaea and the Temple and never returned ownership. There is no way to tell the story any other way in the Bible paradigm. Tacitus and Origen agree. Maccabees is a lie.

THE GEOGRAPHIC MISHAP OF MACCABEES:

When one peruses these Samaritan areas on a map, they quickly realize that Modi'in is parallel with these territories labeled as Samaria and not Judaea by the Book of Maccabees. Most Bible maps include them within Judaea really referring to the time after this annexation joining these three Samaritan governments into Judaea. What Maccabees does is attempts to cover up a considerable conflict with its geography. Modi'in was not in Judaea. Understand this family would be buried and commemorated in Modi'in as their place of origin, not Jerusalem. They had no ties to it historically.

If the Hasmoneans originated in Modi'in as Maccabees itself documents, they were Samaritans or at least a foreign power entering Judaea from Dan's territory illegally in conquest, not rebellion. A rebellion is not defined as an attack on a foreign land, and it is illiterate for so many scholars to blindly follow these blind Pharisees. This is completely evidenced by their taking the Temple and usurping the priesthood which Judas Maccabeus and his brother, Jonathan, both filled such office themselves according to Maccabees. This continued as their rulers, the Hasmonean Dynasty, continued the same as they declared themselves kings and High Priest against scripture. They were not a priestly family, but only in claim.

The Temple Priests, the sons of Zadok, never lived in Modi'in in the territory of Dan according to the Bonne Map of Israel of 1770 and in Ephraim just North of there in the 1850 Mitchell Map of Palestine *(pictured right)*. In either event, it was not in Judaea where the sons of Zadok were. This just so happens to be to the Northwest of Jerusalem exactly as Daniel pinpointed as both are still in Ptolemy's territory.

The sons of Zadok were in Jerusalem in the Temple where they should be. There is no history of their exile during this period until the Maccabees exiled them to the Wilderness of Judaea to Bethabara. That is called Qumran today which proves the original Bible Canon curated by the Temple Priests. This is perfectly predicted in Daniel 8 and Psalm 83 with the Hasmoneans defiling the Temple and affirmed in history by Tacitus, Origen, and the Qumran multiple times. All this history is right under the noses of scholars, but they cannot see it as their noses have grown as they repeat the lies of the Pharisees/Hasmoneans who conquered the Temple.

THE BLOODLINE BLUNDER OF MACCABEES:

Certainly, from their father, Mattathias, it is claimed their lineage originated in Jerusalem from Temple Priests. However, the Bible requirement in that era was far stricter and Maccabees fails to produce valid descendancy of the priesthood for this family. Ezra well documents the need for this evidence even before this time *(1Esd. 5:38-39)*. That is not a small oversight on the part of this illiterate author who does not know the Bible. This alone proves they were not priests. Otherwise, they would have evidence especially since Ezra recorded some tried to return with

Modi'in was NOT in Judaea!

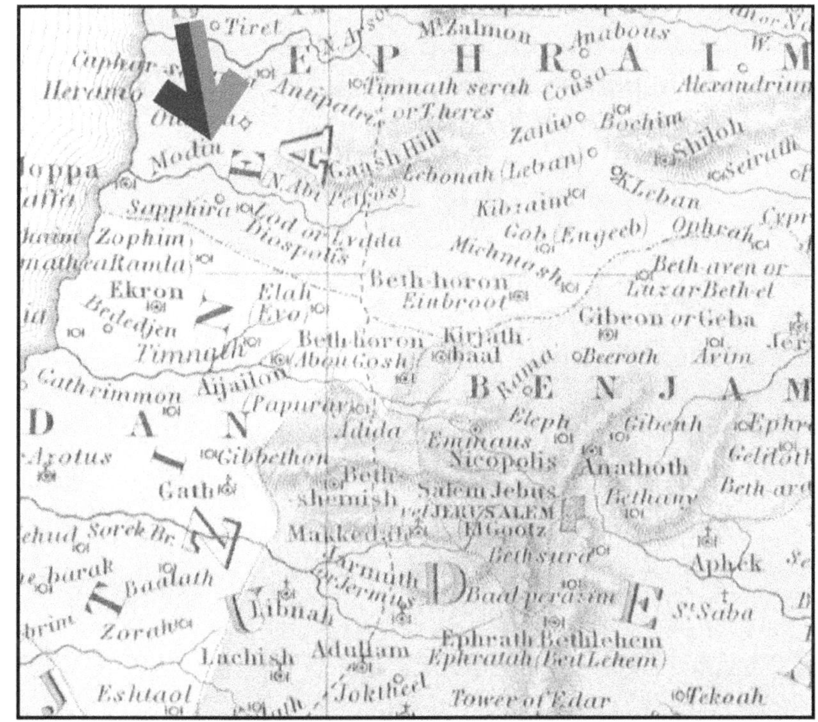

1770, Bonne Map of Israel. Rigobert Bonne 1727 – 1794 [12].

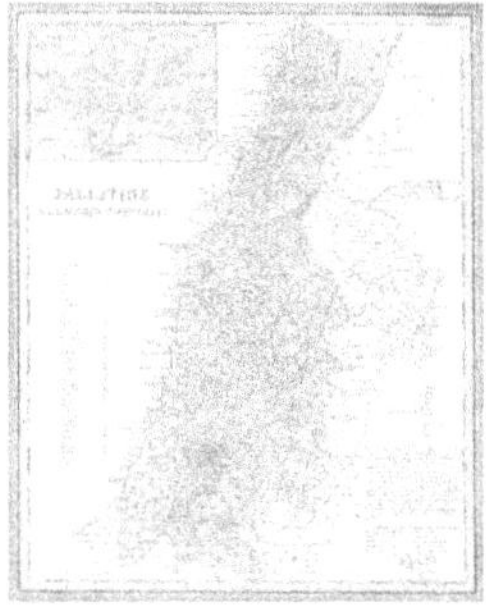

1850, Mitchell Palestine & Adjacent Countries. Published in "A New Universal Atlas Containing Maps of the various Empires, Kingdoms, States and Republics Of The World." (1853 issue) Source: Public Domain. Wikimedia Commons.

the Southern Kingdom from Babylon claiming to be from the priesthood who were rejected because they did not produce ample records. The Maccabees do not either, and their insufficient, scant listing with no real track leaves nothing for debate on the matter. The author was too stupid to understand priestly families did a better job of holding a firm record of their lineages. He was not Hebrew and did not understand the priesthood and its history. That is glaring ignorance.

1 Maccabees 2:1 KJVA 1611:
In those daies arose Mattathias the son of Iohn, the sonne of Simeon, a Priest of the sonnes of Ioarib, from Ierusalem, and dwelt in Modin.

There was a priestly family of Jehoiarib in 1 Chronicles 9:10 and 24:7 which appears to be the attempted connection in claim in Maccabees for Mattathias' bloodline. However, this family is listed with the *"ruler of the house of God,"* the sons of Zadok. This leaves a massive problem for Maccabees as this family would be in the house of Elohim and nowhere else. They dwelt in and did not leave Jerusalem but served in the Temple managing the ministry, but not the Maccabees. A son of Zadok outside of Judaea and outside of Jerusalem in that age, was no holy priest. They ran the Temple already. They did not have to conquer it from a foreign land employing Nephilim tactics and traits as Maccabees asserts.

Read the lineages of priests such as Ezra and they are far more detailed than this clear manipulation like the claims of those who tried to infiltrate the priesthood in Ezra's time *(1Esd. 5:38-39)*. Many generations are missing because this is a contrived lie. If they had shown the detail, it would reveal itself as fraud, so they hide in providing no detail whatsoever. Who was Simeon's father? A priestly line must include all the detail as there were those even in the return from Babylon who made such claim and the detail of their lineage proved they were not. The Maccabees operate in actions as imposters of the same ilk. This is blatant hocus-pocus. However, Maccabees espouses occult doctrine even.

THE PAGAN DOCTRINE OF PURGATORY AND PRAYING FOR THE DEAD IS TAUGHT IN MACCABEES:

As in Catholicism, the occult doctrine from the Egyptian Book of the Dead is prevalent in their culture especially that of purgatory – a place between Heaven and Hell in which souls can work out their salvation and even receive prayers though they are dead. However, the Catholic hierarchy loves Maccabees because it espouses this satanic theology, they prefer over the Bible which never has such. This is an accidental inclusion of a pagan author who did not appear to have enough intellect to recognize he undermined his whole book in doing so. The Maccabees did not even worship Yahuah but were occultists.

Second Maccabees 12:41-45 KJVA 1611

All men therefore praising the Lord the righteous Iudge, who had opened the things that were hid, Betooke themselues vnto praier, and besought him that the sinne committed, might wholy bee put out of remembrance. Besides, that noble Iudas exhorted the people to keep themselues from sinne, forsomuch as they saw before their eyes the things that came to passe, for the sinne of those that were slaine. And when he had made a gathering throughout the company, to the sum of two thousand drachmes of siluer, hee sent it to Ierusalem to offer a sinne offering, doing therein very well, and honestly, in that he was mindfull of the resurrection. (For if he had not hoped that they that were slaine should haue risen againe, it had bin superfluous and vaine, to pray for the dead.) And also in that he perceiued that there was great fauour layed vp for those that died godly. (It was an holy, and good thought) wherupon he made a reconciliation for the dead, that they might be deliuered from sinne.

There are actual scholars who read this plain English and apply witchcraft claiming it does not say they prayed for the dead, yet that is exactly what this says. The language *"to pray for the dead"* is clear enough for most who can read but we will expound for scholars who cannot seem to understand what that means. The passage then says: *"he made a reconciliation for the dead, that they might be deliuered from sinne."* No one needs to explain to anyone. He took up an offering of silver to cover sin which is ridiculous, and then, prayed for the reconciliation of the dead to be delivered from sin they already committed, and their lifetime was ended on Earth. You will never find that in the Bible. Do not allow their illiteracy in propaganda to dismiss what very clear pagan doctrine documented for thousands of years.

Catholics continue to follow this today in ignorance as well against scripture. However, this becomes even more satanic and pagan when one knows the Old Testament's sin offering is not silver. That is ridiculous and leads to the illiterate Catholic doctrine of indulgences Martin Luther protested. No wonder he hated Maccabees. One cannot pay to have their sins removed regardless of the amount. It is well documented throughout that animal sacrifice served this purpose and Yahusha became our final offering as His blood is sufficient for all sacrifices through eternity *(Heb. 10)*. However, there is no prayer for forgiveness of the dead.

Praying for the dead is not just Catholic Doctrine which we have witnessed many times, it is the ancient occult doctrine which has no Biblical root. When man dies, he will be judged by what he did in life as to whether he entered relationship with Yahusha or not *(Matt. 7, John 15)*. We cover this in full in "Where Do We Go When We Die?" Series on YouTube. They either lived the life of a believer while alive or they did not. They were in relationship with Yahusha or they were not.

There is only one way unto salvation and that is Yahusha *(John 14:6; 1 Tim. 2:5-6; Acts 4:12)* which remained the same in the Old Testament as they had the same hope of the Second Coming of Yahusha that we have today. Prayer for the dead is in vain. We die once and that settles it. Whatever happened during that lifetime is not undone by intercession after one is dead. If one can go out and live a satanic life until their death and then, through prayer after death, they can still enter the Kingdom of Heaven, then, we would serve an unjust Elohim who was not committed to righteousness. The next progression after death, is judgment on the Day of Judgment and never before. Yahusha appears a Second Time unto salvation for those who were in relationship with Him while living. They cannot enter such relationship after the die.

Hebrews 9:27-28 KJV
And as it is appointed unto men once to die, but after this the judgment: So Christ was once offered to bear the sins of many; and unto them that look for him shall he appear the second time without sin unto salvation.

Even Ezekiel defines salvation the same in the Old Testament as salvation is not new in the New Testament. In fact, it is not new even to Gentiles who were always included in the promises to Israel under the covenant as the "stranger among you" was always able to be saved *(Exo 12:49 Lev 7:7; Num 15:16, 29)*. In fact, many bloodline Hebrews in Israel over time, were not saved. When Paul defines it does not matter if one is Hebrew or Greek *(Gal 3:28; Col. 3:11)*, he is continuing an Old Testament doctrine not defining anything new to scripture. Paul taught the Law.

Ezekiel 18:20-21 KJV
The soul that sinneth, it shall die. The son shall not bear the iniquity of the father, neither shall the father bear the iniquity of the son: the righteousness of the righteous shall be upon him, and the wickedness of the wicked shall be upon him. But if the wicked will turn from all his sins that he hath committed, and keep all my statutes, and do that which is lawful and right, he shall surely live, he shall not die.

This strange occult doctrine of Maccabees also practiced in pagan Catholicism today has always been rebuked in scripture.

Ecclesiastes 9:5-6 KJV
For the living know that they shall die: but the dead know not any thing, neither have they any more a reward; for the memory of them is forgotten. Also their love, and their hatred, and their envy, is now perished; neither have they any more a portion for ever in any thing that is done under the sun.

What is truly amazing is these imposters invaded the Temple as foreigners installing a Festival of Lights, when there is no light found in them. The Maccabees were not just frauds telling a false history, they were pagans. The obsession with light is Kabbalistic in fact.

Isaiah 8:19-20 KJV
And when they shall say unto you, Seek unto them that have familiar spirits, and
unto wizards that peep, and that mutter: should not a people seek unto their God?
for the living to the dead? To the law and to the testimony: if they speak not according
to this word, it is because there is no light in them.

Who is it that inquires of the dead in this manner? It is called necromancy, an ancient occult practice never supported by any scripture at any time. A Catholic or any other pagan religion praying to or for the dead, is no different than a witch in practice as that is their custom, not the Bible's. That includes Mary and Saints.

Deuteronomy 18:10-11 KJV (Cf. Lev. 19:31)
There shall not be found among you any one that maketh his son or his daughter
to pass through the fire, or that useth divination, or an observer of times, or an
enchanter, or a witch, Or a charmer, or a consulter with familiar spirits, or a
wizard, or a necromancer.

OTHER FALSEHOODS IN MACCABEES:

We covered the Commentary on Nahum from the Dead Sea Scrolls which identifies the Roman Empire as the Kittim even by era as succeeding the Greek Empire, thus not the Greeks. Though Kittim is a son of Javan, founder of Greece in Genesis 10, in prophecy it signifies the coming of the Roman Empire. For instance, in the Dead Sea Scrolls, it is the Kittim who destroy the Temple. That is Rome, not Greece.

Apocalyptic Chronology or Apocryphal Weeks (4Q247):
"... [And afterwards will co]me the fif[th] week ...
four-hundred [and eighty years (after the exodus from Egypt)] Solo[mon]
(built the Temple; cf. 1 Kings vi, 1) . . . (It was destroyed in the time) [of
Zedejkiah king of Judah ... (It was restored by) the Levites and the people of the
Lan[d] ... (Final stage)... kin[g] of the Kittim ..." – Vermes, p. 403 [22].

The Hasmonean Hyrcanus is opposed by the Roman Empire, not the Greeks.

Historical Texts C-E (formerly Mishmarot Ca_c); Text D (4Q332); Fr. 2-3:
... Hyrcanus rebelled ... to oppose ...
... [of the Kit]tim killed ... – Vermes, p. 405-6 [22].

Dated to the First Century B.C., this fragment asserts the Roman Empire as the Kittim, not the Greeks.

Commentaries on Isaiah; Frs. 8-10:
The heart of the forest shall be felled with the axe, th[ey] ...
for the war of the Kittim. And Lebanon through a po[werful one shall fall
(x, 34). Its interpretation concerns the] Kittim who will be given into the
hand of his great one ... – Vermes, p. 498 [22].

In the second half of the First Century B.C., the Kittim are still identified as the controlling Empire and that as well were the Romans, not the Greeks.

Commentary on Nahum (4Q169); Second Half of the First Century B.C. (The
Roman Era):
Its [interpretation: the sea is all the K[ittim who are] ... to execut[e]
judgement against them and destroy them from the face [of the earth,]
together with [all] their [com]manders whose dominion shall be finished.
– Vermes, p. 504 [22].

However, the Books of Maccabees do not know this and falsify history claiming the Kittim as the Greeks. That demonstrates they were not familiar with the Bible.

1 Maccabees 1:1 KJVA 1611:
And it happened, after that Alexander sonne of Philip, the Macedonian, who came
out of the land of Chettum, had smitten Darius king of the Persians and Medes,
that hee reigned in his stead, the first ouer Greece

Greece is not the Kittim and this confuses the narrative and a Bible prophet recording scripture would agree with the sons of Zadok Temple Priests on this. In the next verses, Maccabees misdirected Jerusalem as a Seleucid territory when it fell under Ptolemy instead. That is false as we already proved. It claims a gymnasium was built in Jerusalem by the Greeks, yet no Greek history concurs with this. If it happened, the Greeks would have recorded it, and it would be the matter of record for such details. In fact, it would also likely be known who would have funded such a project. Josephus, the Pharisee and royal Hasmonean does not offer credible information on this narrative but represents the Maccabee family by blood. The New Testament never mentions any portion of this manufactured story.

Greek history does not document their forcing Hellenism on the Hebrews they respected from the highest of authorities. Equally, though they did not practice it, there is no evidence the Greeks had such animosity towards circumcision among the Hebrews. The real question is why would they care that Hebrews continued to practice such? Again, Maccabees is the real source of their supposed hatred of the practice to such a degree that they would persecute those who were circumcised. The problem is that smells of Pharisee leaven as they are the ones who even in Acts 15 claimed that one had to be circumcised to be saved which is never in any Old Testament scripture. It is Pharisee doctrine, not Bible. This exposes Maccabees as a Pharisee fraud. It is not just one doctrine, but their whole false, infused religion.

Maccabees 1:54 invokes Daniel's "Abomination of Desolation" by the Greeks which did not occur even still and does not until the Last Days. They are confusing the "Transgression of Desolation" which they fulfill, not Greece. This is a false reading of Daniel and ridiculous. Greece's hanging *"the infants about their neckes, and rifled their houses, and slewe them that had circumcised them"* is among the dumbest of embellishments in Pharisee leaven. This is false history and sensationalism to invoke a response from the reader which we see in Pharisaism often. It is their public relations staple.

Maccabees makes a claim in 2:7 that the Temple was under the control of strangers and the enemy. However, this is false. The sons of Zadok still controlled the Temple at this time soon to be exiled by the descendants of Mattathias. We have their writings that debunk this. This is a dilemma Maccabees cannot overcome. It is false. If this were true, this would mean Daniel, David and the Qumran Scrolls are all erroneous. They are not.

In addition, as a pagan son of Zadok who failed to execute his priesthood, if even true, Mattathias supposedly cared about the Temple and the law so greatly, he would murder to uphold his erroneous interpretation. Supposedly, while defiling the Temple, the Greeks were not satisfied with a sacrifice of abomination never mentioned by Daniel *(Oops!)* but came into Modi'in demanding that they also offer such defilement *(2:15)* which is more coloring language in propaganda. However, as Modi'in is in Samaria and not Judaea, this is ridiculous and would not even matter in terms of the Temple, nor the religion of Judaea. The area was already pagan, and this is fraud.

What leader would be so stupid as to create such war especially during the fall of the Greek Empire where they were far too busy with Rome at this point to even think about Jerusalem in such terms. This is nonsense. Equally, ludicrous is Mattathias witnessing an altar set up for such sacrifice and a Jew upholding it in the pagan city in which he lived. He, then, reacts by murdering him *(2:24)*. This did not happen and makes no logical sense. Modi'in was never such a holy place. The fact that Maccabees elevates that Samarian, occult city reveals this is no Bible story.

However, he did not stop there, Mattathias then, murdered *"the king's commissioner who compelled men to sacrifice, he killed at that time, & the altar he pulled downe (2:25)."* This is utterly stupid. It was an act of war and what difference would it even make if they forced occult sacrifice in an occult, Samaritan city anyway? This was written by an idiot who only offers sensationalism without any truth in basis.

He and his sons flee to the mountains where others gather with them in rebellion, yet it reads as a triumph for their family all along. That is just as a Pharisee would write because they are oblivious to how a righteous servant of Yahuah would operate. The Maccabees were not righteous. They were foreign Pharisee frauds.

It was not sensational enough to have the onslaught of the Greeks, however. This leaven must then, claim people were slain on the Sabbath of course *(2:41)*. Then, not only were these Hasmoneans murderers, but they go on a mutilation spree cutting the male parts of *"what children soeuer they found within the coast of Israel vncircumcised, those they circumcised valiantly (2:46)."* Is it valiant to chop the male portion of a defenseless child in vain as they were not practicing believers? No! Where does the Bible ever espouse the doctrine of forced circumcision? Is this the Star Trek Borg? It is a choice and anyone going around cutting off portions of the male anatomy of children without their parents' consent, is a satanic tyrant cramming their belief system down the throats of others against the Bible. These were not priests of Yahuah.

This is far too much emphasis on circumcision which is Pharisee, never Bible. Circumcision is not salvation and never was. Only a Pharisee would write something so inept just as their claim in Acts 15. How could anyone in any age view this as inspired scripture? Can you imagine a warrior boasting of chopping the reproductive organs of young children and his friends heralding him for it? That is as satanic as one could ever behave. What a stupid, telling narrative of fools.

In 2:70, Mattathias passes away and was buried, not in Jerusalem where a son of Zadok should be, but in the Samaritan city of Modi'in. This is very stupid and very clearly this was no son of Zadok. Even his family supposedly originated in Jerusalem which this proves untrue, and this writer was oblivious to the Bible paradigm.

In 3:2, the term *"the Battle of Israel"* is used yet this proves this writer is unaware that the Southern Kingdom of Judaea did not call itself Israel any longer which was the Northern Kingdom's connotation and none of the Northern Kingdom were there in the land anymore. The reason this is so easily forgotten is that this was written by a Pharisee from the synagogue of satan who would still try to claim that Samaria was Israel when they were foreign imposters who wished to be Israel but never were. Very oddly, Judas Maccabeus is compared to a Nephilim giant *(3:3)* and when one reads his escapades, perhaps he was. He is given Messianic attributes yet was a warlord. This is a false claim, and it is ludicrous to claim *"because saluation prospered in his hand (3:6)."* Judas was not the Messiah! What blasphemy!

Like a Nephilim, not a righteous man, Judas *"went through the citties of Iuda, destroying the vngodly out of them, and turning away wrath from Israel."* Once again, Judaea did not identify as Israel, and this is an unbiblical Nephilim act of aggression. This writer clearly did not understand that when Israel, such as in the days of King David went around eradicating peoples, it was ridding the land of Nephilim. Now, we have the opposite narrative, where this Nephilim Judas, is killing every non-believer he finds. That is not scripture. Grace exists in the Old Testament as well and salvation was available to Gentiles even in the Exodus and beyond. This is satanic and ridiculous.

However, Judas must have had superpowers or perhaps a fighter jet because he then, becomes *"renowned vnto the vtmost part of the earth, & he receiued vnto him such as were ready to perish (3:9)."* How ridiculous. This is very clear Pharisee fluff of epic proportion and leaven. Continually, one reads how Judas was so feared yet should that not be Yahuah who is feared and became famous? The focus is the Nephilim strength of this hero and not His Elohim who should be the topic if the writer were of Bible caliber and character. He was not.

Antiochus, very stupidly, supposedly advanced his soldiers pay for a year to retain their readiness for battle *(3:28)*. That is fallacious enhancement. Remember, this is the time when Greece was already at war with Rome and already falling. This is insane exaggeration and irresponsible. Maccabees is not scripture. Amid a local war he was losing, he divided his men unwisely, and then, headed further East into Persia to gain more tribute *(3:31)* because of his stupidity. At the same time, Rome was wiping out the Greeks on the Western front. That is nonsense.

At this point, the Temple was completely abandoned which never happened in this age *(3:45)*. Judas then, employs no real strategy whatsoever but with 3,000 men surrounded by the enemy of over 6,000 including 1,000 of the best horsemen *(4:1)* supposedly blew trumpets and that was enough to scare the enemy into a frenzy *(4:13)*. Judas was standing in the middle of the plain with 3,000 men, not on mountains like Gideon, and they supposedly had no swords nor armor, but just trumpets. The enemy simply fled because half their numbers, which they could clearly see were unarmed, blew trumpets at them. They, then, pursue the enemy, yet with their trumpets? Did swords now appear miraculously in their hands? Or was their enemy known for an allergy of trumpets perhaps? This is illiterate nonsense as this enemy were experts of war and this fails. This reads like the Talmud – illiterate.

There is a constant emphasis on the spoils of war throughout this entire story, which is absolutely Pharisee in nature, and not Bible. There is also a consistent lack of detail of these supposed battles as these are not actual historical nor Biblical accounts. The focus on the *"manliness"* of Judas' soldiers and their readiness to *"die valiantly"* is Nephilim in nature and not Biblical. Who cares about Judas' manliness?

Maccabees, then, admits that there was a place referred to as the *"gate of Ptolemais"* near Tyre *(5:22)*. This is very telling because the territory of Ptolemy, not the Seleucids, would have at least continued that far North. This is a problem for Maccabees as that is far North of Modi'in meaning they are the power that rose out of Ptolemy as Daniel predicted. In fact, Simon, Judas' brother then, gathers people from Northern Samaria such as Galilee and Arbattis which have no place in Judaea and relocated them into Judaea *(5:23)*. These were not Hebrews but imposters. Judas also relocated people from Ammon and Gilead *(5:52)* into Judaea. He, too, was bringing in foreigners. This was a foreign invasion much like 1948 which fits Gog of Magog and his allies and powers yet fails Isaiah's prophecy *(Isaiah 11:10-12)*.

There is a great overthrow of the Children of Israel because they did not listen to Judas *(5:60-61)*. One would think that would be Yahuah they were to listen to as the Bible would typically word it in such a way. The emphasis on the great fame of Judas becomes obvious. Somehow priests were not supposed to fight, yet Judas and his brothers were priests even declaring themselves High Priest over time *(5:67)*.

The far too overstated stooge, Antiochus IV Epiphanes, during war with Rome and with a local revolt on his hands, just left his post with half his troops to go collect tribute that did not require his personal appearance. However, he was far too stupid to just do that. With a war on two fronts already, Antiochus supposedly decided to go attack a different land in Persia called Elymais which was renowned for gold and silver *(6:1-4)*. Two wars were not enough. He was so desperate, he had to go start a third war because he was too much of an idiot to realize such a place of riches might be well fortified. We will not even mention war with Ptolemy as well. This brands him one of the dumbest leaders in history leaving his post during a war to go collect money – a function of subordinates which should have been collected all along. We are supposed to believe he had no such system in place. The fact this writer does not know that demonstrates the author of Maccabees is illiterate of how the Greek Empire functioned. He loses that battle because he just loses everywhere as he stumbles and fumbles around like a court jester.

Basically, Antiochus is more a model for Wile E. Coyote from Looney Tunes as he is destined to lose to the Road Runner in every possible way no matter his efforts. Though Wile E. was likely smarter than this character is written, his is fiction all the same just as the Nephilim hero, Judas Maccabeus who conquers against all odds in superhuman ways that are clearly fiction. He is credited as superhuman much as the Book of Modern Jasher's Pharisee embellishment does as well. When one reads these texts, they can observe a common thread of the lunatic writers who clearly thought we were all too mundane and inadept to figure out their nonsense.

Instead of returning to Jerusalem, which was an area of Ptolemy, not Antiochus which this writer also did not know, Antiochus just gives up and grieves to the point of death *(6:9)*. He, then, realizes that all these bad, very poorly fabricated things were happening to him because of his evil acts in the Temple and Jerusalem *(6:12-13)*. Is this really how truly evil men operate? ...Only in the movies. This was just too much. Antiochus gives up the ghost and dies *(6:16)*.

Maccabees would then claim that Romans would *"louingly accept all that ioyned themselues vnto them"* as they conducted their *"warres and noble acts (8:1-2)."* The Maccabees would not trade one empire for another. They created their own though very small.

In consistent Nephilim fashion, Judas refuses to flee a battle he was losing. Instead, he chose to *"die manfully (9:10)"* and Judas was killed *(9:18)*. He is then buried, not in Jerusalem, but in Modi'in *(9:19)* in Samaria demonstrating he was not a Judaean, nor a priest. Judas' exploits are well detailed throughout Maccabees. However, the author has to pump him up even more claiming: *"As for the other things concerning Iudas and his warres, and the noble actes which he did, and his greatnesse, they are not written: for they were very many (9:22)."* This is a tool of excessive fiction. In verse 27, the author mistakenly refers to a nation of Israel yet again in fraud. This union of Samaria with Judaea forced by the Maccabees was not a uniting of Lost Tribes of Israel. It was a conquest of Judaea by the Samaritans whom they would never join. This is even made clear in the New Testament mindset as even in the Parable of the Good Samaritan, what was unthinkable was that a Samaritan could be good.

When his brothers carry the mantle, they chose to war on the Sabbath *(9:43-44)* which is forbidden and a clear demonstration they were not familiar with scripture.

That proves they are not sons of Zadok. At this same time, the enemy Alcimus commands: *"the wall of the inner court of the Sanctuarie should be pulled downe, he pulled downe also the works of the prophets (9:54)."* This never happened. Alcimus supposedly dies as the order is given which is fiction *(9:55-56)*.

A laughable false lineage is then associated in utter ignorance which Maccabees proves to assert Spartans as from the tribe of Abraham. This is extremely illiterate. Indeed, Samaritans may have had such association especially through Nephilim bloodlines. However, Israel never did, and Sparta was not from Abraham.

> *1 Maccabees 12:21 KJVA 1611:*
> *It is found in writing, that the Lacedemonians and Iewes are brethren, and that they are of the stocke of Abraham:*

Upon the death of his brother Jonathan, Simon then reveals his occult leanings in a burial practice that very clearly does not originate in the Bible. This is blatant satanism including seven pyramids. What Bible prophet and author would not know this is the opposite of the Bible practice? This is befitting the prayer to the dead doctrine from earlier as well as it is the same occult paradigm.

> *1 Maccabees 13:27-30 KJVA 1611:*
> *Simon also built a monument vpon the Sepulchre of his father and his brethren, and raised it aloft to the sight, with hewen stone behind and before. Moreouer hee set vp seuen pyramides one against another, for his father and his mother, and his foure brethren. And in these he made running deuices, about the which he set great pillars, and vpon the pillars he made all their armour for a perpetuall memory, and by the armour, ships carued, that they might be seene of all that saile on the sea. This is the Sepulchre which he made at Modin, and it standeth yet vnto this day.*

Also, note this author just admitted in verse 30, this was written later and not at the time of the Maccabees. It would not matter if the tomb stood at the time, it was built which would not be a point. He is admitting this is written well after. This coalesces with what we know as there is no published copy of Maccabees even in part until Josephus in 90 A.D. This book essentially admits that.

The narrative again heralds Simon as a Nephilim hero as he was *"honourable (in all his acts) (14:5)"* and not as a Bible one giving Yahuah the credit. Instead of providing the Law of Moses or things which restore the ways of Yahuah, he provides food and munitions *"so that his honourable name was renowmed vnto the end of the world (14:10)."* Where is Yahuah in that? This is not a Bible narrative.

There are letters mentioned from Spartans especially which there is no evidence those ever existed. They refer to the heathen *(14:36)*, yet Spartans were heathens. This is nonsense. It proves Spartans did not write those. They make a demand that their writings be placed in the Temple which is ludicrous.

THE PREPOSTEROUS FALSITY OF 2ND MACCABEES:

Having been openly rebuked as occult by Martin Luther, we will not even enter 2nd Maccabees in such detail as it is unnecessary at this point. Even from the first verse, 2nd Maccabees opens with a false claim that there were Jews in Egypt at that time. There may have been Samaritan kin there, but there were no Judaeans in Egypt then. Then, it makes a very fraudulent attempt to move the Feast of Tabernacles from Ethanim, the Seventh Hebrew Month which reconciles to September-October, to the ninth Hebrew month of Kislev *(Babylonian name reconciles to November-December)*. Maccabees tries to change the Law. This is idiotic and it failed. One cannot violate the law any worse than to create a new Feast Day except for to attempt to move an existing Feast to the month in support of a false history.

> *2 Maccabees 1:9 KJVA 1611:*
> *Then we prayed vnto the Lord, and were heard: we offered also sacrifices, and fine flowre, and lighted the lampes, and set forth the loaues. And now see that ye keepe the feast of Tabernacles in the moneth Casleu (Kislev).*

However, we see here the root of what would become Hanukkah. They knew they could not move Tabernacles to December, though this book just tried. So, they created a new holiday instead. Why would this be necessary? They would have known the Temple was originally dedicated *(Hanukkah)* during Tabernacles in Solomon's days. Therefore, they needed to move it. This is connected in verse 18.

> *2 Maccabees 1:18 KJVA 1611:*
> *Therefore whereas we are nowe purposed to keep the purification of the Temple vpon the fiue & twentieth day of the moneth Casleu, we thought it necessary to certifie you thereof, that ye also might keepe it, as the feast of the tabernacles, and of the fire which was giuen vs when Neemias offered sacrifice, after that he had builded the Temple, and the Altar.*

This author then, admits he does not know the Bible yet again. He claims the altar of the Temple was hidden in a pit without water by the Temple Priests *(1:19)*. A Temple Priest would know better as well as a prophet or writer of scripture. The Book of 2nd Esdras 10:21 documents the altar was destroyed in the Babylonian destruction of the First Temple.

The Maccabees initially tried to move Tabernacles to Kislev 25 instead of its established date of Ethanim 15 in start. Who did they think they were. This attempt failed but proves how brazenly satanic these non-priests were. Sons of Zadok do not change Feasts nor create new ones. Manipulators do. Even the Second Temple did not follow this timeline, and this is ridiculous. These three major violations of scripture already discount this book from the Bible.

This pattern of violating the Feasts and Sabbath by the Maccabees/Hasmoneans and their priests continued because they were never holy and never priests. The very day they would exile the true Temple Priests from the Temple occurred on the Day of Atonement. That is no observation of that Moed'im in any sense but the opposite. This is why they are called wicked priests and rebuked many times throughout the Dead Sea Scrolls and by Messiah *(charts at end of chapter)*.

> *Woe to him who causes his neighbours to drink; who pours out his venom to make them drunk that he may gaze on their feasts (ii, 15).*
> *Interpreted, this concerns the **Wicked Priest who pursued the Teacher of Righteousness** to the house of his exile that he might confuse him with his venomous fury. And **at the time appointed for rest, for the Day of Atonement, he appeared before them to confuse them, and to cause them to stumble on the Day of Fasting,** their Sabbath of repose. – Vermes, p. 515 [22].*

The Maccabean paradigm is one of a false priesthood never legitimate. They do not know the Bible practices, and this is evidenced many times over in the rebukes of Yahusha as well as the true Temple Priests they exiled. However, nothing is more damning in the consideration of Maccabees as credible, than Hanukkah.

THE HANUKKAH HOAX:

Just as with Purim, modern Judaism has a major conflict with its observation of a new Feast Day never added in any scripture anywhere. Hanukkah is a bit more deceiving because they use the name "dedication" which is the meaning of the word. However, the Feast of Dedication in scripture is never about rededications. There is one for the First Temple in the days of King Solomon on the Feast of Tabernacles. That is not in December but October regardless of their attempting to move it.

Then, the Second Temple dedication occurred when it was built in the twelfth Hebrew month late February to early March and was never changed. Last we checked October nor March did not move to December. Again, 2nd Maccabees does attempt such which failed. When Messiah visited the Temple for the Feast of Dedication in the Winter, He was there in late February to early March, not in December which is illiterate especially when most year's Hannukah falls in early December and that is not even Winter yet. How stupid. Not only was there no rededication of the Temple in the days of the Hasmoneans, but they were also the defilers who usurped the priesthood exiling the true Temple Priests to Qumran/Bethabara. This is why Yahusha chose to launch His ministry there and not the defiled Jerusalem Temple. The following chart *(next spread)* demonstrates how the blind Pharisees of Judaism are leading the blind into a ditch.

There is no Festival of Lights in the Bible. That is a pagan concept, and most Rabbis even know this, but they observe it anyway. This should be no surprise of

Kabbalists who worship such light, not Yahuah. He has never been their Elohim but an infusion with their occult gods from Assyria/Babylon/Persia *(2 Ki. 17)*. This is why the true Temple Priests rail on these Pharisees and the religious system in Jerusalem as it was illegitimate and a different religion. That is why Yahusha chose to launch His ministry in Qumran/Bethabara instead of the defiled Jerusalem Temple. Even Josephus knew better as he tells us this even is not even called Hanukkah, but it is the Festival of Lights known as an occult Feast over thousands of years and never a Bible practice.

"And from that time to this we celebrate this festival, and call it Lights..."
– Flavius Josephus, Antiquities of the Jews, 90 A.D., Book 12.7.7

One of the major blunders by modern Rabbis is their illiteracy of this event in their own Pharisee lore. They refer to the event as Hanukkah by title in fraud, yet that was not even its original name according to Josephus. Basically, this is Josephus' admission that latter Rabbis (Pharisees) even lied further changing the name of this event which he said was called "Lights" or the Festival of Lights, to steal the Feast of Dedication or Hanukkah in name. Are we really surprised by this when we were warned how they operate in leaven?

Anyone who knows even a little about the occult already knows this is the ancient pagan Festival of Lights, never a Bible Feast, and it had nothing to do with the Dedication or Hanukkah of the Temple. Talk about a ridiculous lie easily unraveled. So, this Festival is not even called Hanukkah as that was a deception to grab the Temple Dedication of late February to early March as somehow changed which never happened. Earlier though, they tried to move Tabernacles even.

They label the false Temple leadership with many rebukes such as "Teacher of Lies." Those are they who "banished" the true Temple Priests from their land. They are "seers of falsehoods" or false prophets and occultists. The Pharisees exchanged the Law of Yahuah for the "smooth things" or watered down doctrines that tickle the ears. They "withhold knowledge" as they are not teaching Biblical knowledge and that is right of the Talmudic doctrine in practice. Most of all, the Pharisees *(Rabbinic Judaism)* represents folly concerning their feast days which they use to ensnare the lambs leading them to slaughter. Every Feast Day is wrong and defiled by them as they follow the Babylonian Lunar Calendar and they have never embodied the worship of Yahuah whom they reject and dare not even speak His name that was spoken many times by the patriarchs including Abraham. However, their fraudulent leaven adding Purim and Hanukkah is even worse and that is also covered in this chastisement. The real question is why modern Christian scholars don't know this and how have they lost track of *the synagogue of satan who say they are Yahudim and are not, but do lie (Rev. 2:9, 3:9)."*

*"Teachers of lies [have smoothed] Thy people [with words], and [false prophets]
have led them astray ...
They have banished me from my land like a bird from its nest...
And they, teachers of lies and seers of falsehood, have schemed against me a devilish
scheme, to exchange the Law engraved on my heart by Thee for the smooth things
(which they speak) to Thy people. And they withhold from the thirsty the drink
of Knowledge, and assuage their thirst with vinegar, that they may gaze on their
straying, on their folly concerning their feast-days, on their fall into the snares.
(1QH XII [formerly iv], 7-12). – Vermes, Hymn 12, p. 269 [22].*

Finally, at some point in this satanic celebration, some Pharisee chose to add
leaven even to the seven candles of the menorah. There are never eight in any
scripture ever, but Hanukkah adds an eigth candle. This exposes this false holiday
for what it is. There is no better of example of the illiteracy of Rabbis who are
modern Pharisees. No one could claim such authority to add to scripture in such a
way and this required a blatant satanic mindset to think in these terms.

This is never in question when one reads the words of Messiah and the Qumran
scrolls exposing their physical enemy used by spiritual forces. Many focus on Paul's
telling us we do not wrestle with flesh and blood as an excuse to forget this cult
was well identified throughout scripture. They coalesce to rebuke this cult that
stole the Temple, usurped the Priesthood, and are the synagogue of satan, Sons of
Belial, and much similar language always in exposing them. Today, church scholars
belly up to the synagogue bar and drink much of the Kool-Aid they dispense as if it
is something different. It never is. The synagogue of satan has always been detailed
in scripture and shame on any scholar who lost track of them and then, places the
very physical enemy in positions of influence over their doctrines. This is why so
many church doctrines vet as originating in the occult even from Babylon, Persia
and Egypt. As the Remnant Ekklesia in these Last of Days, we must prove all these
things out for ourselves because scholars are clueless. Hanukkah is a hoax and so
are all the Books of Maccabees.

THE HANUKKAH HOAX

The Feast of Dedication of modern Judaism also originates in the Books of Maccabees, yet Greece did not defile the Temple. However, worse, the Bible gives dates for the Dedication of the First and Second Temples and neither are near December.

הנכח: *chănukkâh, khan-ook-kaw'; from H2596; initiation, i.e. consecration:—dedicating(-tion). H2598.*

FIRST TEMPLE FEAST OF DEDICATION:

Feast of Tabernacles. 7th Hebrew Month (Ethanim)
Modern Calendar: Between Sept. 15 - Oct. 15
1 Kings 8:63, 8:2; 2 Chronicles 5:3

SECOND TEMPLE FEAST OF DEDICATION:

Adar 3 or 23. 12th Hebrew Month (Not December)
Modern Calendar: Between Feb. 15 - Mar. 15
Ezra 6:15-17, 1st Esdras 7:5-8 (Note: March 15 is still Winter)

The Second Temple stood until 70 A.D. Therefore, it's Feast of Dedication remained Late February to Early March *(Winter)*. The history used to redefine this as a rededication proves to be fraud according to the Qumran community *(previous page)*. What the Maccabees did was celebrate their pagan, Persian Winter Solstice Festival and they called it Hanukkah which is the Hebrew word for dedication. However, they defiled the Temple on that date. It is a rather disgusting display in fraud. Some attempt to claim Messiah was celebrating the Hasmonean Hanukkah but that as well is a lie. He was there in the 12th Hebrew Month *(Feb 15-Mar. 15)*.

EXPOSED IN 1ST ESDRAS!

Matthew 15:12-14 KJV
Then came his disciples, and said unto him, Knowest thou that the Pharisees were offended, after they heard this saying? But he answered and said, Every plant, which my heavenly Father hath not planted, shall be rooted up. Let them alone: they be blind leaders of the blind. And if the blind lead the blind, both shall fall into the ditch.

MODERN HANUKKAH IS THAT DITCH!

Messiah Was in The Temple In Adar *(between Feb. 15-Mar. 15)* NOT December!

John 10:22 KJV
*And it was at Jerusalem **the feast of dedication**, and it was **winter**. And Yahusha walked in the Temple in Solomon's porch.*

This is consistent with the Second Temple Feast of Dedication in the Winter in Late February to Mid-March. Messiah did NOT celebrate the Hasmonean Hanukkah nor does He ever embrace their story on any level. He rebukes their priests, their religion and even their lineage. It is time we correct this for good.

PHARISEE FRUITS

These Fruits Match Satan's from John 10:10 not Yahusha's

"Vipers"	"Hypocrites"	"Expand the Word with Leaven"
Matt. 3:7, 12:34, 23:33 Luke 3:7	Matt. 6:2, 6:5, 15:7, 16:3, 22:18, 23:13, 14, 15, 23, 25, 27, 28, 29, 24:51 Mark 7:6 Luke 11:44, 12:56	Matt. 15:6, 16:6, 11 Mark 7:13, 8:15 Luke 12:1
"Lead People to Hell"	**"Operate Against His Commandments"**	**"Blind" "Vain"**
Matt. 23:13, 23:15, 24:51 Luke 11:52	Matt. 15:3-6, 23:4, 23 Mark 7:5-13 Rom. 2:17-20	Matt. 15:12-14, 23:16-17, 23-26 Mark 7:7 John 9:39-41 Rom. 1:21, 2:17-20
"Condemned to Hell Generally"	**"Unclean" "Self-Righteous"**	**"Murderers"**
Matt. 5:20, 23:13-15, 24:51	Matt. 6:5, 23:5, 15, 23-27, 28 Luke 7:29-30, 36-50, 18:9-14 John 8:39-59, 12:42	Matt. 12:14, 21:45-46, 23:31, 26:4 Luke 6:11, 11:47 John 8:44, 11:45-57 Acts 3:14-15, 7:52

"Pharisaism shaped the character of Judaism and the life and thought of the Jew for all the future."
—Jewish Encyclopedia [60]

ACCORDING TO THE BIBLE 

Why Ignore What the Bible Says to Support a False Paradigm?

"Seed/ Synagogue of Satan"	"Devour Widow's Houses/Poor"	"Pray/Give to Be Seen" "Haughty"
John 8:44 Rev. 2:9, 3:9	Matt. 23:14 Mark 12:40 Luke 7:36-50, 20:47, 21:1-6	Matt. 6:2, 5, 16, 23:5-6, 14, 17-22 Mark 12:40 Luke 11:43,16:14, 20:45-47
"Don't Know Prophecy" "Seek Signs"	"Don't Know Scripture"	"Thieves" "Extort"
Matt. 12:14-37, 16:1-4, 27:40-43 Mark 8:11-12 Luke 7:29-30, 11:29-32 John 5:18, 10:24-39	Matt. 16:6-12, 21:23-27, 22:34-46, 23:23-24 , 26:62-68 Mark 3:6; Acts 1:6 Luke 7:29-30, 22:2 17:20-21 John 5:18, 10:24-39	Matt. 21:13, 23:25 Mark 11:17 Luke 19:46
"Stand in the Way of Knowledge"	"Accusers and Liars"	"Fools"
Matt. 23:34-35 Luke 11:52, 22:2 John 12:42	Matt. 12:1-2, 13-17, 22-24, 22:15-22, Mark 3:22 Luke 6:7, 7:39, 11:53, 19:39, 20:20-26 John 8:13; Rev. 2:9	Matt. 23:17, 19 Luke 11:40, 24:25 Rom. 1:22, 2:17-20

Pharisaism Became Rabbinic Judaism After 70 A.D. Pharisees Are Modern Rabbis, Modern Jews.

*Page Number in Paranthesis.

"Sons of Darkness" "Men of the Pit"	"Sons of Belial/ Satan" "Lot of Belial"	"Wicked Priests"
War Scroll, (165-182)	4Q286 (394), 4Q386 (613)	
Dam. Doc. (134, 144)	Dam. Doc. (133)	4Q394-9 (221)
4Q548 (573)	Temple Scroll (212)	4Q448 (340)
Comm. Rule (111)	War Scroll (176)	iQpHab (509-515)
4Q258 (121)	Comm. Rule (99)	4QpPsa (519)
Hymn 9 (265)	Hymn 7 (263)	

"Defilers of the Temple"	"Theives" "Rob the Poor" "Prey on Widows"	"Unclean"
iQpHab (513, 515)	iQpHab (509-515)	iQpHab (513)
Dam. Doc. (133, 137, 148)	Dam. Doc. (134)	4Q174 (525)
4Q174 (525)	4Q163 (499)	Dam. Doc. (133-134)
Temple Scroll (212)	Hymn 13 (273)	4Q286 (394)
	Comm. Rule (113)	

"Vain"	"Strangers" "Men of Perdition"	"Flouters of the Law" (Disregard, Despise)
iQpHab (514)		
Dam. Doc. (134)	4Q174 (525)	iQpHab (509-512)
4Q174 (526)	4Q501 (328)	Dam. Doc. (133)
Comm. Rule (103, 119)	Comm. Rule (113)	4Q163 (499)
War Scroll (171, 176)	4Q 171 (522)	4Q174 (525)
Hymn 14 (276)		11Q13 (533)

"Pharisaism shaped the character of Judaism and the life and thought of the Jew for all the future."

—*Jewish Encyclopedia* [60]

ACCORDING TO THE DEAD SEA SCROLLS

From "The Complete Dead Sea Scrolls in English. Revised Edition" By Geza Vermes. [22]

"Liars" "Spouter of Lies"

4QpPsa (37)
iQpHab (510-515)
Dam. Doc. (137)
4Q 171 (519, 522)
4Q501 (328)
Hymn 14 (278)

"Those Who Seek Smooth Things"

Dam. Doc. (129-130)
Thanksgiving Hymns (262-269)
4Q163, (499)
4Q169, (505-7)
4Q177, (536)

"Scoffers"

Dam. Doc. (129, 137)
iQH, 1Q36, 4Q427-32
Hymn 6 (262)
4Q162 (499)

"Abomination" "House of Guilt"

iQpHab (511, 513)
Dam. Doc. (133)
4Q175 (528)
Temple Scroll (212)
4Q387 (603)
4Q389 (604)

"Enemies"

iQpHab (514-515)
Dam. Doc. (133)
4Q174 (525)
War Scroll (176-177, 184)
Temple Scroll (215-217)

"Oppressive" "Overbearing"

iQpHab (509-514)
4Q448 (341)
4Q508 (383)
4Q504 (378)
4Q 171 (522)

"Unfaithful" "Rebellious"

iQpHab (509-510, 513)
Dam. Doc. (133)
4Q306 (243), 11Q13 (533)
Hymn 14 (278)
4Q332 (405)
Comm. Rule (99)

"Vipers, Spiders, Serpents, Dragons"

Dam. Doc. (133)
Hymn 14 (275)
Hymn 13 (273)

"Men of Violence" "Instruments of Violence"

Hymn 14 (276, 278)
Hymn 7 (263)
4Q 171 (520-522)
Comm. Rule (113)
iQpHab (509-515)
4Q175 (528), 4Q379 (585)

**Pharisaism Became Rabbinic Judaism After 70 A.D.
Pharisees Are Modern Rabbis, Modern Jews**

Martin Luther, 1483-1546:

"The book of Judith is not a history. It accords not with geography. I believe it is a poem, like the legends of the saints, composed by some good man, to the end he might show how Judith, a personification of the Jews, as God-fearing people, by whom God is known and confessed, overcame and vanquished Holofernes—that is, all the kingdoms of the world."
"... `Tis a figurative work..."
"...It is a tragedy..."

– "The Table Talk of Martin Luther." Ch. 24, pp. 27. [110]

DECONSTRUCTING THE BOOK OF
JUDITH

WORK OF FICTION?

WAS JUDITH EVER SCRIPTURE?

THE Levite BIBLE
LeviteBible.com

In defending the Apocrypha books that pass the test of inspired scripture, we find the Book of Judith to be catalogued in the category of indefensible. This is why we will not publish it here, but we will examine this work of fiction. When Martin Luther defined the book as fiction and poetry, he should have rejected it, and this is where we take major issue with those who undermine the sanctity of what is inspired by thinking it acceptable to force even fiction into the mix which the Bible never needed. Scholars have a field day with the number of historical errors in the text of Judith and they are correct on a number of these inconsistencies which do not reconcile as the valid books, such as Tobit can. The book also does not have an ancient track as Bible Canon in historicity. It was not found in Qumran among the Temple Priests who were the only ordained curators of Old Testament scripture.

In fact, if one reads Esther, Maccabees and Judith in parallel, they present themselves to originate in the same Zionist-type propaganda we see today. Judith is a great Hollywood plot of fiction but has no value to the Bible believer on any level. Zionism as a political ideology did not exist then, but it is akin to the message of these books which are not Bible accounts. These represent fake histories and fiction as the Bible is concerned, and with a very evident mission. The synagogue of satan who say they are Yahudim and are not but do lie *(Rev. 2:9, 3:9)* wish to reposition themselves as the Lost Tribes of Israel. They never were and still are not.

One can, then, assess more similar modern embellishments of Pharisees in the Midrash, Talmud, etc. This can be traced in style all the way to the cry in newspaper articles that six million Jews were about to be wiped out in the Russian Steppes published in the mid-1800's decades before World War II. Then, that prophetic warning of these seers of the occult is declared to have come true. Though atrocities definitively occurred indeed, many have noted the numbers do not even match those declared by the museums of the areas involved. It's called math, but propaganda would tell us that we must accept a figure that does not add up. That is called witchcraft. Again, war is evil, and many people died, and far more were not Jews, but that sensationalism does not award them the right to change the facts.

There is no debating that, nor justifying the evil World Wars on any Biblical, nor moral level. That is a standard Pharisee practice exposed by Yahusha who called them out for their leaven, or additives, expanding the narrative. These fictional myths do not belong in our Bibles and have never had a legitimate footprint of revelation. Their Bible interpretation is even worse as Yahusha warned us they were turning Torah against His Commandments 2,000 years ago *(Mark 7:9)*. We need to realize this today but also in history as Pharisees are also historians, academics, and Bible scholars – the Stoics according to Josephus *(see Introduction Vol. 1)*. They are occultists who hate Yahuah and His Word assailing it at every turn. Let us not refer to them as scholars of the Bible as they do not know it.

REJECTED AS INSPIRED SCRIPTURE IN THE B.C. ERA:

Though Judith was added into the Greek Septuagint at some point later, there is no evidence it appeared in the origin translation in 300-200 B.C. Many attempt that position and there is nothing logical about it. Some even posit Maccabees was in the original and its story did not even occur until more than a century after it was translated. Just because it is found in later copies, does not mean it was always there. The LXX is not a definitive list of Canon as first, no one has the original index and second, it was not translated by the Biblically ordained librarians of Bible Canon. It is useful in many ways but not in such determination. We, as well, note the other Apocryphal books found there but never as the measure above the Qumran Temple Priests. There are no fragments nor associations of the Book of Judith in Qumran/Bethabara in any sense. Therefore, Judith was not scripture, and it does not then become scripture as an Old Testament text after that was already well established even in mass archaeology. This alone fails Judith in the most profound sense.

REJECTED AS INSPIRED SCRIPTURE IN THE FIRST CENTURY:

There is not a single allusion to nor quote from the Book of Judith in the entire New Testament. This means Yahusha and the Apostles did not read it nor teach it demonstrating indisputably Judith was never inspired scripture. Debating any reasonable use of the book fails quickly when the Bible does not need this contrived book of fiction to tell its story. The Temple Priests did not keep fiction and anyone believing the Bible to be fiction, is no Bible scholar.

REJECTED BY THE EARLY EKKLESIA AS INSPIRED SCRIPTURE - FIRST TO FOURTH CENTURY:

Indeed, there were early church fathers who treated Judith as inspired scripture. However, without any previous precedence, this also fails. The Catholic Church even documents that "Augustine, Basil of Caesarea, Tertullian, John Chrysostom, Ambrose, Bede the Venerable and Hilary of Poitiers, considered Judith sacred scripture *[Wikipedia]*." Of course, these are all Catholics who even admit they do not follow the Word such as Tertullian's admission in 177 A.D. that the Catholic Church already completely abandoned the Bible's Holy Days by the Second Century. However, these are impertinent and not enough to establish Bible Canon on their own. The Catholic Counsels which followed many of these, had no authority to even take a vote on the topic as the Old Testament was curated by the Temple Priests exiled to Qumran. The fact the Catholic Church would usurp the throne of Yahusha, the Word, to attempt such demonstrates they are the opposite.

"Among the Hebrews the Book of Judith is found among the Hagiographa, the authority of which toward confirming those which have come into contention is judged less appropriate. Yet having been written in Chaldean words, it is counted among the histories. But because this book is found by the Nicene Council to have been counted among the number of the Sacred Scriptures, I have acquiesced to your request, indeed a demand, and works having been set aside from which I was forcibly curtailed, I have given to this (book) one short night's work translating more sense from sense than word from word. I have removed the extremely faulty variety of the many books; only those which I was able to find in the Chaldean words with understanding intact did I express in Latin ones."
– Jerome, Prologue to Judith [131]

We cite Jerome with the understanding he was no expert on the books of the Bible, and 382 A.D. is far too late to have a discussion on what the Temple Priests included in Old Testament Bible Canon, which no one can change. He had no authority to censor books, nor add more even set aside. He never should have included Esther, Maccabees nor Judith as "Apocrypha" as neither had the historicity in projecting the Bible Canon of the Temple Priests. The Jews he mentions as Hebrews are Pharisees, and never the keepers of Bible Canon. He basically admits he is following the wrong source propagating the Pharisee Canon as he was disconnected from the true Biblical ekklesia and their practices. That should not manifest as shocking to anyone who understands the era after the Apostles which we cover in our YouTube Series, "After the Apostles." The Catholic Church was never built on the foundation of Yahusha's ekklesia but stood against it as early as the time the New Testament was being written. The fact that this documentation exists in writings like the Didache illustrates these were those who "crept in unawares" *(Jude 1:4)* whom the Apostles warned against over 2,000 years ago.

However, in this quotation, we find in the late fourth century, Jerome was only aware of a copy of Judith written in "Chaldean words." That is the Babylonians, not Hebrews. The speculative commentaries that assume this book written in Hebrew or Greek in origin are unsupported and unfounded. He said he translated it because he was "forced" to do so. Even he knew this was not inspired scripture. He further noted the corruptions were of "extremely faulty variety" in this book which was being massively manipulated prior to his era.

We find the Syrian word for the Chaldeans as well, *"sonnes of Chelod (1:6),"* which is an odd way to render them if Judith were a Hebrew. The reason is this is a Pharisee document and those are intended to evolve and be altered over time. Those that try to apply that Pharisee reasoning to the Bible are not Bible scholars. Just read the Talmud and one sees one rambling after the other in which the Rabbis do not even agree, but that is their useless paradigm. It is never that of the Bible! There is no such thing as "almost scripture" and the Temple Priests were not frauds operating as Pharisees who find it acceptable to alter and even fabricate entire texts long after. Their accusation of the holy Temple Priests as forgers is demented and deranged. Only a demon would think in such terms which may well be why they are referred to as the synagogue of satan by Yahusha *(Rev. 2:9, 3:9)*. It matters not whether they have been influenced or possessed, that is their doctrine.

> *"Carey A. Moore argued that the Greek text of Judith was a translation from a Hebrew original, and used many examples of conjectured translation errors, Hebraic idioms, and Hebraic syntax. [6] The extant Hebrew manuscripts are very late and only date back to the Middle Ages. The two surviving Hebrew manuscripts of Judith are translated from the Greek Septuagint and the Latin Vulgate. [7] The Hebrew versions name important figures directly, such as the Seleucid king Antiochus IV Epiphanes, and place the events during the Hellenistic period when the Maccabees battled the Seleucid monarchs. However, because the Hebrew manuscripts mention kingdoms that had not existed for hundreds of years by the time of the Seleucids, it is unlikely that these were the original names in the text." – Wikipedia.*

Understand that one in Babylon can still write using Hebrew idioms in the Chaldean language to try to sound like a Hebrew wrote it. That should not be news to a scholar who can think. This one cannot. That does not prove the book written in Hebrew at all. It is also a false paradigm to make a point of this as it does not matter if the original was written in Hebrew. Some Pharisee liars could write in Hebrew as well. The content of the book remains a lie regardless of the language in which it originated which they have no evidence to disprove Jerome's only finding the book in the Chaldean language in his age. That is what history says.

The fact that the Hebrew versions date to the Middle Ages and offer corruptions inserting characters of the Maccabean age around 165 B.C., attests the true intent of this book in Pharisee circles. Those offer evidence to the contrary regarding Hebrew origins. It was perhaps the first draft of the fraudulent Books of the Maccabees. Esther, Maccabees, and Judith seem to be a fabrication from this cult of sorcerers whom our Messiah and the Qumran Temple Priests so strongly rebuked with the sharpest of language *(see "Pharisee Fruits" and "Who Were the Pharisees and Hasmoneans?" on pages 286-289).*

CLASSIFIED AS FICTION BY MARTIN LUTHER IN THE 1500S:

> *Martin Luther, 1483-1546:*
> *"The book of Judith is not a history. It accords not with geography. I believe it is a poem, like the legends of the saints, composed by some good man, to the end he might show how Judith, a personification of the Jews, as God-fearing people, by whom God is known and confessed, overcame and vanquished Holofernes—that is, all the kingdoms of the world." "... 'Tis a figurative work..." "...It is a tragedy..."*
> *– "The Table Talk of Martin Luther." Ch. 24, pp. 27. [110]*

In the 1500's, Martin Luther labeled Judith essentially as a work of fiction along the lines of Saint legends which are never scripture either. He called it a *"tragedy,"* *"figurative work,"* and *"poem."* He appears to have viewed it as allegory, in which vein, it becomes useless when the account is complete fiction. The Bible does not need a book for such. It has direct prophesies that have materialized as truth and others being revealed as such in these last days. The Bible generally represents accurate histories and geographies though many scholars do not present them accurately. We have well proven that in our previous books that deal with the geography and history of antiquity. Luther rightly noted, *"the book of Judith is not a history"* and *"It accords not with geography."* As with Esther and Maccabees, these quotes from Luther lack detail, but the evidence is not a great burden to bring to light.

However, Martin Luther was no authority on Old Testament Bible Canon, and we are not treating him as such. That ordination belonged exclusively to the sons of Zadok who lived in Qumran/Bethabara. They did not keep Judith as scripture and Luther admitted the book is fiction with erroneous history and geography.

1611 KJV ANCHORS NO NEW TESTAMENT QUOTES TO THE BOOK OF JUDITH:

In the 1611 Authorized King James Version, unlike the larger books of Apocrypha it's size, the Book of Judith does not have a single anchor in the New Testament attributed to it in origin. That is very revealing. The only book written after Judith to quote it is the false history of 2nd Maccabees 15:35 in reference to 14:1. This is a huge sign that the Bible paradigm did not treat Judith as scripture, or one would expect much more affinity. It appears to be in the same genre with Maccabees and Esther. It is rather odd that Esther is 16 chapters with its additions and Judith is the same length as is 1st Maccabees. Perhaps they became innovative when they made 2nd Maccabees only 15 chapters. This does not seem coincidence.

One of the worst forms of scholarship is the justification of a fictional text one knows is fiction yet continues to force into the Bible practice. Judith is fiction period. Fiction has no place in the Bible. Certainly, Yahusha taught in the form of parables at times which are used to effectively demonstrate a narrative. However, Yahusha did not make up an entire book and call it valuable fiction. There is no such thing. If any book of the Bible tests as a work of fiction, it is not Bible period. It never belonged there nor in a category called "Apocrypha." One article published in a journal of theology from South Africa presents such a position in the most illiterate, unacademic approach imaginable. Is the Bible known for fiction? No. If a scholar believes that, they are no Bible scholar and they are an unbeliever. This is a major problem with modern scholars. Many are not even believers.

> *"The book of Judith is a work of fiction (Efthimiadis-Keith 2004:15, 153). This work of fiction, however, remains a literary text before us and it deserves to be approached with respect and be appreciated as it is. Narratives do not have to be historically true to have an impact on the community in either a positive or a negative way. Therefore some overarching questions around the Judith narrative should be addressed. For example: What is the intended purpose of this work of fiction (Judith)? What were the probable religious challenges that the author*

of this fictional text sought to address in the home community? In which time or period is this fictional text set? – Risimati S. Hobyane, HTS Theological Studies, School of Biblical Studies and Ancient Languages, Faculty of Theology, North-West University, Potchefstroom Campus, South Africa. [133]

When one placates such ignorance as to propagate fantasy as a valid part of the Bible, they undermine the sanctity and the truth of scripture. How has this even become a discussion in any circle? This has become a clown circus, and the prime jester of origin was the Catholic Jerome in 382 A.D. His creation of a subgroup of hidden books was a manipulative mixing of the holy with the profane demonstrating that imbecile had not even a remote clue as to what was or was not inspired. He was an unqualified novice and an occult sorcerer employing witchcraft into the Word. His category of "hidden" books was a sham from its inception as there is never a classification of "maybe scripture" in the Bible practice. These are the same kind of question marks scholars often strive to create in their unintelligent, dense fog of confusion while they rarely bother to research further and explore answers to their own questions. That is not scholarship and certainly not academic.

JUDITH FAILS AS BIBLE AND SECULAR HISTORY:

As we have seen in Tobit, Nabuchodonosor *(Judith 1:1)* can be the Babylonian King Nebuchadnezzar, or his father, Nabopolassar. Many forget Assyria was first sacked by Nabopolassar and he responded to the Median conquests, before Nebuchadnezzar was king. That is the better timeline for this story, but nothing fixes Judith's lack of historic knowledge. The Medes did attack the Assyrian city of Assur in about 614 B.C. followed by their conquest of Nineveh about 612 B.C. during Nabopolassar's reign, not Nebuchadnezzar. Nabopolassar reigned from 626-605 B.C. in whole. His twelfth year recorded in Judith 1:1, would be about 614 B.C. which does match the conquest of Assur by the Medes indeed.

However, the Mede king at this time was Cyaxares *(625-585 BC)* and so many Bible dictionaries are oblivious to history claiming it to be his father or someone else when the timeline is very clear. This places Judith's timeline at the very end of the captivity of the Northern Lost Tribes when they were about to be released. That is the same time the Southern Kingdom was about to be taken into Babylonian captivity. However, this is an obstacle for this entire story as Judith could not even be a Tribe of Israel nor could her city possess actual Israelites. That was a Samaritan stronghold of imposters, not part of Israel anymore and no Lost Tribes were released yet, nor would they return there even after.

There is no documentation of a King of the Medes named Arphaxad *(Judith 1:2-4)* in any historical text and this is a timeline that only fits Cyaxares *(625-585 BC)* who was not known as Arphaxad and was not killed in battle *(Judith 1:15)* as Judith claims. Nabopolassar did not kill him either as Judith asserts since he died in 605 B.C. and Cyaxares still alive, reigned for twenty years after that. This is an erroneous history. This is why Martin Luther and others tell us Judith is not history because it is false. His father was Phraortes but the sad attempts at the backwards, false etymology of "PHRA" being "ARPH" is nonsensical and not scholarship.

There is no evidence suggesting Phraortes was known as Arphaxad either and he is the wrong king in the wrong time. Judith fails. He did die in battle with the Assyrians which is used by some scholars to try to stretch this, but that does not fit the story of Judith either as that would not be the twelfth year of Nabuchodonosor whether one viewed that as Nabopolassar, nor Nebuchadnezzar. Whomever wrote Judith was unaware of history proving they did not even live in that era. This is no surprise as there is no possibility of Judith being written in the 600 B.C. era. If it were and as inspired scripture, it would be quoted elsewhere, and it simply is not. In either era over a 150-year period around the supposed time of Judith, the kings of Media were known as Deioces, Phraortes, Cyaxares, and Astyages according to Herodotus *(Herodot. 1:102)*. Neither of these are Arphaxad in any etymological sense.

It was then, in the eighteenth year of Nabopolassar (608 B.C.), that Nabopolassar *"called Olofernes the chiefe captaine of his army (Judith 2:4)."* The challenge for Judith once again is this General has no record. He did not exist, and her story never happened. There is mention of a General named "Holofernes" during the reign of Artaxerxes III Ochus, but that would be over two hundred years too late as he reigned from about 359-338 B.C. This General did not exist in Judith's time in history and this narrative fails.

In addition, in this timeframe according to 2 Chronicles 35 *(1Esd. 1:26–27)* which were the days of Josiah the king of Judaea *(610 B.C.)*, Josiah sided with the Babylonians or Nabopolassar against Pharaoh Necho of Egypt and the remaining Assyrians who fled making their last stand at Carchemish. Holofernes was with Nabopolassar and Babylon also. He was not actually Assyrian though Judith makes this connection backwards as well. Judith is the opposite of scripture and fact. However, the largest problem Judith will never overcome is that Holofernes cannot replace Nebuchadnezzar as that was his role in that era. Holofernes did not exist! This becomes one of the most illiterate attempts to fraud the Bible and the Catholic Church has fallen for this Pharisee lie that even Jerome knew as false in 382 A.D.

> *The most famous of the kings of Babylon, the second of that name, ruling from c.605 bc through to 562 bc. His father, Nabopolassar, ejected the Assyrians to restore Babylon's independence and to found the Neo-Babylonian kingdom. During his father's reign Nebuchadnezzar defeated the Egyptian Pharaoh Necho at Carchemish in 605 bc, thus giving him control over a wide area of western Asia.*
> *– Oxford Reference [137]*

Holofernes supposedly enters Judaea *(3:9)* at this point which did not happen and flies against history. In fact, it was Nabopolassar's son, the future king, Nebuchadnezzar who with Judaea at his side would defeat the Egyptians and Assyrian remnant at Carchemesh around 605 B.C. Notice the sensational tell when

Judith claims Judaea was mostly concerned that Holofernes was there to attack the Temple *(4:2)* which was false, but the exact kind of sensationalism propagandists use. We see this same kind of embellishment as a tool in Maccabees and Esther, just as in modern times regarding *"the synagogue of satan who say they are Yahudim and are not, but do lie (Rev. 2:9 and 3:9)."* This really reveals those behind this fallacious narrative and the purpose of this fraud becomes apparent. Judaea was allied with Babylon in the battle which took place in North Samaria which Judith tells the opposite story with major missing details in fraud. This is because Judith never existed.

Judith 4:3 offers a complete blunder claiming that some living in Judaea had returned from captivity. From where, and why does the Bible never say this? The only captives at this point were the Northern Tribes who had not returned yet and did not return to Judaea especially where they were not welcome. However, let us not confuse the geography here as Judith places this event in North Samaria in the most illiterate fashion imaginable. The North and South of Israel were not allies in those days and will not be until the End Times return and regathering which has not occurred even now.

They did not return to Samaria because they were replaced, and their land was given by the Assyrians to imposters who would try to infuse their Babylonian/Assyrian religions and gods with YHWH *(2 Ki. 17)*. Yahuah always rejected that, yet it continues today. That is the origin of Pharisaism which is the origin of what is called Rabbinic Judaism today even in the Jewish Encyclopedia. Yahusha rebuked them so many times for good reason. They were always the physical enemies of Israel, and they remain so today even in abundant prophecy. There is no Bible, nor historic narrative, that demonstrates that ever happening, but the opposite. We are aware many scholars do not know this and that is their negligence that becomes evident.

The Southern Kingdom and the Northern were not allies. No Northern Tribes were freed yet in any narrative, and none returned to Northern Israel where they were replaced and their lands given away and more so, they were not welcomed into the Southern Kingdom either. This confuses the entire narrative of the divide of the North and South of Israel since the days of Solomon and they never reunite in any sense until the Day of Judgment. If the insinuation here is that those of the Southern Kingdom returned from Babylon before they were ever taken captive, that defies all logic as well.

This gets even worse as whomever wrote Judith did not know that the Samaritans at this time were not Tribes of Israel and this conflict cannot be overcome, nor ignored. They were enemies since 2 Kings 17 and Judaea did not set up military camps and even possess *"into all the coasts of Samaria (Judith 4:4)"* as claimed in Judith, or they would have created war with the Philistines, Tyre, Sidon, etc. To claim such, is to completely misunderstand the dynamic of the time as Samaria was no longer part of Israel and possessed no Israelites, but only enemies. Yes, Josiah did go up there and destroy idols that were formerly made by Northern Israel, but no Northern Tribes were left there. They were gone and replaced *(2 Kings 17)*.

ALL the Northern Tribes were taken captive into Assyria and *"there was NONE left (2 Kings 17:18)."* Even in this age that Jeremiah wrote Kings, which is after the time of Judith, *"Israel was carried away out of their own land to Assyria UNTO THIS DAY (2 Kings 17:23)."* They did not return, and Judith is a lie. 2nd Esdras defines these Northern Tribes remain exiled from Northern Israel until the *"latter time (2Esd. 13:43-47)."* Isaiah 11 clarifies the Northern Tribes will not return to the Promised Land until the very End Times as well. For Judith to make this claim exposes the agenda to mix and confuse the enemy Samaritans as Lost Tribes falsely.

This is where it aligns with the fraud of Esther and Maccabees trying to infuse the synagogue of satan, originally Samaritan imposters *(2 Ki. 17)*, as Lost Tribes of Israel when they never were. All the claims you see along these lines such as their building another Temple in Northern Israel is equally false to scripture, and an attempt to mislabel Samaritans as Lost Tribes when they are not since the time of the captivity of the Northern Kingdom *(2 Ki. 17)*. They are the imposter replacements Yahusha exposed in Revelation 2:9 and 3:9 and no wonder we see them trying to inject a fraudulent Book of Judith to make such a connection which cannot be made.

This is why Yahusha rebuked them as exposing they "say they are Yahudim and are not, but do lie *(Rev. 2:9, 3:9)*." Messiah was directly rebuking Maccabees and Judith outright as those are the books making the claim that Samaritan imposters, or Pharisees, are Tribes of Israel when they are not. They are replacements and imposters. Esther is the same as it is claiming some faction in Persia to be Israelite when the last migration of the return of the Southern Kingdom of Israel already returned before Esther ever entered the palace. This is the major expressed theme of these four books of propaganda and neither ever belonged in the Bible even as "Apocrypha." They are false and not inspired in any sense.

Add to this, Judith claims Joacim was High Priest in Jerusalem *(4:14)* in these days and the Bible is clear it was Hilkiah *(2 Ki. 22; 2 Chr. 34)*. Judith's entire case that Holofernes came to attack the Temple is erroneous. The Assyrians who fled to the area during that time which brought the Babylonian forces whom Judaea joined sides, are absent in Judith's false narrative. The writer simply did not know.

In Judith 5, the writer becomes absolutely senile. "Achior, the captaine of all the sonnes of Ammon" recites Genesis as he goes on to tell the story of Israel in Abraham's migration into Canaan and Israel into Egypt. However, in a lapse in judgment, the writer goes too far beyond the days of Judith to the destruction of the Temple and into the return from Babylon, which had not happened yet. This is a sign of fraud and a very poor one. Somehow this Ammonite captain knows of things that had not happened and he is informing a Babylonian General who would know this if it already happened. Babylon destroyed the Temple.

Even if one warped Judith into the days of Nebuchadnezzar, one must wonder why an Ammonite would have to inform a Babylonian General of Babylonian conquests and exploits. This is a typical mark of a hoax especially when it has Judaea already returning from Babylonian captivity when Babylon is in the height and really beginning of its ascent. That is ludicrous. It is equally inept that this writer identifies Achior as a hireling of Ephraim when the Northern Tribes were gone and replaced and not even in the land *(6:2)*. It would be Judah as only Judaea was left. It reads as if Achior is an ally to Judaea which is against scripture. Ammonites were not allies, but enemies.

Again, after the exile of the Northern Kingdom who never returned to Samaria, Judith invokes *"Ozias the sonne of Micha of the tribe of Simeon(6:14)"* as a *"governor"* of the city of Bethulia. There were no Northern Tribes left in Samaria and none that remained as governors of any city at that point. This is fiction. However, this city is also a fabrication. Bethulia is supposedly the "house of Israel" which again, was already exiled from the land long before and never returned. Even in verse 21, Ozias *"made a feast to the Elders(6:21)."* This is not a Biblical practice but rings of paganism as well as Catholicism's veneration of saints or elders which one will never find in the Bible as its practice. This is another indication; this was written by an occultist.

THE TWISTED GEOGARPHY OF JUDITH:

Unfortunately, not only is Bible and secular history a challenge for Judith, but so is geography. In fact, this exposes the entire narrative as a hijacking of the name Israel by the synagogue of satan in Samaria. The city of Bethulia is not located in Judaea and is not a realm of the Lost Tribes of Israel either. It is a Samaritan stronghold and somehow, we are supposed to be believe the Temple High Priest by the wrong name wrote to warn those Samaritans who were their enemies. That is especially laughable when Josiah was there in that same place fighting on the same side of those who were supposed enemies. What nonsense. This writer of Judith has no understanding of geography either just as Luther also noted accurately.

Judith 2:25 places the border of Japheth at Arabia which is ludicrous. Noah set these territories in Jubilees 8-9 *(see The Book of Jubilees: The Torah Calendar for full mapping)* and Japheth is far North of there ending at the Russian Steppes. However, Madai, son of Japheth did encroach taking land from Shem in this territory called Media after him. This was not legal and never Japheth's territory. However, even with Media as Japheth's, it does not border Arabia, and this fails. It is Northeast Iraq into Northwestern Iran ending at the Tigris River in the middle of Iraq, never Arabia.

One of the worst manipulations in this story is the city called Bethulia. It did not exist as defined and if it did, it was contrary to the story. Scholars have attempted to embellish etymologies that it may be another name for Jerusalem which is false and as illiterate as one can operate when there are markers associated, they should have been grown up enough to test before positing incoherent theories. They try to force it into Judaea which is their negligence failing to even read the text on a basic level. They have claimed it must be the Temple, yet people lived there and there was a battle there so no, that is not the Temple. These are poor, unsupported guesses of those incapable of actual research.

Dothaim is mentioned as an anchor for this location near Bethulia and this becomes very evident. Dothan is a preserved area in history located in the Northern hills of Samaria. This means this Bethulia being mentioned was not in Judaea, and not even Southern, but in Northern Samaria. This is another indicator that the imposters of Samaria wrote this narrative to attempt to rebrand themselves as Israelites. They never were. They were imposters in the land.

There is mention of another place named Belmaim which is either fiction or lost to history and then, *"unto Cyamon which is over against Esdraelon (7:3)."* Esdraelon is well documented in scripture as a large plain in Northern Samaria as well near Galilee. This is known as Jezreel today and that is a center for the occult which really leads to Judith's origin. Bethulia is located in the occult center of Samaria controlled by the enemies of Israel and their replacements. One could not be more illiterate to claim that as a territory of or close to Judaea which is nowhere nearby. The obvious intent is to claim Northern Israel, no longer Israel anymore, possessed Northern Tribes who were not even in Northern Israel then.

This false history is an attempt to infuse and reposition the synagogue of satan as Israelites and Judith fails. Notice the pattern with Maccabees and Esther which do the same. Josiah did meet the Egyptians in that area in 610 B.C. or so indeed, but he fought on the side of Babylon in that battle, and this is the opposite. The claim that *"the children of Israel which were in Bethulia (7:6)"* is a fairy tale. They were Samaritans, not Israelites, and most scholars do not know the difference as they forget 2 Kings 17 happened and do not understand the era. More profound, modern scholars place these Pharisee imposters of the synagogue of satan as their advisors which is why they know so little of this dynamic. It is as if they never read Messiah's warnings.

> *"The plain west of the Jordan which divided Galilee from Samaria. Esdraelon was the Greek name for Jezreel though strictly it was the marshy area adjacent to the more fertile Jezreel. Many conflicts were fought in the area; Deborah against Sisera (Judg. 4), Saul against the Philistines (1 Sam. 29: 1), and Josiah against the Egyptians (2 Kgs. 23: 30); in modern times (1917) the British against the Turks. The name does not appear in the Hebrew OT but is used in the LXX at Judith 1: 8. '*Armageddon' (REB) of Rev. 16: 1 is a mountain on the plain of Esdraelon."*
> *– Oxford Reference [134]*

Is it not odd to see that Gog of Magog who controls Britain chose this same area to stage a battle with Turkey at the end of World War I in which it would, then, advance further into Palestine fulfilling the prophecy of Ezekiel 38? Palestine was not truly in the war, yet Britain stole Palestine and gave the deed to Lord Rothschild in the Balfour Declaration later that same year. Most do not realize this is merely a continuation of this same story where the synagogue of satan so desires the land once called Biblical Israel. They have always been enemies of true Israel, and this is why Revelation 11 defines modern Israel in our time, as spiritual *"Sodom and Egypt (Rev. 11:8)."*. In addition, Judith even appears to contain occult concepts as well such as its story of the seven walls of Ecbatana which derives from Sabaean legends.

"It is contended by Rawlinson (Geogr. Jour. 10, 127) that this story of the seven walls is a fable of Sabaean origin — the seven colors mentioned being precisely those employed by the Orientals to denote the seven great heavenly bodies, or the seven climates in which they revolve."
– McClintock and Strong Biblical Cyclopedia [135]

This also resounds similar to the legend of the occult ancient Atlantis and its concentric rings. Herodotus *(Herodotus 1:98)* does mention these rings in Ecbatana as well but likely his source was the occult, not the Bible, and certainly not Judith which did not exist yet at that time.

THE SORTED NEPHILIM GENEALOGY OF JUDITH:

Deeper research reveals that in the ancestral lineage of Judith, there is a massive dilemma. First, there is a son of Israel named *"Salasadai"* never documented in any scripture which is very problematic. Scholars attempt to erroneously connect this name to the Septuagint's rendering of Zurishaddai, father of Samuel, but these do not connect especially since this was supposed to be the son of Israel. The timeline is far off. Judith renders Sama'el, not Samuel and that is no coincidence. Israel had plenty of sons, but never onc named Salasadai, nor anything similar. This is a manufactured, anemic lineage which oddly includes two Nephilim very ignorantly. It is as if they wish to be caught and they are.

> *Judith 8:1 KJVA 1611:*
> *Now at that time Iudeth heard thereof, which was the daughter of Merari the sonne of Ox, the sonne of Ioseph, the sonne of Oziel, the sonne of Elcia, the sonne of Ananias, the sonne of Gedeon, **the sonne of Raphaim**, the son of Acitho, the sonne of Eliu, the sonne of Eliab, the sonne of Nathanael, **the sonne of Samael**, the sonne of Salasadai, **the son of Israel.***

In the entire Bible, the only Rephaim are the Nephilim giants. Chedorlaomer defeated the Rephaites at Ashteroth-Karnaim *(Gen. 14:5)* in this same area that Judith, the Rephaim, lived. This is affirmed many times in Genesis 15:20; Deuteronomy 2:10-21, 3:11; Joshua 12:4, 13:12, 15:8, 17:15, 18:16; 2 Samuel 5:18-22, 23:13; and 1 Chronicles 11:15, 14:9 and 20:4. Og, the Nephilim giant king of Bashan, just North of Gilead in this same area, is recorded in Deuteronomy 3:11 as the last of the Rephaim. That lineage does continue but becomes labeled as the sons of Rephaim such as Anak. He is found in Joshua multiple times even with the extremely large size of his bed. They are not Israelites, and it is no enigma the Rephaim are found in this city in Northern Samaria in the same area known to be a Nephilim site. Benjamin did have a son named Rapha, but the timeline does not work as that is off by more than 5 generations. There is a son of Micah named Rapha but again, both are completely different family trees and do not work. Rephaim is the only logical conclusion here.

The problem is Judith descended from Nephilim and lived in Nephilim territory which fits this entire circus of fiction. The Rephaim originally inhabited from Ammon to Mt. Hermon in the Canaan area, but many still remained as Israel never vanquished them all. Multiple references included the area of Jezreel as well. Jubilees nails this down as one can see Edrei or *Esdraelon,* and that surrounding area identified in Judith, as the land of the Rephaim. That happens to be in Judith's bloodline. This is very bad news for the Book of Judith which proves false anyway, but now we know why this is so far off from inspired scripture. Her story seems palatable on the surface, but not when one drills down into research.

Jubilees 29:9-11:
But before they used to call the land of Gilead the land of the Rephaim; for it was the land of the Rephaim, and the Rephaim were born (there), giants whose height was ten, nine, eight down to seven cubits. And their habitation was from the land of the children of Ammon to Mount Hermon, and the seats of their kingdom were Karnaim and Ashtaroth, and Edrei, and Mîsûr, and Beon. And Yahuah destroyed them because of the evil of their deeds; for they were very malignant, and the Amorites dwelt in their stead, wicked and sinful, and there is no people today which hath wrought to the full all their sins, and they have no longer length of life on the earth.

Rephaim are Nephilim giants. This is why Yahuah told Abraham to completely wipe out the Nephilim tribes including the Rephaim. However, Judith, who appears a Nephilim in lineage, somehow rebrands them as Lost Tribes of Israel. She was no Israelite inhabiting Rephaim territory in the wrong era with the wrong history, and all this vets as a Nephilim narrative to claim they are Lost Tribes of Israel. It is sad that scholars have never seemed to research this.

Jubilees 14:18:
And on that day Yahuah made a covenant with Abram, saying: "To thy seed will I give this land, from the river of Egypt unto the great river, the river Euphrates, the Kenites, the Kenizzites, the Kadmonites, the Perizzites, and the Rephaim, the Phakorites, and the Hivites, and the Amorites, and the Canaanites, and the Girgashites, and the Jebusites."

This is such a clear example of a manufactured lineage as Elihu is the critic of Job from before the days of Abraham which does not fit this era and no one of that time occurs otherwise. They seem to just borrow names that have no tie and do not even match the family. However, Rephaim are the post-flood Nephilim giants. Sama'el is the most revealing as he is known in demonology as "king of all demons." This is another name for Asmodeus or Ashmadai whom the Septuagint ties with the Hasmoneans or *"the Chasmoniim (whence came forth Phylistiim) and the Gaphthoriim (Gen. 10:14 LXX Greek Sept.)"*. Yes, the Hasmoneans were not Hebrews, but foreigners who attacked Judaea and the Temple in 165 B.C. *(see Introduction of Apocrypha Vol. 1)*. Their bloodlines are the origin of the Philistines and the Gaphthoriim from where Goliath and his five Rephaim giant brothers originate. This area of Bethulia is another Nephilim stronghold just as Modi'in, named for Ashmodi, the prince demon. This is not even hidden, but in plain sight.

According to tradition, Samael is the king of all demons, the angel of death, the husband of the demonic Lilith, and the archenemy of Michael the archangel and of Israel. – Encyclopaedia Britannica [136]

Judith was a Nephilim, and the inference is that is a Northern Tribe of Israel. This is one of the most disgusting claims imaginable. She was married to a fictional man named Manasseh to give the further appearance of a Northern Lost Tribe, yet no Lost Tribes were in Bethulia at this time in history. Nephilim and Samaritans were.

Another odd occurrence in Judith demonstrating the writer was not even Hebrew and did not understand the customs, is that of her mourning her husband's death. One puts on sackcloth and places ashes on her head. In her case she removes the sackcloth *(9:1)* which is the opposite of Bible mourning. Instead of living in her house, Judith set up a tent on the roof *(8:4)*. No Hebrew prior ever did so that we can find, and this appears another example of an author who is oblivious to the rituals of the Bible. He was likely confusing the oath of a Rechabite with this Rephaim or perhaps the tradition of the Feast of Tabernacles. This demonstrates Judith was not holy and had no clue how the mourning process worked for Israel.

This widow supposedly *"fasted all the dayes of her widowhood (8:6)"* in which this passage tells us that is three years and four months *(8:4)* at this point in the story. That is a lie. That means there is nothing to discuss because Judith was already dead. No one ever fasted that long in history. That is not a Bible practice for widows to fast. We find it assumed by many regarding Hinduism, but not in the Bible. This is the same kind of disconnect that Esther has to scripture. They both represent different worship than that of the Bible. Fasting can be a Bible practice, but not for widows and Esther as well was not fasting to Yahuah whom she never mentions, worships, praises, thanks, nor credits as He is not a part of her entire narrative.

She, then, tips its poker hand and reveals its writers were Pharisees or Babylonians which are one in the same. The only exception in Judith's supposed three-year plus fast, in which she would likely be dead, was *"save the eves of the Sabbath, and the Sabbaths, and the eves of the newe Moones, and the newe Moones, and the Feasts, and solemne dayes of the house of Israel (8:6)."* This exposes the writers of Judith were using the Babylonian Lunar Calendar and not the Bible calendar which always begins at sunrise. We fully define that position in "When Does the Bible Day Begin" Series on YouTube as well as in REST: The Case for Sabbath free in eBook at RestSabbath. org. Also, when Yahusha and the Prophets fasted long-term, that practice trumps the Sabbath in regard to food and they would still fast on the Sabbath for that special observance only. Fasting is not a Sabbath practice but when continuing a fast beyond six days into a Sabbath, one does not end the fast in Bible history.

Judith supposedly "feared God greatly" yet was not following His customs. As with Esther, she uses sex appeal to gain influence and then, to kill. Understand that Yahuah was very adamant throughout Jeremiah especially that the Southern Kingdom must accept its punishment and go into captivity *(Jer. 42:12-22)*. Her story of attempted deliverance he condemned and told Israel he would destroy all who tried to escape captivity, is once again the antithesis. Yahuah is not involved in subverting His own will and Judith is false. Her Moussed/CIA plot makes for great spy craft of freemasons but fails Bible literacy.

Judith 8:18 then unfolds a massive lie that the Northern Kingdom no longer worshipped idols, yet none of the Northern Kingdom were even in North Israel at this time and the Samaritans who were, were documented in scripture to have worshipped idols to this time of Jeremiah *(2 Ki. 17)*. She compared this time to the trials of Abraham, yet he was actually holy, and this people were not. She married Judaea and Samaria together as if they are even the same people and they are not in scripture. They remain divided at this point and no Northern Tribes are in Samaria yet. This whole story is based on nothing but lies, false history, false Bible practices, and even the Nephilim lineages of Judith.

Judith continually repeats the false claim that the Assyrians who are really the Babylonians in that age, are out to defile the Temple *(9:8)*. She lives in North Samaria and has no connection to the Jerusalem Temple. The Bible proves this is a false narrative. She prayed for Yahuah to smite the Babylonians, yet He had given them license to carry out His judgment on the Southern Kingdom at that point. Judith did not get that because she was no Israelite. She would know the time of judgment had come which the prophesies of Jeremiah and the other prophets of this era are concise and plain. Judith does not represent the Bible paradigm and she is no prophet.

As with Esther, Judith is claimed to be one of the most beautiful women ever which is a sign of Pharisee embellishment. She uses her beauty as a superpower as a Nephilim would. Perhaps for a Nephilim she was, but this is no Bible story. However, perhaps she was even giant in size because for some odd reason, it took one hundred men of Holofernes to escort her which is utterly excessive and a very stupid embellishment like the Talmud exposing the cult that wrote this trash.

In 11:10, Judith continues to embellish repeating the lie that Israel could only be conquered if they sin forgetting that had already happened and judgment was already upon them. The statement was true, but its time already passed as the Southern Kingdom was about to enter captivity and the Northern Kingdom had already been in captivity and had not been released yet making this nonsensical. Again, it is as if this writer had no familiarity with the Bible. Judith commits to be the prophetess to whom Yahuah will tell whether Israel sins when they already had. It is extremely hard to believe a General would fall for such a simplistic claim from Judith who was no prophetess and had nothing but beauty to offer. Sure, the words would sound good but no one who rises to the greatest General in Babylon could be so naive. Then, he rashly and without any real thought commits that if

Judith would tell him when to attack after Israel sinned, he would convert to her religion even. This is ridiculous. It sounds like witchcraft, not Bible.

It is completely unbelievable that Holofernes, a General about to go to battle, would have not just drunk too much, but more than he had ever drank before. Nothing about that makes sense and it is another sign of Pharisee embellishment. For the guard to leave an enemy, regardless of beauty, alone with a drunken General, would be uncharacteristic and negligent *(13:2-4)*. That is nonsense.

In two blows, Judith supposedly severed the head of Holofernes which she was supposedly strengthened by Yahuah. Either she was a Nephilim as her lineage suggested, or this is fiction. It takes several blows for a skilled assassin to remove a man's head. Though Yahuah certainly could, this goes against His decree in this same era that Babylon would conquer Judaea with his permission. Judith then leaves abruptly as if the garrison of one hundred soldiers who were required to escort her, did not see her exit it appears. This is make believe indeed.

Judith is exalted and the Ammonite, Achior, bows at her feet which is not Bible *(14:7)*. She is directly praised again by the elders from Jerusalem to "salute her *(15:8-10)*." They blessed Judith and not Yahuah which is the wrong paradigm again. However, this is not a Bible account which would spend no time on such, and all praise would go to Yahuah.

One of the most illiterate of positions in Judith has a Hebrew practice of tearing one's garments in mourning *(14:19)*, but not as that of Hebrews. It is ascribed as an action of Bagoas when he discovers Holofernes dead. He is not a Hebrew and Assyrians are not known to mourn that way. This story is indeed fiction. Even the thirty days to spoil the camp seems embellished *(15:11)*. Afterwards, Judith ends with a celebration dance with her and the women and soldiers using garland of olive and singing *(15:13)*. This is not Bible worship. This is a pagan ritual fitting to the Nephilim from which tribe Judith originated. The Greeks used wreathes of olive leaves in the same fashion in their victory celebrations.

Though Yahuah is generally credited against His will, Judith is extoled directly and in an unbiblical fashion. They make a big deal of her putting off her garment of widowhood, yet it was over 3 years and that is nonsense. Verse 9 credits *"her beautie tooke his minde prisoner,"* which is very distasteful to include as worship of Yahuah. It does not belong, nor does verse 10 which reads: *"The Persians quaked at her boldnesse, and the Medes were daunted at her hardinesse."* Should not this read Persians quaked at Yahuah's miracle and the Medes at His resolve to protect His people? In fact, as Holofernes was a Babylonian General, what does that have to do with Persia, nor Media regarding the Southern Kingdom which has no pertinence?

Judith 16:7 KJVA 1611
For the mighty one did not fall by the yong men, neither did the sonnes of the Titans smite him, nor high gyants set vpon him: but Iudeth the daughter of Merari weakned him with the beautie of her countenance.

At the time when Yahuah had already begun to decree the captivity of the Southern Kingdom into Babylon and the Northern Kingdom was still in bondage, we are supposed to believe this fabrication of a fictional deliverance He had already judged righteously against. Then, their celebration in Jerusalem supposedly lasted three months *(16:20)* which is further embellishment. If one was going to make up such a story as this one is a fairy tale, they would know better than to render the account fiction so many times in so many ways. This writer lacked even that amount of wisdom. This very legend of Judith supposedly kept Israel safe the rest of her entire 105 years of life *(16:25)*. The only problem is the Southern Kingdom was taken captive into Babylon during that time thus, this is a lie from start to finish.

It is evident there is no truth in this entire story. Judith's challenges with history and geography cannot be overcome. The conflicts with Bible doctrine are too overwhelming to consider this as inspired or even "almost inspired." It fails even as "Apocrypha" and never should have been placed there anywhere near scripture. When scholars do so in any paradigm, they deprecate the whole of scripture in association with occult rubbish.

In conclusion, the Books of Esther, Maccabees and Judith all fail any examination as inspired scripture. The rest of the 1611 King James Apocrypha tests as what was and still should be Bible Canon. In other words, this entire category titled "Apocrypha" is the biggest lie. The Temple Priests never recognized such and not a single book labeled so, even belongs there whether pass or fail. Jerome and the Pharisees before him assembled a hidden paradigm to set aside some of scripture as questionable. We have proven, those books which vet as Canon never belonged. They added in occult books they well knew would lessen the value of the entire category in one of the greatest frauds in history. What they did was change the Bible and they, and those who follow, will suffer that curse. The good news is we can all restore His Word to its original status and our research will continue. Yah Bless.

Over 300 pages. 6"x 9" Paperback.
© 2021

Most of us have been taught the Sabbath passed away.
Is that what the Bible says? Review the evidence for
yourself in this comprehensive Bible Case for Sabbath.
This will change your life.

Now Available in Print and in eBook at:

RestSabbath.org

International:

Philippines:

eBooks:

○ ISSUU

TheGodCulture.com

▶ YouTube *The God Culture*   f *The God Culture - Original*

BIBLIOGRAPHY:

Translation Originally From:
1611 King James Version

Other General Sources of Note:
The Complete Dead Sea Scrolls in English. Revised Edition. By Geza Vermes. Penguin Books. London, N.Y. Revised 2004. Originally Published 1962. Page number in reference. [22]
The Book of Jubilees: The Torah Calendar. By Timothy Schwab and Anna Zamoranos. 2021. Based on the Original Translation by R.H. Charles, 1903. Free eBook: www.BookOfJubilees.org
2nd Esdras: The Hidden Book of Prophecy. By Timothy Schwab and Anna Zamoranos. 2021. Based on the Original 1611 King James Version. Free eBook at www.2Esdras.org
The Book of First Enoch: The Oldest Book In History. By Timothy Schwab and Anna Zamoranos. 2021. Based on the Original Translation by R.H. Charles, 1912. Free eBook at www.firstenoch.org
Apocrypha, Vol. 1. By Timothy Schwab and Anna Zamoranos. 2023. Based on the Original 1611 Authorized King James Version. Free eBook www.ApocryphaTest.com

Cited, Numbered Sources:
1. "The Canon of Scripture." Blue Letter Bible citing "What Everyone Needs To Know About The Bible." By Don Stewart. The Basic Bible Study Series. Publisher Dart Press, Orange, California. https://www.blueletterbible.org/faq/canon.cfm
2. Clark Pinnock, Biblical Revelation, Grand Rapids: Baker Book House, 1973, p. 104. Quoted by Blue Letter Bible.
3. 2014 Lecture at University of Chicago Divinity School sponsored by Jewish Federation of Chicago. Rachel Elior. Professor, Hebrew University of Jerusalem. https://www.youtube.com/watch?v=wLit979B60Y&t=3621s
4. Strong's Concordance "Awan" #H5770. Blue Letter Bible. (Note Ancient Hebrew never had a "V" so the word is Awan not Avan).
5. 1. "Where to See Some of the World's Oldest and Most Interesting Maps." By Jennifer Billock. Smithsonian Magazine. July 18, 2017.   2. "Geography and Ethnography: Perceptions of the World in Pre-Modern Societies." By Kurt A. Raaflaub & Richard J. A. Talbert. 2009. John Wiley & Sons. p. 147. 3. Map from: Wikimedia Commons. Map of the World from Sippar (Tell Abu Habba), Iraq, 6th century BCE. On display at the British Museum in London. By Osama Shukir Muhammed Amin.
6. "Books of Enoch Collection." By Scriptural Research Institute. 2020. p. 106.
7. "Rapha." Abarim Publications.
8. "The Dead Sea Scrolls and the Christian Myth." By John M. Allegro. 1992.
9. "The Mystery of the Essenes." By H. Spencer Lewis, F.R.C. From "The Mystical Life of Jesus." Rosicrucian Digest No. 2. 2007. p. 3.
10. "Natural History." Pliny the Elder. Book V. p. 277.
11. "The Life of Flavius Josephus." 1:2. The Genuine Works of Flavius Josephus the Jewish Historian. Translated from the Original Greek, according to Havercamp's accurate Edition.
12. 1770, Bonne Map of Israel. Rigobert Bonne 1727 – 1794. AdobeStock.
13. Madaba Mosaic Map(left), c. 6th century A.D. St. George's Church. Jordan. AdobeStock.
14. 1836, Tanner Map of Palestine, Israel, Holy Land. AdobeStock.
15. NASA/Goddard Space Flight Center Scientific Visualization Studio U.S. Department of Commerce, National Oceanic and Atmospheric Administration, National Geophysical Data Center, 2006, 2-minute Gridded Global Relief Data (ETOPO2v2). Horace Mitchell (NASA/GSFC): Lead Animator.
16. 1845, Chambers Map of Palestine, Israel, Holy Land. AdobeStock.

17. *1852, Philip Map of Palestine, Israel, Holy Land. AdobeStock.*

18. *Ein Gedi Photos: Chalcolithic Temple, Essene Synagogue, Tile mosaic Peacock symbols. AdobeStock.*

19. *Antiquities of the Jews — Book VIII, Chapter 6:4 and 7:1. Flavius Josephus.*

20. *"Enoch and Qumran Origins: New Light on a Forgotten Connection." Gabriele Boccaccini, Editor. William B. Erdemans Publishing Co. Grand Rapids, MI and Cambridge, UK. 2005. p. 137.*

21. *"The Complete Dead Sea Scrolls In English Revised Edition." "The Damascus Document." Translated By Geza Vermes, 2004, Penguin Classics Books. London, England. First Published 1962. Revised Edition 2004. p. 139.3. Flavius Josephus, Antiquities of the Jews, 18:16.*

22. *The Complete Dead Sea Scrolls in English. Revised Edition. By Geza Vermes. Penguin Books. London, NY. Revised 2004. Originally Published 1962. Page number in reference.*

23. *"The World's Largest Caldera Discovered In The Philippine Sea." By David Bressan. Forbes Magazine. Oct. 21, 2019.*

24. *"Dudael." Wikipedia. Feb. 24, 2022.*

25. *Strong's Concordance. Blue Letter Bible.*

26. *Ancient Hebrew Research Center. By Jeff A. Benner. Ancient-Hebrew.org. 2019.*

27. *Philippines #1 in Gold in History. The Search for King Solomon's Treasure. The Lost Isles of Gold and the Garden of Eden. By Timothy Schwab and Anna Zamoranos. 2020. 1. "Ancient Mining: Classical Philippine Civilization." Wikipedia. Extracted August 9, 2019. and "Cultural Achievements of Pre-Colonial Philippines." Wikipedia. Extracted August 9, 2019. 2. "The Edge of Terror: The Heroic Story of American Families Trapped in the Japanese-occupied Philippines." By Scott Walker. Thomas Dunne Books. St. Martin's Press. New York. Chap. 3 - The Gold Miners, 1901-1937. p. 44.*

3. *"Philippine Civilization and Technology," By Paul Kekai Manansala. Asia Pacific University.*

4. *"Encyclopedic Dictionary of Archaeology – Philippines, the." Compiled by Barbara Ann Kipfer, Ph.D. Kluwer Academic/Plenum Publishers. New York, London, Moscow. 2000. p. 436. 5. "Miners Shun Mineral Wealth of the Philippines." By Donald Greenlees. NY Times. May 14, 2008. Citing The Fraser Institute. 6. "Trillion – Dollar Philippine Economic Goldmine Emerging From Murky Pit." By Ralph Jennings. Forbes Magazine. Apr. 5, 2015. 7. "Mining for Gold in the Philippines." By Nicole Rashotte. Gold Investing News. Sept. 10th, 2019.*

28. *Philippines #1 in Pearl. The Search for King Solomon's Treasure. The Lost Isles of Gold and the Garden of Eden. By Timothy Schwab and Anna Zamoranos. 2020. 1. "This $100 Million Pearl Is The Largest and Most Expensive in the World." By Roberta Naas. Forbes Magazine. Aug 23, 2016. 2. "Pinoy in Canada Discovers Strange Family Heirloom is Actually a Giant Pearl Worth $90 Million." Buzzooks.com. May 23, 2019.*

29. *Romblon Philippines Strongest Onyx. The Search for King Solomon's Treasure. The Lost Isles of Gold and the Garden of Eden. By Timothy Schwab and Anna Zamoranos. 2020. 1. "ROMBLON: 8 Awesome Places You Should Visit in Romblon!" Our Awesome Planet. Sept. 7, 2016. 2. "The Romblon Marble." Ellaneto Tiger Marble Trader, Romblon. 2010. 3. "Marvelous Marble" By Robert A. Evora. Manila Standard. Jan. 16, 2014.*

30. *"The Center of the Center of Marine Biodiversity on Earth." 1. "Environmental Biology of Fishes." K.E. Carpenter and V.G. Springer. 2005. 72: 467-480. 2. "Center of the Center of Marine Diversity." CNN. Apr. 30, 2012. 3. "100 Scientists Declare RP as World's 'Center of Marine Biodiversity." By Katherine Adraneda. June 8, 2006. The Philippine Star reporting on "Philippines Environmental Monitor, 2005" by the World Bank.*

31. "Havilah." Hitchcock's Dictionary of Bible Names from BibleHub.org and KingJamesBibleDictionary.com, Strong's Concordance #H2341. Blue Letter Bible.

32. "Eve - Havah." Strong's Concordance #H2332. Blue Letter Bible.

33. "Alabaster, Mineral." and "Marble, Rock." By Editors of Encyclopaedia Britannica. Encyclopaedia Britannica. Updated Jan. 24, 2018 and Jan. 24, 2020.

34. "Indonesia's Mountains of Fire." By Daniel Quinn. Indonesia Expat. June 30, 2014. Indonesia's Volcanological Survey. Laporan Kebencanaan Geologi. Apr. 2, 2019.

35. "." Wikipedia.

41. "The giant undersea rivers we know very little about" By Richard Gray. BBC News. July 6, 2017. Citing Dan Parsons, PhD, Sedimentologist, University of Hull, UK.

42. "The Thanksgiving Hymns (1QH, 1Q36,4Q427-32). Hymn 14." The Complete Dead Sea Scrolls. By Geza Vermes. Penguin Classics. P. 278.

43. "Chapter Eight. Traditions Common To 4 Ezra And The Dead Sea Scrolls." By E.J.C. Tigchelaar and F. García Martínez. Qumranica Minora I. Qumran Origins ,and Apocalypticism. Series: Studies on the Texts of the Desert of Judah, Volume: 63. Publisher: Brill. 01 Jan 2007. 153–168.

44. F. García Martínez, "Qumran Origins and Early History: A Groningen Hypothesis," Folia Orientalia 25 (1989): 113–36.

53. "Commentary on Habakkuk." The Complete Dead Sea Scrolls in English. Revised Edition. By Geza Vermes. Penguin Books. London, NY. Revised 2004. Originally Published 1962. p. 510-511.

54. Commentary on Nahum, P. 505. The Complete Dead Sea Scrolls in English. Geza Vermes. Penguin Classics. Revised Edition. Published 1962. Revised 2004.

55. Commentary on Habukkuk, P. 515. The Complete Dead Sea Scrolls in English. Geza Vermes. Penguin Classics. Revised Edition. Published 1962. Revised 2004.

56. "Blessings (iQSb=iQ28b), The Blessing of the Prince of the Congregation." The Complete Dead Sea Scrolls in English. Geza Vermes. Penguin Classics. Revised Edition. Published 1962. Revised 2004. p. 389. 100 B.C. dating: J. T. Milik (DJD, I, 118-29).

60. "Antiquities of the Jews — Book XI." Josephus. Chapter 3.1. Chapter 11.133.

61. "Euergetes" Encyclopedia of The Bible citing R.H. Charles, The Apocrypha and Pseudepigrapha of the Old Testament, I (1963), 293. Bible Gateway.

62. "3,000-year-old Canaanite temple discovered in buried city in Israel." By Tom Metcalfe. Live Science. Feb. 24, 2020.

63. "The Gilgamesh Epic And Old Testament Parallels." By Alexander Heidel. Tablet VIII, Col. 11:4-5, p. 62; Tablet IX, 15-16. p.65; Tablet X, Col. 3:40-44, p.76.

64. "Cyrus the Great, King of Persia." By Richard N. Frye. Fact-checked by The Editors of Encyclopaedia Britannica. Apr 1, 2023.

65. "Psittacosis." Centers forr Disease Control nd Prevention. Last Reviewed: March 17, 2022. Content Source: National Center for Immunization and Respiratory Diseases.

66. Satpathy G, Behera HS, Ahmed NH. Chlamydial eye infections: Current perspectives. Indian Journal of Ophthalmology 2017;65:97-102

67. "Fish bile and cautery: trachoma treatment in art." By Johnson HA. Journal of the Royal Society of Medicine. 2005 Jan;98(1):30-2.

68. "Raphael, רפאל." Abarim Publications.

69. "Nineveh and Babylon." Austen Henry Layard. P. 168. London, 1853. On the spot drawing of Plate 6 (cropped) from bas-relief from the Palace of Sennacherib in Tobit's era. The fish is believed to be a mangar fish from the Tigris-Euphrates basin.

70. Özgür, M.E. (2016). The Luciobarbus esocinus (Heckel, 1843) from the Euphrates River Basin: An introduction about its past, present and future. Proceedings of the 2nd International Congress on Applied Ichthyology & Aquatic Environment 10 - 12 November 2016, Messolonghi, Greece. Cited on Wikipedia.

71. "River Monsters: Discover the Largest Fish in the Euphrates River." by Brandi Allred A-Z Animals. Feb. 6, 2023.

72. "Prison of Solomon." Wikipedia. Citing Encyclopaedia Iranica, & Tehran Times.

73. "Antiquities of the Jews." By Flavius Josephus. Book 4:22.

74. Origen's "Letter to Africanus." By N.R.M. de Lange, Cambridge Studia Patristrica. Vol. XVI. PATRISTICA. STUDIA. Oxford 1975. p. 244.

75. "Letter to Africanus." Translated by Frederick Crombie. From Ante-Nicene Fathers, Vol. 4. Edited by Alexander Roberts, James Donaldson, and A. Cleveland Coxe. (Buffalo, NY: Christian Literature Publishing Co., 1885.) Revised and edited for New Advent by Kevin Knight.

76. "The Genuine Works of Flavius Josephus The Jewish Historian." Translated from the Original Greek, according to Havercamp's accurate Edition. By William Whiston M.A. University of Cambridge. London. 1737.

77. "Baruch Is There, Just Sometimes As Part of Jeremiah." By Tom Nash. Catholic Answers.

78. Bar 3:36 (Athenagoras, Legatio pro Christianis 9,2 [98,11–12 P.]). Cf. Cyprian, Testimonia ad Quirinium 2,6 (CChr.SL 3,1, 35,17–36,20 Weber); Lactantius, Divinae institutiones 4,13,8 (SC 377, 114,30–34 Monat); Bernard Pouderon, "Les citations scripturaires dans l'oeuvre d'Athénagore: leurs sources et leur statut," Vetera Christianorum 31 (1994): (111–153) 112; Sean A. Adams, Baruch and the Epistle of Jeremiah: A Commentary on the Greek Texts of Codex Vaticanus (Septuagint Commentary Series; Leiden: Brill, 2014), 17.

79. "Baruch and the Epistle of Jeremiah." By Sean A. Adams. Brill. 2014. p. 17.

80. Decretum Gelasianum. https://www.tertullian.org/decretum_eng.htm.

81. The Apocrypha and Pseudepigripha of the Old Testametn In English. R. H. Charles, D.Litt., D.D. Vol. 1. Oxford at the Claredon Press. 1913.

82. "Of the Thundering Legion." By William Whiston. London. 1726. pp. 47-63.

83. "Apocrypha: Biblical Literature." Written and fact-checked by The Editors of Encyclopaedia Britannica. Last Updated: May 12, 2023.

84. "On the Patristic Old Testament Canon." By Admin. Classical Chritianity. Eastern Orthodoc For Today. Dec. 21, 2011.

85. "Susanna" Early Jewish Learning citing "Introduction to the Old Testament," By James King West. p. 458.

86. "Bel and The Dragon" Early Jewish Learning citing "Introduction to the Old Testament," By James King West. p. 458.

87. "The Pope and the Mithras Cult: Part II." By Jon Sorensen. Catholic Answers. Sept. 23, 2013.

88. "HAS 'Esther' BEEN FOUND AT QUMRAN? '4QProto-Esther' AND THE 'Esther' CORPUS." By Sidnie White Crawford. Revue de Qumrân 17, no. 1/4 (65/68) (1996): 307–25.

89. Bibilical Intertextuality Forum. intertextual.bible.

90. The Instructor (Book II), Chapter 1. The Paedagogus (Clement of Alexandria). Translated by William Wilson. From Ante-Nicene Fathers, Vol. 2. Edited by Alexander Roberts, James Donaldson, and A. Cleveland Coxe. (Buffalo, NY: Christian Literature Publishing Co., 1885.) Revised and edited for New Advent by Kevin Knight.

91. "Deuterocanonical Books In The New Testament." ScriptureCatholic.com.

92. "Polycarp and Paul: An Analysis of Their Literary and Theological Relationship In Light of Polycarp's Use Of Biblical and Extra-Biblical Literature." By Kenneth Berding, Brill. 2002. p.105.

93. "The Epistle of St. James." By Joseph B. Mayor, M.A. OAMB, LITT.D. DuBL. Macmillan and Co. London, NY. 1897. pp.76-77.

94. "An Analysis of 4Q Instruction" By Torleif Elgvin. Doctoral Thesis Submitted to the Senate of the Hebrew University of Jerusalem. 1997. 5.1.3. p. 172.

95. "Mystery" in the Wisdom of Solomon and 4QInstruction. By Benjamin Wold. Journal for the Study of the Pseudepigrapha. Sage Journals, Vol. 31. Iss. 1. Sept. 9, 2021.

96. "Book of (The) Wisdom of Solomon." McClintock and Strong Biblical Cyclopedia. The Cyclopedia of Biblical, Theological, and Ecclesiastical Literature. James Strong and John McClintock; Haper and Brothers; NY; 1880.

97. Deuterocanonical and Cognate Literature Yearbook 2019.

98. "Torah and Divine Revelation in Three Jewish Texts: 4QInstruction, Wisdom of Solomon and the Fourth Gospel." By Jeffrey Hubbard. Journal for the Study of the New Testament 44, no. 4 (June 1, 2022): 561–79.

99. "The Wisdom of Solomon." By The Rev. J. A. F. Gregg, M.A, Cambridge University Press. 1909.

100. "Adam, The Angels and Eternal Life: Genesis 1-3 in the Wisdom of Solomon and 4QInstruction." Matthew Goff. Florida State University.

101. "4QInstruction." By Matthew J. Goff. Wisdom Literature From the Ancient World; No. 2. Society of Biblical Literature. 2013.

103. "Baruch" by P. P. Saydon, revised by T. Hanlon, in A New Catholic Commentary on Holy Scripture, ed. Reginald C. Fuller, Thomas Nelson, Inc. Publishers, 1953, 1975, §504j. The same source states that "[t]here is also evidence that Baruch was read in Jewish synagogues on certain festivals during the early centuries of the Christian era (Thackeray, 107-11)", i.e. Henry St. John Thackeray, The Septuagint and Jewish Worship, 1923.

104. "Baruch and the Epistle of Jeremiah." By Sean A. Adams. Brill. 2014. p. 1.

105. VanderKam, James C. "The scrolls, the Apocrypha, and the Pseudepigrapha." Hebrew Studies, vol. 34, annual 1993, pp. 35+. Gale Academic OneFile. Accessed 1 June 2023.

106. Collins, John J. Dead Sea Discoveries 17, no. 2 (2010): 231–33. http://www.jstor.org/stable/20787404.

107. Dead Sea Scrolls Translated. The Qumran Texts In English. By Florentino Garcia Martinez Wilfred G. E. Watson Translator E. Jf. Brill Leiden, New York, Cologne. 1994.

108. "Nicene and Post-Nicene Fathers." Ser. 2. Vol. 1. Church History of Eusebius. Bk. 3. Ch. 39.

108. A Collation of Variants from 967 to Ziegler's Critical Edition of Susanna, Daniel, Bel et Draco. By Tim McLay. p. 121-125.

109. Christian Stadel. "The Judaeo-Syriac Version of Bel and the Dragon: An Edition with Linguistic Comments." Mediterranean Language Review 23 (2016): 1–31.

110. "The Table Talk of Martin Luther," By Martin Luther, Translated by William Hazlitt, Esq. Of God's Word, Ch. 24, p. 27-28. Philadelphia: The Lutheran Publication Society. From Christian Classics Ethereal Library.

111. "Archaeology and the Book of Esther." By Carey A. Moore. The Bible Archaeologist, Gettysburg College. Vol. 38. 1975, 3-4.

112. "Highlight of the gods?" By Shammai Engelmayer. Jewish Standard, May 16, 2021.

113. "The Book of Esther In Light Of History." By Jacob Hoschander. The Jewish Quarterly Review, July-Oct., 1918, New Series, Vol. 9, No. 1/2, pp. 1-41, Ch. 1. University of Pennsylvania.

114. "Why Were the Books of the Old Testament Apocrypha Rejected as Holy Scripture by the Protestants?" By Don Stewart. BlueLetterBible.org.

115. "Does the New Testament Quote the Old Testament as Authoritative Scripture?" By Don Stewart. BlueLetterBible.org.

116. "Sirach, The Wisdom of Jesus the Son of (Hebrew, Ḥokmat ben Sira; Latin, Ecclesiasticus)." By Crawford Howell Toy, Israel Lévi. Jewish Encyclopedia.

117. "Ahasuerus." McClintock and Strong Biblical Cyclopedia citing Herod. 1, 106.

118. *"Apocrypha, Bible Manuscripts and Textual Questions, Daniel, General, Reliability of the Bible." By John Oakes. March 18, 2013 Evidence For Christianity. "Are the additions to Daniel (Azariah, Suzannah, Bel and Dragon) inspired and reliable?"*

119. *"New Light on the Book of Daniel from the Dead Sea Scrolls." By Dr. Gerhard Hasel, Past Dean of the Seventh Day Adventist Theological Seminary. Originally republished in Bible and Spade, January 1992.*

120. *"Could any creature evolve to breathe fire, like a dragon?" By Luis Villazon, Zoologist. BBC Science Focus Magazine.*

121. *"What Does Science Say About Flying and Fire Breathing Dragons?" By Anne Marie Helmenstine, Ph.D. ThoughtCo. Dotdash Meredith Publishing. Updated Feb. 03, 2020.*

122. *"Josephus and the Twenty-Two-Book Canon of Sacred Scripture." By Duane L. Christensen. Journal of the Evangelical Theological Society 29/1, March 1986. p. 39-41.*

123. *"The Book of Esther and the "Enūma Elish." By Adam Silverstein. Bulletin of the School of Oriental and African Studies, University of London, Vol. 69, No. 2 (2006), pp. 209-223.*

124. *"Esther & Canon?" By John Anthony Dunne, PhD, University of St Andrews. December 27, 2011.*

124. *"Highlight of the gods?" By Rabbi Shammai Engelmayer. Jewish Standard. March 14, 2014.*

125. *"Esther." By: Emil G. Hirsch, John Dyneley Prince, Solomon Schechter. Jewish Encyclopedia.*

126. *"aššatum." Wiktionary citing R. Borger, Mesopotamisches Zeichenlexikon (MZL), Münster (2003); A. Deimel, Šumerisches Lexikon (Deimel), Rome (1947); and Chr. Rüster, E. Neu, Hethitisches Zeichenlexikon (HZL), Wiesbaden (1989).*

127. *"Myrtle: The Provenance and Meaning of a Plant." By Julia Blakely. Smithsonian Libraries and Archives. June 28, 2018.*

128. *"The Book of Esther in the Light of History." By Jacob Hoschander. The Jewish Quarterly Review, Jul.-Oct., 1918, New Series, Vol. 9, No. 1/2. pp. 1-41. Published by University of Pennsylvania Press.*

129. *"Joseph Goebbels: On the "Big Lie." Jewish Virtual Learning. Citing "Mein Kampf," By Adolf Hitler. Vol. 1, Ch. 10.*

130. *"Damaspia," "Amestris," and "Stateira" Encyclopaedia Iranica. Vol. VI, Fasc. 6, p. 626 citing Ctesias from Jacoby, Fragmente, vol. III.C, p. 468, frags. 15, 47; Herodotus 7.61.2, Ctesias, fragment 14 ; and DB 4.84-85: Vidarna, Ctesias, 53-55, and Jacoby, 688 F15.*

131. *"Prologue to Judith," By Jerome. Translated by Kevin P. Edgecomb. Tertullian. org.*

132. *"Of the Thundering Legion," by William Whiston. London: 1726. Of Alexander the Great's Meeting the High-Priest of the Jews at Jerusalem. Pages 47-63. Citing Josephus in Antiq. XI.8., Origen Contr. Cels. V. p. 265. [V.50], and Eusebius Chronicon.*

133. *"Clashing deities in the book of Judith: A Greimassian perspective." By Risimati S. Hobyane. HTS Theological Studies. School of Biblical Studies and Ancient Languages, Faculty of Theology, North-West University, Potchefstroom Campus, South Africa. http:// dx.doi.org/10.4102/HTS.V71I3.2893*

134. *"Esdraelon." Oxford Reference Quick Reference. Oxford University Press. Citing "A Dictionary of the Bible (2 ed.)." W. R. F. Browning. 2009.*

135. *"Achmetha." The Cyclopedia of Biblical, Theological, and Ecclesiastical Literature. James Strong and John McClintock; Haper and Brothers; NY; 1880.*

136. *"Samael." By Rebecca M. Kulik. Encyclopaedia Britannica. Updated 2023.*

137. "Nebuchadnezzar." Oxford Reference Quick Reference. Oxford University Press. Citing "The Concise Oxford Dictionary of Archaeology (2 ed.)." Timothy Darvill. 2008.

138. "Rule of Rome Timeline." Jewish Virtual Library.

139. The Histories of Tacitus, Vol. 3, Book 5.8.1. Loeb Classical Library edition of Tacitus, 1931.

140. "Dialogue with Trypho." Justin Martyr. C.71-3.

141. "The Tale of Susanna: A Story about Daniel" By Dr. Malka Z. Simkovich.

INCREASING INSIGHT
THE REMNANT IS AWAKENING

Apocrypha: Vol. 1
7" x 10"

Apocrypha: Vol. 2
7" x 10"

2nd Esdras:
7" x 10"

▶ YouTube *The God Culture*   f *The God Culture - Original*

International:

amazon

Philippines:

Shopee

eBooks:

issuu

PAPERTURN

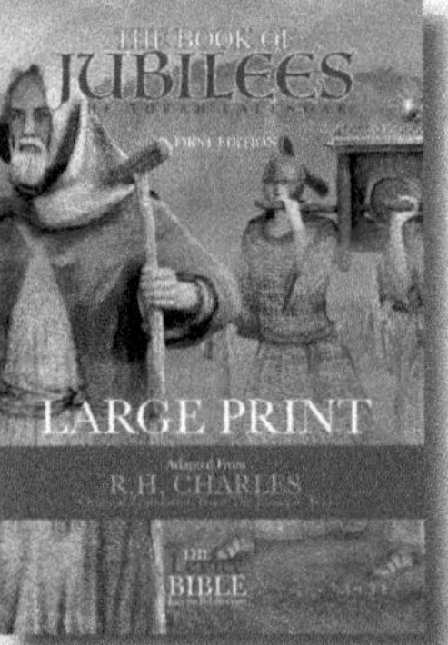

The Book of Jubilees:
7" x 10"

Bible History Illustrated:
7" x 10"

First Enoch:
7" x 10"

www.OphirInstitute.com

REST: Sabbath
6" x 9" Paperback

The Full Case:
6" x 9" Paperback

Coffee Table Book:
8.25" x 11" Hardcover